Politics and the Pound

Philip Stephens is an Associate Editor and Political
Commentator at the *Financial Times*. He was previously the
newspaper's Economics Correspondent and its Political Editor. He
was educated at Wimbledon College and Worcester College,
Oxford. He lives with his family in London.

PHILIP STEPHENS

POLITICS AND
THE POUND

THE TORIES, THE ECONOMY AND EUROPE

PAPERMAC

First published 1996 by Macmillan

This Papermac edition published 1997 by Macmillan
an imprint of Macmillan Publishers Ltd
25 Eccleston Place, London SW1W 9NF
and Basingstoke

Associated companies throughout the world

ISBN 0 333 63297 4

1 3 5 7 9 8 6 4 2

A CIP catalogue record for this book is available from
the British Library.

Typeset by CentraCet Limited, Cambridge
Printed and bound in Great Britain by
Mackays of Chatham plc, Chatham, Kent

FOR MY LATE FATHER AND MOTHER

TO WHOM I OWE SO MUCH

Contents

ACKNOWLEDGEMENTS

This book owes much to the *Financial Times*. For the past thirteen years I have written for the newspaper about events economic and political. It has been a privileged vantage point from which to peer into the fast-turning kaleidoscope of modern Britain. I was first urged by a former editor, Sir Geoffrey Owen, to make more of it. His successor, Richard Lambert, provided the time and encouragement for me to do so.

Many other people at the *FT* helped, directly or indirectly, wittingly or unwittingly. We may not always agree, but Sir Samuel Brittan has long been an invaluable source of guidance and encouragement. So too have been Peter Norman and Joe Rogaly. David Snaddon and his colleagues in the newspaper's library never fail to turn up an obscure quotation or a yellowing newspaper cutting.

In the worlds of Westminster and Whitehall, dozens of politicians and officials have offered assistance. Many helped at the time the events took place; most gave additional valuable time during the past year. Once or twice I was lucky enough actually to participate in an event which subsequently found a place in the history books – or at least in the political memoirs. Then, or more recently, I have heard at first hand the views of the leading dramatis personae – Margaret Thatcher, Geoffrey Howe, Nigel Lawson, John Major, Michael Heseltine, Douglas Hurd, Norman Lamont and Kenneth Clarke among them. Needless to say, that does not imply that they will agree with my analysis and conclusions. Many other ministers and Conservative advisers have provided enlightenment. Sometimes the occasion has been an on-the-record interview, often a lunch or a late-night chat in the lobby of the House of Commons. For their insights over many years, I hope I can thank without in any way incriminating Chris Patten, Richard Ryder, Sarah Hogg, Tessa Keswick, Edward Bickham, Andrew Tyrie, Michael Maclay, Tom Arnold, Maurice Fraser, Tim Yeo and the late Judith Chaplin.

Sadly, our politics is not sufficiently mature to admit a thriving discourse between journalists and the civil service. Dozens of officials, senior and junior, in the Treasury, the Foreign Office, the Bank of England and the prime minister's office offered information and insights for this book, but, absurdly, to name them might be to cast a shadow over their careers, so I thank them anonymously.

At Macmillan, I would like to thank Tanya Stobbs, who has been perceptive and patient. The text was professionally and painstakingly copy-edited by Bob Davenport. Two friends Anthony Teasdale and Wolfgang Rieke read much of the book and made valuable suggestions. Everyone mentioned above, of course, is blameless as regards mistakes or misjudgements. This updated edition of *Politics and the Pound* takes the story to the autumn of 1996, with the threatened collision between British politics and Europe's plans for a single currency looming ever closer. Doubtless there will be more to add at a later stage.

In so far as it is possible to discard one's preconceptions and prejudices I have sought to present an objective account. This book is not intended as a grand polemic but to shine some light on the important but neglected world where economics and politics collide. I hope it will illuminate one or two lessons which might usefully be drawn by politicians of all persuasions. The big mistakes in economic management are made when politicians become prisoners of ideological certainties or of simple pride. Both life and economics are more complicated than our politics allows.

Finally, and most importantly, I must acknowledge my personal debt to Patty, Jessica and Benedict for putting up with me while I was I never there.

PHILIP STEPHENS

Autumn 1996

PREFACE

There is no more potent symbol of Britain's postwar decline than sterling. The relentless depreciation of the pound has paralleled the nation's retreat from influence. In 1960 one pound bought nearly twelve Deutschmarks or fourteen French francs; in mid-1995 it was worth a little over two Deutschmarks and just seven francs. The fall against the dollar, from $2.80 to around $1.50, was less dramatic, but sterling lost five-sixths of its value against the Japanese yen. Little more need be said about Britain's relative economic performance over the same thirty-five years.

The story is about more than economics, however. It is one in which politicians – prime ministers and chancellors – have been in turn mesmerized, bewildered and destabilized by the exchange rate. Politics and the pound have proved an unpredictably explosive mixture. At different moments, the government has sought to sustain sterling's exchange rate, to ignore it, and to devalue it. Sometimes the pound has been given an exalted role in economic management; at other times it has been treated as no more than one indicator among many. Occasionally the policy has been one of complete indifference. These approaches have been repaid at different times with economic upheaval and political convulsion. And, as ideology has alternated with pragmatism, sterling has continued to depreciate.

The governments of Margaret Thatcher and John Major have suffered as much as those of any of their predecessors – perhaps more. Uncertain of the economics and vexed by the politics, they have veered between parading a strong currency as an emblem of national renaissance and delighting in a competitive (the politicians' word for weak) exchange rate. Nowhere was that contradiction more apparent than in the aftermath of Black Wednesday, the moment on 16 September 1992 when sterling was ejected from the exchange rate mechanism of the European Monetary System. Days earlier, John Major's administration had been certain that the pound must stand alongside the Deutschmark in Europe's strong-currency club. Days afterwards, it was lauding the gains for British industry which would flow from sterling's enforced return to the second division.

That was only the most dramatic of many such swerves. At the outset of her premiership the free-market monetarism at the centre of Margaret Thatcher's project persuaded her to let the pound find its own level. For a brief moment at the start of the 1980s a surging pound was viewed as proof positive of the national revival she had promised. But Thatcher discovered soon enough that the price of political pride was the deepest economic recession since the 1930s. It was not long before the exchange rate resumed its fall. Nigel Lawson, among the most formidable of modern chancellors, was first trapped and then destroyed by his attempts to stabilize sterling.

Next, and most dangerously, came a crossover between the economics of the pound and the politics of Europe. Sterling became for many in the Conservative Party a badge of sovereignty. The pound may have been daily losing value against the Deutschmark and the French franc, even the lira and the Belgian franc, but it would never be surrendered. The entanglement, embedded in sterling's ill-fated membership of the ERM and later in the Tory civil war over a single European currency, did as much as anything to destroy Thatcher's premiership. It also drained the authority of John Major's administration.

The purpose of this book is to trace the policies and mistakes made by the Conservatives during the seventeen years from the start of Margaret Thatcher's first government in 1979. The text focuses on the power struggles over sterling which eventually saw the dramatic departures of Nigel Lawson, Geoffrey Howe and Margaret Thatcher, on the humiliation of Black Wednesday, and on the ideological divide over Europe which might yet break the Conservative Party. It examines the confusion in the minds of the politicians about the role of the exchange rate in a modern economy and its worth as a symbol of sovereignty. It points up the tensions and conflicts to come if Germany and France manage to rescue their ambition of a single European currency.

But, briefly at least, the picture should be painted on rather a broader canvas. Thatcher and Major were not the first prime ministers to be vexed by the exchange rate, and they certainly will not be the last. Events since 1979 exemplify a much more enduring tension in the nation's political psyche as it has been forced to admit to a much-diminished status as a middle-ranking power on the edge of the European continent. They symbolize Britain's ingrained ambivalence towards Europe, and its reluctance to accept the loosening of transatlantic ties and a less audible voice on the wider international stage. Not so long ago it was the pound's rate against the dollar that counted. Now it is that against the Deutschmark.

So a longer account might have started as far back as 1925, with Winston Churchill's appallingly misguided attempt to return sterling to the gold standard. For the previous century the convertibility of sterling into gold had encapsulated the strength and stability of Britain's imperial economy. After the guarantee had been suspended following the First World War, the attempt to restore it represented a last attempt to defy the emerging new economic and political order of the twentieth century. It also encapsulated the most oft-repeated of mistakes of Churchill's successors at the Treasury – the belief that, if the value of the pound is fixed, the real economy will adjust accordingly.

Churchill thought long and hard before announcing that sterling's gold convertibility would be restored at its pre-war rate of $4.86. When he announced the decision in the House of Commons, he was frank enough to admit his doubts. But his advisers – and above all Montagu Norman, the governor of the Bank of England – assured him that Britain's standing in the world depended on unshakeable confidence in the currency. It was a tragic error, born of the vanity of a political and economic establishment still living the glories of empire. An increase of about 10 per cent in the external value of sterling drove British exports from world markets and the domestic economy into brutal slump. In his famous tract of the same year, *The Economic Consequences of Mr Churchill*, John Maynard Keynes justly ridiculed the assumption that prices, costs and pay in the economy would adjust automatically to the higher exchange rate. But it took the Great Depression and a doubling of unemployment to the then extraordinary level of 2.5 million to persuade Ramsay MacDonald's national government to break with gold in 1931. The economic lesson of this dismal episode – that politicians cannot escape the hard truths of the real economy by pulling on the straitjacket of a high exchange rate – should have been better learned by Mr Churchill's successors. So too should have been the political moral that, in managing sterling, nothing is more dangerous than pride.

The Bretton Woods arrangements set up at the end of the Second World War marked an attempt to provide a more rational alternative to the gold standard. Established at a conference in the New Hampshire town of that name in 1944, this system of fixed but adjustable exchange rates aimed to combine the stability of the gold standard with the flexibility demanded by the changing geography of the world economy. In the most explicit acknowledgement of the political and economic hegemony of the United States, the dollar provided the formal anchor for this new international monetary system (although the US currency was backed in turn by the racks of gold bars at Fort Knox). For a quarter of a century, until the system's breakdown in the early 1970s, Bretton Woods did indeed help build stable international foundations for economic reconstruction. But the system failed to end the confusion among British politicians between cause and effect in economic management. In the newly created Federal Republic of Germany and in Japan, appreciating currencies reflected the success of their postwar economic policies. The strong Deutschmark and yen, however, were a measure of that success, not the cause of it. In Britain during the same period, a weak pound mirrored a weakening economy. Attempts to deny that reality by sustaining an overvalued parity within the Bretton Woods system served only to delay the inevitable reckoning.

Sterling was fixed initially at $4.03 – a rate which was too high, but one which reflected Britain's understandable, but ill-judged, perception that, as a victor of the war, its future economic prosperity was assured. Despite substantial financial assistance from the US, maintaining that parity placed a permanent balance of payments constraint on the pace of growth in the British economy. Exports were too expensive, imports too cheap. Sterling's role as a widely traded international reserve currency – another legacy of empire – tightened the noose on British policy-makers. The so-called 'sterling balances' in the hands of past and present overseas dominions would haunt successive governments until they were finally dispersed by James Callaghan during the late 1970s.

Bretton Woods had another weakness so far as British governments were concerned – it hardened the equation between devaluation and political humiliation. Thus Clement Attlee's Labour government never fully recovered from the devaluation of 1949, when it was obliged to lower sterling's exchange rate against the dollar to $2.80. Two years later Attlee went into opposition. Nor did the devaluation solve the problem. The 1950s are remembered now as a golden age, when output grew steadily and prices were more or less stable. In fact the period was punctuated by frequent speculative onslaughts on the pound, resisted only at the expense of deflationary domestic policies and repeated outflows from the Bank of England's foreign currency reserves. Sterling's weakness then, as later, was a symptom of a more fundamental malaise – a failure to re-equip and invest, the increasing polarization of industry between management and unions, and a mistaken assumption that the export markets of empire could be taken for granted in a post-imperial world.

These were not problems which could be solved by sustaining a high exchange rate. But the politicians had stigmatized devaluation. The failure of the first years of Harold Wilson's administration was due more than anything else to to his determination that, come what may, he would not be the second Labour prime minister since the war to devalue the pound. Of course, he was eventually forced to do just that. And the political backlash when he bowed to the inevitable in November 1967 was all the more intense because of his previous insistence on equating devaluation with national humiliation. It seems absurd that an adjustment in sterling's exchange rate from $2.80 to $2.40 could so cripple the Wilson government. But then John Major made the same mistake twenty-five years later, allowing an unsustainable Deutschmark parity of DM2.95 to define the difference between the failure and success of his administration. Perhaps both men would have done better had they been willing subsequently to apologize for their mistakes.

To be fair, if the first quarter of a century after the war illuminated the futility of seeking to build economic success on the single plank of a strong exchange rate, the next twenty-five years carried a rather different message. A falling exchange rate was no more a cure for relative economic decline than a fixed parity. Anthony Barber, the chancellor in Edward Heath's Conservative government, saw the break-up of Bretton Woods in the early 1970s as a cost-free liberation. No longer would the pace of economic expansion be constrained by the balance of payments; instead a floating exchange rate could take the strain if demand in the domestic economy outpaced that in Britain's main competitors. It was a short-lived dream. The Barber boom collided with the first oil-price shock and ended in the new economic phenomenon of the 1970s – stagflation.

Heath's successor, James Callaghan, discovered at similar cost that a floating pound did not exempt the government from the laws of economics. The sterling crisis of 1976 was spread over weeks and months rather than concentrated in a single act of devaluation. It was the trigger none the less for his government's crushing submission to the International Monetary Fund. The IMF experience reinforced once again Labour's reputation as the party of devaluation – a legacy which stayed with subsequent leaders. Had Attlee not devalued in 1949, Wilson might well have pre-empted the humiliation of 1967 by adjusting sterling's parity as soon as he took office three years earlier. And, had Callaghan not been humbled by the IMF, the

Labour Party might not have allowed itself to become so closely identified fifteen years later with the Conservatives' policy of sustaining sterling's position in the ERM.

Free-floating, of course, coincided with monetarism – the revival in Britain of the belief that the scourge of the 1970s, inflation, could be defeated by quantitative restrictions on the supply of money in the economy. For a brief period it looked as if sterling might slip into the background of economic policy-making. But the early 1980s also saw the dawning of the global capital market, injecting a new volatility, and unpredictability, into currency relationships. The long-assumed relationship between the exchange rate and the underlying performance of the economy was fatally fractured.

Under Bretton Woods and the gold standard, the value of sterling had been a reliable proxy for shifts in the balance of payments. A falling pound would signify a deficit on external trade, a strong pound the reverse. The scrapping of international controls on capital flows and an explosion in the turnover of foreign exchange trading transformed the financial markets. In a world of footloose capital looking for the best, short-term, return, the old assumptions no longer held. The value of sterling might still reflect over the long run the balance between the nation's exports and imports. In between times, however, investor fashions and the relative returns offered in inter-national bond markets could drive the currency in the opposite direction. The traders hunched over their flickering screens in the world's financial centres might well attach more weight to arbitrage opportunities or to the political mood than to the state of the balance of payments.

The 'overshooting' of the dollar during the first Reagan presidency was the most obvious example of this phenomenon, but sterling was not immune. The apostles of floating rates had argued during the 1970s that sound management of the domestic economy would guarantee a stable currency. If that was ever true, it was not so for most of the 1980s. By 1992, when the markets brushed aside Europe's central banks to fracture the ERM, the daily turnover of foreign exchange transactions had reached $1,200bn.

In this bruising world of mobile capital and instantaneous transactions, the exchange rate also became one of the most important conduits of inflation. It is to fall into the trap of oversimplification to argue that a falling exchange rate was of itself the fundamental cause of inflation. Although it must be said that the steady decline in the internal purchasing power of the pound matches almost precisely the fall in sterling's value against the Deutschmark, it was the performance of the real rather than the monetary economy that remained the decisive influence on prices as well as output. But, in an open economy like that of the UK, sterling's role as a transmission mechanism for domestic price changes was incontrovertible.

It was with these complexities that the Conservatives grappled after 1979 and which are the theme of this book. If there was a single thread, it was the mistaken assumption that the exchange rate, strong or weak, could solve the daunting problems still facing the British economy. There has been a constant confusion between sterling's role as an indicator and as an instrument of economic policy – between cause and effect.

The future holds no easy answers. At the time of writing, Germany and France seem ever more determined to meet the deadline of the Maastricht treaty for the creation of a single European currency before the end of the century. Nothing is certain, but the odds are that they will be joined by upwards of five other members of the EU. It is apparent also that, whatever the outcome of the general election due in the late spring of 1997, Britain is unlikely to be in the vanguard of economic and monetary union.

A decision to join would break the Conservative party. John Major has said privately that he would never make it. Mr Major has no intention of appearing in the history books as the prime minister who abolished the pound. Tony Blair has struck a positive rhetorical note. He appears certain that if the project proceeds, Britain will have to be part of it at some stage. But Mr Blair has signalled also that there would be formidable obstacles to British participation in 1999. After what will be eighteen years in opposition, an incoming Labour government would be justifiably wary of gambling its future so quickly on such a momentous decision. Jean Monnet, the founding father of the European Community, remarked soon after its inception that the British, being realists, would join after the new organization had proved its worth. Perhaps the same will be true of a single European currency.

What is dispiriting is the absence of serious and measured debate. The political issues are susceptible neither to the nationalist slogans trumpeted by many on the Tory right nor to the wide-eyed enthusiasm of those who cling on to a federalist ideal born of the 1950s rather than the 1990s. The horrors of the Bosnian conflict offer ample testimony to the need to preserve the postwar cohesion in Europe which was the central ambition of the European Community's founding fathers. The post-communist world demands that it extend its frontiers to central and eastern Europe, but does not undermine the central importance of Franco-German rapprochement. Britain least of all would benefit from a fragmentation of the post-Maastricht European Union which saw Germany looking east rather than west. It cannot wish away the reality that Europe will shape its future. Margaret Thatcher feared above all a German Europe. In applauding the virtues of the nation state she ignored the risk of a resurgence of German nationalism. And those on the Eurosceptic right of the Tory party who espouse a return of the balance-of-power diplomacy of the nineteenth century rarely extend the historical perspective to 1914.

But neither do the enthusiasts for a single currency tell the whole story. A successful, and inclusive, economic and monetary union would require a degree of political integration which may run well ahead of the present mood of national electorates, particularly in Britain. A single currency of itself would not submerge national identites and cultures in a European superstate. To operate successfully, however, it would presume a degree of supra-national co-ordination of economic, and particularly fiscal, policy which would extend significantly beyond the narrowly defined parameters in the Maastricht treaty. There is no reason why this should not command the consent of the people in time. But that consent should not be taken for granted.

The economic debate has been enveloped in a similar fog. Those who demand that Britain save sterling at all costs ignore both its history of depreciation and the transformation of the financial markets. Much of the sovereignty they seek to retain passed long ago from the hands of the government to international investors and markets. And those who believe that a weak pound will ensure Britain's economic success need only to look again at the exchange rates quoted at the outset of this preface. If Germany and France press ahead with economic and monetary union, the result of staying outside is as likely to be higher inflation and interest rates as a competitive edge in European markets. A single currency, however, cannot be used as a instrument to force convergence among disparate economies. If it is, the consequences in Britain at least will be similar to those endured under the gold standard. The economic convergence must be real; and any objective analysis of the state of the British economy suggests that will take some time yet. If Europe creates a single currency and it works, Britain will certainly join at some point. To remain outside for ever would be take the path of progressive detachment from the European continent and to

surrender British influence in events which will none the less determine the
nation's destiny. But as the politicians debate the issue, they would do well
to learn one small lesson of history. So far as sterling is concerned dogma is
the most dangerous enemy of the rational decision.

CHAPTER ONE

CONVICTION

MARGARET THATCHER entered Downing Street in May 1979 with all the certainties of opposition. James Callaghan's Labour administration had had its spirit broken during a term never free from economic or political crises. It had survived rather than governed. As it happened, the economic outlook in the summer of 1979 was improving. The annual inflation rate had fallen to below half the rates of 20 per cent and above seen in the mid-1970s. North Sea oil would soon dispel the balance of payments deficits and repeated sterling crises which had plagued the Callaghan and Wilson administrations. But the 1978 winter of discontent, the strife within its own ranks at Westminster and sheer exhaustion had drained the Labour Party of the will to govern. Callaghan forecast the election defeat in a famous remark to his political adviser Bernard Donoughue. The tide of history was running against them, he said. A sea-change in the public mood of a kind seen only once in every thirty years or more would carry the Conservatives to office.[1]

Thatcher's radicalism was circumscribed during these early years by a cabinet largely inherited from Edward Heath. The rose-tinted spectacles through which many Conservatives now view this first administration obscure the contemporary uncertainties, mistakes and divisions. The new prime minister was sure of her fundamental agenda, however. The defeat of inflation, the taming of the trade unions, the scrapping of a panoply of state controls over the economy, and the re-establishment of incentives for personal initiative provided the core of the prospectus. Her government would create the conditions under which individuals would reclaim control of their lives from the state. Pre-eminent among these conditions was control of inflation: sound money was the slogan which echoed through the Thatcher years. As the 1979 Conservative election manifesto stated, 'The pound today is worth less than half of its 1974 value. On present form it would be halved in value yet again within eight years. Inflation on this scale has come near to destroying our political and social stability.'

It was the internal purchasing power of the currency – what Harold Wilson had unwisely referred to as 'the pound in your pocket' after the 1967 devaluation – rather than sterling's exchange rate against the currencies of its international competitors which preoccupied the incoming government. As it turned out, however, an unprecedented surge in sterling's value against the dollar and the Deutschmark would prove the decisive factor in the rapid disinflation of the domestic economy during the early 1980s. The exchange rate returned to centre-stage by accident rather than design. Thatcher's predecessors had been haunted by regular speculative storms on the currency markets. For its first few years North Sea oil would spare the incoming government such humiliations. But Thatcher would discover quickly that a strong pound created almost as many problems, and that, rising or falling, the exchange rate could not be ignored.

Sterling had floated freely since the summer of 1972 after a short-lived attempt by the Heath administration to tie it to other European currencies in the so-called 'Snake'. The wider Bretton Woods arrangements had begun to fracture some years earlier as the dollar, the anchor for the system, came under increasing pressure on financial markets. The international monetary arrangements agreed at Bretton Woods in 1944 anchored the world's currencies to the dollar in a system of fixed but adjustable exchange rates. The dollar's value was in turn guaranteed by its convertibility to gold. But the financial burdens imposed on the United States by the Vietnam War obliged President Richard Nixon to abandon this convertibility in August 1971. Four months later the dollar was devalued against other major currencies in an attempt to salvage the relative stability provided by the system during the previous quarter-century. The Smithsonian Agreement in December 1971 also introduced new rules to allow wider margins of fluctuation either side of the agreed rate for each currency against the dollar. In May 1972 the six founding members of the European Community sought to buttress these more flexible arrangements by establishing a separate grid to promote stability between European currencies. Initially, the six – Germany, France, Italy, The Netherlands, Belgium and Luxembourg – were joined in the Snake by Britain, Denmark and Ireland, which were due to accede to the Community the following January. Anthony Barber, the British chancellor, managed to keep sterling within the Snake mechanism – the precursor of the European Monetary System – for only six weeks. In a move which foreshadowed the subsequent 'Barber boom', the government announced on 23 June that the pound would henceforth float freely against other currencies. Barber wanted the freedom to devalue the currency and reflate the economy. During the following year, sterling depreciated by 20 per cent against the strongest European currencies. Denmark and Ireland followed Britain out of the system, undercutting its credibility at the outset. The intention to create a zone of European currency stability was then undermined fatally by the formal abandonment in March 1973 of the Bretton Woods system. The Snake did survive in a much narrower form until the creation of the European Monetary System in 1979, but by then France and Italy had also been driven out.

Floating exchange rates gave the Heath and subsequent Wilson and Callaghan governments a degree of flexibility, but did not grant them immunity from the foreign exchange markets. The era of empire had left sterling with a disproportionately prominent role in the international financial system. Until the late 1970s it remained the world's second reserve currency. The sterling balances held by overseas central banks left the pound particularly vulnerable to any deterioration in the nation's balance of payments position and to short-term shifts in sentiment on foreign exchange markets. The Labour government elected in late February 1974 soon discovered that the exchange rate continued to impose a powerful restraint on its freedom of manœuvre.

Five months earlier, in October 1973, the Yom Kippur War between Israel and her Arab neighbours had set the stage for the first international oil-price shock. By the start of 1974 the price charged by the Arab-dominated Organisation of Petroleum Exporting Countries had more than quadrupled, from $2.50 to over $11 a barrel. The Labour administration responded by seeking to maintain the level of demand and employment in the domestic economy through higher spending and borrowing. Most other leading industrial nations took the opposite course, reacting to higher fuel costs by deflating their economies. The result was an increase in Britain's current-account deficit, which could be financed only briefly by the recycling of the huge financial surpluses accumulated by the OPEC countries. The government failed to prevent the economy from moving into recession, but the inflation rate accelerated rapidly, ushering in an unprecedented period of 'stagflation'.

By the autumn of 1976 the government, now headed by James Callaghan, was engulfed by a full-scale sterling crisis. It was forced to call in aid from the International Monetary Fund – a political humiliation from which it would never recover. As the price of the credits needed to restore confidence in the pound, the IMF imposed sharp reductions in government spending and borrowing and demanded a medium-term commitment to curb the growth of private credit. In effect, the Fund obliged Denis Healey, the then chancellor, to put in place the framework for economic policy which would provide the foundation for Thatcher's subsequent monetarist experiment. For her part, the leader of Her Majesty's Loyal Opposition did not lose an opportunity to remind Callaghan of the national defeat represented by the submission to the IMF.

Sterling's depreciation was quickly reversed once the government had bowed to the Fund's demands (in 1977 the Treasury found itself cutting interest rates to prevent the pound rising too fast), but the episode remained a potent symbol of economic failure. As had happened in 1949 and in 1967, a Labour government had been bloodied by the foreign exchange markets. At the height of the crisis, in September 1976, Healey was obliged to abandon at the last moment a trip to Manila for the annual meeting of the IMF. His humiliating about-turn at Heathrow Airport joined Wilson's televised address to the nation after the 1967 devaluation as one of the more haunting images in the scrapbook of modern British politics. The economists and policy advisers who were shaping in opposition the economic approach which Thatcher would take to 10 Downing Street were strong advocates of a floating pound. She could never quite erase, however, the image of devaluation as a mark of national decline.

*

During the late 1970s Giscard d'Estaing of France and Helmut Schmidt of Germany determined to restore order to European currency markets. In 1972 the European Community had endorsed an ambitious proposal for economic and monetary union known as the Werner Plan, after the Luxembourg prime minister Pierre Werner. But the breakdown of the Bretton Woods system had obliged it to abandon the project. So in 1978 the French president and German chancellor determined to replace the Snake with a more robust mechanism – the European Monetary System (EMS). The concept was similar to that of the Snake: currencies in the exchange rate mechanism (ERM) of the new system would be allowed to fluctuate by 2.25 per cent either side of an agreed central parity against the European Currency Unit, itself a composite of the nine European Community currencies. The Deutschmark, whose value had been protected during the postwar period by the Federal Republic's success in controlling inflation, would act as an anchor for the system in a role similar to that of the dollar under the Bretton Woods system. Efforts to maintain the agreed parities through concerted central bank intervention would be buttressed by the pooling of a fifth of all national foreign exchange reserves in a newly created European Monetary Cooperation Fund. This would offer substantial short- and medium-term credit facilities to governments whose currencies faced speculative attack. At the Brussels summit in December 1978, six of the nine European Community governments – Germany, France, The Netherlands, Belgium, Luxembourg and Denmark – agreed to join. Those of Italy and Ireland initially reserved their position, but decided soon afterwards to participate.

Callaghan, however, kept sterling outside the ERM, while indicating his readiness to participate in the pooling of currency reserves and the medium-term credit facilities of the wider EMS. He told the House of Commons on his return from the Brussels summit that an attempt to tie the pound to the Deutschmark would be needlessly deflationary. Britain's industrial competitiveness was already being undermined by a weak dollar, and in Callaghan's view the ERM 'would place obligations on us that might result in unnecessary deflation and unemployment'.[2]

At the Treasury, Denis Healey drew the same conclusion after a remarkably frank admission from Manfred Lahnstein, the head of the West German finance ministry, of his government's motivation. Lahnstein acknowledged that the Bonn government expected that, over the medium to long term, the ERM would cap the value of the Deutschmark against other European currencies, delivering to West Germany a sustained competitive edge over its neighbours.[3] Membership of the system would involve other, more short-term, risks. Treasury officials had been scarred by the experiences of 1967 and 1976: a fixed parity in the ERM would give the financial markets a target, leave sterling vulnerable once again to the speculative pressure which had proved so destructive of the government's economic strategy in the past. The economic case against membership was reinforced by the government's precarious political position. In the late 1970s the Euroscepticism which would later flourish on the Conservative back benches at Westminster was far more prevalent on the Labour side. By staying out of the ERM, Callaghan avoided a rebellion among his own MPs.

Given her later antipathy to Europe in general and to the ERM in particular, Thatcher's response in the House of Commons exchanges in December 1978 is fascinating. While the prime minister stressed that he had acted in the 'national interest', Thatcher lamented Britain's exclusion from the European Community's first division. 'This is a sad day for Europe,' she began. The Labour government was 'content to have Britain openly classifed among the poorest and least influential members' of the Community. What was it that had prevented Callaghan from signing up, she asked rhetorically: 'Was it economic weakness and lack of competitiveness?'[4]

Within only a few years, during her protracted struggle with Nigel Lawson over ERM membership, she would be echoing the Labour leader, admitting that the economy was not strong enough to bear a formal link between sterling and the Deutschmark and citing the national interest for her refusal to join the ERM. In late 1978, however, Thatcher had yet to develop fully the visceral distrust of attempts to peg the exchange rate and the deep antipathy towards European integration which would later break her cabinet and precipitate her own downfall. Formally at least, the Conservatives were committed both to greater exchange rate stability and to closer cooperation in Europe. Geoffrey Howe, then shadow chancellor, set out the position in the first House of Commons debate on the EMS, held just before the Brussels summit. Howe told MPs that 'A set of rules applying nationally and internationally should be respected and would show a desire to eliminate inflation within the national boundaries and to secure as far as possible stability between currency units.'[5]

The Conservative Party took the same approach in its manifesto for the first direct elections for the European Parliament, held only weeks after Thatcher's entry into 10 Downing Street. By now the ERM, which had been formally inaugurated in March 1979, included the currencies of every EC country except Britain. The manifesto for the June 1979 elections said that the government 'supported the objectives of the new system', which included closer coordination of national economic policies as well as greater currency stability. 'We shall look for ways in which Britain can take her rightful place within it,' the manifesto added.[6] The statement was the precursor to the subsequent formula that sterling would join the system when the time was 'ripe' (or 'right'). This particular phrase would in time become Thatcher's excuse to defer indefinitely a decision, providing the spark for her fatal confrontation with Nigel Lawson and Geoffrey Howe.

Whatever Margaret Thatcher's longer-term intent, there was general agreement that a target for the exchange rate would not slot easily into the economic framework envisaged by the incoming government. It determined to defeat inflation by imposing strict limits on the growth of the money supply. Thatcher was no trained economist, but she had embraced with enthusiasm the monetarist theory which had become fashionable during the early 1970s. This prime minister took her anti-statist philosophy from the teachings of Friedrich von Hayek, and her economics from the monetarism of Milton Friedman. The texts were Hayek's *The Road to Serfdom*, the Austrian-born libertarian's assault on proposals for postwar state planning, and Friedman's *Studies in the Quantity Theory of Money*, the Chicago-school economist's redefinition of eighteenth-century monetarism.

The idea of controlling inflation by reining back the amount of money in circulation had an instinctive appeal for a politician who saw no reason why the nation's finances should not be managed on the same basis as those of any prudent household or corner shop. So her economic strategy drew on principles first enunciated in the 1750s as the quantity theory of money by the Scottish philosopher David Hume. This theory, developed at the time when currencies were anchored to the gold standard but then updated by Friedman, saw strict control of the domestic money supply as the prerequisite for stable prices. In the simplest terms, if the government was successful in restricting the supply of money in the economy, there would be no threat of inflation. The international value of the pound would also be safeguarded. In Friedman's later interpretation, 'The central fact is that inflation is always and everywhere a monetary phenomenon. Historically, substantial changes in prices have always occurred together with substantial changes in the quantity of money relative to output.'[7]

In fact Hume's proposition had been overturned in the intellectual revolution marked by the publication in 1936 of John Maynard Keynes's *General Theory of Employment, Interest and Money*. Keynes challenged the basic assumption of early monetarism: that there was a stable causal relationship between the stock of money in an economy and the level of national income and prices. The classical economic tradition which developed alongside the gold standard made two assumptions which did not hold in the more complex world of the 1930s. Classical theorists based the arguments for a stable link between money and prices on the premise that economies tended naturally to operate at full capacity and that money, backed by gold, could be easily defined and readily correlated with the volume of transactions in the economy. During the 1930s, mass unemployment and the growing sophistication of financial markets had undercut both assumptions. Keynes demonstrated that in a modern, credit-based economy, money was as much an instrument for speculative investment as a means of facilitating transactions in the real economy. Interest rates were the critical influence and, depending on their level and the volume of spare capacity in the economy, an increase in the supply of money could just as well lead to increased holdings of bonds and other financial instruments as to higher spending and inflation. So the supply of money could not be taken as a reliable proxy for the level of output and prices in the economy. Keynes did not conclude that money was irrelevant, but his analysis provided the basis for a postwar economic consensus in which fiscal rather than monetary policy became the primary instrument of government attempts to regulate the economy.

As David Smith recounts in *The Rise and Fall of Monetarism*, it was this consensus that Friedman and his colleagues in the Chigaco school of economics sought to overturn during the 1950s. Friedman's restatement of the quantity theory sought to answer Keynes's critique, arguing that Keynes had overstated the influence of interest rates, and that the relationship between the money stock and prices had survived rapid financial innovation. Initially there was little enthusiasm for Friedman's analysis: the Bretton Woods exchange rate system was widely seen as an adequate financial discipline on the major industrial economies. Nor did Friedman answer more basic critiques of monetarism. It may be statistically accurate that if growth in the money supply far exceeds increases in national output, inflation by definition will accelerate. The link, however, is as coincident as it is causal. For any given increase in the supply of money in a particular economy, a myriad of other factors – the level of spare capacity, wages, investment, competitiveness – will determine whether the result is faster economic growth or accelerating prices. It is as true that the behaviour of output and prices determines the amount of money as vice versa. The attractive simplicity of the new monetarism also ignored the difficulties of choosing the right measure of money to target and of establishing whether it maintained a reasonable correlation with price changes. That particular dilemma was identified during the 1970s in what became known as Goodhart's Law. Formulated by Charles Goodhart, a senior economic adviser at the Bank of England, it stated with some prescience of the supposed link between money supply targets and inflation that 'Any observed statistical regularity will tend to collapse once pressure is placed on it for control purposes.'[8]

In 1979, however, the incoming government was not intimidated by such complexities. The runaway-inflation of the 1970s and the perceived failure of Keynesian fiscal policies to shield the economy from recession provided fertile ground for Friedmanite monetarism. The inflationary boom which had followed Anthony Barber's decision to float the pound had been widely associated with a rapid expansion

of domestic credit. Efforts to contain inflation through direct controls
on incomes and prices were proving ineffectual. For the Conservatives, monetarism offered an answer which could be translated readily
into an explicable political slogan: if the government stopped printing
money, inflation would be tamed. It also provided the intellectual
framework to jettison the postwar consensus that governments could
ensure adequate demand in the economy through higher public
spending and borrowing. The free-market Institute for Economic
Affairs and two prominent economic writers, Samuel Brittan of the
Financial Times and Peter Jay of *The Times*, took a rather more
sophisticated version of Friedman's approach to a wider audience.
Henceforth, macro-economic policy would be directed not at maintaining any particular path for growth but at curbing inflation.

The Callaghan government had managed to reduce the annual
inflation rate from 24 per cent in 1976 to an average of a little over 8
per cent in 1978 before it began to pick up again during the first half
of 1979. When Thatcher entered Downing Street, however, several
developments gave new momentum to the acceleration. Abroad, the
overthrow of the Shah of Iran and the subsequent Iran–Iraq war
delivered a second oil shock to western economies. Oil prices during
early 1981 would touch $40 a barrel, up from $12 three years earlier,
before plummeting again in the middle of the decade. At home, a
large shift from income to value-added tax in Geoffrey Howe's first
Budget in June 1979, the breakdown of the Labour government's
incomes policy, and the Conservatives' pre-election commitment to
honour large public-sector pay awards all pushed up domestic prices.
The annual rate of increase in the retail price index, which had crept
up to 11.4 per cent in June 1979, jumped to 15.6 per cent in the
following month after Howe almost doubled VAT from 8.5 to 15 per
cent. The rate continued to accelerate for nearly a year, reaching a
peak of 21.9 per cent in May 1980.

The particular monetarist framework adopted by Howe had its
origins in the 1976 IMF crisis. Howe chose to set targets to constrain
the growth of one of the broad measures of the money supply, known
as sterling M3. He planned to buttress those targets with a much
tighter grip on public spending and borrowing. Sterling M3 measured

the amount of money circulating in the economy as notes and coins as well as the much larger liquidity base represented by deposits with the banking system. Its growth rate could be calculated fairly readily through analysis of its principal 'counterparts' – the level of government borrowing, the volume of lending by the banks, and financial flows across the foreign exchange markets. Sterling M3's performance had been monitored by the Treasury for several years, and its annual rate of expansion had shown a reasonably stable correlation with the general pace of price increases in the economy. The assumption was also that the government could effectively regulate the growth rate of sterling M3 both by adjusting interest rates and by reducing government borrowing.

Though still regarded with some scepticism by many senior Treasury officials, sterling M3 had first been targeted by Denis Healey as part of the price of the IMF credits. Healey had little confidence in the money supply as a guide to policy, but understood well enough that to restore the confidence of the financial markets the Treasury needed a visible lodestar for its economic policy. In his own words, Healey was an 'unbelieving' monetarist – an opportunist rather than a convert to the new economic fashion. Once he had left office, he was to comment laconically of his flirtation with the theories of Milton Friedman that 'A government takes great risks when it flies in the face of market opinion . . . however misguided that opinion may be.'[9]

Howe's team at the Treasury was made up of 'believing' monetarists. While Healey set goals for sterling M3 in order to appease the financial markets (and then, by some quirk of fate, managed to hit them), Howe announced targets with the intention of meeting them (and inevitably missed). A barrister by profession, Howe was never a doctrinaire monetarist. He soon tired of the arcane intellectual arguments which developed almost as soon as the strategy was put in place, remarking in his 1980 Budget speech that 'monetarism means curbing the excessive expansion of money and credit . . . It is a great pity that its practical, common-sense importance has been so confused by arid, theoretical disputes.'[10] But he was persuaded that sterling M3 had proved its worth during the last years of the Callaghan government and that a clear target was essential to deliver low inflation.

Nigel Lawson, then financial secretary to the Treasury, was the real intellectual enthusiast. As he remarked in a lecture to the

Conservative Bow Group, the government's economic strategy was founded on two basic propositions: 'The first is that changes in the quantity of money determine, at the end of the day, changes in the price level; the second is that government is able to determine the quantity of money.'[11] In these early years Lawson was technically the third-ranking minister in the Treasury, but he was to prove the driving force behind the new strategy.

The appeal of a money supply target went beyond the promised short-cut to lower inflation. It provided a direct bridge to the government's other ambition – to shrink the size of the state and lower taxes by cutting public spending and borrowing. The public-sector borrowing requirement (PSBR) – the gap between government spending and revenues – was a key counterpart of sterling M3. So the two objectives dovetailed neatly – reducing public borrowing was integral to controlling the government's chosen measure of money. The Treasury, which has always seen its most vital task as reining back the demands of the Whitehall spending departments, was enthusiastic about the symmetry. Douglas Wass, the permanent secretary, and other senior officials did not share Lawson's monetarist zeal, but they recognized the potential advantages of a policy which promised clarity and simplicity. The message to the cabinet was unequivocal: unless it reined back spending, the growth rate of sterling M3 would overshoot its targets. That would lead to higher interest rates – the only other instrument available to the Treasury to rein in monetary growth. Monetarism, as one senior official put it, 'provided just the right structure of incentives . . . we never really believed in sterling M3, but it was helpful that ministers did'.

The targets for sterling M3 were formally enshrined in the Medium Term Financial Strategy (MTFS), drafted by Nigel Lawson and published alongside the March 1980 Budget. Henceforth the MTFS would be updated annually to provide a permanent framework for policy. The first MTFS set descending target ranges for the growth rate of sterling M3 during the following four years. It was to be allowed to expand by between 7 and 11 per cent in the 1980/81 financial year, but by 1983/84 its rate of growth would be restricted to 4 to 8 per cent. Those targets were accompanied by a commitment to parallel reductions in public borrowing. The PSBR was to be cut from nearly 5 per cent of national income in 1979/80 to 1.5 per cent by 1983/84.

The overall aim was to achieve a decisive downward shift in inflationary expectations among managers and trade union negotiators. The logic was that if both sides of industry could see in advance that the government would not allow excessive pay awards to feed through into higher prices they would adjust their behaviour accordingly. The cost in terms of lost output and higher unemployment of squeezing out inflation would be correspondingly less. The belief that expectations were central to a successful counter-inflation strategy had been foreshadowed in *The Right Approach to the Economy*, published in 1977, which stated, 'Monetary targets openly proclaimed can have a crucial effect in reducing inflationary expectations.'[12] Lawson pressed initially for a still more rigid framework in the MTFS, suggesting a single target for monetary growth rather than a series of permitted ranges. The idea was opposed by the Bank of England. Gordon Richardson, the Bank governor, and his deputy, Kit McMahon, raised powerful objections to an excessively doctrinaire approach. Conscious of the disinflationary impact of a sharp rise in the exchange rate, they argued to some effect that the signals provided by the money supply should be interpreted more flexibly.[13]

Even before the ink was dry on this first MTFS, its foundations had been cracked by the government's separate drive to liberalize the economy. Six months earlier Howe, urged on by Lawson, had taken the dramatic step of scrapping the controls on foreign exchange transactions which had been in place since the Second World War. Industry, banks and individuals henceforth were free to borrow and lend in the currency of their choice. Individuals no longer faced any limits on the amount of sterling they could take abroad. The change rendered ineffectual parallel restrictions on the lending operations of domestic banks, because these banks could now move their operations offshore to evade them. So the dismantling of foreign exchange controls was followed in mid-1980 by the abolition of the Supplementary Special Deposit Scheme, the so-called 'corset' restrictions on domestic credit expansion. Taken together the two measures undermined decisively the Treasury's ability to keep within its self-imposed monetary straitjacket. As the economist Christopher Johnson puts it in a crisp account of this ill-fated monetarist experiment in *The Economy under Mrs Thatcher*:

The government's aim of reducing inflation had to be reconciled with its other main economic principle, that of the free market. Conservative policy-makers failed to spot the incompatibility of abolishing controls and restrictive practices in markets such as those for credit, foreign exchange, securities, housing and labour, yet seeking to retain strict official curbs on one key market – that for money.[14]

The 7 to 11 per cent annual target range set by Howe in the MTFS for the growth rate of sterling M3 was quickly exceeded. In two months alone, July and August 1981, the measure rose by 10 per cent as a result of the abolition of the corset. During the 1980/81 financial year as a whole it expanded by 18.4 per cent – more than seven percentage points above the top of its planned range. As Keynes had explained fifty years earlier, the use to which money is put is as important as the overall amount.

This rapid growth of the money supply, however, belied the draconian financial squeeze applied by high interest rates and, above all, by an unprecedented surge in the value of sterling. It was this rise in the exchange rate rather than any success in meeting its money supply targets which would deliver the low inflation the government promised – but at an unexpectedly and unnecessarily high price in terms of lost output and employment. Interest rates were raised to record levels (17 per cent in November 1979) in an attempt to rein in monetary growth. The high cost of borrowing did not constrain the growth of liquidity (perversely, it contributed to still faster growth because it attracted more bank deposits), but it did deliver a powerful upward jolt to the exchange rate.

The value of the pound stood at DM3.80 and $2.10 when Margaret Thatcher entered 10 Downing Street. It had climbed steadily since the beginning of 1979, in anticipation of the economic benefits of North Sea oil and of the election of a Conservative government committed to low inflation. The reality of the election victory and the Thatcher government's pledge (backed by higher interest rates and immediate reductions in public spending) to put the defeat of inflation above all other priorities added powerful momentum to the appreciation. So for a time did the weakness of the dollar at the end of Jimmy Carter's presidency. The abolition of exchange controls provided a partial safety-valve for the foreign currency income from the North Sea as companies and financial institutions built up new overseas assets. It succeeded only briefly in checking sterling's rise.

The incoming government did briefly consider joining the ERM. It agreed in the summer to endorse Callaghan's decision that, even while it stayed out of the exchange rate arrangements, Britain should participate in the wider EMS credit arrangements and deposit 20 per cent of its foreign currency reserves with the new European Monetary Cooperation Fund. At a subsequent meeting at 10 Downing Street in October 1979, Gordon Richardson put the case not for immediate entry but for the government to keep open ERM membership as a real option. Peter Carrington, the foreign secretary, took a similar tack. But, with the inflation rate still rising, sterling emerging as a petrocurrency and the Treasury developing the domestic monetary framework which would be enshrined in the MTFS, there was little real enthusiasm. In 1977 the Treasury and Bank had attempted to cap the sharp appreciation in the value of sterling which had followed the return of confidence after the previous year's IMF package. The Callaghan government had cut interest rates by an unprecedented ten percentage points to 5 per cent, and the Bank of England had bought more than $15bn of foreign currency for its reserves. The strategy had been abandoned, however, when the pound's depreciation threatened an acceleration in the inflation rates. So now, two years later, sterling was to be allowed to float freely upwards. It surged.

What was termed 'benign neglect' of the exchange rate also fitted the Thatcher government's monetarist strategy. Friedman and his colleagues in Chicago had long argued that fixed, or semi-fixed, exchange rates hindered the necessary adjustments between economies when they became misaligned because of variations in inflation rates. Governments would do better to concentrate on stabilizing the money supply and let currencies find their own equilibrium. The underlying assumption was that control of domestic inflation would translate into a relatively stable exchange rate. Nigel Lawson was among those to take Friedman at his word.

Much later Lawson would disclose that by the summer of 1981, soon after the government had begun to quietly ignore its monetary target in favour of ending the recession, he had flirted with the idea of ERM membership. As financial secretary, he raised the option during an internal Treasury review of monetary policy in 1981. One of the officials present recalls that his colleagues 'fell off their chairs' at the suggestion, since, publicly, Lawson had been one of the strongest defenders of a free-floating rate. Another saw the intervention as symptomatic of Lawson's desire to remain at the centre of attention, to establish his reputation as the government's principal economic thinker. In his memoirs, *The View from No. 11*, Lawson says that he also sent a private note to Howe in June 1981, advocating ERM membership during the second half of that year. He admits, however, that he was not entirely convinced by his own arguments. The note concluded, 'I have very mixed feelings about the course I have sketched out.'[15]

Whatever his private doubts, Lawson never showed them in his public statements. While Treasury and Bank officials were increasingly troubled by the damaging impact of a rising exchange rate on economic output and employment, the financial secretary was unyielding. During his days as a journalist he had dreamed of getting his hands on the levers of power; he was not inhibited by the responsibility. For its first two years, the MTFS did not bother to mention the exchange rate. Nor was Lawson shy then of justifying the official policy of letting the exchange rate find its own level. He tackled the pound's appreciation in a major economic policy speech delivered in Zurich two months before the 1981 Budget.

By then, Howe, with the support in 10 Downing Street of Alan Walters, Thatcher's economic adviser, was preparing to quietly ignore the rapid growth in sterling M3 and to respond to the strength of the pound with lower interest rates. Lawson, however, concluded a lengthy analysis of the government's strategy with the assertion 'It is essential from now on to secure a lower rate of growth of broad money, and indeed, over the three remaining years of the MTFS, it might well be prudent to claw back at least some of the excess growth that has already occurred.' As for the exchange rate, the sharp appreciation during 1980 should not be cause for concern as it was the result of the 'free play of market forces'. There was no alternative to domestic monetarism, he concluded:

The present government has no exchange rate policy as such – for the simple reason, as Switzerland among others has experienced, that the attempt to have such a policy greatly complicates (if it actually does not make it impossible) the difficult enough task of pursuing a sound monetary policy, without, at the end of the day, having any significant effect on the real exchange rate.[16]

Lawson could not have given a clearer, if soon redundant, defence of the neglect of sterling – intentionally benign but in practice malign – which characterized the first Thatcher years.

By the beginning of 1981, eighteen months after the election, sterling had risen to DM5.00 and to $2.40. Its overall value, measured against a basket of leading currencies, had increased by about 30 per cent. The appreciation, alongside the credit squeeze imposed by high interest rates, delivered the biggest deflationary shock to the economy since Winston Churchill's return to the gold standard in 1925. The higher exchange applied direct downward pressure to the inflation rate by reducing the price of imports, more than offsetting the higher cost of oil (which in turn fuelled sterling's appreciation). Indirectly, but more importantly, it undercut sharply the ability of companies to compete with overseas suppliers in both domestic and international markets. The damage to industrial competitiveness was compounded by the high level of pay settlements which followed the acceleration of inflation between mid–1979 and mid–1980. Between 1979 and 1981 the loss of international competitiveness suffered by some sectors was as much as 50 per cent. Predictably, companies reacted by cutting back output, closing plants and shedding labour at an unprecedented pace. The effect on the economy was startling. In direct response to the squeeze imposed by the exchange rate, national output fell by 5.5 per cent between the summer of 1979 and the first three months of 1981. Unemployment more than doubled, reaching 2.3 million by the end of 1981, and twelve months later it exceeded 3 million. It would not be until 1986 that the dole queues began to shrink again. Inflation, it was true, soon began to fall steeply (to 13 per cent in January 1981 and to 5 per cent by the end of 1982), but the cost of that success in terms of the real economy was much higher than either predicted or necessary.

The fact of the pound's appreciation was hardly surprising. Interest rates were at record levels, and the combination of the development of the North Sea and the second oil-price shock had transformed in the short term the outlook for the balance of payments. Terence (later Sir Terence) Burns, recruited by Howe in January 1980 from the London Business School as the government's chief economic adviser, belonged to what was known as the school of international monetarists. At the LBS, he had developed a model of the economy which identified the exchange rate as the principal 'transmission mechanism' for domestic price changes. Peter (later Sir Peter) Middleton, then the senior official in charge of monetary policy and the successor in 1983 to Sir Douglas Wass as permanent secretary, took a similar view. Middleton had been a pivotal figure in the establishment of the monetary framework put in place by the Callaghan government after the IMF crisis. He was not, however, a purist and he readily acknowledged a role for the exchange rate alongside targets for sterling M3. He had remarked in a speech to the Institute of Fiscal Studies in March 1978 that any change in interest rates had 'a rapid impact on the rest of the economy through its effects on the exchange rate and thence through the effects of changes in the exchange rate on prices, the current account balance and the level of activity.'[17]

What shocked the Treasury, and enraged industrialists, was the speed and extent of sterling's appreciation. At first most of the rise was attributed to the windfall gain to the balance of payments from North Sea oil. Only during the second half of 1980 did the government recognize that the high interest rates it had imposed in a vain attempt to control the money supply were the more significant factor. By then, manufacturing industry had responded with a massive retrenchment which would see eventually the loss of 2 million jobs and nearly a fifth of its pre-recession output. Blue-chip companies like ICI recorded losses for the first time in their history. The engineering industry was virtually destroyed. At the Confederation of British Industry's annual conference in November 1980, its director-general, Terence Beckett, summed up the mood of industry by calling for a 'bare-knuckle fight' with the government. The Treasury did respond, cutting interest rates twice in 1980, to 16 per cent in July and to 14 per cent in November. Lawson, however, forbade the Bank from admitting publicly that the moves were linked to the strength of sterling.

Lawson, in the intellectual driving-seat at the Treasury, favoured sticking with the policy, arguing that it was essential to break the inflationary psychology which had taken hold during the 1970s. Later he would keep faith with that judgement, seeing the pound's appreciation as the catalyst for a long overdue onslaught on decades of overmanning in manufacturing and for a decisive improvement in industrial productivity. He would admit, however, that 'Like everyone else I failed to see how high and for how long it [the pound] would continue to rise.'[18] Others in the cabinet were not quite so charitable in their interpretation. The then employment secretary, James Prior, demoted in 1981 for his opposition to the economic strategy, commented in his memoirs, *A Balance of Power*, that:

> All through the early period of Margaret's government I felt the Treasury team were out of their depth. They were all theorists – either barristers or, in the case of Nigel Lawson, a journalist. None of them had any experience of running a whelk stall, let alone a decent-sized company. Their attitude to manufacturing industry bordered on the contemptuous.[19]

During the autumn of 1980 Thatcher was not about to embark on a fundamental U-turn of the sort which had discredited the Heath government a decade earlier. As the criticism of her government mounted, she replied with the most famous phrase of her premiership, telling the Conservative Party conference at Brighton in October 1980, 'To those waiting with bated breath for that favourite media catch-phrase, the U-turn, I have only one thing to say. You turn if you want to. The lady's not for turning.' Behind the bravado, however, Thatcher was as concerned as any of her colleagues to bring down interest rates. By now her government was desperately unpopular, she was facing persistent cabinet revolts, and sterling M3 was quite obviously under-stating the intensity of the deflationary squeeze on the economy. For all her public scorn of U-turns and the oft-repeated commitment to sound money, her anxiety to reduce interest rates would prove one of the more enduring features of Thatcher's premiership. Home-owners were 'her people': they expected her to keep mortgage rates low. For that reason she had at first opposed the MTFS, agreeing only when Howe convinced her that a medium-term framework for policy would provide a sounder basis for lower interest rates.

Thatcher's first response to the gathering political storm in the summer of 1980 was to press for a more fundamentalist approach to control of the money supply. The shared assumption of monetarists about the link between money and prices disguised deep disagreements over the available techniques for restraining monetary growth. Some favoured targets for broad measures of liquidity; others preferred much narrower guides, such as the quantity of notes and coins. Milton Friedman was among those convinced that the government had chosen the wrong target and the wrong methods. Alan (later Sir Alan) Walters, who would join Thatcher in Downing Street as her economic adviser at the beginning of 1981, shared Friedman's view that the Treasury should switch to a target for a much narrower definition of money – the monetary base. This comprised notes and coins in circulation and the balances which commercial banks were obliged to keep at the Bank of England. It represented only a small proportion of money and credit in the economy, but it had the virtue of being easy to control. Paul Volcker, the chairman of the US Federal Reserve, had experimented with monetary base control, and the technique was favoured by the Swiss academic economists, notably Jurg Niehans, who were now welcome visitors to 10 Downing Street. Gordon Pepper, a prominent City economist, helped to persuade Thatcher to take up the idea, arguing that it would deliver more effective control of the money supply at a lower level of interest rates.

The proposal was, however, vehemently opposed by the Bank, which saw it as a particularly primitive form of monetarism, and it was regarded with deep scepticism in the Treasury, because it would leave the determination of interest rates to the financial markets. The Bank had always paid more attention to the idea that output and prices determined money rather than vice versa. Nor was the Treasury establishment imbued with the ideological zeal of Friedman and his allies. It did agree to float the possibility in a Green Paper published in the spring of 1980, but privately it was hostile. It wanted to retain the link between money and public borrowing provided by sterling M3, and was not prepared to leave to financial markets the level of the exchange and interest rates. Middleton responded to a study by Niehans on the subject by commenting that it was 'strong on views but not on analysis and evidence'.[20] After a lengthy and semi-public debate, Thatcher was persuaded to drop the idea only after she had been convinced that the technique would lead to frequent and unpredictable changes in mortgage rates.

By the autumn of 1980 Douglas Wass shared the general alarm in the country at the damage being inflicted on industry by the strong pound. Lawson was regarded as clever but impetuous by the Treasury establishment. It had not escaped the officials' attention that, for all his certainty now, he had regularly changed his views over the previous two decades. At the Bank, Richardson's instinctive suspicion of monetarist blueprints was reinforced by Kit McMahon's scarcely concealed scorn for Lawson and his fellow ideologues. Wass persuaded Howe to commission an internal Treasury analysis of the impact of sterling's appreciation on Britain's competitive position. In December 1980 the report concluded that the long-term damage to the trade balance foreshadowed by the scrapping of industrial capacity held out the risk of large future devaluations of sterling. Wass argued that the higher the pound rose initially, the greater the eventual deterioration in the balance of payments and the more likely it would fall sharply in subsequent years. This was an approach similar to the one that Lawson would deploy many years later when he attempted to cap sterling's value against the Deutschmark. In 1980, however, the young financial secretary was scornful, dismissing the Wass analysis as typical of what he referred to as the Treasury's 'devaluationists'.

Nevertheless, in the March 1981 Budget the central thrust of the MTFS shifted from control of the money supply to a more determined medium-term effort to reduce the level of public borrowing. This particular Budget – seen by some as a turning-point in the country's economic fortunes and by others as one of the worst examples of the triumph of ideology over economic common sense – is best remembered for its swingeing tax increases. Its longer-term significance, however, lay in a rebalancing of the government's economic strategy. Henceforth the Treasury would relax the monetary squeeze on the economy, paving the way for a steady devaluation of the pound, while imposing progressively tighter curbs on government borrowing. The policy was never explicitly stated in those terms, and the Treasury continued to experiment with sterling M3 and other monetary targets for several years. As Christopher Johnson puts it, however, monetarism gradually gave way to fiscalism.[21] An analysis published during the same year by the Treasury economist Simon Wren-Lewis signalled the gradual rediscovery of economic realities: 'Money seems to be important,' his paper said, 'but it is certainly not the only variable that may be significant in determining prices.'[22]

By the beginning of 1981 sterling M3 was growing at an annual rate of 20 per cent – far outside its official target range – but the pound was still rising and the two reductions in interest rates during 1980 had signally failed to provide a respite for industry. The most ardent monetarists, including Niehans, had concluded that the monetary straitjacket had been too tight. While the government had thought that the pound's rise was a natural consequence of North Sea oil, Niehans concluded in early 1981 that the main reason for the high exchange rate was not oil but the high level of interest rates. His report, commissioned by Thatcher, provided the backdrop for the tax increases and interest rate cut in the 1981 Budget. It was not until a year later, however, that the Treasury would acknowledge explicitly a significant role for sterling in the formulation of monetary policy, admitting in the MTFS which accompanied the 1982 Budget that 'The exchange rate is a route through which changes in the money supply affect inflation ... the government considers it appropriate to look at the exchange rate in monitoring domestic monetary conditions and in taking decisions about policy.' Sir Ian (later Lord) Gilmour, sacked from the cabinet in the autumn of 1981 for his opposition to the Thatcher experiment, was later to remark caustically, 'So strong was the dogma that only after ... Jurg Niehans had reported the real world to be correct did the Treasury concede that conditions were far tighter than they had intended.'[23]

The quid pro quo for this looser monetary policy was the package of tax increases in the 1981 Budget. The public-sector borrowing requirement in the 1980/81 financial year had originally been set at just under 4 per cent of national income. The impact of the recession on spending and revenues pushed the actual out-turn to 6 per cent. Geoffrey Howe resolved to bring it back down to a fraction over 4 per cent in 1981/82. His decision to raise taxes during what still seemed to be the trough of the recession overturned the conventional economic wisdom. The additional £4.5bn in taxes – equivalent to nearly 2 per cent of national income – defied the accepted view that public borrowing should be allowed to rise during a recession. A parallel squeeze in public spending provoked horror within the cabinet, where the so-called 'wets' were preparing for a final confrontation with Thatcher. In a famous letter to *The Times* on 30 March 1981 no fewer than 364 economists warned that the Budget would prolong unnecessarily the recession. The economists, including four former chief economic advisers to the Treasury, proclaimed that 'There is no basis in economic theory or supporting evidence for the government's belief that by deflating demand they will bring inflation permanently under control and thereby induce an automatic recovery in output and employment.' Instead, the Budget measures would further erode the country's industrial base and threaten further political and social stability (the previous year had seen serious rioting on Merseyside). Many in the government shared that fear, and the Budget was followed in July by a large-scale cabinet revolt against the £5bn of spending cuts that Howe deemed necessary to meet his new borrowing target. Jim Prior, Peter Walker and Ian Gilmour led the opposition in one of the most dramatic confrontations of Thatcher's premiership. The three had been among the most prominent figures in a series of struggles with the Treasury the previous year. In the autumn of 1980 they had successfully beaten back Howe's demands for further cuts in Whitehall budgets, forcing him instead to raise National Insurance contributions. Thatcher, however, was gradually consolidating her authority. In September 1981 the critics of her economic strategy were summarily sacked or demoted in a wide-ranging cabinet reshuffle and the spending cuts were driven through.

Conservative folklore identifies the 1981 Budget as a defining moment after which Britain's economic recovery was soon under way. While the government had failed to meet its money supply targets, the reduction in public borrowing did provide the backdrop for sustained improvement in its fiscal position. As it turned out, however, the package was neither the triumph claimed by the government nor the unmitigated disaster alleged by its critics. Alan Walters, now working for Thatcher at No. 10, insisted that the tax increases be accompanied by a two-point cut in interest rates to 12 per cent – a move designed to reverse some of sterling's earlier appreciation. Interest rates would rise again later the same year, but by then a weakening pound had loosened the deflationary coils around the

economy. So ultimately the significance of the March 1981 package
lay in the subsequent fall in the exchange rate. At the time the
government was steering blind, but there is some truth in Thatcher's
remark in the first volume of her memoirs, *The Downing Street Years*,
that 'Far from being deflationary our Budget would have the reverse
effect ... it would allow interest rates and the exchange rate to fall,
both of which had created severe difficulties for industry.'[24] The
MTFS, conceived as a monetarist blueprint, evolved into a strategy
designed essentially to reduce the level of public borrowing.

Sterling's progressive devaluation over the two years from the spring
of 1981 liberated the economy from the monetarist straitjacket of the
first Thatcher years. In part the fall was simply the obverse of an
unprecedented rise in the value of the dollar. The combination in
Washington of Ronald Reagan's expansionary fiscal policy and the
fierce anti-inflationary squeeze imposed by Paul Volcker at the US
Federal Reserve provided the backdrop for an unprecedented appreciation of the US currency which was to last for four years. In 1981
alone, the pound dropped from its high of $2.40 at the beginning of
the year to $1.80 by the end. But sterling also weakened more
generally, depreciating by nearly 20 per cent against the Deutschmark
to just over DM4.00 at the end of 1981. At times the Treasury
became as alarmed by the speed of the depreciation as it had been by
the extent of the earlier rise. Howe twice raised interest rates in 1981
– from 12 per cent to 16 per cent – as the fall accelerated, just as he
had cut them a year earlier in an effort to slow sterling's appreciation.
As he commented in his memoirs, *Conflict of Loyalty*, 'We had all been
obliged to recognize that our benign neglect of the exchange rate and
other market pressures could continue no longer.'[25] The intention,
however, was to brake rather than to reverse the trend. Despite
occasional rebounds, sterling continued to depreciate over the next
eighteen months before stabilizing in the second half of 1983. Its
average trade-weighted value during that latter year was little different
from that in 1979. The foreign exchange markets' flirtation with a
strong pound had been brief but damaging. The cost in terms of lost
industrial capacity for this lower inflation rate was much higher than
was paid by any of Britain's major trading-partners. As Wass pre-

dicted, the government's indifference to the fate of manufacturing industry would play a significant part in the rapid deterioration of the current account in the second half of the 1980s. The experience also foreshadowed the subsequent conversion of Howe and Lawson to active management of the exchange rate.

The government did once again consider, albeit briefly, joining the ERM during this first Thatcher term. Sterling's fall in the autumn of 1981 had prompted a Treasury study of the option. Gordon Richardson saw an opportunity to put an effective floor under sterling's value. The consensus among Treasury officials, however, was that it was too soon to consider such a major policy shift. More by chance than by design, the government had begun to hit its (much amended) money supply target (1981/82 and 1982/83 turned out to be the only years that the Treasury met its prescribed goals). More fundamentally, inflation remained well above German levels and sterling appeared vulnerable to unpredictable fluctuations in the oil price. Terence Burns and Peter Middleton, by now the two most influential figures in the Treasury, were still committed to making the MTFS work. Sir Kenneth Couzens, the senior official in charge of international policy, was also cautious. Couzens argued that joining the ERM might well be seen as an admission by the government of the failure of its initial strategy.

The Treasury raised its objections during a formal discussion with the prime minister in January 1982. Gordon Richardson and Peter Carrington backed entry, but Howe said he was unconvinced. He was sympathetic to the demands of industry for a more competitive exchange rate, and, as he recounted subsequently, 'I remained unable to reconcile membership with the management of domestic monetary policy.'[26] Senior Treasury officials believed that the pound's rate against the Deutschmark, which had recently rebounded to DM4.40, was likely to prove too high to lock in permanently. They were also keen to pursue a more broadly based monetary strategy, taking into account fluctuations in the exchange rate, rather than return to policy to a single 'hook'. Thatcher also was antipathetic, warned by Alan Walters that the pegged, or semi-fixed, exchange rate arrangement represented by the ERM would fatally undermine her economic strategy. She concluded that tying sterling to the Deutschmark would limit the government's freedom of manœuvre. It would be better to wait until British and German interest and inflation rates were brought much more closely into line. At this meeting there were also early signs of her growing mistrust of her European partners. Thatcher regularly faced direct pressure from Chancellor Helmut Schmidt to bring sterling into the ERM, but her experience during 1979 and 1980 in fighting for a rebate on Britain's contributions to the Brussels budget had not enhanced her enthusiasm for closer cooperation with other EC governments. She had got back 'our money', but she had discovered in the process that others had fundamentally different ambitions for the future of Europe.

The ERM could not anyway claim to have been an unalloyed success in its early years. By the autumn of 1981 there had been no fewer than four realignments of the currencies within the mechanism. President François Mitterrand's determination to pursue an expansionary economic policy led to repeated devaluations of the franc's parity against the Deutschmark. The lira and the Danish krone were also subject to frequent realignments. As a neutral party, Howe was often asked to chair the acrimonious meetings of finance ministers at which the precise details of such realignments were hammered out. His private secretary at the Treasury, John (later Sir John) Kerr, was deputed to write the subsequent reports to Thatcher. By complete chance, Kerr's subsequent career as one of the brightest of Whitehall officials would provide a single thread through the Thatcher and Major governments' struggle with sterling. Some years later, as a senior official in the Foreign Office, Kerr would draft the fateful ultimatum on ERM membership delivered to Thatcher by Howe and Lawson. He had become by then a powerful and eloquent advocate within the Whitehall establishment of the benefits of engagement with Britain's European partners. So it was ironic that in these early years Kerr was content to record in his reports to Thatcher how fortunate the government was to be free to stand aside from the bitter wrangling about exchange rates which plagued the ERM.

CHAPTER TWO

NAVIGATING WITHOUT A COMPASS

THE MOMENT WHICH CRYSTALLIZED Nigel Lawson's decision to put the exchange rate at the centre of his economic strategy came in January 1985, eighteen months into his chancellorship. Sterling crises had traditionally provided a stick with which Conservatives could beat Labour administrations. Now Lawson learned that the financial markets did not distinguish between free-market friend and interventionist foe. His ambition for radical reform of the tax system and for deep cuts in income tax rates would take second place to the financial markets' unpredictable attitude to the pound.

The chancellor had called a January Budget-planning meeting with his officials and junior ministers. Following tradition, the foreign secretary's country house in Chevening, Kent, had been borrowed for the occasion. Sterling had been under pressure since the previous month, a victim of an inexorable rise in the value of the dollar, of weakening oil prices, and of doubts about the government's anti-inflation resolve. On Friday 12 January, before travelling to Chevening, Lawson had raised interest rates by one percentage point to 10.5 per cent in an attempt to halt the slide. Now, as he discussed with his officials the scope for tax reductions in his second Budget, the markets, with help from 10 Downing Street, were preparing to wreck his strategy.

The trigger was the weekly briefing given to Sunday newspaper journalists by Bernard Ingham, the prime minister's press secretary. The pound had fallen by that Friday afternoon to $1.12 – less than half its value four years earlier and perilously close to parity with the US currency. The unease among currency traders had been reinforced on the previous Sunday by a front-page report in the *Sunday Times*. This had declared that the government was determined to maintain a 'hands-off' policy and allow the exchange rate to find its own level. On this following Friday, Ingham repeated the message. Unaware of the changed circumstances, he offered the standard line that the government was not in the business of trying to defend any particular level for sterling. His remarks, attributed to 10 Downing Street, duly appeared on the front pages of most of the Sunday newspapers on 13 January. William Keegan, the economics editor of the *Observer*, was alone in reflecting the real anxiety within the government over the prospect of a one-dollar pound.

Ingham's version dominated the BBC news on Sunday morning. In the habit of listening to the first bulletins of the day, Thatcher was instantly alarmed, telephoning Lawson in a state of extreme agitation. She was horrified at the prospect of becoming the first prime minister in history to preside over a one-dollar pound. The chancellor scrapped the remainder of the Chevening meeting and rushed back to Downing Street. After hurried consultations with Treasury and Bank officials, Thatcher endorsed another rise in interest rates – to 12 per cent – at the start of Monday's trading. Robert Culpin, Lawson's usually taciturn press secretary, overturned Ingham's briefing in a frantic series of telephone calls to economics correspondents. Breaking with the hallowed tradition that officials never foreshadow the Treasury's tactics in financial markets, Culpin said it was ready to support the pound by selling foreign currency from the Bank's reserves and by raising interest rates. 'You can quote me,' he added, in an effort to secure maximum impact on the following morning's front pages. The dismay in Whitehall was shared at the Bank. Robin Leigh-Pemberton, who had succeeded Gordon Richardson as governor in 1983, was horrified that the pound might soon be worth only one dollar.

The interest rate rise provided only temporary respite: the episode had severely shaken confidence in the government's grip on its economic policy. Within days a further rise in the value of the dollar and a fall in oil prices provoked a new run on sterling. The government stood by powerless as aggressive intervention by the Bank failed to stabilize the position. Lawson learned what James Callaghan had meant when he wrote of the Wilson government's experience, 'It was like swimming in a heavy sea. As soon as we emerged from the breaking of one wave, another would hit us before we could catch our breath.'[1] On 28 January Lawson was obliged to raise borrowing costs for the third time in as many weeks. At 14 per cent, base rates were now back to their highest level for three years.

The Chevening weekend was a salutary shock to Margaret Thatcher. In her mind, letting the pound find its own level did not include the humiliation of parity with the dollar. Ingham, strongly rebuked afterwards by Lawson for his comments, had reflected accurately her preference for a free-floating exchange rate. For that reason she held no grudge against her press secretary. He had simply not grasped on this occasion the important distinction between eschewing a specific exchange rate target and complete indifference to the value of the pound. Within days the prime minister had told a BBC Radio interviewer, 'In my view sterling has gone down too far. I do not like it down at this rate'. Higher interest rates had been necessary, she added, because 'one has to have regard to the exchange rate'. Privately, her mood was less controlled. At one point during the crisis she demanded of Lawson why sterling was not already in the ERM, 'protected from all this'. The official monitoring this particular telephone conversation was stunned. At Lawson's instigation, she also wrote to President Reagan, complaining of the havoc wrought by the seemingly inexorable rise in the dollar.

This initial reaction revealed the underlying tension in Thatcher's attitude to sterling's exchange rate. She was infuriated by the government's vulnerability to speculative attacks on sterling – and never more so than when a falling pound forced it to put up interest rates – but in calmer moments an instinctive mistrust of attempts to target the exchange rate would dominate her approach. In her mind, fixing a particular rate for sterling would give the speculators an easier target and leave the government with even less discretion over the cost of borrowing for home-owners. Another confusion ran through her premiership: she would celebrate the 'international confidence' in her economic strategy demonstrated by the occasional rise in the exchange rate only to express concern later that sterling might be 'uncompetitive'. As one of her aides in 10 Downing Street was to remark, 'She knew what she wanted, but that was not always consistent.' Robin Leigh-Pemberton was confronted with the contradiction at the meeting in late January 1985 called to discuss the rise in interest rates to 14 per cent. Convinced that sterling needed the shelter of the ERM, he suggested as a prelude giving sterling a more formal place in monetary policy – the Bank could operate a 'sub-target' for the exchange rate, to reassure the financial markets. Anticipating a hostile reaction, Eddie George, the official in charge of the Bank's markets division, had warned the governor beforehand to choose his words carefully. George had been right: 'She would not have it,' Leigh-Pemberton reported when he returned to Threadneedle Street.

There was another lesson from the January 1985 sterling crisis, however, which both Thatcher and Lawson ignored to their cost in subsequent years: financial markets need reassurance, and nothing is more destabilizing than open conflict between 10 and 11 Downing Street.

On his return to the Treasury after the 1983 election Lawson had brought to the chancellorship the self-confident pugnacity which was to become his political trademark. Here was a politician without a hint of self-doubt. He had a grasp of the intellectual framework for economic management rare in his predecessors, and he intended to cast aside the postwar economic consensus. However, a precipitate slide in sterling's value during the following year provided the first of many painful lessons in the ease with which the financial markets in which he had so much faith could dislocate his economic strategy.

Lawson would claim subsequently that his enthusiasm in 1985 for an exchange rate target was entirely consistent with his previous thinking. For politicians, of course, consistency has a looser meaning than for the rest of us, and the Treasury is the natural home for Whitehall's sophists. Its approach to economic policy-making has long demonstrated an easy mastery of the art of illusion. It is adept at performing regular U-turns while persuading the outside world that it never drives but in a straight line. A favourite technique is to change the substance of a policy while sticking at first with the rhetoric applicable to its earlier position. When the new approach is firmly in place, ministers and officials modulate their public pronouncements accordingly. They emphasize all the while a spurious consistency, sprinkling public statements with phrases like 'as the government has always said'. By such routes, 180-degree policy reversals become mere shadings of previous policies.

The new chancellor was a master of such casuistry, employing it to the full in the progressive abandonment of primitive monetarism in favour of an exchange rate target. As William Keegan points out in an admirable account of the evolution of Lawson's economic thinking, *Mr Lawson's Gamble*, this chancellor had never been shy of changing his mind.[2] During a spell as a young economic journalist in the early 1960s his column in the *Sunday Telegraph* was one of the few places where the then chancellor, Reginald Maudling, could be accused of timidity rather than of recklessness in his efforts to stoke the fires of economic expansion. Lawson later used the editorship of the *Spectactor* as a platform to castigate Harold Wilson for his refusal to devalue the pound to make room for faster economic growth. Yet by the early 1980s he had concluded that attempts at reflation were futile. Hardened Treasury officials would continue to marvel at the ease with which his restless intellect could jettison one set of economic rules for another. As Keegan puts it, 'His officials were continually surprised at the facility with which Lawson managed to rationalize almost any action, in the face of a check to progress, as being entirely in keeping with previous plans.'[3] Or, as one of these officials remarked with the merest hint of sarcasm some years later, 'Nigel has been in favour of most things at one time or another.'

By the summer of 1983 even the most fervent monetarist found it difficult to deny the pre-eminent role of the exchange rate first in the 1980/81 recession and then in promoting the subsequent economic upturn. By mid-1983 sterling had fallen to around \$1.50 from its early 1981 level of \$2.40. Against the Deutschmark it had slumped from its high of DM5.07 to DM3.90. It was no coincidence that the economy's recovery from the deepest recession since the 1930s mirrored step by step the progressive devaluation of the pound.

So one of Lawson's first acts as chancellor was to commission from officials a thorough review of monetary policy. The review provided the occasion for a lengthy internal debate on whether the government could carry through into its second term the threadbare economic ideology of its first. It was widely accepted in the Treasury and the Bank that financial liberalization had injected an inherent instability into the behaviour of the money supply. Persistent overshoots in the growth rates of sterling M3 reflected no more than increased cash balances held by financial institutions in response to high real, or inflation-adjusted, interest rates. The surge in bank deposits held the potential to reignite inflation if the government dropped its anti-inflation guard, but there was no immediate threat.

The Bank of England favoured a formal place in policy for the exchange rate. Thatcher had chosen Leigh-Pemberton to succeed Gordon Richardson as governor in an attempt to weaken an institution which she saw as a rival source of policy-making. The battles with Richardson in the early 1980s, during which he had blocked the move to monetary base control, were fresh in her mind: she wanted the Bank to carry out her policy, not to press its own. Leigh-Pemberton, a former chairman of National Westminster Bank and an unexpected choice, was widely seen as a more pliant figure than his predecessor. A lord lieutenant of his home county of Kent, he brought to the role an unfamiliar courtesy and diffidence. He had had extensive connections with the Conservative Party and no real experience in the formulation of macro-economic policy. On the issue of Europe and the ERM, however, he had unexpectedly firm views. Leigh-Pemberton believed that Britain's economic and political future lay in Europe; sterling should be part of the ERM at the earliest practicable opportunity.

The governor did little to disguise his preference during a detailed exposition in the autumn of 1984. At this point Nigel Lawson was still publicly committed to domestic monetarism, but Leigh-Pemberton mused on the alternatives in a lecture delivered to the University of Kent at Canterbury.[4] One option would be 'the adoption of an exchange rate target', he said: 'For the United Kingdom, with its close political and economic ties with our European neighbours, there could be a number of attractions in taking a full part in the exchange rate mechanism of the EMS.' He found strong support within the Bank. Kit McMahon, the deputy governor, was a scathing critic of the ideology of the first Thatcher term. McMahon was a moving force behind the post-election review of monetary policy, pressing for a more prominent role for sterling.[5] Anthony Loehnis, the Bank director in charge of overseas policy, was another advocate of the economic and political benefits of ERM membership.

One senior Bank official, Eddie George, was much less enthusiastic. The director in charge of the money markets division, George did not want to replace an inflexible money supply target with a rigid goal for the exchange rate. His view, unchanged ten years later when he replaced the retiring Leigh-Pemberton as governor in 1993, was that policy should be based on a pragmatic assessment of a range of monetary and economic indicators rather than on a single 'hook'. Confident – critics would say arrogant – in his own opinions, George preferred discretion to rules. He was to become a pivotal figure in the events of the late 1980s and 1990s. A cool public persona earned him the flattering soubriquet 'Steady Eddie', but a more volatile temperament emerged in several behind-the-scenes clashes with the Treasury. Leigh-Pemberton would joke that George had discovered the perfect monetary strategy: as the most experienced practitioner in the financial markets, decisions about interest rates and sterling should be left entirely to his judgement. Despite their disagreements over the ERM, George was the Bank official most respected by Lawson.

In the summer of 1983 the relevant Treasury officials shared George's scepticism. The connection between the growth rate of sterling M3 and government borrowing remained an important lever over spending and borrowing: the rest of Whitehall was still told that higher spending would necessitate higher interest rates. This neat analysis of the relationship between budget deficits and interest rates owed more to the Treasury's convenience than to empirical evidence. Much freer cross-border capital flows had undercut the long-assumed relationship between the amount a government borrows and the level of domestic interest rates. The Treasury, however, was not prepared to cede such a useful weapon.

Peter Middleton, by now permanent secretary in place of Douglas Wass, had also invested substantial intellectual capital in the targeting of broad money. He would irritate Lawson by pointing out that the basic framework had been put in place long before the Conservatives' 1979 election victory. No zealot, he was content for the Treasury to adopt an entirely pragmatic stance, reviewing the whole range of financial and economic indicators in its private deliberations on the level of interest rates. Middleton wanted also to keep open the option of adjusting what was known as the 'policy mix' – the balance between monetary and fiscal policy. As in 1981, a tighter fiscal policy might allow lower interest rates and a weaker pound without risking higher inflation. The pragmatism, however, was strictly for internal consumption: he saw distinct advantages in a more inflexible public approach. A transparent commitment to restrain the money supply was useful in dealing with the markets. True, the sterling M3 target might have been missed more often than it had been hit, but to abandon it would undermine confidence none the less. 'Having a target and missing it turned out to be quite a good policy. It allowed for flexibility,' Middleton subsequently told colleagues.

Terence Burns's contribution to the 1983 review also came down in favour of a broadly based monetary policy. Taking up the chief economic adviser's post at the age of only thirty-five, Burns quickly established himself as one of the principal architects of the government's economic strategy. Along with Middleton, he was one of Lawson's most trusted advisers. A down-to-earth grammar-school boy from the North East with a sharp and flexible intellect, Burns would emerge from the economic policy débâcles of the late 1980s and early 1990s as one of Whitehall's great survivors, replacing Middleton as permanent secretary in 1991. Eight years earlier he was sceptical about basing economic policy on an explicit target for sterling. He wanted instead a policy which gave substantial weight to the exchange rate, but one which did not set any 'hard margins' for fluctuations in the pound's value. The government could choose to respond to trends on the currency markets with offsetting changes in interest rates, but should not bind itself to a sterling target. Burns wanted also to pay close attention to one of the narrow measures of money, known as M0. Comprising the notes and coins in circulation in the economy, this took no account of the creation of credit by the banking system, but Burns considered that its behaviour had a good coincident relationship with price changes in the economy.

Neither Middleton nor Burns shared Lawson's preference for unbreakable rules. The chancellor's priority, and later his obsession, was to create what he called an 'over-arching financial framework' – an unequivocal and transparent set of guidelines by which financial markets could assess the government's performance. As early as 1978 he had stated in an article in *The Times* that 'The secret of practical economic success, as overseas experience confirms, is the acceptance of known rules. Rules rule: OK?'[6] In his officials' minds, rules were useful but discretion in their application could be equally so. In 1983 Geoffrey (later Sir Geoffrey) Littler, who had replaced Kenneth Couzens as the senior official responsible for international economic affairs, was almost alone among the Treasury mandarins in being an enthusiast for the ERM. Littler's contribution to the review acknowledged that there were still objections to sterling's participation. He pointed out that the dollar's ascent could not continue indefinitely and, when it went into reverse, it would create tensions between European currencies. Littler thought, however, that most of the obstacles could be removed within a year.

Lawson would suggest later that the early doubts of Burns and Middleton reflected the influence of a 'devaluationist' tendency within the Treasury.[7] More a strand of thinking than a cohesive group of officials, this tendency favoured a tight fiscal policy with, in relative terms, lower interest rates and a weaker exchange rate. In part this mirrored a puritanical bias in the Treasury which always favoured the promotion of exports over domestic consumption – hardly surprising, perhaps, after decades of intermittent balance of payments crises. Burns, however, has denied with some indignation the idea that he ever sought a lower exchange rate. Other officials suggest that Lawson's intense preoccupation with sterling often blinded him to wider economic realities. It was true, though, that the culture in the Treasury – its historical baggage – leaned towards a pragmatic approach to the exchange rate. Its collective memory was scarred by previous failed attempts to sustain a fixed rate. In the words of one senior adviser to Lawson, 'We were always worried about getting caught on a sterling hook ... our emotional experiences were the humiliating past retreats from a fixed rate. We wanted to take the exchange rate into account, but in a miasmic way.'

In the event, the 1983 review was inconclusive. Lawson's address to the Lord Mayor's banquet in October of that year – the annual Mansion House speech at which the chancellor sets out his financial strategy for the coming year – contained changes of emphasis rather than of direction. Sterling M3 was downgraded from its earlier pre-eminence but retained as an 'important indicator'. M0, the narrow money supply measure favoured by Burns, was given a more prominent role. Sterling's performance was also to figure in interest rate calculations. Lawson added of the exchange rate, however, 'There will as before be no target for it, nor, contrary to some ill-informed speculation, any complicated mechanical formula linking it with other indicators.'⁸ One of the officials responsible for drafting the speech summarized succinctly the new policy: the Treasury had decided on 'pragmatism dressed up as monetarism'.

The chancellor was not ready even a year later to abandon his public faith in domestic money supply targets. Addressing the same audience of City bankers in October 1984, Lawson recited the monetarist credo which the Conservatives had brought to office in 1979:

> It is the monetary aggregrates that are of central relevance to judging monetary conditions and determining interest rates. That has always been our policy and it remains so. We take the exchange rate into account when its behaviour suggests that the domestic monetary indicators are giving a false reading, which they are not. Provided monetary conditions are kept under firm control, excessive movements, whether in the money or exchange markets in response to outside influences, will tend to correct themselves relatively quickly.⁹

By now there was the beginning of a substantial lobby at Westminster and in the City for ERM membership, but Lawson brushed aside the argument in a letter to David Owen, the leader of the Social Democratic Party. Owen was among those who thought that the ERM would provide a reliable anchor for anti-inflation policy and a more stable environment for business. Lawson was dismissive, replying that currency misalignments would quickly correct themselves.

The reality was otherwise. A few months earlier, in July 1984, he had suffered his first sterling crisis. A sharp rise in US interest rates in the early summer had given fresh impetus to the dollar's appreciation. Simultaneously, confidence in sterling was undercut by the wayward behaviour of the money supply and by a national docks strike. In early July the Treasury was forced to raise interest rates from 9 to 10 per cent. Within a week the pound was under renewed pressure. The markets anticipated a second rise in borrowing costs, to 12 per cent. Treasury officials were initially reluctant to endorse the increase, fearful of being driven into defending a particular level for sterling. The Bank, however, warned that resisting would undermine the credibility of the government's anti-inflation strategy. Lawson concurred. Most of the increase was reversed over the following months, but there could not have been a clearer demonstration of the destructive power of the currency markets.

Much later Lawson would comment that his 1984 Mansion House speech had been his last 'significant utterance as an unreconstructed, parochial monetarist'. Displaying disarming, if belated, frankness, Lawson reflected on his comments about sterling, 'This line was a fiction even when I uttered it, as the exchange rate played a much larger part in policy than I was prepared to admit in public.'[10]

By the time of the sterling crisis of January 1985 the pound had been falling almost continuously for four years. At $1.10 it was 55 per cent below its high point against the dollar in late 1980. A rate of DM3.50 represented a fall of 30 per cent against the West German currency. The sterling index, measuring the pound's value against a basket of currencies weighted according to Britain's overseas trade, was 28 per cent lower than its peak in early 1981. A government which proclaimed above all a commitment to sound money had presided over an unprecedented fall in the external value of the pound.

To a significant extent the depreciation represented a reversal of the rise in the first two years of the Thatcher administration. Sterling's average rate in 1979, for example, had been DM3.90. The pound's fall against the US currency was also a reflection of the dollar's dramatic climb against all currencies. The monetary squeeze in the US imposed by Paul Volcker to counterbalance President Reagan's fiscal expansionism triggered a 60 per cent rise in the dollar's trade-weighted value between 1980 and early 1985. The focus in Britain on the dollar/sterling rate meant that the US currency's strength was often misinterpreted as representing a weakening of the pound. Encouraged by the chancellor, Peter Middleton launched a campaign to persuade the media – and in particular the broadcasters – to pay more attention to the pound's average value. The old 'trade-weighted' index was renamed as the more media-friendly sterling index, and was calculated and published more frequently throughout the day by the Bank of England. This more flattering presentation, however, could not disguise the fact that sterling's weakness reflected also the relaxation of the government's anti-inflation policy.

From the moment he became chancellor, Lawson emphasized that he would not rest on the progress made in reducing inflation during the first Thatcher term – chancellors must always sound tough about inflation. Measured by the retail price index, the inflation rate had fallen to a low of 3.6 per cent in June 1983. That figure, artificially depressed by falling mortgage rates, understated the true position: the underlying rate of price increases was running at just over 4 per cent. Lawson insisted that that was not good enough, remarking in his 1983 Mansion House speech that there 'could be no relaxation of the pressure to keep inflation moving down'. A 5 per cent inflation rate would have been considered excessive only two decades earlier, he continued: 'It is too high . . . the government's ultimate objective is price stability.'

The fullest exposition of Lawson's rejection of the post-war Keynesian consensus came the following year, when he delivered the Mais Lecture at the City University Business School. The instruments of macro-economic policy – taxation, public spending and interest rates – were no longer directed towards regulating demand in the economy, he said. They would be used instead to fight inflation. Micro-economic, or supply-side, policy had in the past been used to try to suppress inflation through direct controls on prices and wages, but would now be directed at promoting faster growth. The new doctrine said the government would increase the potential for faster economic growth through deregulation and by freeing the labour market with an assault on the trade unions.[11]

This typically bold assertion of strategy was one of principle rather than precise practice. Lawson was correct that, in the more open, competitive world of the 1980s, the scope for governments to regulate demand in their economies had much diminished. His confidence that the goals of economic management could be so neatly divided between macro- and micro-economic policy did not, however, match the complex reality. In truth, Lawson was purist in public and pragmatic in private. Unemployment in 1985 was above 3 million and still rising, despite the government's repeated attempts to massage the official statistics. Output was rising by an annual 3 per cent, but progress in making good the losses of the 1980/81 recession was painfully slow. Lawson believed that, over the medium to long term, there was indeed no trade-off between inflation and economic growth:

inflationary booms led inevitably to recessionary busts. But he accepted that too harsh an anti-inflationary squeeze would stifle recovery and discourage investment in new capacity. Whatever the rhetoric, he wanted lower interest rates. Sterling's weakness was the principal obstacle.

The dilemma in early 1985 was that, while the exchange rate was now the key influence on interest rate decisions, the government did not acknowledge that reality. The Treasury experimented unsuccessfully with different monetary aggregates. Sterling M4, another broad measure, which included building society as well as bank deposits, proved as suspect as sterling M3. M0, the narrow aggregate favoured by Burns, failed to win credibility in the financial markets or within the Treasury. One official was fond of remarking that computer models of the economy demonstrated that the price of a medium-sized can of baked beans was as reliable a guide to inflation. He was only half joking.

The fruitless excursions along these monetary motorways sent a confused message to financial markets. On occasion they suspected that the Treasury had an undeclared target for sterling. It was widely known that officials had calculated that a 5 per cent fall in the exchange rate would add eventually one percentage point to the recorded inflation rate. Other, semi-official, ready reckoners suggested that the inflationary effect of such a depreciation could be offset by a one-point rise in interest rates. So sterling frequently came under speculative fire because the markets judged that the government was indifferent to its fate.

Lawson's first public acknowledgement of his interest in the ERM came at the end of January 1985, in evidence to the all-party Treasury and Civil Service Committee. Mindful that Thatcher was still far from convinced, Lawson agreed there were still significant obstacles to ERM membership. He told the MPs that the fall in the value of the pound which had forced that month's interest rate rises, in part, had reflected sterling's peculiar status as a petrocurrency. The tone of his evidence to the MPs, however, hinted at a pivotal role for the exchange rate in setting interest rates. Asked whether sterling should be in the ERM, he replied with deliberate ambiguity, 'I think that this matter is continually under review, and I do not wish to prejudge what will eventually happen.'[12]

He had raised the issue of ERM membership with Thatcher two weeks earlier, on 11 January, the day which had seen the first of that month's three interest rate increases to defend the pound. He told her that doubts about the government's anti-inflation resolve were leading to ever more frequent speculative attacks on sterling. The resulting falls in the exchange rate threatened in turn to trigger the accelerating inflation which the markets feared. That in turn forced the Treasury to increase interest rates. No one could doubt the correlation between sterling and changes in interest rates. As George Blunden, the deputy governor of the Bank during the second half of the 1980s, told the Treasury and Civil Service Committee many years later:

> Interest rate movements hitherto have very rarely been made just for domestic reasons. Nearly always they have been made in relation to sterling and what is happening to sterling. It may be that to satisfy the jargon of the day the explanation did not always refer to sterling but, actually, in the discussions which led to the interest rate movements, sterling has always been a commencing point.[13]

Burns made the same point in a similar review of policy when he described the exchange rate as probably 'the dominant mechanism' in the link between interest rate changes and inflation.[14]

The handful of purists who kept faith with the early Thatcher years disputed this analysis. Their view was that, if the domestic money supply was kept under tight control, exchange rate fluctuations would not affect the overall level of prices. Instead they would lead only to shifts in relative prices as between imported and domestically produced goods. Such views, however, belonged to the world of long-run abstract theory rather than that of medium-term reality. The surge in the exchange rate during the early 1980s provided unequivocal evidence of sterling's role. Then the high exchange rate had driven down the inflation rate. In the second half of the 1980s a falling pound threatened the reverse.

*

Lawson eventually concluded that, if he had no choice but to operate an exchange rate policy, a formal link with the Deutschmark provided the best hope of entrenching the government's earlier success against inflation. The Federal Republic of Germany had an enviable inflation record. The postwar political settlement, entrenching the duty and authority of an independent Bundesbank to contain price rises, had shielded it from the inflationary excesses of the 1970s. There were occasional blips, but the Bundesbank had more often than not met its target of ensuring that prices rose no faster than 2 per cent a year. In Lawson's mind, pegging sterling's value to the Deutschmark would import into Britain the same anti-inflationary discipline.

True, some sectors of the economy are not directly affected by the level of the exchange rate – most basic service industries, for example. In an open economy like that of Britain, however, enough of industry is exposed to international competition to ensure a predictable relationship between movements in the exchange rate and in domestic prices. A commitment to German-style price stability would enhance greatly the credibility of the government's resolve. The ERM thus promised in the 1980s what the gold standard had provided until the 1920s and what Bretton Woods had offered in the postwar years but with greater flexibility. The rules of the system, a semi-fixed rather than a fixed-rate regime, allowed for periodic realignments of parities. This was a remarkable break with the philosophy of the late 1970s and early 1980s. Then the government had proclaimed that, if the money supply were kept under control, sterling's exchange rate could safely be left to the markets. Now Lawson's argument was that, if the exchange rate was fixed, the money supply would look after itself.

Following their first discussion, the chancellor raised the issue of ERM membership several times with Thatcher during January and February 1985. Shaken by the pound's weakness, she was prepared to listen. Sterling fell to a low of around $1.05 towards the end of February. She repeated her concern about the dollar in talks with President Reagan during a visit to Washington at the end of the same month. She was worried about the high interest rates needed to prop up sterling. The spread of home-ownership was central to her project; rising mortgage rates delivered a direct blow to 'her people'.

Otherwise, however, her instincts remained firmly against an exchange rate target. She preferred the illusory certainties of the domestic money supply to the risk of attempting to buck the foreign exchange markets. If sterling was locked into the ERM, she might be forced to accept still higher borrowing costs.

These early discussions in Downing Street were inconclusive, because Lawson did not press for an immediate decision. During a seminar on the subject at 10 Downing Street in February 1985, his view that the balance of the argument had shifted in favour of membership was supported by Geoffrey Howe (by now foreign secretary) and by Robin Leigh-Pemberton. Lawson accepted, however, that entry would anyway have to await some recovery in sterling's value. Also the Treasury would need to start rebuilding the foreign exchange reserves. The reserves of gold and foreign currencies held at the Bank of England had stood at $22bn when the government first took office in 1979. They had risen subsequently to $28bn in the first few months of 1981. But, having declared its indifference to the exchange rate, the government had then made a political virtue of repaying the foreign currency debt incurred by the previous Labour administration. In these early years it dismissed intervention in the markets as a hangover from the 1970s. At the end of 1984 the reserves were down to $15.6bn, so when Lawson confronted the speculators the following month he found that he had precious little ammunition. The Bank's intervention during the first three months of 1985 dangerously depleted the remaining reserves. At $13.5bn by the end of March 1985, they were at their lowest since 1977. Less than half of that figure was available in readily convertible currencies for intervention on the markets. Thatcher agreed that the Treasury could begin the first programme of official overseas borrowing since 1976.

Hopeful if not entirely confident that the prime minister could be persuaded of the virtues of the ERM later in the year, Lawson set about shading the public presentation of policy. In his March 1985 Budget the money supply targets were downgraded by the addition of a parallel series of medium-term projections for nominal, or money, gross domestic product. This provided a target in cash terms for the country's national income – the sum of the real growth in the economy and of any increase in prices. Adopting a target for money GDP involved an explicit commitment to use monetary policy to sustain as well as to curb demand in the economy. Samuel Brittan, the economics commentator of the *Financial Times*, described Lawson's post-monetarist approach as 'a reinstatement of demand management in nominal terms'.[15] The chancellor also stressed sterling's new role, commenting in the Budget speech that 'Significant movements in the exchange rate, whatever their cause, can have a short-term impact on the general price level and on inflationary expectations. So benign neglect is not an option.'[16] His conversion brought wry approval from Leigh-Pemberton, who, during an appearance before the Treasury and Civil Service Committee the following month, told MPs that he welcomed the 'reinstatement' of the exchange rate in the Treasury's policy calculations.[17]

There was another important ingredient in Nigel Lawson's conversion. After its earlier studied indifference, the US administration began to understand the damage that the dollar's relentless rise had inflicted on the US economy. A growing budget deficit as a result of the Reagan tax-cutting programme, high interest rates and a surging dollar had led to an unprecedented increase in the US trade gap. By 1984 the annual current account deficit had reached $100bn and was still increasing. The dollar's strength was driving US manufacturers out of their export and home markets while the strong domestic growth generated by the Reagan administration's tax cuts sucked in cheaper imports.

The juxtaposition of a large trade deficit and a rising currency defied the traditional economic logic. For most of the postwar period governments had discovered to their cost how quickly a deteriorating balance of payments position would translate into devaluation. But the world was entering an era in which massive capital flows across the foreign exchanges were becoming divorced from the underlying trade patterns which had once determined them. Global bond markets were coming of age, and daily transactions on the foreign exchange markets now totalled hundreds of billions of dollars. Relative interest rates were often more important than current-account positions in determining the direction of vast, often speculative, capital flows. In this dawning world of hot money less than 5 per cent of foreign exchange transactions were linked to longer-term patterns of trade and investment. The massive expansion of capital markets also injected a new volatility into currency movements. The early 1980s regularly saw daily fluctuations in the value of the dollar of as much as 1 or 2 per cent. On one memorable day in September 1984 a raid on the speculators by the Bundesbank triggered a fall of over 4 per cent.

The January 1985 sterling crisis coincided with a crucial change of policy and personnel in the US administration. The first signs came on 17 January, at a meeting in Washington of finance ministers of the Group of Five – the US, West Germany, France, Japan and Britain. (The larger G7 includes also Canada and Italy.) Margaret Thatcher's protest to Reagan about the dollar's strength prompted Don Regan, the US Treasury secretary, to take a cooperative approach to intervention in the exchange market. As a result, the G5 finance ministers, who had preferred previously to meet secretly, issued their first-ever communiqué. They recorded that they would work towards 'greater exchange market stability', and signalled that they were prepared to intervene if necessary to halt the dollar's rise. The meeting was followed by a series of coordinated raids by the central banks, including for the first time the US Federal Reserve, in which they sold more than $1bn from their reserves. The aim was to break the markets' confidence that the US currency's appreciation had become a one-way bet.

A more important shift came the following month with Regan's replacement at the Treasury by James Baker, formerly the White House chief of staff. Baker, a pragmatist and a fixer rather than an economic theorist, saw the dangers of the dollar's appreciation. The worsening trade position had led to a wave of protectionist pressure from US industry and in Congress. The White House faced persistent calls to take unilateral action to reduce the country's bilateral trade deficit with Japan and to impose new restrictions on imports from Europe. Baker determined on a plan which he hoped would both restore order to world currency markets and allow the US to re-establish its leading role in management of the world economy.

Whether by free-market coincidence or central bank design, the dollar's rise halted in March 1985. The US currency fell from a peak of DM3.40 and 263 yen to DM3.05 and 250 yen by the mid-summer. Sterling recovered strongly, allowing Lawson to reverse part of the January interest rate rise. However, the dollar's decline, particularly against the yen, was not enough to make even a small dent in the US trade deficit. The administration was unwilling to make substantial reductions in the burgeoning federal budget deficit, the fundamental cause of the worsening trade position. Baker first toyed with the idea of calling an international monetary conference as the prelude to the establishment of a new international exchange rate regime. The idea had been long favoured by the French government, which saw the ERM as a basis for a wider international system of currency management embracing the dollar and yen. Others – particularly Germany – were doubtful about the prospect of rebuilding Bretton Woods.

The eventual compromise was a meeting of G5 finance ministers in New York which unveiled in September 1985 what was to become known as the Plaza accord. Just as Lawson's March 1985 Budget foreshadowed the end of Britain's monetarist experiment, the Plaza accord, named after the New York hotel at which the G5 met, signalled an end to Washington's unthinking faith in the wisdom of financial markets. The ministers and their central bankers planned what Lawson termed subsequently a 'six-week blitz' against the dollar. Their communiqué on 22 September said, in the opaque jargon beloved of central bankers, that 'some further orderly appreciation of the non-dollar currencies against the dollar is desirable'. Behind the communiqué lay an unannounced commitment to sell up to $18bn from the central banks' reserves in order to secure an immediate 10 to 12 per cent devaluation of the dollar. There was a more fundamental message: the G5 was no longer content to stand on the sidelines of international markets – it would be a participant rather than a spectator. The markets took fright, and by the end of 1985 the US currency had fallen by 15 per cent.

The first, and last, serious cabinet discussion during Margaret Thatcher's premiership of whether Britain should join the ERM took place in November 1985. A number of factors had coalesced during the late summer to persuade Nigel Lawson, and many of his senior colleagues, that the time was now 'ripe' for sterling's entry. The dollar's fall during most of 1985, given fresh momentum by the Plaza accord, had seen a return of confidence in sterling. From March onwards it recovered most of the ground lost during the previous winter of devaluation. The sterling index (average for 1985=100) jumped more than 10 per cent from a low of 92.9 in the first three months of 1985 to 104.6 in the third quarter. The rise against the dollar was more dramatic, from an average of $1.11 to $1.38. Sterling also rose from a low point of less than DM3.50 to DM3.92. The recovery allowed a gradual ratcheting down of interest rates from the high of 14 per cent in January to 11.5 per cent in late summer. Industrialists and back-bench Conservative MPs wanted a sharper reduction, but Lawson, badly scarred by the January crisis, was cautious. A demand from the Confederation of British Industry for another two-point cut in the cost of borrowing was brushed aside. Thatcher, worried about an acceleration in the headline rate of inflation to 7 per cent, insisted that the rise in the exchange rate was not damaging industry. Business should take note that it was 'not advisable to rely on the exchange rate for competitiveness,' she told the House of Commons.[18]

Sterling M3 was beyond reinstatement as a reliable guide to future inflation. Its annual growth rate had accelerated to 20 per cent, compared to a guideline of 5 to 9 per cent set in the March Budget. In June, Lawson secured Thatcher's agreement to end the practice under which the Bank of England sought artificially to contain its expansion by mopping up funds with massive sales of gilt-edged securities – known as 'overfunding'. In his Mansion House speech in October, the chancellor dropped the sterling M3 target. It was revived briefly the following year, but Lawson had effectively buried the British monetarist experiment. Ian Gilmour, the former cabinet minister, offered a damning judgement: 'The doctrine of monetarism was so comprehensively disproved by its practice that both a consider-able effort of memory and a suspension of disbelief are needed to recall that, in the opening years of the Thatcher government, monetarism was its guiding doctrine and principle.'[19] The chancellor shed few tears at its demise. 'The acid test of monetary policy is its record in reducing inflation,' he told the assembled bankers at the Mansion House. 'Those who wish to join the debate about the intricacies of different measures of money and the implications they may have for the future are welcome to do so. But at the end of the day the position is clear and unambiguous. The inflation rate is judge and jury.'[20] However, the bold rhetoric disguised the absence of any alternative policy to replace the Medium Term Financial Strategy, and his challenge to his monetarist critics would later return to haunt Lawson.

The chancellor had again raised the issue of ERM membership with the prime minister in early September. She was sceptical, but agreed that the issue should be discussed at a Downing Street seminar on 30 September. Lawson prepared carefully, marshalling his arguments in close cooperation with the Bank of England. Robin Leigh-Pemberton was enthusiastic, while Eddie George was prepared to mute his opposition. The thrust of the chancellor's presentation at the seminar was that the principal obstacles to membership had been removed. Sterling had recovered from its low point. He had begun earlier that month the process of replenishing the foreign exchange reserves with the successful issue of floating-rate notes, or short-term bonds, worth $2.5bn. The Plaza accord provided a favourable international backdrop to more active currency management. The discrediting of broad money and the failure to establish M0 as a credible alternative meant that the government had anyway been obliged to give weight to the exchange rate. Lawson sought also to answer in advance one of Thatcher's principal political objections to the ERM – that sterling might come under speculative attack immediately before a general election if the Labour Party was faring well. Her fear was that a falling pound within the ERM might force the government either to raise interest rates or to devalue during the election campaign. Either course might hasten a Labour victory. Lawson asked Geoffrey Littler to devise an insurance policy. Littler responded by suggesting that the pound could be temporarily suspended from the ERM during an election campaign, re-entering at the same exchange rate immediately after the assumed Conservative victory.

By now Lawson had secured the support of Burns and Middleton, though neither shared his zeal. As one of the officials most closely involved in the debate remarked: 'By the autumn of 1985 no one in the Treasury was opposing membership. We were resigned to it, and content to get on with it. But I wouldn't say we were enthusiastic.' There were political as well as economic arguments in favour. The European single market was coming into view – a development which would bind Britain's economic future still more closely to that of the continent. The Foreign Office saw valuable political leverage in participation in the ERM. Middleton's view was fairly typical of the

Treasury: the issue was not whether the ERM offered an easy escape route from the monetarist muddle but whether anti-inflation policy could be run instead with an exchange rate target. There were risks, but on balance he thought the answer was yes.

Thatcher's contribution to the seminar, however, reflected the advice of Alan Walters and of Brian Griffiths, the head of the No. 10 policy unit. Walters had left No. 10 in 1983 to take up a post at the World Bank in Washington, but he remained a regular visitor to 10 Downing Street and kept in close touch with Griffiths, who shared his antipathy to the ERM. They warned the prime minister beforehand that the corollary of a more stable exchange rate would be increased volatility of interest rates. Tying sterling to the Deutschmark could also impose a deflationary bias on economic policy in the approach to the next general election. The advice strengthened Thatcher's own doubts, and she summed up at the end of the seminar by saying that further deliberation was necessary.

The consequent ministerial meeting took place six weeks later, on 13 November, in No. 10 Downing Street. It was attended by Geoffrey Howe; Lord Whitelaw, the home secretary and deputy prime minister; Leon Brittan, the trade and industry secretary; John Biffen, the leader of the House of Commons; Norman Tebbit, the party chairman; and John Wakeham, the chief whip. Lawson was accompanied by Peter Middleton and Terence Burns; Leigh-Pemberton by Eddie George. The prime minister was joined by Brian Griffiths. Lawson had spoken individually beforehand to all of the ministers except Biffen. He had answered in detail a series of questions which Thatcher had sent him in advance. The Treasury, with the cooperation of the Bank, prepared three separate papers – an overview pressing the case for early membership, another answering each of Thatcher's questions, and the last detailing the relative performance of currencies in the ERM since 1979.

The overview paper, published subsequently in Lawson's memoirs, was carefully argued and crisply written.[21] It displayed his technical grasp, his presentational skills and an easy ability, when it suited him, to make a natural elision between good economics and political advantage. Above all, it underlined his passionate conviction that economic management could be effective only under 'a set of anti-inflationary rules'. During its first term the government had provided this with the MTFS, but the unreliability of sterling M3 had driven it back on to a policy of discretion. The rules had inevitably lost much of their original clarity, and he was now steering the economy without a compass: 'I have in any case to recast the presentation of policy fundamentally between now and the Budget following the patching-up job I did at the Mansion House.' The exchange rate was the most readily comprehensible target for monetary policy, so ERM member-ship would buttress the MTFS. It would also provide the necessary 'shot in the arm – a touch of imagination and freshness' – to improve the presentation of the Treasury's anti-inflation strategy, and to ensure that government policies carried conviction. There were risks, of course, but they had much diminished. Sterling's status as a petrocurrency had been significantly reduced, Britain's relations with its European partners had improved. At DM3.70 the pound was now in the lower half of the DM3.60–4.00 range in which it had fluctuated for the previous three years. 'We should take the opportunity to join at around this rate.' If sterling remained outside the ERM, the financial markets inevitably would begin to ask why. 'And the only conclusion they can reach, aided and abetted by periodic moans from industry, is that we may wish to see the exchange rate lower, if not now, then before too long.' As a result, interest rates outside the ERM would have to be higher than if sterling were inside. 'I am forced to the conclusion that not to join now would be a historic missed opportunity in the conduct of economic policy, which we would before very long come bitterly to regret.'

Lawson made plain that he was not speaking simply for himself: 'My judgement . . . is shared not only by the governor of the Bank of England but also by senior officials in both the Treasury and the Bank. They all believe it makes operational sense to join, and that we can now deliver our policy objectives more effectively in the EMS than if we remain outside it.'

As expected, John Biffen, a convinced monetarist with a dis-tinguished record in advocating free-floating exchange rates, opposed the chancellor, but the others present offered strong support. Howe and Brittan were natural allies. Howe had wrestled with the com-plexities of the money supply for most of his chancellorship, and towards the end he had reached the conclusion that an exchange rate anchor was the obvious alternative. As foreign secretary he was increasingly conscious of the need to maintain Britain's influence within Europe. Leigh-Pemberton, deeply concerned about the lack of clarity and transparency in official policy, emphasized that the balance of risks was firmly in favour of ERM membership. The officials present were mildly surprised to hear Norman Tebbit offer his backing. Later he would change his mind and become one of the most vehement critics of the ERM.

The return to a fixed exchange rate undoubtedly would have provoked some opposition among back-bench MPs at Westminster. Biffen represented a strand of monetarist thinking which still commanded the support of a few dozen Tory MPs, and a report published later the same month by the Treasury and Civil Service Committee voiced concern that sterling's rate against the Deutschmark was unsustainably high. The report accepted most of the arguments for eventual membership, but the committee's chairman, Terence Higgins, warned that, at DM3.70, the pound's rate against the Deutschmark was uncompetitive.[22] Lawson, however, could rely on strong support from the business and financial community. Wakeham, who as chief whip was best equipped to gauge the likely reaction on the Conservative back benches, thought any revolt would be modest. Whitelaw, as was the normal practice, summed up the discussion. Lawson's report of his conclusion is not disputed: 'If the chancellor, the governor and foreign secretary are all agreed we should join the EMS then that should be decisive. It has certainly decided me,' Whitelaw said.[23]

It had not decided Margaret Thatcher. She had resolved even before Lawson had spoken that she would not consent. Walters and Griffiths had equipped her with a long list of objections. Falling oil prices argued for delay; the government would lose its control over interest rates if sterling was bound to the Deutschmark; there would be serious risks in the run-up to the general election; sterling's entry into the ERM might destabilize the whole system. The practical objections were in one sense a cover: her instincts – and she was a politician whose instincts provided her philosophy – were against joining. She harboured a fundamental objection: she could not understand why the Bundesbank should be allowed to determine British monetary policy unless 'we had no faith in our own ability to control inflation'. So she insisted on sticking to the formal position of joining 'when the time was right', even though 'most of my arguments applied to principle as much as timing'.[24] As soon as Whitelaw had finished speaking, she brought the meeting to an abrupt end. Her ministers and officials were left stunned by her final remark: if they wanted to join the ERM they would have to find a new prime minister, she told them. There was, said one of the officials present, 'a glazed determination in her eyes which I had never seen before'; she was 'shaken but immovable'.

This would be the only occasion during her eleven years in Downing Street when Thatcher would stand alone against the expressed will of her most senior ministers on such an important issue. For all her convictions, when it counted she usually preferred retreat to isolation. The ERM was the exception. Lawson and Howe would both reflect after their resignations some five years later that, had she given way in 1985, the economic boom and bust of the late 1980s might well have been avoided. Perhaps.

Lawson, joined in 11 Downing Street by Howe, Whitelaw and Tebbit immediately after the meeting, considered resignation. He had been rebuffed on a central issue of the policy for which he bore responsibility. He was persuaded to stay: it was too soon to give up the prize of the chancellorship. Howe, among others, thought that the prime minister might yet be brought round. Intriguingly, no one considered seriously the other option – forcing the issue on to the agenda of the full cabinet to see whether Thatcher would indeed resign rather than give way. Instead, Lawson set about rebuilding an economic strategy in the hope that she would change her mind. His officials did not share his optimism. As one said, 'I don't think any of us thought it would happen unless she fell under a bus – and Howe took over.' Lawson, as an official from the Bank put it, had 'reached the gates of Moscow and been turned back'.

There was a postscript to this confrontation which would prove an important, and malevolent, influence on the later conflict between chancellor and prime minister. Lawson was aware that Walters had sent Thatcher a note of his objections in advance of the November meeting. He also discovered soon afterwards that a draft of Walters's forthcoming book on Thatcher's economic management, *Britain's*

Economic Renaissance, had been circulating among officials in White-hall.[25] The book, a warm account of the transformation of Britain's economic prospects under her premiership, included a strong attack on the ERM.[26] Walters argued that the mechanism was fundamentally flawed. He contended that, if financial markets attached credibility to the currency link between two or more countries, interest rate levels in those countries inexorably would converge, even if their respective inflation rates were markedly different. Countries with low inflation rates would be forced by the ERM to maintain interest rates at higher levels than necessary to meet their domestic policy objectives, while those with high inflation rates would be obliged to adopt too lax a policy. Walter's thesis had more to do with abstract economic theory than with reality: in practice, the system allowed for substantial variations in interest rates. To Lawson, however, Walters's intervention seemed a serious threat. He thought Thatcher's adviser had added the exchange rate section to the book at the last moment in a deliberate effort to thwart his ERM ambitions. Walters denied the charge, and complained later that the Treasury had anyway forced large cuts in the final text. The incident none the less sowed dangerous seeds of mistrust which would have an important influence on the later clashes between the two men.

CHAPTER THREE

A DEVALUED CURRENCY

NOTHING IS SO INCONSTANT AS the attitude of politicians to sterling. During its early years the Thatcher government had exulted in a strong pound. The confidence of the international investors who poured their funds into sterling was irrefutable proof of the soundness of the government's economic strategy, a symbol of national revival. In its second term, the same government presided over an unprecedented fall in the exchange rate. Margaret Thatcher never really understood the inconsistency.

Nigel Lawson would look back on sterling's devaluation in 1986 as the most significant error of his chancellorship.[1] It was this episode more than any other which exposed the underlying tension in his management of the economy. Lawson the ideologue was unshakeable in his public insistence that the defeat of inflation offered the only route to economic success. Lawson the pragmatist understood that the real world demanded that he sustain the economic recovery and turn the tide of rising unemployment. So the Treasury borrowed from St Augustine the principle of virtue deferred: the Holy Grail of permanently low inflation was always only a year or two away. The devaluation would have another significance: it hardened the chancellor's conviction that a stable pound could provide the only firm anchor for a credible anti-inflation policy. Sterling's fall in 1986 led inexorably to Lawson's policy the following year of 'shadowing' the Deutschmark outside the ERM. That in turn would provide the catalyst for his explosive departure from the Treasury.

The trigger for the pound's slide in 1986 was a collapse in the oil price. A barrel of crude oil which had cost nearly $30 in the last weeks of 1985 was worth less than $10 by mid-1986. Sterling, still regarded on international markets as a petrocurrency because of the large contribution made by North Sea oil to Britain's trade balance, inevitably came under pressure. The chancellor was left with two options. He could defend sterling, as he had done in January 1985, by pushing up interest rates. In those circumstances Britain would pocket the benefits of cheaper fuel in the form of a lower overall inflation rate. Alternatively he could allow the pound to fall and calculate that higher import prices for other goods would be offset by the benign impact on inflation of cheaper oil. In this second scenario the net effect on inflation would be neutral, but economic growth would benefit from a more competitive exchange rate. The chancellor chose higher growth over lower inflation. Between the last three months of 1985 and the final quarter of 1986 the trade-weighted sterling index fell by more than 16 per cent – from 101.5 to 85.1 (1985=100). Against the Deutschmark the pound fell 25 per cent to DM2.85 during the same period. The devaluation left sterling for the first time well below its level in 1979, when its index value had been 107.

This was a momentous, heretical decision, but, as the American economist John Kenneth Galbraith once remarked, nothing is so admirable in politics as a short memory. Since 1979, despite its evolving role in interest rate decisions, sterling had been viewed as essentially a monetary indicator. The pound's value was treated as an indicator of the tightness of the government's anti-inflation stance. In 1986 that changed. The reversal was never admitted, but sterling became instead an instrument of macro-economic management, just as it had been before the Conservatives' monetarist revolution. Devaluation was seen as a necessary stimulus to higher output and, more specifically, to an improvement in the country's trade position. The practice as distinct from the rhetoric of official policy towards sterling in 1986 was little different from that of the Labour government in 1977 when Denis Healey engineered a deliberate devaluation. Like Healey, Lawson discovered that once the financial markets sense that a government wants a lower exchange rate it becomes impossible to control the speed of descent.[2]

He was not alone in judging that the diminishing worth of North Sea oil should be offset by an increase in the competitiveness of Britain's manufactured exports. Many Treasury officials, less dismissive than the chancellor of the damage inflicted on manufacturing industry by the recession of 1980/81, thought the fall in value of Britain's North Sea oil assets made devaluation inevitable. The alternative was a return to the balance of payments crises which had dogged the economy during the 1960s and 1970s. Their counterparts at the Bank of England were more cautious. Bank officials, caught off guard by an acceleration in price rises during 1985, were nervous about loosening the anti-inflationary reins. The differences, however, tended to be about how far and how fast sterling should be allowed to fall rather than about the principle.

Previously, the chancellor had publicly scorned the idea that a high exchange rate was the cause of Britain's industrial weakness. He had directed particular contempt at the conclusions of a report into the future of British manufacturing industry of a House of Lords committee headed by Lord Aldington. The committee, looking ahead to the run-down of North Sea oil exports, had concluded in July 1985 that determined action was needed to rebuild and modernize industry. It called for an expanded government role in promoting the growth of high-technology industries, in sustaining research and development and in improving education. It highlighted also the need for a stable and competitive exchange rate.[3] The chancellor dismissed the report as a 'mixture of special pleading dressed up as analysis and assertion masquerading as evidence'.

He had an escape route, however, against the time when the terms of the economic debate shifted. In 1984 he had responded in a speech in Cambridge to the growing political debate about how Britain should make best use of the finite wealth below the North Sea. The thrust of his argument was that oil exports inevitably would displace overseas sales of manufactured goods. Over time, however, the position would be self-correcting.[4] He took up the theme in his evidence to the Aldington committee in May 1985. Speaking before the peers had finalized their report, he argued that gradual decline of North Sea revenues would be accompanied by an equally sedate fall in sterling's real (or inflation-adjusted) exchange rate. This improvement in competitiveness might result from a fall in the exchange rate, but it could also come from improved productivity. If industry kept increases in its costs below those of overseas rivals, then its competitiveness would improve without any fall in sterling's nominal value. Lawson's model was West Germany: the Deutschmark had been strong throughout the postwar period, but remained competitive because of the country's strong inflation and productivity performance.

At the beginning of 1986 this theoretical option was not on offer. Instead of facing a gentle run-down of its North Sea resources over decades, Britain found that its oil revenues had more than halved within a matter of months. The case for devaluation was reinforced by other indicators. The economy had grown steadily during 1984 and 1985, but the recovery was now in its fifth year. There were visible signs that the pace of growth was slowing, and there was a question mark over whether the upturn would be followed soon by a cyclical down-swing. It was an alarming prospect. Unemployment had been rising without a break for six years and a general election was looming into view. The Treasury insisted that the economy was experiencing no more than a temporary pause in the upturn, but privately it was far from certain of the claim. One adviser recalls that the Treasury was steeped in gloom: 'That is why we allowed sterling to fall. Everyone was pessimistic. It was the mood of the building.'

Lawson blames others for the devaluation: the message of his memoirs is that he acquiesced against his better judgement on the advice of Peter Middleton and Terence Burns. The charge is strongly denied within the Treasury. Its appearance, long after Lawson's resignation, provoked anger among the officials with whom he had worked most closely. Burns and Middleton made no secret of their antipathy to a formal exchange rate policy outside of the ERM, but officials insist that this did not amount to a policy of seeking a weaker pound, covertly or otherwise. As one of their number puts it, 'What we wanted was a policy which gave a substantial weight to the exchange rate but one without any hard margins. We wanted to take account of all the indicators in setting interest rates. We did not want to be forced into raising rates every time there was a flurry of speculation against sterling.' There were undoubtedly also officials in the Treasury and Bank who thought that fiscal policy should be tighter and monetary policy looser in order to tilt the balance in the economy away from domestic consumption and towards investment and exports. One former Bank official recalls that even before the oil price fall some in Threadneedle Street thought sterling was overvalued by about 10 per cent. And Lawson could in any case have overruled official advice. In the words of one former aide, 'I don't recall this particular chancellor ever finding it difficult to overturn the views of his officials.' Whatever their respective views about the exchange rate, Lawson and Burns did differ over fiscal policy. Burns proved a consistent opponent of the programme of income tax cuts on which the chancellor embarked in the spring of 1986.

By an unhappy coincidence, the oil-price fall was accompanied by an unexpected political crisis for Margaret Thatcher's government – the so-called 'Westland affair'. A seemingly trivial cabinet dispute over how best to rescue an ailing West Country helicopter company erupted into a perilous row. It led to the enforced departure in January 1986 of two of Thatcher's most senior cabinet ministers, Michael Heseltine and Leon Brittan. Heseltine, a passionate believer in the need to build new industrial alliances in Europe, was obliged to quit as defence secretary after failing to secure Thatcher's support for a European rescue operation for Westland. Her natural Atlanticism, cemented by a close relationship with President Reagan, spoke in favour of a rival deal with a US manufacturer. Thus the Westland crisis provided an early preview of the later divisions over Europe which fatally divided Thatcher's cabinet. Heseltine exacted his revenge in 1990, when his challenge for the leadership ended her premiership.

In January 1986, however, there was a more immediate threat to her premiership. Her handling of the dispute between Heseltine and Brittan, the trade and industry secretary, appeared to breach all of the normal cabinet rules. There were charges that she had been directly involved in the illicit Whitehall campaign to discredit Heseltine which eventually obliged Brittan to resign. If Neil Kinnock had pressed home the Labour Party's attack more effectively, Thatcher might have been forced from Downing Street at that moment. Understandably, in such circumstances she was in no mood to deepen her unpopularity by increasing interest rates.

Lawson had in fact raised rates from 11.5 to 12 per cent on 8 January, just before the Westland row burst into the public domain. The pound had fallen sharply in the previous few weeks, mirroring a drop in the oil price to $22 a barrel. The Treasury feared sterling might go into free fall. However, the small rise in borrowing costs was calculated to brake rather than reverse sterling's decline. By the last week of January the pound had lost 4 per cent of its value in as many weeks. There was no second or third rise in interest rates as there had been in similar circumstances a year earlier. Lawson disclosed subsequently that he had pressed for a one-point increase on 24 January. Thatcher had assented only with 'bad grace', but before the Treasury had announced the rise sterling had stabilized momentarily. The chancellor rescinded the planned announcement. It was a mistake, he said later, he had 'regretted ever since'.[5] As the pound fell in subsequent months, however, he did not attempt to rectify it.

Sterling's depreciation in 1986 did not take a smooth path. Periods of turbulence, and occasionally panic, were punctuated by intervals of calm. The perception that the government would tolerate a significant depreciation was reinforced by the Treasury's decision to publicize the concept of an 'oil-adjusted exchange rate'. This acknowledged that the time-scale for the economy's necessary adjustment to falling oil revenues had been telescoped into a matter of months. It held that, as long as sterling's depreciation did no more than mirror lower oil prices, the adjustment need not lead to higher inflation. The analysis was no more than common sense, but it was also as far removed from monetarism as anything propounded by the previous Labour administration.

The official inflation figures underpinned the new strategy, as the benefits of lower oil prices were felt much sooner than the higher import costs from a weaker pound. The annual inflation rate had reached 7 per cent in mid-1985, but it fell to a low of 2.4 per cent in July 1986. The decline in the value of the dollar since the Plaza accord provided additional comfort. By April 1986 the pound, at $1.55, was nearly 50 per cent higher against the US currency than in February 1985. The rise against the dollar would do something to soften the impact of sterling's depreciation against other currencies.

Nigel Lawson meanwhile showed no hesitation in extolling the benefits of his new sterling policy. His Budget speech in March 1986 declared that the oil price fall and sterling's devaluation offered an 'outstanding opportunity' for industry to increase its exports and to reduce import penetration.[6] If he harboured any self-doubt about the strategy, he did not display it at his post-Budget briefing for economic correspondents. Criticisms of his policies were dismissed as 'claptrap', the outlook for the economy was the best for a generation. As for the less sanguine forecasts of economists in London's financial markets –

dubbed by the chancellor 'City scribblers' – they should be consigned to the dustbin: 'Anyone who just feeds data into a model [of the economy] and believes what comes out is an idiot.'[7] He took advantage of a brief period of calm on the foreign exchange markets to bring down interest rates to 10 per cent by June 1986. Unemployment had at last started to fall. The growth pause turned out to be just that – a pause.

The chancellor had still not given up on the idea of ERM membership. In the wake of Margaret Thatcher's rebuff in the autumn of 1985, Lawson had pressed ahead with preparations against the day when he might persuade her otherwise. In December 1985 Peter Middleton and Geoffrey Littler from the Treasury had travelled with Anthony Loehnis, the Bank director responsible for international relations, for secret talks in Bonn. They met with Leonard Gleske, a Bundesbank director, and Hans Tietmeyer, the state secretary in the federal ministry of finance who, some years later, would become Bundesbank president. Their talks, at Tietmeyer's house in the Bad Godesberg suburb of Bonn, secured German backing for sterling's membership. Tietmeyer voiced doubts about the suggestion that the pound might temporarily be suspended from the mechanism during an election campaign. The Bundesbank thought such a provision a dangerous precedent. The following year Tietmeyer would also raise with Littler his concern that the rapid build-up of liquidity in the British economy was storing up inflationary pressures. The basic message, however, was that Lawson could expect German backing. One of those present at the December meeting in Bad Godesberg recalls that the mutual assumption was that sterling would enter the ERM at between DM3.45 and DM3.60 – a tough but acceptable rate for the British.

By March 1986 the pound had already fallen sharply, but Lawson made no secret of his ERM ambitions. The Budget saw a brief reinstatement of sterling M3. The planned target range of 11 to 15 per cent, however, was twice the 4 to 8 per cent foreshadowed in the previous year's Medium Term Financial Strategy and anyway had only guideline status. The chancellor made it plain that lower oil prices had weakened objections to ERM entry by diminishing sterling's status as a petrocurrency. Treasury officials let it be known that Geoffrey Howe at the Foreign Office backed strongly Lawson's view on the issue. Pressed after his Budget speech on the prime minister's view, Lawson was coy: 'As you know ... the government is totally united on everything.'[8] By the following month, chancellor and foreign secretary were coordinating the pressure on the prime minister.

Addressing the Lombard Association on 16 April 1986, Lawson stated clearly his own preference, before hinting that the prime minister was the last remaining obstacle to ERM membership. He told his City audience that, over the medium term, 'maintaining a fixed exchange rate against countries who share our resolve to reduce inflation is a pretty robust way of keeping domestic policy on the rails'. He then added, 'The government does not believe the time is yet right for us to join the EMS.'[9] Robert Culpin, the Treasury press secretary, left economics journalists in no doubt of Lawson's meaning. In this context 'the government' did not include the chancellor: it referred only to Thatcher. Culpin also alerted correspondents to a speech which Howe was delivering that same night to the Conservative Group for Europe. Britain, the foreign secretary said, could not go on indefinitely saying it would join the mechanism only when the time was right. In a pointed message to Thatcher, Howe added that the final decision on timing should be left to the Treasury.

Lawson insisted in his Lombard Association speech that the advantages of replacing a domestic monetary framework with an exchange rate target were available only within a formal system. There could be no halfway house short of full membership of the ERM: 'I see no role for an exchange rate target outside a formal exchange rate system, shared by other countries and supported by a coordinated approach to economic management and intervention. And that, for the United Kingdom, means outside the exchange rate mechanism of the EMS.' This was Treasury orthodoxy. Rachel Lomax, one of the Treasury's ablest officials and much respected by Lawson, had drafted the text. Within a year, however, the chancellor would take a different view. Even as he spoke Thatcher was telling MPs that the pound's fall against the Deutschmark over the previous winter had vindicated her doubts about the ERM.[10] Faced with her persistent opposition, Lawson would ignore his own strictures and attempt to shadow the Deutschmark from outside the ERM.

Lawson's enthusiasm was reinforced once again by events on the international stage. The Plaza accord to drive down the value of the dollar was perceived as a great success. Concerted raids by the Group of Five's leading central banks injected a powerful uncertainty into markets in which the speculators had hitherto been unchallenged. Between September 1985 and March 1986 the dollar fell by nearly 20 per cent against the currencies of its main trading-partners. Looking back, it is questionable that the central banks wielded as much influence as it seemed at the time: their intervention may have been as much a coincident as a causal factor in the dollar's decline. In early 1986, however, the finance ministers and central bankers recaptured the illusion if not the reality of power. For most of the 1970s and for the first half of the 1980s they had been spectators on the world's money markets; now they had become participants, and they enjoyed the experience.

In Europe, the ERM had provided some shelter against the storms on international markets, particularly after the spring of 1983, when François Mitterrand abandoned his expansionary economic policy in favour of a strong franc – the so-called 'franc fort' policy. But the mechanism could still fall victim to unpredictable shifts in the dollar's value. When the US currency rose, the ERM tended to be stable; but when the dollar fell, a consequent rush of funds into the Deutschmark placed strains on the weaker European currencies. France, long committed to a system of rules to constrain the excesses of financial markets, argued during the early 1980s for a series of international currency zones, grouped around the dollar, the ERM and the yen. Nods in that direction were made by leaders of the G7 leading industrial nations at the Versailles and Williamsburg summits in 1982 and 1983. Supporters of free-floating exchange rates had argued that prudent economic policies would iron out occasional fluctuations in exchange rates. The evidence from the dollar, however, was that currencies could be subject to long, and dangerously disruptive, periods of 'overshooting' which bore little relationship to underlying economic conditions.

James Baker saw in international coordination of economic policy an opportunity to reassert US leadership. As well as seeking to defuse protectionist pressure in Congress, he wanted to ensure that his efforts to reduce the twin US budget and trade deficits, the legacy of Reaganomics, did not lead to a hard landing for the US economy. He wanted a more competitive dollar and faster economic growth in Europe and Japan. Baker was suited to the role he now assumed. Unversed in the minutiae of economics, he was a politician in the activist mould who revelled in the spotlight which now turned on the world's finance ministers. The success of the Plaza accord convinced him there was more to be done. At the Tokyo summit in May 1986 he unveiled a plan for 'multilateral surveillance' of economic policies in the big industrial nations, supervised by the International Monetary Fund. The proposal was for each government to frame its domestic economic policy within an agreed international framework. The IMF would track a range of indicators – from budget deficits and borrowing costs to growth and inflation rates – in each of the G7 countries. Its analysis would tell policy-makers in Washington, Tokyo, Bonn and elsewhere whether their individual strategies matched the common interest of sustained, non-inflationary growth. With unblushing hyperbole, Baker hailed the Tokyo initiative as the most important development in international monetary cooperation since the Bretton Woods conference forty years earlier.

This was a brand of economic activism far removed from the minimalist vision offered by Nigel Lawson in his 1984 Mais Lecture. Lawson, however, was caught up in a mood of infectious enthusiasm for this new attempt to restore a semblance of order to the ever more anarchic behaviour of international markets. The chancellor enjoyed his membership of an exclusive club of men (there were no women) whose brief public statements seemed capable of sending billions of dollars cascading in this direction or that across world currency markets. In January 1986 he hosted a meeting of G5 finance ministers in 11 Downing Street. In early September, at a meeting in Gleneagles, he coordinated efforts by European finance ministers to smooth over one of the frequent squalls which accompanied the efforts to enhance international cooperation.

As they surfaced publicly, such disagreements provoked bouts of turbulence on the foreign exchange markets. Sterling, which tended to be pulled down alongside the dollar when the US currency weakened, was more than once caught in the crossfire. At the annual meeting of the IMF just weeks after the Gleneagles talks, the growing tension between Bonn and Washington spilled over into a public dispute between the Bundesbank and the US administration. The German government, backed by Japan, thought that the dollar had fallen enough since the Plaza accord. It wanted Washington to concentrate on reducing the federal budget deficit. Baker thought the priorities lay elsewhere: he demanded cuts in West German interest rates to increase the pace of European growth, and fiscal expansion in Japan to curb its huge bilateral trade surplus with the US. The public squabble undermined both the dollar and sterling. Such episodes, however, did not dispel Lawson's enthusiasm for a new world order. He liked the limelight abroad, and it suited his cause at home.

Thatcher remained resolute in her refusal to countenance British membership of the ERM. Lawson's clever insinuations that it was only a matter of time before sterling was tied to the Deutschmark were frequently undercut by her public statements. Thus on 10 June 1986 she told the House of Commons:

> At present there is no intention of joining the European Monetary System. To do so would deny us an option we have at present. If there was speculation against sterling there would be only two ways of dealing with it if we joined the EMS. One would be to use up precious reserves, which could be done only to a very limited extent. The second would be by sharply increasing the interest rate. We should be denied the option of taking the strain on the exchange rate. I do not think it right to deny us the option at present.[11]

Her priority before the general election was faster economic growth, and if that required a weak pound so be it.

The financial markets took her at her word. After a respite during the spring and early summer, sterling resumed its slide. Between June and September 1986 it lost 10 per cent of its value on a trade-weighted basis. The pressures of lower oil prices on sterling were compounded by unease in the financial markets at the still rapid growth in the broad money supply measures. By September sterling

M3 was growing at an annual rate of 18 per cent. The Treasury insisted once again that the pace of credit expansion represented a structural shift in the economy rather than latent inflation. The markets were only half convinced. There were other worrying signs – the beginnings of the take-off in house prices, buoyant earnings, and early indications of capacity shortages. September 1986 saw also tangible evidence of the deterioration in Britain's trade position. The provisional statistics showed a record £886m deficit for the month of August. The figure would later be revised downwards, but now it focused the attention of financial markets on the weakening of Britain's trade balance following the collapse of North Sea oil revenues.

By the time Nigel Lawson reached the annual IMF meeting on 26 September, sterling was under siege. The row between the Bundesbank and the US administration had left a vulnerable pound in the speculators' crossfire. For a self-consciously proud chancellor the five days spent in Washington were a humiliating episode. Anxious to avoid a rise in interest rates before the Conservative Party conference the following week, Lawson spent much of his time trying to shake off the economics correspondents who attend such gatherings. As the chancellor darted from meeting to meeting refusing comment, Robin Leigh-Pemberton was left to deal with the press – only to be unfairly rebuked later for being rather too frank in his comments. Heavy intervention by the Bank of England proved futile as the pound fell for the first time ever below DM3.00.

The Bank, selling hundreds of millions of dollars in its efforts to halt the slide, was running down its currency reserves at an alarming rate. The Treasury had raised an additional $4bn earlier in the month as the second instalment of Lawson's plan to replenish the Bank's ammunition, but the markets were unimpressed. Lawson, sensing the scale of the crisis, was obliged to ask for assistance from the Bundesbank. At hastily arranged talks with Gerhard Stoltenberg, the West German finance minister, and Karl Otto Pöhl, the Bundesbank president, the central bank agreed to a show of support for the beleaguered pound. A foreign currency swap arrangement gave the Bank of England some much-needed ammunition against the speculators. The Bundesbank agreed also to buy sterling immediately in the markets. The Bank of England was obliged ultimately to pick up the bill for such intervention, but the Bundesbank's purchases gave the speculators pause for thought – and bought the chancellor some precious time.

Pöhl, who earlier the same week had complained that the Bank of England's intervention in support for sterling had been undercutting Bundesbank efforts to prop up the dollar, relished Lawson's predicament. A self-possessed central banker who enjoyed the Bundesbank's status and authority in international monetary affairs, he had become irritated by Lawson's equally certain confidence. Always in some awe of Margaret Thatcher, he would never become an admirer of her chancellor. Lawson recounted subsequently an interesting footnote to the affair. His initial overtures had drawn a cool response from the Bundesbank and he had telephoned Thatcher to apprise her of the difficulties. She was furious, warning that she would pull out the British army from the Rhine if the Bundesbank would not offer assistance.[12] The threat was never tested, but it offered an early clue to her deep distrust of Germany.

The respite for the pound provided by the Bundesbank proved predictably short-lived. By mid-October, with the annual Conservative Party conference out of the way, the Treasury bowed to the inevitable and raised interest rates from 10 to 11 per cent. Lawson used his annual speech at the Mansion House during the same month to nail his colours yet more firmly to the mast of a stable currency. He acknowledged that sterling's devaluation in response to the collapse in the oil price had been 'inevitable and indeed necessary'. He added, however, that 'There are clearly limits to the necessary and desirable extent of that fall.'[13] The message was echoed at the same event by Leigh-Pemberton. By now the Bank was seriously concerned by the relaxation of the anti-inflation reins. The governor stressed that the pound's depreciation had been 'fully sufficient' to offset the impact on the current account of lower oil prices.[14] The implication was that a further depreciation would be swiftly countered by higher interest rates.

Leigh-Pemberton meanwhile presided over the final rites for sterling M3. In a lecture delivered at Loughborough University a few days after the Mansion House speech, he set out in detail the factors behind the rapid growth in the broad money supply over the previous few years. His speech, drafted by Eddie George, explained the monetary overshoot as reflecting in large part the build-up of cash holdings by financial institutions. Deregulation, high real interest rates and intensified competition had increased the attraction of bank deposits relative to other financial assets. He concluded that it was 'perfectly fair to ask whether in these circumstances a broad money target continues to serve a useful purpose'. But Leigh-Pemberton offered also a note of caution. He compared the build-up of liquidity with an 'overhanging glacier'. It was safe for the moment, but if interest rates were not kept high enough the frozen bank deposits would become a flood of inflationary demand. He concluded, 'It would be just as unwise to pay insufficient regard to the behaviour of broad money ... as it would be to lay too much or too precise emphasis upon it.'[15] The authorities, however, had nothing to take its place in policy-making. Lawson wanted a stable exchange rate, while low interest rates were Thatcher's priority. As the Treasury and Civil Service Committee remarked in its report on the 1986 Autumn Statement, 'Monetary policy is uncertain because the government wishes both to prevent interest rates from rising and the exchange rate from falling ... by not committing itself firmly to either objective, [the government] may weaken market confidence to such a point that neither is achieved.'[16]

It was unfortunate that Leigh-Pemberton's Loughborough speech coincided with more robust indicators of an impending boom. The earlier growth pause had been replaced by an acceleration in consumer spending and borrowing. Once sterling had stabilized after its initial fall during January and February 1986, Lawson had lost no opportunity in reducing interest rates. By May, borrowing costs had been lowered in half-point stages from 12.5 per cent to 10 per cent, reflecting Lawson's anxiety about the durability of the economic recovery. His concerns proved misplaced. With earnings rising much faster than prices, real personal disposable income was growing strongly. The housing market had begun its ultimately disastrous ascent. The intense competition for customers between banks and building societies had greatly increased the availability of credit, and rising house prices prompted a surge in equity withdrawal – the use of mortgage advances to finance a much broader range of spending. The current account of the balance of payments was in deficit for the first time since the 1979 election. Lawson also loosened the reins of fiscal policy, using his Autumn Statement to add £10bn to public-spending targets during the following three years.

The prime minister felt uneasy, but, looking ahead to the possibility of an election the following summer, she did not want a rise in mortgage rates. At a seminar at Chequers during November, Thatcher recalled the Barber boom of Edward Heath's government in the early 1970s. Was there not a danger of history repeating itself? she asked Lawson. But her analysis was confused. She suggested a tighter fiscal policy in the Budget the following spring, apparently unaware that public borrowing was already undershooting the official forecasts. She did not want an increase in interest rates to defend the pound. Brian Griffiths, an ally in her opposition to the ERM, reinforced her resistance. She repeated her preference for lower public borrowing in December, when, for the second time during 1986, she rebuffed a proposal from Lawson for a rise in interest rates. At the end of the year sterling was trading at a record low of DM2.85 – some 25 per cent lower than a year earlier.

By now it was clear that the conflict with Lawson had become one of personal pride as well as economic philosophy. In October 1986 Karl Otto Pöhl visited London, intending to take the case for ERM membership directly to Thatcher. In a speech to the Anglo-German Chamber of Commerce he highlighted the potential advantages of sterling's participation. His speech was careful not to cross the line between encouragement for his British hosts and presumption, but his audience was left in no doubt of the Bundesbank's stance. As soon as Pöhl crossed the threshold of 10 Downing Street a few hours later, Thatcher made it clear that the ERM was not on the agenda for their discussion. Bernard Ingham relayed the message to political correspondents, ensuring Thatcher's rebuff of both her guest and her chancellor made the headlines the following day. The battle of wills had gone public; henceforth Thatcher and Lawson would engage in a struggle over the direction of policy which was as remarkable for its openness as for its destructiveness.

Thatcher chose to restate her position a few weeks later. The prime minister told the *Financial Times* that there was no question of ERM membership before the general election. The British economy was not strong enough: 'We are not quite the same as West Germany yet. I wish we were.' She went on to list several further objections, revealing a hostility which went far beyond the mere issue of timing. Sterling was still a petrocurrency; some other members of the ERM operated exchange controls; the government would be vulnerable to set-piece devaluations. 'What we are talking about is a D-mark standard, and then you have all the problems that we used to have with devaluation, if it comes.' She remembered the humiliation of sterling's departure from the Snake in 1973: 'You know, we came out of the Snake. It is etched on my mind. We went in and we came out. When we go in [to the ERM] we will go in strong and stay in.' There was yet another problem: she wanted to retain the freedom of manœuvre to set interest rates. ERM membership might mean 'I have to swing up interest rates very high, regardless. They might fluctuate much more because we would be tested. I do not want interest rates any higher.'[17]

Such comments persuaded senior Treasury officials that Lawson should retire from the fray. Peter Middleton's relationship with the chancellor was becoming cooler. He was unhappy with the breach between 10 and 11 Downing Street, fearing its corrosive influence on wider economic decision-making. Geoffrey Littler, though still an enthusiast for participation, shared Middleton's view that the cause was hopeless until Thatcher departed. The chancellor had allies in the cabinet, but, though he consulted occasionally with Lord White-law and liaised with Geoffrey Howe, he was reluctant to recruit others to his cause. His differences with Thatcher were common knowledge in Whitehall, but there too his naturally secretive style spoke against Lawson recruiting new supporters for his cause. Over lunch in December 1986, a cabinet colleague remarked on the growing tension between prime minister and chancellor but added that Lawson was unwilling to discuss the dispute with others.

Lawson became increasingly secretive about his intentions, even within the Treasury. He had chosen since 1983 to spend most of his working day in the study at 11 Downing Street rather than in the grand wood-panelled office reserved for the chancellor at the Treas-ury. He tended to work with a small group of trusted officials rather than more widely within the institution. As one senior adviser remarked, 'He would sit for days in his No. 11 study, calling over this group or that group to discuss this or that issue. But unless you were in the inner circle you could never see the whole picture.' The inner circle was tight, comprising Burns, Middleton, Robert Culpin and, at different times, Rachel Lomax, Alex Allan and Geoffrey Littler. Lawson also had great respect for Eddie George, despite the latter's antipathy towards the ERM. George had a technical expertise which fascinated Lawson. Breaking with the protocol which decrees that the chancellor's contacts with the Bank should be through the governor, Lawson held as many semi-clandestine meetings with George as monthly lunches with Robin Leigh-Pemberton. The Treasury adviser quoted above was certain that the chancellor's secretive style was a source of political weakness: 'I always thought afterwards that it was a great pity that Nigel had not done more to gather his friends around him to press the [ERM] case then ... history might have been different if he had done so earlier.'

Lawson would not give in easily. On the day after Thatcher's interview with the *FT* he said the opposite to the House of Commons Treasury and Civil Service Committee, telling the committee, 'I think there is clearly a case for being part of an explicit regional fixed exchange rate system.' The MPs were left in no doubt that he was referring to the ERM, as Lawson went on to emphasize that he now intended to put a floor under sterling, which by then had fallen to DM2.80.[18]

For a brief period after the June 1987 election it seemed to some of his cabinet colleagues that Lawson might defy the predictions of his officials and win the struggle over the ERM. He was the hero of the election campaign. He had cut 2p from the basic rate of income tax in his March Budget, adding to the 1p reduction announced in 1986. The reductions were the springboard for the election victory and, with the basic rate now down to 27p, the government was at last in sight of the 25p first promised by Geoffrey Howe in 1979. Superficially, the economy had recovered its equilibrium. Inflation seemed steady at around 4 per cent, output was rising at an annual rate of more than 3 per cent, the pound had started to rebound strongly in anticipation of a third Conservative election victory. Unemployment was at last falling month by month. Sterling's recovery had allowed successive cuts in interest rates to a level of 9 per cent by May 1987. And, in the final days of the campaign itself, a concerted attack by

Lawson's Treasury team on the Labour Party's spending and tax plans had destroyed the remaining slim chance that Neil Kinnock might replace Margaret Thatcher in Downing Street.

By now the chancellor was widely acknowledged as the intellectual force behind many of the other reforms which made up the Thatcher revolution. His Budgets had combined income tax cuts with a radical shake-up of the structure of business and personal taxation. The City's so-called 'Big Bang' in the autumn of 1986, which scrapped traditional Stock Exchange demarcation lines and opened the market to overseas banks and securities companies, completed the process of financial liberalization. Lawson was the most powerful advocate of the privatization programme, one of the firmest enemies of trade-union power, the standard-bearer of 'popular capitalism' for the masses. It was hardly surprising that for a few months after the 1987 election victory Lawson was seen, for the first and only time in his political career, as a potential prime minister. The mass-circulation *Sun* newspaper, not known until then as one of his greatest admirers, caught the Tory mood in a lavishly complimentary editorial which concluded, 'When at last Mrs Thatcher does step down they need look no further than Mr Lawson to find a leader of equal calibre.'[19] More aware than some of his admirers of his lack of a firm political following at Westminster, this was not an image Lawson cultivated, but he became ever more sure of his own convictions.

The policy of shadowing the Deutschmark which would bring such grief to chancellor and prime minister had started with the Louvre accord to stabilize the dollar. The 22 February agreement was reached by the G5 finance ministers from the US, Japan, Germany, France and Britain plus Canada. (Italy boycotted the meeting because it had been left outside the inner circle, but it would later be admitted when the G5 finance ministers' group was formally enlarged to mirror that of the G7 heads of government.) The essence of the pact was a commitment to stabilize the dollar. Since the Plaza accord in September 1985, the US currency's value against the Deutschmark and the yen had more than halved. Putting aside the tension of the previous autumn between the Bundesbank and Washington, the finance ministers agreed on a new phase of cooperation. Japan and

Germany offered further action to sustain growth in their economies, and the US signed up to a commitment to joint intervention by the central banks to prop up the dollar. Politically the moving force was once again James Baker, but the mechanics of the agreement, settled during talks at the Louvre headquarters of the French finance ministry, were hammered out by the central bankers. Karl Otto Pöhl, Jacques de Larosière, the governor of the Banque de France, and Paul Volcker of the Federal Reserve were the guiding forces. The deal involved a series of loose target zones for the dollar against the German and Japanese currencies. If the dollar moved by more than 2.5 per cent above or below DM1.825 or 152.5 yen, the central banks would consider intervening to support it. If the movement was as much as 5 per cent, central bank intervention up to a total of $4bn would be obligatory. In the tradition of the Plaza accord, the agreement was announced with a fanfare to persuade financial markets of the central banks' resolve. Some saw it as a decisive step on the road to a return to an international system of managed, if not fixed, exchange rates.

Nigel Lawson was little more than a bystander at the main event, but a shrewd one. Sterling's rate against the dollar was not included in the new 'reference ranges' agreed by the finance ministers, but the chancellor saw an opportunity to harness the fire-power of other central banks to his own cause of putting a floor under the value of the pound. Sterling by now stood at below DM2.80. The Treasury had made it clear it would resist any further depreciation, and an undershoot in the public-sector borrowing requirement helped to underpin the confidence in the pound. The chancellor, however, knew from experience the fragile nature of such confidence, and that a renewed bout of speculation would threaten both his March Budget and the government's electoral strategy. So, at a private briefing for British journalists in one of the Louvre's splendid staterooms, Lawson dropped a heavy hint that sterling would indeed enjoy protection from the international accord. He indicated that he would now set a ceiling as well as the previously announced floor for fluctuations in sterling's value. Reminding the journalists that he had made it clear for several months that he did not want to see any further fall in the exchange rate, Lawson said, 'By the same token I have no wish to see a substantial rise.'[20] The message journalists duly took to the financial markets was that, while he would be happy to see some appreciation in the exchange rate, the chancellor was ready to resist too sharp a rise.

He had now chosen, in effect, to ignore the advice he had offered less than a year earlier in his Lombard Association speech. Then he had said it would be impossible to set any target range for the pound as long as it remained outside the ERM; now he did just that. It was not long before the currency markets put in place the ceiling which Lawson saw as the counterpoint to the DM2.80 floor. The pound rose strongly in the weeks after the agreement, quickly reaching DM2.95. The Treasury responded with two half-point cuts in interest rates in quick succession. The markets saw the cuts as signalling that the chancellor had in mind a ceiling of DM3.00. By his own account, Lawson decided to validate this assumption during a meeting of senior Treasury and Bank officials on 18 March.[21] The Bank was instructed to intervene by selling sterling in the markets if it approached DM3.00.

Lawson meanwhile did his best to entrench in the minds of the media and the financial markets the fact that he was serious about stabilizing the pound. The economic forecasts in his Budget on 17 March included for the first time an explicit assumption that the exchange rate over the following year would remain close to its existing levels. Speaking to economics correspondents the next day, the chancellor went as far as he could towards admitting a firm target for the pound. He would not confirm the existence of a precise range, because 'Unless you are part of a formal exchange rate mechanism ... then tactics in the foreign exchange markets are assisted if you don't try to be precise.' But, yes, it was 'certainly conceivable' that the Treasury had more specific private objectives.[22]

Another such encounter came at the beginning of April. Lawson was attending a meeting of the National Economic Development Office (NEDO), the tripartite forum for government, industry and trade unions. Setting out his hopes for exchange rate stability, he remarked that sterling's value against the Deutschmark was 'the most important single rate we want to concentrate on'. Stability would be achieved by 'an appropriate mixture of interest rates and intervention in the foreign exchange markets'. For those at the NEDO meeting who did not follow day-to-day fluctuations in the pound's value, he added that it currently stood at around DM2.90 and $1.60. His press secretary did nothing to dissuade journalists from believing that Lawson had now established an informal target range for the currency, centred on a mid-rate of DM2.90.

This time the tactic backfired. The appearance of his remarks on newspaper front pages on 2 April was received frostily in 10 Downing Street. Margaret Thatcher, who had just returned from a trip to Moscow, left the Treasury in no doubt of her anger that a new economic policy appeared to have been put in place during her brief absence. Lawson was obliged to retract. Briefing economic journalists that same day in the drawing-room of 11 Downing Street, ahead of a meeting of the IMF in Washington, he blamed the press for misinterpreting his comments. The precision attributed to his desire for exchange rate stability was spurious invention, he said – he had done nothing more than remind NEDO members of the prevailing rates on the market. His officials knew otherwise, and Brian Griffiths in 10 Downing Street made no secret of the prime minister's ire. There was another awkward coincidence for the chancellor. Statistics published on the same day showed that the Bank's foreign currency reserves had risen by $1.8bn in March – the largest increase in a single month for a decade: proof, if any was needed, of the policy which Lawson had been obliged to disavow. The row over sterling was becoming ever more public.

The real battle of wills, however, came later – after the general election victory on 9 June 1987. Lawson had headed the group of ministers, advisers and MPs drafting the economic section of the Conservative Party's manifesto for the election. He had secured the agreement of the group that the manifesto should include a firm commitment to take sterling into the ERM. Thatcher insisted on its deletion from the final document. She would remark caustically in her memoirs, 'This approach never made its way into the manifesto but somehow it made its way into policy.'[23]

During the campaign, Lawson promised a thorough review of the ERM once the Conservatives had secured a third term. Business leaders and bankers were pressing actively for sterling's membership, to put an end to the rollercoaster of unpredictable fluctuations which they had endured since 1979, but Lawson's candour alarmed some Treasury officials. They were pessimistic about the prospects of a change of heart in No. 10 and did not want to raise expectations in the markets. In mid-campaign, on 2 June, Lawson offered an unequivocal commitment to a detailed post-election review. On the same day the monthly statistics for the foreign exchange reserves showed an unprecedented increase of $4.8bn in May – the result of massive Bank of England intervention to keep sterling below DM3.00. On the election trail Lawson was not shy of taking the credit for the flood of overseas money into the pound. A rising exchange rate was evidence, he insisted, of the widespread confidence in his economic management. Watching from the relative tranquillity of the Treasury, his officials were quietly amused at this new yardstick for his performance. What would the chancellor say when sterling fell again – that investors had lost confidence?

Lawson waited until July, the month after the election, to raise formally the ERM issue with the prime minister. Intervention to cap the pound's value had added $9bn to the reserves since the spring. The dollar had stabilized in the wake of the Louvre accord, and industry seemed content with an exchange rate of just below DM3.00. In the chancellor's mind, that rate was also in line with a sustainable level for sterling over the medium term. Purchasing-power parity calculations, measuring the relative spending power of different currencies at particular exchange rates, appeared to support that view. So too did more direct comparisons of the competitiveness of British and West German industry. By now, of course, Lawson had discarded the studied indifference to Britain's manufacturing performance which characterized the first years of his chancellorship. It seemed to make good sense to shield British industry from a sharp rise in sterling's value if the odds were that it would soon be followed by an equally precipitate fall. There were other favourable indicators. Inflation was steady at around 4 per cent, and public borrowing once again seemed set to undershoot its £4bn target for the year.

Margaret Thatcher was not interested in the backdrop, favourable or otherwise. In her mind Lawson's constant pressure now represented a challenge to her authority to which she could not yield. When he broached the subject on 23 July 1987 she dismissed his arguments. Once again she was forearmed with ammunition supplied by Alan Walters and Brian Griffiths. She said that joining the system would be an admission that the government could not run its own anti-inflation policy. It would limit its flexibility over interest rates, and force higher borrowing costs when sterling was under pressure. Lawson asked for a further review in the autumn, but she was not prepared to discuss the subject again until the new year. Nor, the prime minister insisted, would there ever be another ministerial review along the lines of that in November 1985.

At a Whitehall cocktail party some weeks later one of her aides confided that Thatcher had indeed decided when the time would be right for entry to the ERM – never. By now she habitually reminded colleagues of sterling's fall since the autumn of 1985, when she had last been pressed to bind sterling to the Deutschmark. Had she given way to Lawson then, she would remark, the government would have been humiliated by at least one and probably two or three enforced devaluations within the ERM. The architect of the election victory, the hero of the Tory back benches, Lawson was left with a painful choice. He could persist with his policy of stabilizing the exchange rate outside the system or he could admit defeat and seek to construct an entirely new economic strategy. The chancellor was as strong-willed as the prime minister he confronted. He took the former course.

CHAPTER FOUR

SHADOWS IN DOWNING STREET

THE MOST REMARKABLE FEATURE of Nigel Lawson's ill-fated attempt to shadow the Deutschmark was that it was never formally enunciated as government policy. For a year from the spring of 1987 the effort to hold sterling steady against the West German currency was the centre-piece of the Treasury's economic strategy. It was the first time since the short-lived experiment with the European Snake in 1973 that a British government had set a firm target for the exchange rate. There could be no secret about its actions: the Bank of England's extraordinary and unprecedented intervention in foreign exchange markets to cap sterling's value could not be concealed from the outside world. The Bank's foreign currency reserves more than doubled within a year as it sought to keep the pound below DM3.00. The conflict between Nigel Lawson and Margaret Thatcher, however, required that the policy was never officially proclaimed.

Treasury policies are generally the product of exhaustive internal debate, first between the chancellor and officials, then between Treasury and Bank, and finally between the chancellor and the prime minister. Papers are drafted, meetings held, arguments encouraged, and political compromises reached before a policy is unveiled publicly. Important policy pronouncements are delivered in set-piece speeches by the chancellor, typically in the Budget or in the annual address at the Mansion House. There was no such detailed discussion about capping the pound at DM3.00, nor was there any formal announcement: this policy just happened. This central plank of the government's economic strategy was never spelled out, never buttressed by detailed analysis or parliamentary debate.

Robin Leigh-Pemberton and Eddie George, responsible for the massive intervention needed to implement the policy, regularly discussed the operational issues. As one Bank official puts it, 'Our intervention instructions were clear – don't let the pound rise above DM3.00.' Leigh-Pemberton was content with the strategy until early 1988, hoping it would act as a catalyst for sterling's eventual entry into the ERM. He was, however, never asked to consider at the outset the basic proposition that the anchor for the government's anti-inflation policy should be an unannounced target for sterling. Eddie George would later tell colleagues, 'At no point did Nigel Lawson tell us there was to be a policy of shadowing the Deutschmark.'

Peter Middleton and Terence Burns at the Treasury were closest to Lawson as the policy evolved. When the chancellor saw in the Louvre accord the opportunity to stabilize the pound, his senior officials were in broad agreement. The devaluation of 1986 had gone further than the Treasury had expected, prompting fears of accelerating inflation. The international agreement to stabilize the dollar offered a convenient shelter for sterling. But the internal discussions did not keep pace with changing circumstances: what started off as a useful tactic became, almost by a process of osmosis, a central strategic goal. The initial aim of preventing any further depreciation had developed into one of halting an appreciation. As one official intimately involved in operating the policy would reflect ruefully, 'We all knew what we were doing. The mistake was never to analyse why we were doing it.'

Lawson subsequently insisted that there had been a solid official consensus behind the strategy at every stage, but others have a slightly different recollection. One official insists, 'It was exclusively a Lawson policy ... You will not find any papers in the Treasury setting out the policy of shadowing the Deutschmark.' As time went by some senior officials began to voice serious misgivings. Memories of past failures to outwit the financial markets were etched on the Treasury's collective memory. Harold Wilson's humiliation in 1967 was part of the folklore of the building, as was the capitulation to the IMF in 1976. Another senior official explains the position thus:

> The approach until 1987 had been to ride with the markets. At difficult moments, policy would give a bit – on interest rates, on public borrowing or on the exchange rate. The key point was we were not trying to beat the markets. The problem with an exchange rate target is that it quickly develops into a trial of strength with the markets. They usually win.

There was no clear perception of where the policy would lead. No one anticipated a struggle with the financial markets lasting more than a year. There were also moments early on when the DM3.00 ceiling might have been lifted. One such occasion was in May 1987, when Eddie George, established as the Bank's most influential adviser in its dealings with Lawson, voiced concern about the implication for inflation. He saw the logic of seeking to avoid before the election a sudden surge in the pound's value which might be followed by an equally precipitate post-election fall; by mid-May, however, he was worried about the scale of the required intervention and advised the Treasury that the pound should be uncapped. Events dictated otherwise: three days after the Bank's warning, Thatcher set the election date for 9 June. Any change in economic policy would have to wait.

Nigel Lawson had good reason not to unveil formally the policy of shadowing the Deutschmark: to have done so would have required the approval of the prime minister. An undeclared strategy avoided, for a time, the inevitable confrontation. It helped that the upward pressure on sterling came in fits and starts: the Bank's purchases of foreign currency to maintain the ceiling were massive but irregular. In August 1987 it actually sold some of the newly acquired reserves when the pound, temporarily, fell against the dollar. Margaret Thatcher's later claim that she was unaware of Lawson's strategy until questioned about it in November 1987 by journalists from the *Financial Times* is challenged by officials. If it was true – and it was – that she did not receive any formal presentation, most of the Bank's intervention showed up in the published figures for the official currency reserves: they soared from $22bn at the end of 1986 to $35bn in September 1987. In addition, 10 Downing Street received daily, confidential, break-downs of the Bank's operations in the currency markets. Thatcher's private office included a senior official on secondment from the Treasury whose role was to keep her closely in touch with economic policy. Brian Griffiths had a similar responsibility, and on occasion Thatcher would talk to Peter Middleton directly. More prosaically, the front pages of most newspapers carried regular reports of the unprecedented efforts being made to stabilize the pound.

Whatever their doubts about his sterling policy, the more serious disputes between the chancellor and his closest advisers during 1987 were over fiscal rather than monetary policy. Burns opposed the 2p cut in the basic rate of income tax which preceded the general election. He argued in the autumn against the dramatic package of tax reductions which followed in the 1988 Budget. He was never convinced by the argument that a shrinking tax base would provide the Treasury with additional ammunition in the constant battle to contain the growth of public spending. He believed the government should first set its spending target and only then fix the appropriate levels of taxation.

The chancellor was not alone during 1987 in promoting the benefits of a stable pound. After the wild gyrations of the previous eight years, industry craved a period of order. The Confederation of British Industry's support for sterling's participation in the ERM was echoed widely by chief executives of large corporations and banks. Most of the City's influential economists joined the chorus. The disintegration of the government's domestic monetary policy had left the exchange rate as the only obvious anchor for an anti-inflation strategy. Most economists agreed with Lawson that, outside of the shelter of the ERM, it was only a matter of time before sterling would once again begin to depreciate.

The political background was also favourable. There were some on the Conservative back benches who would always lament the passing of monetarism. Nicholas Budgen, a member of the Treasury and Civil Service Committee, was among those who always looked for opportunities to harass the chancellor during his appearances before MPs, and two other right-wing MPs on the committee, Neil Hamilton and John Townend, were similarly critical. All three combined an allegiance to the monetarist cause with a deep scepticism about Britain's entanglement in Europe. Their views were not, however, representative of the broad mass of opinion on the Tory back benches. This held that, as long as the chancellor delivered economic success, there was little point in ideological disputes about the precise means. The party was at a point when it still looked to the advantages of Europe rather than the intrusions, and the Eurosceptics, rather than the Europhiles, were in the minority.

There was a similar mood within the cabinet. Jealous of his

prerogative, Lawson rarely discussed his economic strategy with colleagues. Lord Whitelaw and Peter Brooke, a middle-ranking Treasury minister and, for a time, party chairman, were his only real confidants. The balance of the cabinet, however, was pro-European. Lawson's reappointment to the Treasury after the 1987 election was accompanied by Geoffrey Howe's return to the Foreign Office. Douglas Hurd, a staunch European who had served as an aide to Edward Heath during the negotiations on Britain's entry, was given the third great office of state, the Home Office. Kenneth Clarke, rising fast through the ministerial ranks, was still more enthusiastic about closer cooperation. Others who counted themselves in the same camp were Peter Walker, George Younger and Malcolm Rifkind. Nicholas Ridley, Lord Young and Kenneth Baker were early members of the sceptical camp, but there was little doubt that, if the issue had been put to cabinet, Lawson would have won overwhelming support for ERM membership.

The Labour Party meanwhile was on the threshold of a major shift in policy which, within two years, would reverse its previous hostility to a fixed exchange rate. It was partly opportunism: once it was clear that the prime minister had overruled her chancellor on the issue it made good political sense to maximize the significance of the division. Neil Kinnock, however, also had more fundamental reasons. Labour's defeat in the 1987 election had been assured by the voters' perception that it had dumped the form rather than the substance of the earlier anti-European, interventionist, policies which had led to its brutal defeat in 1983. Labour was seen as the party of high spending, high taxes and high inflation, and a readiness to devalue the pound appeared to offer evidence that it had not mended its socialist ways. John Smith, appointed shadow chancellor after the 1987 election, came quickly to the view that support for the ERM would be a powerful symbol of the party's return to economic orthodoxy.

Despite Thatcher's rebuff in July 1987, Lawson continued to insist that the question remained *when* rather than *if* sterling would join the exchange rate mechanism. The upward pressure on sterling had eased during August, and the Treasury had taken the opportunity to raise interest rates from 9 to 10 per cent in response to evidence that the economy had begun to expand at an unsustainably rapid pace. At a September meeting of European Community finance ministers in Nyborg, Denmark, Lawson joined several other finance ministers in pressing the Bundesbank for a series of technical changes to the ERM. The adjustments – strengthening the intervention arrangements to support weak currencies in the system – were hardly revolutionary, but they tilted the balance of mutual obligations. Central banks with weaker currencies could in future expect more help from the Bundesbank. Lawson thought the accord bolstered further the case for sterling's membership. He told his European colleagues in Nyborg that the issue was 'closely under review' and encouraged Karl Otto Pöhl in the view that the decision to join would soon be made.

The tension between 10 and 11 Downing Street re-emerged at the end of September 1987. Lawson, now relishing the world stage, used the annual meeting of the IMF in Washington to set out his ambitions for a new international economic order. This was the moment when the Thatcher government's claim to have effected a renaissance in Britain's economic and political performance was gaining acceptance. The economy was strong and the prime minister's unchallenged political authority at home and her close relationship with President Ronald Reagan appeared to have restored Britain's international influence. The chancellor enjoyed the new-found esteem. In his IMF speech he called for a decisive break with the system of free-floating exchange rates which had replaced Bretton Woods in the early 1970s. To the surprise of many among his fellow finance ministers and central bankers, Lawson proposed that the informal bands for the dollar, yen and Deutschmark established six months earlier at the Louvre should form the basis of a shift to a permanent regime of 'managed exchange rates'. Urging an agreed economic framework among the G7 nations, he said, 'Our objectives should be clear: to maintain the maximum stability of key exchange rates and to manage any changes that may be necessary in an orderly way.' An extension of the disciplines of the ERM to include the dollar and the yen would allow governments to contain movements in their currencies within relatively narrow bands constructed around agreed central rates. 'Henceforth, larger fluctuations in the value of the world's major currencies would be on the basis of periodic realignments of these central rates.'[1] It was a bold proposal, even if it echoed the long-standing French demand for international currency target zones (which Lawson had previously scorned) and coincided with a call by James Baker for a new exchange rate system anchored to the prices of basic commodities, including gold.

Lawson had thought carefully about the idea during a summer break in Sardinia. Returning to the Treasury in early September he had handed Terence Burns a sheet of paper with a list of the points he wanted to make in the IMF speech. The text then went through a number of drafts over several weeks in close consultation with Burns and Robert Culpin. Despite his doubts about the ERM, Burns had become increasingly interested in the possibility of a new international framework for international exchange rates. He had long seen the exchange rate as the principal transmission mechanism for domestic inflation. The speech had not won universal approval in the Treasury, however. Peter Middleton had been happy with the early drafts but became increasingly uneasy as the proposals became more ambitious. Geoffrey Littler, better placed than anyone else to judge the reaction of the finance ministers of the other main industrial nations, was sceptical that the idea would go anywhere. There was also disquiet in the Bank of England. Eddie George was alarmed at a section which suggested that domestic inflation objectives would occasionally have to be sacrificed to the goal of exchange rate stability. He feared Lawson was preparing to give priority to sterling's Deutschmark ceiling over the interest rate rises which might be needed to forestall an upsurge in inflation. In the chancellor's mind, George appeared too anxious not to offend Thatcher: George's promotion hopes rested on maintaining a good relationship with the prime minister.

Lawson did not inform the prime minister in advance of what, by any standards, was a radical scheme. The final draft was completed only in Washington, and Thatcher received her copy as the speech was delivered. She was furious, convinced that the chancellor was seeking to circumvent her veto of ERM membership – a view shared, incidentally, by some of his own officials. Brian Griffiths soon let it be known on Thatcher's behalf that Lawson's grand design did not meet with her approval. In the event, she need not have worried. As it turned out, the September 1987 IMF meeting would mark the high-water mark of international economic cooperation. The differences between Washington and Bonn which triggered the world stock markets' crash a few weeks later and the departure of Baker from the US Treasury the following year saw the grand international designs of the mid-1980s give way to a sombre realization that governments had neither the will nor the wherewithal to tame the markets they had set free fifteen years earlier.

There were other points of strain in Lawson's relationship with the Bank. Leigh-Pemberton, more perceptive than sometimes assumed but lacking a formal grounding in economics, was no match for a self-assured, economically literate chancellor determined to keep a personal grip on the levers of power. The governor understood the constraints on his authority. He decided at the outset that he could not win a confrontation with Lawson. The Bank of England Act, under which the Bank had been nationalized in 1946, was clear: real power rests with the Treasury. The Treasury owns the foreign currency reserves, has responsibility for any decisions on interest rates, and has the final say over operations in the government securities, or gilt-edged, market. The Bank essentially is its agent. The governor, formally, is appointed by the monarch, but in reality the choice lies with the prime minister.

Leigh-Pemberton's view was that any trial of strength would further weaken the Bank by provoking Lawson into a more formal assertion of Treasury control. His caution was reinforced by the chancellor's frequent public assertion of his authority. Leigh-Pemberton's colleagues, worried about the erosion of the Bank's standing in its traditional spheres of influence, thought the relationship should be tested. The chancellor's insistence on directing short-term tactics in the money and foreign exchange markets as well as longer-term strategy caused intense irritation. Protracted discussions about the principle of interest rate decisions would be followed by long, technical, arguments over just how and when the Bank should signal the agreed decision. Lawson insisted also on dictating the Bank's 'line to take' when briefing journalists on such decisions. On other occasions he would break with the carefully agreed conventions and telephone directly the traders in the Bank's money market and foreign exchange dealing-rooms. The Bank's frustration sometimes showed: during one meeting in 1987, Eddie George called an abrupt halt to

Lawson's interference. 'I think that decision can be left to us, Chancellor,' he snapped.

The Bank's irritation was reinforced by the chancellor's vetting of its public statements. By custom, a draft copy of the Bank's *Quarterly Bulletin* was sent to the Treasury in advance of publication. The introductory commentary, written at the time by John Flemming, the chief economist, gave the Bank's view of the balance of monetary and fiscal policy and of the economic outlook. Its phrasing was consciously elliptical, but for close observers of the economic scene the *Bulletin* was a useful counterpoint to the unalloyed optimism of ministerial speeches. Lawson saw no reason why it should question, even delicately, the strategy he was pursuing. The advance drafts would be returned by Alex Allan, Lawson's private secretary, with demands for substantial amendments. To the chagrin of many of his officials, Leigh-Pemberton usually bowed to Lawson's demands. Bank officials responded by 'decoding' the text in the off-the-record briefings for journalists which preceded publication of the *Bulletin*.

The atmosphere was not improved by other disputes, most notably over the government's sale of its remaining shareholding in BP immediately after the stock-market crash in the autumn of 1987. The Bank wanted to abort the flotation; Lawson insisted it went ahead. It was rescued by the establishment of a sophisticated safety-net to limit the potential losses of the merchant banks and securities houses committed in advance to buying the shares. The successful arrangement, however, was followed by a petty but bitter dispute between the Treasury and Bank over the authorship of the scheme. Lawson suggested George had unfairly claimed the credit for the idea. The two men had clashed before, but George regarded Lawson's behaviour over BP as of a different order. Fuming for several weeks afterwards, he seriously considered resignation.

The row in Downing Street over Lawson's IMF speech coincided with Thatcher's growing unease about the level of intervention. It was a concern, incidentally, which appeared to undermine Thatcher's later insistence that she had been unaware of Lawson's strategy. Her attitude to intervention, like her responses to fluctuations in the value of the pound, was unpredictable. Instinctively, she welcomed the accumulation of large amounts of foreign currency by the Bank. During the early months of 1987 she was fond of asking Leigh-Pemberton how much he had 'taken in' to the reserves on this or that day.

During the autumn of 1987, however, her attitude changed. A renewed slide in the value of the dollar – encouraged by another spat between the US administration and the Bundesbank – meant that the Bank of England was accumulating a depreciating asset. The dollars piling up in the reserves were falling in value day by day. The objective was to stabilize the pound against the West German currency, but the Bank did so by buying dollars – the medium for the vast bulk of foreign exchange transactions. Thatcher did not much approve of the idea of filling the vaults of the Bank with a currency whose value was depreciating. Griffiths and Walters warned her of another danger: intervention boosted the domestic money supply as the Bank supplied sterling in exchange for the foreign currency. The excess cash could be mopped up over time by sales of gilt-edged securities – the so-called 'sterilization' process – and Lawson offered frequent assurances that the intervention would indeed be sterilized, but unreconstructed monetarists still saw an inflationary threat.

The world stock-market crash on 19 October briefly forestalled a clash between Lawson and Thatcher. The chancellor announced two successive half-point reductions in interest rates between mid-October and early November as Britain's contribution to an international effort to restore confidence. The trigger for the collapse in world equity markets was the unresolved dispute between the US and West Germany. This undercut confidence in the commitment to a stable dollar, and Wall Street and other world stock markets followed the US currency down. For a short period, there were fears of a 1930s-style depression. However, the crisis passed more quickly than most had imagined, and by December the G7 nations had restored a façade of unity in their policy towards the dollar. Later Lawson would cite the misleading signals from the crash – the economy recovered rapidly from the blow to confidence – as a significant factor in the late 1980s boom. His justified anxiety to avoid a 1930s slump persuaded him to cut interest rates for a third time in early December.

At 8.5 per cent, borrowing costs were at their lowest level since 1984. Lawson, it would turn out, had taken his foot off the monetary brake at just the wrong moment.

On 22 November Margaret Thatcher used what had become an annual interview on economic policy with the *Financial Times* openly to disavow the exchange rate policy of her chancellor. Lawson, in his Mansion House speech less than three weeks earlier, had reinforced his commitment to a stable pound. He told his audience on 4 November that they should be in no doubt about the government's commitment 'to maintain a stable exchange rate, with the rate against the Deutschmark of particular importance.' He repeated his call for an international system of 'managed floating' for the most important currencies, and underscored a continuing commitment to the Louvre framework. As for sterling, stability 'gives industry what it wants, and provides a firm anchor against inflation'.[2] The day before, the Treasury had announced that the currency reserves had risen by a record $6.7bn in October as a result of the Bank's intervention to cap the pound.

The prime minister, however, denied in the strongest terms that there was any target for sterling. 'The Deutschmark at the moment is slightly deflationary. That means that the whole of Europe is geared to a slightly deflationary policy,' she told her *FT* interviewers. She was eager to elaborate: 'Now, we have not been so geared and we have had a greater degree of freedom in relation to both the dollar and the Deutschmark and I just think that I am grateful for that.' And then, 'There is no specific range [for sterling] . . . We are always free.' Thatcher was by now challenging the basic commitment to eventual participation in the ERM: 'We are not confined to any particular limits and I do not like us to be, because to do that is to tempt people to have a go and you cannot beat a speculator except over a short period.' Whatever the Treasury might say, there was no long-term commitment to shadow the West German currency. Everyone knew that the government could 'come off' the present policy whenever it wanted. As for grandiose schemes to fix international exchange rates, she was dismissive. 'Sound' policies were what counted.[3]

The Treasury was horrified by her remarks. It employed all of its Jesuitical talents to argue that the differences between Downing Street neighbours were of tone rather than substance. Over lunch the following day, a senior Treasury official offered a franker assessment: 'She has blown him [Lawson] out of the water,' he commented. 'The only thing I cannot understand is why people are still buying sterling.'

The chancellor's annoyance revealed itself two weeks later, when, on 9 December, he appeared before the Treasury and Civil Service Committee. Lawson was distinctly tetchy. Under pressure from Neil Hamilton, a right-wing Conservative, he restated his commitment to exchange rate stability: 'Keeping the pound in line with the Deutschmark is likely to be over the medium term a pretty good anti-inflationary discipline.' Pressed repeatedly by Giles Radice, one of the Labour MPs on the committee, about the differences with Thatcher revealed by her interview, Lawson replied abruptly: 'If you want any further elucidation of the prime minister's remarks, I suggest you invite her to appear before this committee.' It was during this session with the committee that Lawson admitted also that he had effectively abandoned any predetermined framework for interest rate decisions. The economy was being run on the basis of his subjective assessment of the balance between growth and inflation. As far as interest rates were concerned, 'When I think they ought to go up they go up and when I think they should come down they come down.'[4]

Thatcher recorded subsequently that it was only during the *FT* interview that she discovered that Lawson was pursuing a 'personal economic policy' by shadowing the Deutschmark.[5] A Whitehall aide offered a more plausible explanation: 'The prime minister wanted to change Lawson's policy. The best way to do that was to state publicly that it did not exist.'

The row over the Deutschmark exposed more fundamental differences in their approach to economic management. Lawson was forever in search of sophisticated intellectual frameworks – rules to contain public spending, balanced-budget doctrines, exchange rate systems – into which he could slot day-to-day management of the economy. Thatcher's instinct was to hang on to a few eternal verities. She was attracted to the 'flat-earth' monetarists who inhabited the fringes of economics during the 1970s and 1980s. As one Treasury official put it, 'Swiss academics in pebble glasses would forever be turning up at No. 10.' Thatcher was not self-conscious about the apparent contradictions in her approach. Her government had thrown off the regulatory shackles which had rationed credit throughout the 1960s and 1970s, but she was horrified when banks sent customers unsolicited credit cards. She demanded low inflation but also low interest rates. She was impressed by the anecdotal evidence proffered by a stream of admiring visitors to No. 10, and would respond to Lawson's careful expositions by recalling that this or that businessman thought growth too sluggish or credit expansion too fast. For all his loyalty to the prime minister, Charles Powell, Thatcher's favourite private secretary, was among those who sympathized with Lawson's frustration when a careful, intellectually coherent case, was dismissed with a dubious anecdote. Sometimes, however, her intuition was underestimated: she was worried before many others about the credit explosion and the widening trade gap which proved to be cause and symptom of the late 1980s boom.

As Thatcher became ever less restrained in her public comments, Lawson became ever more determined not to give in. He looked forward to the 1988 Budget as the apogee of his chancellorship. Public borrowing was falling rapidly, providing the scope for the radical cuts in income tax at the centre of his ambitions. The monetary side of the original Medium Term Financial Strategy was in ruins because of the wayward behaviour of the money supply, but the fiscal position was better than Lawson had ever hoped for. The public-sector borrowing requirement had been all but eliminated, and in the 1987/88 financial year the Treasury would record a surplus (a public-sector debt repayment, or PSDR) for the first time since Roy Jenkins's chancellorship. These were heady days. The buoyancy of tax revenues meant that Lawson could promise the 'hat trick' of a budget surplus, increased public spending and sizeable reductions in income tax rates. Meanwhile, the bubble of confidence in the foreign exchange markets meant that, for once, the pressure on sterling was upwards. Interest rates were as low as they had ever been since the Conservative victory in 1979. After stumbling briefly in the wake of the stock-market crash, the economy had resumed its strong growth. In retrospect, these were the ingredients for an unsustainable, inflationary boom; but at the end of 1987 the prospects seemed intoxicating.

There was a moment in December 1987 when Lawson did consider 'uncapping' the pound. By now some of his advisers had become distinctly nervous about the build-up of credit in the economy, reflected in an annual growth rate for sterling M3 of more than 20 per cent. There were other warning signals – from soaring house prices and from a deteriorating trade position. The current account had gone into deficit in 1986 for the first time since 1979. In 1987 the gap was £5bn. It was widening rapidly, and was to reach an unprecedented £22bn two years later. Eddie George voiced concern that policy had become too loose despite the blow to confidence caused by the stock-markets crash. The massive intervention needed to hold sterling below DM3.00 threatened to reignite inflation. One of the informal group of outside independent advisers – the so-called 'Gooies', whom Lawson now consulted regularly on his economic strategy – also warned of the risk of accelerating price rises. Samuel Brittan, the economics commentator of the *Financial Times*, was one of the staunchest supporters of Lawson's attempts to stabilize the exchange rate. In 1987, however, he wondered whether the chancellor's chosen ceiling for sterling was not too low. The intervention required to maintain stability had reached unprecedented levels. On one day alone, 3 December, the Bank was obliged to buy more than $1bn in foreign currency. At a meeting ten days later at the Treasury, Lawson accepted the advice of his officials that sterling should be allowed to breach the DM3.00 ceiling. But the upward pressure on sterling temporarily eased, and the cap was kept in place.

Thatcher returned in December to the issue of intervention. Alan Walters, still in touch from Washington, warned that the Treasury was trying to 'bounce' her into ERM membership. She also became alarmed about the potential losses faced by the Bank on its dollar purchases. The Bank's intervention since the beginning of the year had totalled $27bn, though the full amount had not yet shown up in the published figures for its reserves. Some of the increase could be attributed to the international support operation to prop up the dollar, but most was a direct consequence of shadowing the Deutschmark. With the US currency worth nearly 8 per cent less than at the start of the year, back-of-an-envelope calculations circulating in the City suggested that the Bank faced unrealized exchange rate losses of between $1bn and $1.5bn.

Reports of the putative losses began to appear in the press. Lawson insisted that it was impossible to calculate potential losses or gains but, under pressure, agreed that the Bank should switch its intervention to the sterling/Deutschmark market. The move provoked strong protests from the Bundesbank, which invoked a long-standing convention that intervention in a particular currency can take place only with the permission of the issuing central bank. The Bundesbank had long been hostile to the accumulation by other central banks of large Deutschmark deposits, fearing they would weaken its control over its domestic monetary policy. It held its own reserves entirely in dollars. Though not a member of the ERM, Britain was bound by the rules of the wider European Monetary System. The Banque de France, fearful that Bank of England purchases of Deutschmarks would put downward pressure on the franc, also protested. Leigh-Pemberton, more conscious than Lawson of the need to preserve the goodwill of other European central banks, insisted on a written Treasury instruction before he would agree to carry out the new policy. With Thatcher determined not to allow further purchases of dollars, Lawson finally settled on a compromise under which the Bank's intervention was spread across several currencies, including the French and Swiss francs and the Japanese yen as well as the Deutschmark. Leigh-Pemberton remained far from happy with the outcome, and the protests from the Bundesbank continued, but Lawson was adamant.

The real trial of strength between Lawson and Thatcher, however, took place in early March 1988. The first weeks of the year had seen the upward pressure on sterling abate, largely because a fall in the value of the dollar triggered a more general appreciation of the Deutschmark. Under pressure from his Treasury and Bank advisers, Lawson nudged up interest rates from 8.5 per cent to 9 per cent in early February. The Bank was concerned none the less about the visible inflationary pressures in the economy and the prospect that Lawson would compound the risks of an unsustainable boom with large tax cuts in his March Budget. Lawson had laid out his tax-cutting strategy at the traditional Chevening meeting with his advisers in January. He was determined to reduce the top rate from 60p to 40p and, to balance the clear benefits for the wealthy, to reduce the basic rate from 27p to 25p. Terence Burns was deeply uncomfortable with the proposals, wanting a tighter fiscal stance, but his own, wayward economic forecasts suggested that the cuts could be accommodated. Because revenues were so buoyant, the forecasts indicated that the tax cuts, worth £6bn in a full financial year, could be made without actually reducing the overall share of national income taken by tax. As for the inflationary consequences, the Treasury's economists thought that the economy was certain to slow down during the following year. The errant forecasts would cost dear.

Burns's discomfiture was shared in Threadneedle Street. At the briefing which accompanied the publication in February of the *Quarterly Bulletin*, senior officials indicated they had pressed Lawson to adopt a 'prudent' fiscal stance.[6] Some time afterwards a Bank official would charge that a similar warning in the Bulletin itself had been 'toned down' on the instructions of the chancellor. Provisional figures for gross domestic product meanwhile confirmed the rapid pace of growth in the economy: output had risen by over 4.5 per cent in 1987 – the fastest rate of expansion since the Barber boom. Provisional trade figures showed a widening in the current-account deficit to a record £900 million in the single month of January. The signs of an overheating economy were multiplying.

By the time sterling threatened once again to break through the DM3.00 ceiling, during the first week of March, the Bank was extremely uncomfortable with Lawson's policy. An acceleration in the pace of pay awards had confirmed its conviction that interest rates should rise, but that conflicted directly with the cap on sterling. During the two days of 2 and 3 March the Bank was forced to buy $1.8bn worth of foreign currency to hold the pound steady. At a meeting in the Treasury on Friday 4 March, Eddie George recommended that the pound should be uncapped: intervention on this scale was unsustainable. Easing the pressure would require a cut in interest rates, when what the economy required was an increase. Burns and Middleton took the same view, but Lawson wanted to hold the line until his 15 March Budget. He was pre-empted by Thatcher, who summoned him later on the same day to a meeting in No. 10. Her instructions were blunt: the intervention should cease on the following Monday morning. After what Lawson was subsequently to call an 'unpleasant' 30-minute meeting, she agreed that the Bank could intervene with small foreign currency purchases to smooth the pound's ascent, but there was no question of maintaining the Deutschmark ceiling. She also wanted half-hourly reports on the level of intervention. To Lawson's intense irritation, Peter Middleton would occasionally play up to Thatcher by addressing her by her formal title of First Lord of the Treasury: now she had decided to exercise the authority the title bestowed.

The uncapping of sterling was a bitter blow to the chancellor, the end of a year-long struggle to defy the foreign exchange markets. He would remark subsequently that the decision forced upon him by Thatcher removed a major plank of his anti-inflation policy. When the mood turned against sterling, as it surely would, the markets would not forget that he had been driven off his declared policy of stability. If he could not stop the pound rising, what chance had he of resisting the inevitable fall?[7] During the final few days before the Budget he was steeped in gloom. It was ironic, though, that a chancellor who prided himself on his intimate knowledge of the financial markets had given his adversaries such an easy target. Between the summer of 1987 and March 1988 the pound fluctuated in the narrowest of bands – DM2.95–3.00. On the single occasion when it appeared to be weakening, at the beginning of February, Lawson had raised interest rates. The signal could not have been clearer: investors in sterling were offered a one-way bet. They could take advantage of real interest rates in Britain which remained significantly higher than those in West Germany in the confident knowledge that there was no exchange rate risk in holding sterling. If the pound fell, the Treasury would support it with yet higher rates. If the currency rose, the investors would pick up a windfall profit. There was a quite different, but equally salutary, lesson in the episode. The markets, credited frequently with perfect foresight, were entirely oblivious to the economic realities which would ensure that sterling's strength was characteristically short-lived.

At this stage Lawson still hoped something could be salvaged from the wreckage. When the pound rose to DM3.05 on the following Monday, the Treasury briefed journalists to the effect that it was still committed to managing the exchange rate. The goalposts had been moved, but the objective was to seek stability at a slightly higher level.

Lawson had decided on a shadow 'realignment' of sterling – the sort that might well have taken place within the system. The new ceiling Lawson had in mind was DM3.10, but that too would soon be breached.

The policy shift might have been successfully managed, but Thatcher's aides left no doubt that she had overruled the chancellor. A façade of unity depended on a degree of self-restraint that she found impossible. Her authority was at its peak, and she was less and less inclined to heed the advice of her ministers. She had developed the habit of 'performing' at the daily meetings of cabinet committees which set the direction of government policy. Frequently she would seek to humiliate unwary colleagues. Geoffrey Howe was a regular victim. She saw also less and less reason to moderate in public the force of her private convictions. In the spring of 1988 she would constantly undercut her chancellor as the dispute over sterling unfolded. By the summer, Lawson's economic strategy and his reputation would face ruin.

The first outburst came on 8 March at prime minister's question time in the House of Commons. Thatcher was pressed by Neil Kinnock on the apparent confusion over sterling policy. Her response was uncompromising: excessive intervention or cuts in interest rates to cap the pound would risk a resurgence of inflation, she replied. Within minutes Treasury officials launched a damage-limitation exercise, pointing out that the prime minister, in departing from her prepared text, had not conveyed the subtlety of the new policy. Two days later, however, there was worse. Lawson, answering questions to Treasury ministers, stressed his determination to prevent an unsustainable rise in the value of the pound. Facing what were soon to become familiar taunts from Labour MPs that he had been overruled by the prime minister, Lawson responded, 'While stability does not mean immobility, any further significant rise in the exchange rate, certainly against the Deutschmark, would, in my opinion, be unlikely to be sustainable.'[8] Within minutes, Thatcher had denied him. Pressed by Neil Kinnock on whether she agreed with the chancellor, Thatcher insisted the defeat of inflation was the government's priority. 'There is no way in which you can buck the market,' she declared.[9] The phrase, which visibly stilled the House of Commons, undercut the central plank of Lawson's economic strategy. He returned to the Treasury in despair. The most important Budget of his chancellorship was just days away, and Thatcher was wrecking his economic policy.

Aides attempted to minimize the impact of Thatcher's comments by briefing journalists that the chancellor would reinstate his sterling policy in the Budget speech on the following Tuesday. In the event, even that option was blunted by No. 10. Acting for the prime minister, Brian Griffiths insisted on diluting Lawson's initial text. The Budget speech, on 15 March, included general backing for international efforts to promote currency stability but no specific reference to the policy of shadowing the Deutschmark.[10] Despite wild acclaim from the Tory back benches for the dramatic package of tax cuts in the Budget, the strain of the battle with Thatcher had begun to show. Briefing economics correspondents after the Budget, Lawson declined to repeat the unequivocal commitment to a stable pound which he had given the previous autumn in his Mansion House speech. He appeared tired and defensive. He was also clearly irritated by the fact that the journalists who pressed him on the exchange rate did so in the knowledge that he had been instructed to keep his counsel. Pressed on his own future at the Treasury, he was evasive. For the first time in his political career he had the look of a beaten man. There was, though, one spark of defiance. Those who wanted further clarification of the government's economic policy, he said finally, should wait and see: 'Actions are far more important than words.'[11]

The action came twenty-four hours later. On 17 March Lawson announced the first of a fateful series of interest rate cuts designed to demonstrate that, whatever Thatcher might say, he still controlled the levers of policy. The cut, from 9 per cent to 8.5 per cent, had been approved by Thatcher, but the chancellor's aides seized the opportunity to present it as a reassertion of his authority. In the House of Commons, Thatcher praised Lawson's Budget before declaring without any audible trace of sarcasm that the cabinet was 'a big happy family'.[12] Others joined the public dispute, however, overturning almost daily the Treasury's attempts to restore a sem-blance of coherence to the government's economic strategy. Lord Young, the trade and industry secretary, infuriated Lawson by pub-licly backing Thatcher's position. On three separate occasions within a week, Young dismissed attempts to 'buck the market'. While governments liked to think they could set the value of their currency, 'We long ago found the pound seems to rise and fall to its own level,' he commented at one point.[13] The interjection provoked a furious protest from Lawson and a subsequent 'clarification' from Lord Young's office. The latter's advisers, however, were careful to tell journalists that Lord Young would not apologize to the chancellor. Geoffrey Howe, meanwhile, returned to Lawson's defence. On 24 March he used a speech in Zurich to applaud 'the increasingly valuable experience of stability in the EMS'. Of British policy, he remarked, 'Exchange rates have necessarily come to play a more significant role in both domestic monetary decisions and international policy cooperation.'[14]

A day later, on Friday 25 March, the chancellor and governor, accompanied by a phalanx of Treasury and Bank officials, trooped in to 10 Downing Street for an extraordinary meeting. Lawson, in the words of one of the officials accompanying him, was 'seething with frustration'. It was a difficult, bruising, encounter. Leigh-Pemberton was due on the following Monday to give evidence to the Treasury and Civil Service Committee and, with the government's policy in complete disarray, it was essential that his appearance dispel the confusion. Lawson presented Thatcher with a number of options – including that of finally joining the ERM. This last the prime minister dismissed without discussion.

During what another official described as 'really a rather nasty' exchange, a form of words eventually was settled upon. On the following Monday, Leigh-Pemberton spelt out the terms to the Treasury and Civil Service Committee. Sticking, slightly nervously, to the agreed text, he told the MPs, 'We do give as much consideration to stability of the exchange rate as we can within the overall context of the anti-inflationary stance.' The emphasis of his remarks was Thatcher's: control of inflation was the first objective. Subject, however, to that overriding goal, 'I think stability of the exchange rate is very desirable.' The governor acknowledged that during the year preceding the decision to uncap the pound the aim had been to hold it in a range between DM2.80 and DM3.00. The decision to let it move out of the range had been taken because the intervention required of the Bank risked reigniting inflation. Under close cross-questioning, he stressed that there was no longer a precise target for the pound, and that the authorities were not shadowing the Deutsch-mark. Some of the MPs, however, detected the Bank's private concern that Lawson had put his exchange rate policy ahead of efforts to control the inflation rate. Nicholas Budgen extracted at least a partial admission from the government that the Bank's *Quarterly Bulletin* in February had contained a clear warning that the economy was at risk of overheating.[15]

Appearing two days later before the same committee, Lawson confirmed that nothing really had been settled. His agreement with the prime minister was based on the assumption that a stable pound would henceforth take second place to the fight against inflation. However, the chancellor told the MPs what he really believed: 'Exchange rate stability – I would like to emphasize this – is in no sense an alternative to anti-inflation strategy. The whole point is that in the right circumstances it reinforces it.' He was determined not to surrender to the prime minister, but nor could he respond to the MPs' questions about when and if sterling would join the ERM. Asked if the time would be 'right' before 1992, the date set for the completion of the single European market, he replied simply, 'I cannot answer that question.' For their part, the MPs did not fail to notice that the chancellor's rhetoric on inflation did not match the reality. Their report concluded that in the conduct of economic policy 'the dogmatism of earlier years has gradually given way to a somewhat obscure pragmatism.' As for the record, on the basis of its own stated ambitions, the government was three years 'behind schedule' in curbing inflation. Using methodology suggested by the Bank, the MPs also calculated that the foreign exchange intervention ordered by Lawson during 1987 was showing a loss to the Treasury of £1.3bn as a result of the subsequent depreciation of the dollar.[16]

The obvious tension at the heart of the government did not immedi-ately prick the speculative bubble in the financial markets. By the end of the first week of April sterling was at its highest for two years, reaching DM3.15. Lawson cut interest rates to 8 per cent – the lowest level for a decade. The Treasury sought to explain the move on the basis that sterling's rise had tightened the overall approach to monetary policy. It produced a new rule of thumb to underpin the justification – a 4 per cent rise in the exchange rate could be offset by a one-point cut in interest rates without any weakening of the anti-inflation stance. The evidence of overheating in the economy was mounting, however, and Lawson's tax cuts threatened another burst of consumer spending and borrowing. An ill-judged Budget decision to delay until August new restrictions on mortgage interest tax relief had given a further upward push to the housing market. Officials at the Bank made no secret of the fact that they were far less sanguine than they were sometimes obliged to sound. The economy was in the midst of a boom, and the chancellor was cutting interest rates. Personal pride now came before reasoned decision-making.

As the headlines following each interest rate cut proclaimed that Lawson had prevailed over the prime minister, Thatcher found it increasingly difficult to conceal her anger. On 12 May Neil Kinnock again put her under pressure in the House of Commons. The question was straightforward: Did Thatcher agree with her chancellor that any further increase in the pound's value was unsustainable? She could not bring herself to support Lawson, avoiding three times an unequivocal answer.[17] The following day Geoffrey Howe added fuel to the fire by dropping an unscripted sentence into his speech to the Conservatives' Scottish conference in Perth. His remark, that the government could not delay indefinitely a decision to join the ERM, ensured that the cabinet row continued to dominate the headlines in the weekend press.[18] At a meeting in No. 10 on the evening of Sunday 15 May, Lawson and Thatcher agreed another truce. She would back the chancellor in her next encounter with Kinnock. There could be no repeat of the earlier, massive, intervention, but he could cut interest rates still further to contain sterling's appreciation.

Publicly, Lawson continued to talk down sterling, warning that any further rise against the Deutschmark would prove 'unsustainable'. Lawson said subsequently that the initiative on interest rates was Thatcher's. He had accepted a 'poisoned chalice'.[19] Treasury officials are less sure of the precise sequence, while Thatcher later described the reduction as 'the price of tolerable relations with the chancellor'.[20] Either way, the cut in rates to 7.5 per cent, announced on 17 May, was a terrible mistake. In the House of Commons, Thatcher told Kinnock that 'It would be a great mistake for any speculator to think at any time that sterling was a one-way bet.'[21] The headlines once again declared Lawson the victor of the titanic struggle in Downing Street. Seeking refuge at a meeting in Paris of the Organization for Economic Cooperation and Development, however, the chancellor was awkwardly evasive. His relationship with Thatcher had become so fragile as to preclude further comment on the central issue of his economic management. 'I have no comment to make on that,' he replied when pressed to repeat remarks he had made only days earlier: 'I do not think it is sensible to say anything more.'[22]

Lawson considered resignation after his 1988 Budget. His wife, Thérèse, advised him it was time to bow out. By the end of May it was too late. The Budget had been overshadowed both by the row over the exchange rate and by the ever-clearer indications that the economy was growing much too fast. The Budget tax cuts were small in relation to the overall pace of credit expansion in the economy, but they sent a dangerously optimistic message to consumers. Within two weeks of making it, Lawson had been obliged to reverse the May cut in interest rates. By early August he had pushed up interest rates in half-point stages to 11 per cent – the highest level for two years. At the end of the same month, official figures showing a record £2.2bn current-account deficit in July forced another one-point rise. The deficit in October was even more frightening – £2.4bn. By the end of November interest rates were up to 13 per cent after a steady stream of increases. Lawson's standing among Tory back-bench MPs was falling as fast as it had risen. Edward Heath, in a jibe which would stick, accused the chancellor of being a 'one-club golfer' after he refused to explore alternative methods of reining back the rapid expansion of credit.

Inflation – the judge and jury of Lawson's policy – was rising fast, reaching 6 per cent at the end of the year. The current account was heading for a record £15bn annual deficit. The Treasury's forecasts at the beginning of the year had proved hopelessly wrong. Instead of the predicted gradual deceleration, the economy had expanded faster than at any time since the Barber boom. The consequences would be the same. Lawson at this stage still thought he could steer the economy towards a soft landing. His speech to the annual meeting of the IMF, held that September in Berlin, displayed typical bravado.

Developing a theory which Burns had enunciated within the Treasury, Lawson sought to pretend that, in the brave new world of footloose capital, the mounting current-account deficit provided no real cause for concern. In the past, he said, Britain's balance of payments crises had reflected irresponsible fiscal policies. On this occasion the deficit was entirely a private-sector phenomenon and, as such, would prove 'self-correcting'.[23] He was entirely unconvincing, but sounded as if he believed it. For a time at least during 1988 it seemed that Lawson was persuaded by his own rhetoric that the economy had undergone a permanent transformation which would free it from the shackles of the past. He had been unwise enough in the aftermath of the 1988 Budget to declare that Britain was experiencing an 'economic miracle' comparable to that experienced by West Germany in the immediate post war years. Its exposure as a mirage took only a few months. He would be proved right in his assertion that a rise in the exchange rate would be unsustainable. He did not predict, however, the dire circumstances which would trigger the subsequent fall.

CHAPTER FIVE

HUBRIS

AT THE BEGINNING OF 1989 Margaret Thatcher looked forward to the tenth anniversary of her first election victory with satisfaction and with apprehension. It would offer eloquent testimony to her unchallenged command of British politics, but it would also invite questions as to how long she would, or should, remain in Downing Street. The delicate balance between celebration and presumption would not be easily struck. She did not foresee that 1989 would bring a fatal entanglement between Europe and the economy which would fracture first her cabinet and then her premiership. The debate over the ERM would assume a still more dangerous guise, emerging as the symbol of the looming struggle in the cabinet and in the Conservative Party over Britain's place in Europe. Abroad, she would wage war against Jacques Delors, the president of the European Commission. At home, she would do battle with her foreign secretary and her chancellor. What had once been a fierce but, for most people, arcane debate over the role of the exchange rate in economic management would become the most damaging and divisive issue of her premiership.

Already the strains in the cabinet were apparent. The row over sterling had transformed Thatcher's relationship with Nigel Lawson into one of mutual resentment. He had remained in No. 11 only because to have left while the economy was running into serious problems would have been an admission of failure – and of responsibility. He was at once beleaguered and embittered; she blamed him for the renewed upsurge in inflation. Their regular weekly meetings were businesslike but tense affairs, and at larger gatherings she did little to restrain herself. Leaving one such encounter at No. 10, Robin Leigh-Pemberton turned to Lawson and asked quizzically how he put up with it. 'I may not for much longer,' was the response. 'Let me know if you hear of any openings in the City.'

Thatcher was increasingly distrustful of Geoffrey Howe. His preoccupation with maintaining Britain's influence in Europe was mirrored by her ever-hardening conviction that its interests lay across the Atlantic, not across the Channel. Her early suspicions about the ambitions of Britain's European partners had by now hardened into deep antagonism. Delors's influence was reinforced by the burgeoning alliance between François Mitterrand and Helmut Kohl. The Franco-German alliance, the backbone of the Community, at once vexed and perplexed her. In December 1985 she had signed the Single European Act, the most fundamental revision of the Treaty of Rome since the creation of the Community. Its principal objective was to create a single market, dismantling the trade and other barriers which stood in the way of a true Common Market. It had been a British project, driven in Brussels by Lord Cockfield, a former cabinet minister. It involved, however, a major extension of majority voting in the Brussels Council of Ministers – a constitutional shift whose importance Thatcher had underestimated. A deadline of 1992 for the dismantling of all internal barriers provided both the framework and the momentum for those seeking to build an identifiably federal Europe. Thatcher considered that she had been misled by the Foreign Office in the negotiations which had led to the Single European Act. In truth her own bargaining style in Europe was aptly described some time later by Douglas Hurd: the most familiar sequence was 'No, No, Yes.'

Thatcher, however, blamed the Foreign Office. It seemed to have escaped her revolution; it had not noticed that she had made Britain great again. In her view, the genteel diplomats of the FCO preferred appeasement to confrontation. She had at first found it difficult to build alliances in Europe; now she saw little purpose in the attempt. She noted that Howe's foreign travel diary included long spells without visiting Washington – he always seemed to be in Brussels or in other European capitals. There was also a problem of personal chemistry. Thatcher, ever more imperious, was enraged by Howe's quietly dogged approach in their frequent disputes. However much she ridiculed him in front of colleagues, the foreign secretary stuck to his carefully prepared arguments.

Lord Whitelaw's illness and departure from the cabinet in December 1987 had removed a powerful force for restraint and moderation. The business of government increasingly was conducted by small ad-hoc groups of senior ministers instead of through the formal cabinet machinery. Thatcher's unchallenged authority was accompanied by growing isolation. Norman Tebbit had left the cabinet after the 1987 general election and would refuse more than once her offers to return. Lord Young, another trusted ally, was preparing to return to the private sector. She had decided to promote the career of John Major as a possible successor, but he was by no means a close friend. Nicholas Ridley, the environment secretary, was almost alone among senior ministers in being invited to her flat in No. 10 for a late-evening glass of whisky. Ridley had once proclaimed himself a European federalist, but now he shared her visceral dislike of Delors and deep mistrust of Germany. He had never lost faith with monetarism and was appalled at Lawson's preoccupation with sterling. His lunches with political journalists were punctuated with tirades against the chancellor's attempt to target the exchange rate. Thatcher soon followed his example, blaming the return of rising inflation on Lawson's attempts to shadow the Deutschmark.

In July 1990 Ridley would be forced to resign after the *Spectator* printed one of his intemperate outbursts. He told Dominic Lawson, the magazine's editor and coincidentally Nigel's son, that European integration was 'a German racket designed to take over the whole of Europe'. On the day he left, a cabinet colleague remarked laconically on the unfairness of politics: after all, Ridley had been 'speaking with his mistress's voice'.

Thatcher's closest advisers in 10 Downing Street – Bernard Ingham, her press secretary, and Charles Powell, the private secretary responsible for foreign affairs – were much closer to their mistress than most of her ministers. The two men had long since ceased to be conventional civil servants. Ingham, a bluff Yorkshireman who had once been Tony Benn's press officer, had become a devoted Thatcherite. During his legendary briefings for the political journalists in the Westminster lobby it was frequently impossible to disentangle Ingham's views from those he relayed as the property of the prime minister. Since there was rarely any contradiction, the distinction was usually superfluous.

Powell, an urbane and extremely intelligent official, had arrived in Downing Street in 1984 on temporary assignment from the Foreign Office. Thatcher trusted his judgement, and he understood how to operate the levers of power. He had no intention of returning to the duller diplomacy practised in King Charles Street. From a younger generation, Powell had wider horizons than the prime minister, and few of her reflex prejudices; he operated with a sharp intellect and an elegant pen. In theory he was a middle-ranking official; in practice he often wielded greater influence than the cabinet secretary. With just a hint of bitterness, Nigel Lawson would comment of Powell, 'He never saw it as his role to question her prejudices, merely to refine the language in which they were written.'[1]

At the start of 1989 Thatcher believed she had won the battle of wills over the ERM. There would be no more arguments, she assumed, because there would be no further discussion. Her antagonism towards the mechanism had become pathological. Once she might have seriously considered joining, if only to prove that under her leadership the British had become every bit as strong as the German economy. Now entry would be a humiliating admission of failure. The Paris and Bonn governments were also planning something which, from 10 Downing Street, seemed yet more threatening to Britain's control over its economic destiny: the ERM was to be the basis for a single European currency. Alan Walters, preparing to return to London as her personal economic adviser, kept her well supplied with objections should the Treasury seek to reopen the ERM debate. Her aides sought to persuade her, not always success-fully, to keep her counsel in public statements. Officials in Lawson's private office were in constant contact with their counterparts in No. 10 to avoid a repeat of the open confrontations of the previous year. Treasury officials were also under instruction to monitor Thatcher's every utterance at prime minister's questions in the House of Com-mons on Tuesday and Thursday afternoons. 'We need to know if our policy has changed,' Peter Middleton would comment with only the merest hint of irony.

The efforts to rebuild a semblance of unity had only limited success. Once in the open the rift was constantly exploited by the Labour opposition and featured regularly on the front pages. In one of her now-frequent exchanges on the issue with Neil Kinnock in the House of Commons, on 12 January 1989, the prime minister could not disguise her true feelings. At this stage the pound was still rising against the Deutschmark. Acting on Lawson's instructions, the Bank was intervening to contain the appreciation. Thatcher, however, appeared dismissive of the intervention, telling Kinnock, 'You cannot in fact have two priorities, and the priority is getting inflation down.'[2] The listening Treasury officials groaned in frustration: any impact the intervention might have made in limiting sterling's rise had been neutralized. Middleton determined in his own mind that she should make a choice – between supporting the chancellor's policies and replacing him. At one point he broached the issue with the prime minister. Her response was brusque: it was none of his business.

Her irritation with the continuing speculation that sooner or later she might be forced to admit 'the time was right' to join the ERM bred a growing indiscretion at private gatherings. One such occasion was a Lobby reception in the House of Commons soon after her public exchange with Kinnock. Thatcher was in relaxed mood, reflecting on the momentous events in Mikhail Gorbachev's Soviet Union. Then conversation turned to the ERM. 'I won't have the Belgians decide the value of the pound,' she stormed. 'You shouldn't pay attention to what they say in the Treasury.' Her interlocutors – journalists – were startled. She launched next into a detailed account of the 'national humiliation' of Britain's withdrawal in 1973 from the European Snake. She had been education secretary at the time, a junior member of Edward Heath's cabinet, but she spoke as if it had been a moment of personal shame. Then there was the contradiction she had pointed out in the House of Commons – tackling inflation was the main priority. She continued with her unprompted list of objections. The dismantling of capital controls by other European nations to create the single market would destabilize the ERM. The pressure on governments in the system to follow a recent rise in West German interest rates had shown once again the ERM's inherent inflexibility. Finally, she was not at all certain that she would join even if, as she fully expected, she won a fourth term of office at the next general election.

These sentiments duly appeared on the front pages of two national newspapers the following morning – attributed as her views but without direct quotation.[3] The Treasury was baffled and annoyed. A senior official suggested that the report was out of date, based probably on a misinformed or mischievous briefing by one or other of the prime minister's Downing Street aides. Thatcher's own stance on the ERM was softening, the official insisted, and the names of Powell and Ingham were mentioned as the most likely source of the report. It was not until some time later that the Treasury discovered that the words had come directly from the prime minister herself. Such was the way economic policy was now made in Margaret Thatcher's government.

The chancellor's problems were mounting. The pace of growth during 1988 had been much faster than Lawson had predicted. The Treasury's forecast in the 1988 Budget had been for the economy to expand by a healthy but sustainable 3 per cent. A year later it was clear that the actual growth rate had been closer to 5 per cent – Lawson had been driving blind. The government had only itself to blame, as some years earlier, as part of one of its periodic 'efficiency' drives, it had ordered deep cuts in the resources allocated to gathering economic statistics. Consumer spending had jumped by more than 6 per cent in 1988, fuelled by surging house prices and easy credit. Consumers could spend their new-found wealth by taking advantage of equity-release schemes on offer at every building society and bank. Oblivious to the mistakes of the past – and to warnings from the Bank of England – the high-street banks ignored traditional prudential standards. They assumed, wrongly, that 100 per cent mortgages were risk-free. Average house prices had risen by more than 15 per cent in both 1986 and 1987 and by more than 20 per cent in 1988. The indifference of consumers and lenders alike to a massive build-up in personal debt had been encouraged by the tax cuts announced in the 1988 Budget. The size of the give-away – £6bn in a full year – was minuscule relative to total spending in the economy, but the income tax reductions were a powerful stimulant to the careless confidence of the time. So too was the chancellor's chimeric promise of a virtuous circle of lower taxes, higher public spending and government debt repayment. The Treasury repaid nearly £15bn of debt in the 1988/89 financial year, but the supposed transformation in the public finances was illusory, and by the early 1990s the Treasury would be borrowing as much as £45bn in a single year.

By May 1989 Lawson had been obliged to raise interest rates to 14 per cent – the highest level since early 1985. The tightening of the monetary ratchet was in deliberately small steps, as the chancellor wanted a 'soft landing' for the economy. His hopes that the boom would be followed by only the mildest of hangovers were soon disappointed. Retail price inflation reached an annual rate of 7.9 per cent in March 1989 – the highest level since 1982. The figure was exaggerated by the inclusion of the impact of higher mortgage interest rates, but the underlying inflation rate had crept up to nearly 6 per cent and was set to go on rising. There were also strong warning signals from the labour market. After thirty-two successive monthly falls since July 1986, recorded unemployment still stood at nearly 2 million. The early-1980s recession, however, had left hundreds of thousands of workers stranded outside the employment market without appropriate skills or training. The result was a serious mismatch between the jobs and the jobless, leading to labour shortages in several key industries. Average wage settlements had crept up from 5 to more than 7 per cent, and increases in earnings were running at more than 9 per cent a year. The spending spree had fed through into a rapid increase in Britain's current-account deficit – forecast in the March 1989 Budget at £14.5bn, but in fact heading towards £20bn. It was back to the bad old days of boom and bust.

In an incautious moment Nigel Lawson had described the upsurge in inflation as a temporary 'blip'. Thatcher, warned by Alan Walters that the Treasury was too sanguine, was not assuaged. She regarded the taming of inflation during her first term in Downing Street as a proud personal achievement. Her understanding of economics was shot through with contradictions: the public champion of lower taxes, she regarded the tax increases in the 1981 Budget as her greatest triumph, always emphasizing her own role in the decision which had attracted the wrath of 364 economists. From that moment she had a naïve faith in the efficacy of fiscal policy in squeezing out inflation – a faith which underpinned her hostility to higher interest rates. She was confused too about the logic of locking sterling's exchange rate to the Deutschmark: sometimes she thought it would be too deflationary; on other occasions she would argue it would risk reigniting inflation. Thatcher never doubted the end of low inflation; she was equivocal at best about the means.

Lawson's discomfiture was increased by the return to the House of Commons in early 1989 of John Smith, the shadow chancellor. Recovered from a heart attack in the previous October, Smith channelled his formidable debating skills into undermining his opponent's confidence and reputation. He ridiculed the chancellor at every opportunity about the prime minister's interference, and constantly played back Lawson's previous claims that the economy had been transformed. There were moments now when the chancellor visibly wilted before the onslaught from the opposition dispatch-box.

A clue to the shadow of Lawson's depression during the spring of 1989 came in the aftermath of the 14 March Budget. It had been a dull affair after the tax-cutting excitement of the previous year. There was some long-overdue help for workers at the bottom end of the income scale, and extra assistance for pensioners, but the package essentially was a holding operation. Six years into his chancellorship, Lawson had to admit that inflation was once again the main problem. At his post-Budget press conference he appeared weary and disillusioned, sidestepping questions about his own future and volunteering, 'This is certainly my last Budget for this year.' During off-the-record lunches with journalists, his cabinet colleagues speculated regularly about possible successors as chancellor, while Ridley promoted his own claim to the post. Ominously, March 1989 also saw the start of a sustained turn-round in the opinion polls. For the first time since the 1987 election, Labour pulled level with the Conservatives. The opposition would swiftly move into a commanding lead as the economy, Europe and the poll tax sapped the authority of Thatcher's government.

The economic backdrop could hardly have been less auspicious for the looming confrontation with Britain's European partners – a confrontation which would crystallize the conflict in Margaret Thatcher's cabinet and bind fatally the economics of the ERM to the politics of Europe. The *casus belli* was the publication in April 1989 of the report of the Delors Committee on Economic and Monetary Union. It was the route map for a single currency managed by a supranational central bank. The committee had been established at the Hanover summit in June 1988. Thatcher had tried initially to block the initiative, but had been outmanœuvred. Curiously, she had agreed that the group be chaired by Jacques Delors. He had just been reappointed as president of the European Commission – a decision she had reluctantly endorsed as a means of preventing the post from falling into German hands.

This was the era of optimism among federalists, and Delors would quickly emerge as the symbol of all that the prime minister feared and despised in Europe. In July 1988 Delors marked his reappointment by predicting a massive extension of the Community's authority. He forecast that within ten years it would be the source of 80 per cent of economic legislation affecting member states. Its social dimension would be greatly expanded. His speech to the European Parliament in Strasbourg ended with a warning: 'We are not going to manage to take all the decisions needed between now and 1995 unless we see the beginnings of European government.'⁴ Thatcher was furious; in a BBC Radio interview she dismissed his vision alternately as 'extreme' and 'airy-fairy', and hardened her own public position against European integration.⁵ Delors compounded the crime by bringing the message directly to Britain. The presence of the Commission president at the annual conference of the Trades Union Congress in early September 1988 was insult enough to a prime minister who saw the humbling of the unions as central to her achievement. Using such a platform to celebrate the onward march of a federal, socialist, Europe was a declaration of war. Within weeks she had countered with an alternative vision. It was to prove a defining moment in the government's relations with the rest of Europe.

The first draft of the speech which would be delivered to the College of Europe in Bruges was written by Charles Powell, Thatcher's foreign affairs private secretary, at the end of August. That in itself was strange, since by custom the Foreign Office would provide an initial draft for the prime minister's office to work from. The copy sent to Geoffrey Howe's office set alarm bells ringing through the Foreign Office. Howe sought substantial revision, and the task was allocated to John Kerr, the FCO official responsible for European affairs. Kerr, a former private secretary to both Lawson and Howe, made substantial changes. The central message of the speech – that Thatcher would never accept the replacement of de Gaulle's Europe des Patries by the Delors vision of a United States of Europe – remained, but in the amended text it was in softer focus. It began with a long résumé of the contribution which Britain had made to Europe's development and of the need to extend the benefits of

Western democracy to the East. Her Europe was one which did not stop at the Berlin Wall but would stretch eventually from the Atlantic to the Urals. Powell accepted 80 per cent of Kerr's amendments. Even if there was still a coded hostility, it was difficult to quarrel with the call for a wider, liberal, less intrusive Community open to the East as well as the West.

The Foreign Office believed its damage-limitation exercise had been successful. It was mistaken. On 20 September 1988 Margaret Thatcher laid the foundations for the rebirth of Tory nationalism. The officials had underestimated how just a few phrases could define a speech. Bernard Ingham would ensure that it was Thatcher's 20 per cent – with some particularly acerbic lines added at the last moment – not the diplomats' 80 per cent which grabbed the headlines. Ingham's briefing left no doubt that Thatcher intended the speech as a direct attack on Delors. Thatcher railed against a European 'identikit' and the threat of endless regulation replacing the free cooperation of independent nation states. She concluded:

> It is ironic that just when those countries such as the Soviet Union which have tried to run everything from the centre are learning that success depends on dispersing power and decisions away from the centre, there are some in the Community who seem to move in the opposite direction. We have not successfully rolled back the frontiers of the state only to see them reimposed at a European level, with a European superstate exercising a new dominance from Brussels.[6]

This was Thatcher breaking free of the Foreign Office, wrenching back, as she saw it, control of Britain's destiny from those who would stand unquestioningly on the escalator to a European superstate. The Whitehall establishment was aghast. As Hugo Young puts it in his seminal biography of Thatcher, *One of Us*, 'The Bruges speech looked like a watershed in September 1988, and time has not altered that assessment.'[7] To Geoffrey Howe it represented something else too: Thatcher's rediscovery of a latent hostility to Europe which had always been there but had hitherto been kept under control. It was her escape from 'the collective responsibility of her days in the Heath cabinet – when European policy had arrived, as it were, with the rations'.[8]

*

The Bruges speech encapsulated Thatcher's frustration at past defeats as much as a new determination to draw a line. At the Hanover summit in June 1988 she had found herself outwitted and outgunned by Paris and Bonn over economic and monetary union. A European currency had been a long-standing Franco-German aspiration. It had been formalized by President Georges Pompidou and Chancellor Willy Brandt nearly twenty years earlier. The idea had been incorporated into the Werner Plan in 1970, and had been endorsed by Edward Heath at the Paris summit in October 1972, when Britain stood on the threshold of membership of the Community. The ambition had, however, fallen victim to the breakdown of Bretton Woods and the economic dislocation caused by the instability of the dollar and the 1973 oil-price shock. The creation in 1979 of the EMS had marked a return to the effort to stabilize exchange rates, and the concept of economic and monetary union had been revived during the negotiations for the Single European Act. President Mitterrand had by then set in place the *franc fort* policy to weld the French currency to the Deutschmark. After a series of bruising encounters in the early 1980s, Mitterrand concluded that the Bundesbank's jealously guarded independence could not be chipped away gradually. Instead it would be subsumed in the new European-wide institution needed to manage a single currency. Chancellor Kohl's motives were different. He came from the generation which still feared the resurgence of German nationalism. The answer was to bind Bonn more closely into the institutions of Europe through a federal political structure: to create a European Germany rather than a German Europe. Bonn would demand political union as the price for the monetary union sought by France. Between Kohl and Mitterrand, Delors seized the chance to promote his vision of an integrated Europe.

Lawson had warned Thatcher against acceptance of any commitment within the Treaty of Rome to economic and monetary union. Despite his hopes of persuading her to take sterling into the ERM, he also argued against treaty changes which would make British membership obligatory.[9] On the latter point she took his advice. But, during the Luxembourg summit in December 1985 at which the single-market programme was agreed, France and Germany secured overwhelming backing to formally incorporate the goal of monetary union. Britain had paid lip-service to the idea when it joined the

Community but now Thatcher conceded its inclusion in the preamble of the Single European Act and thus its embodiment in the treaty. She succeeded in adding some deliberately vague wording about economic and monetary 'cooperation' as opposed to 'union', but the pass had been sold. The retreat in Luxembourg provided the lever for Kohl and Mitterrand two and a half years later.

At the Hanover summit in June 1988, Thatcher was left to argue only about the composition of the group which would give shape to the idea of a single currency. Her aim was to ensure that any report would be grounded in pragmatic analysis rather than in political ambition, and she insisted that the study be conducted by the Community's central bank governors, albeit under the chairmanship of Delors. She was relying in particular on Karl Otto Pöhl. The Bundesbank had made no secret of its distaste for the monetary dreams of French politicians. It regarded itself as in effect already Europe's central bank – the anchor for the currencies and monetary policies of its neighbours. It had no wish to relinquish its authority to an institution which would dilute its hegemony. Pöhl would tell visitors to his twelfth-floor office in the Bundesbank that of course he supported the idea of a European central bank. Glancing down at the car park below, he would remark that there was plenty of space for a small annexe to be attached to his Frankfurt headquarters. Thatcher thought she could put another brake on the committee's deliberations by directing Robin Leigh-Pemberton's contribution. She had not mentioned her plans that he should join the committee in advance of the summit – the Bank governor was informed only by telephone from Hanover – but she never considered he might take a view different from her own.

The prime minister underestimated the central bankers. As the committee's work progressed, Pöhl did express reservations. Once or twice he threatened not to attend future meetings unless the minutes of their deliberations, drafted by Delors, reflected the actual proceedings rather than the chairman's personal views. However, Pöhl decided not to obstruct the work and signed up to the final eventual blueprint on the basis that it had been the central bankers' task only to describe how a single currency might be achieved. The Bundesbank doubted whether the ambition could or should be realized, but that was a matter for the politicians to decide. In a public display of independence, Leigh-Pemberton resisted pressure from Thatcher and Lawson to submit a dissenting report and, after a discussion with Pöhl at the beginning of April 1989, he endorsed the report on the same basis as his German colleague. The prime minister was never told that the final text of the report was 'polished' by officials in the Bank of England. For much of his first term Leigh-Pemberton had chosen to do the government's bidding. Once reappointed in 1988 for a second term his confidence grew, and with it his intense distaste for the prime minister's view of Europe. He wrote a detailed letter to Thatcher explaining his decision to sign the report. She never replied. When the governor asked a Downing Street official about her silence, he was advised it would be prudent to let the matter drop.

The Delors scheme was for a three-stage move to monetary union. During the first stage all the remaining countries (in practice Britain, Portugal and Greece) would join the ERM, all capital controls would be dismantled, the single market would be completed, and greater use would be made of the European Currency Unit to enhance monetary cooperation. Stage two would see the creation of a European Monetary Institute – an embryonic central bank. Stage three would mark the transition from permanently locked exchange rates to a single currency, managed by a European central bank. Crucially, the report said that a decision to start stage one should also enshrine a commitment to the entire process. Delors's intention was to ensure that, once governments had embarked on the relatively innocuous preparatory phase, it would be impossible for them to turn back.[10] Thatcher was appalled. Here was the proof that Delors was set on the creation of no less than a European government which would destroy Britain's right and ability to rule itself. She had been right in Bruges, and she resolved that she would never again bend in her opposition to his federalist blueprints.

The foreign secretary and the chancellor approached the Delors report from different perspectives. Lawson was as passionate in his public opposition to a single currency as he was privately determined to win the argument with Thatcher over the ERM. He set out his objections to monetary union in a lengthy exposition to the Royal Institute of International Affairs in January 1989. The core of his argument was that the transfer to Europe of the key levers of economic management would strike at the heart of the nation-state. The ERM, Lawson said, was an agreement freely entered into by sovereign states. Monetary union would imply the transfer to a supranational body of authority over interest rate policy. Governments would lose de-facto control of fiscal policy – of taxation, spending and borrowing: 'It is clear that economic and monetary union implies nothing less than a European government – albeit a federal one – and political union: the United States of Europe.'[11] Lawson has never shifted from that position, but his officials detected a tactical ploy in the timing and prominence of this particular speech. It would be easier, he thought, to persuade Thatcher to drop her objections to the ERM if the Treasury was seen to be as resolute as she in its opposition to a single currency.

Howe instinctively was a pro-European. His views had been shaped while working for Edward Heath in the early 1970s. He found little problem with the notion that Britain could enhance its influence in the world by sharing sovereignty with its European partners. He rejected the *dirigiste* blueprint produced by Delors, but the long-term ambition of economic and monetary union did not cause him nightmares. His growing conviction that the alternative to Europe was isolation and impotence was spelled out in a speech to the Confederation of British Industry in May 1989: 'Outside the Community, we could no longer influence, as we should, the vigorous mainstream of growing European consciousness and prosperity. Outside the Community, our standing, before our allies and our adversaries alike, would be seriously diminished. Already it is becoming impossible to imagine a future for Britain without the Community.'[12]

The two men had not cooperated systematically in their efforts to persuade Thatcher to take sterling into the ERM, but there had been occasions when they had coordinated their public declarations. The press secretary at the Treasury would call journalists to draw attention to speeches from Howe which were supportive of Lawson's position. After his comments in support of Lawson's position at the Scottish party conference in Perth in May 1988, Howe had suggested to Thatcher that all three meet to settle a common position. Suspecting a plot, she had bluntly rejected the idea. More often than not, however, Lawson and Howe had ploughed their own furrows, concentrating on winning bilateral disputes with No. 10 rather than acting in concert. Until 1989 at least, Lawson was suspicious of Howe's resolve: he doubted that his colleague was ready to risk his career. These two ministers in Thatcher's government were not alone in choosing to operate alone. Here was a central weakness of her third administration. As she retreated into her Downing Street bunker, turning to her aides rather than her colleagues for advice, most of her ministers could be heard in private complaining about her imperious leadership, but only on the rarest of occasions would they come to the aid of a colleague at odds with the prime minister. The completion of the Delors report in the spring of 1989 provided the occasion for such a rare endeavour. Lawson and Howe decided, albeit from their different perspectives, that it was essential to harden the commitment to take sterling into the ERM. The calculation was that a signal that the government was ready to join the first stage of economic and monetary union was essential to give Britain the political influence it needed in order to prevent the other eleven signing up now for the full Delors project.

The idea of a joint paper to shape the government's position at the forthcoming Madrid summit in June was first raised during a series of private meetings between the chancellor and the foreign secretary during the spring and early summer of 1989. It followed an abortive attempt by Ruud Lubbers, the Dutch prime minister, to persuade Thatcher of the merits of taking sterling into the ERM. Lubbers was the closest Thatcher had to an ally in the councils of Europe. His commitment to integration was never in doubt, but his staunch support for NATO and for the American military presence in Europe led Thatcher to place him apart from other 'federalists'. With encouragement from Howe, Lubbers had explained during an Anglo-Dutch summit at Chequers that the effectiveness of Britain's opposition to a single currency would be greatly enhanced by ERM membership. Thatcher's response, in Lawson's presence, was to blame the upsurge in British inflation on attempts to shadow the Deutschmark – a charge which she would soon lay publicly. A few days later Lawson raised the issue once more in his weekly meeting with Thatcher. He relates her reaction in his memoirs: 'I do not want you to raise this subject ever again . . . I must prevail.'[13] He chose to ignore her.

Lawson recalled subsequently that Howe was the moving force in the Madrid *démarche*. The Whitehall record, however, shows that it was the chancellor who formally made the first move. He instructed Timothy Lankester, the Treasury official responsible for monetary affairs, to start work on a memorandum. It was Lankester who first contacted John Kerr at the Foreign Office. The memorandum was to be presented to Thatcher before European leaders discussed the Delors plan at the Madrid summit. The early versions of the document were evenly balanced between the foreign policy and the economic case for ERM membership. In the Treasury's initial draft there was much emphasis on the role the ERM might play in avoiding any repeat of the upsurge in inflation. The Treasury admitted that monetary policy had been too lax during the period when sterling had been shadowing the Deutschmark. It then reached the ingenious conclusion that, had sterling been within the ERM at the time, the problem would not have arisen: Germany would not have demanded a revaluation. That particular thought was dropped long before the final document reached the prime minister.

The Madrid memorandum was a remarkable document, distilling in thirty-five terse paragraphs the conflict at the heart of Margaret Thatcher's cabinet. Its innocent title, 'EC Issues, and Madrid', belied the explosive nature of its content. Its final sentence, 'Could we discuss this with you?', offered a vivid image of the breakdown in relationships at the heart of the government. Thatcher had long since abandoned the practice of holding ministerial meetings in advance of such European summits. Instead she met with her advisers. Brian Griffiths, the head of the No. 10 policy unit, would join Alan Walters in reassuring Thatcher she was right to ignore the advice of her most senior ministers. Ostensibly, however, the strategy that Howe and Lawson now outlined was tailored to the prime minister's objectives. Here was a scheme to delay if not derail any timetable for economic and monetary union (EMU): Britain would play an active part in the relatively innocuous stage one of the process and, in so doing, it might detach that phase from the more threatening stages two and three. The principal danger for Britain was Delors's insistence that agreement to embark on the process would be a commitment to complete it. The goal of British diplomacy in Madrid must be to break that link.

The memorandum went well beyond that. In terms which were soon to find a constant echo among pro-Europeans on the Conservative back benches, it carried a deeper warning about the risks of isolation in Europe. The choice was between engagement in the debate and banishment to the sidelines. A threat to veto EMU would be a futile gesture: there was a real prospect that the other eleven governments would establish new arrangements outside the Treaty of Rome to create a single currency. Accepting banishment to the sidelines would involve a heavy political and economic price. If Britain became a 'semi-detached' member of the Community it would soon find it had lost influence in Washington as well as in Brussels. Japanese investment in Britain would be threatened, and so too would the prosperity of the City of London. The document concluded that a pledge that sterling would join the ERM by July 1992 – three years hence and the date set for the completion of the single market – was conceding 'very little'. By contrast, seeing off the – potentially very damaging – debate over EMU for an even longer time by so doing would be a 'major prize'.

Howe and Lawson suggested that Thatcher attach two conditions to the ERM pledge: all member states must dismantle their remaining capital controls well before July 1992; and sterling would be admitted to the mechanism with the wide, 6 per cent, margins of fluctuation enjoyed by Italy, rather than the 2.25 per cent bands applicable to other currencies. Britain also would need to reduce its inflation rate, but that was a matter for its own government.

Lawson initially had wanted a shorter time-frame. An early Treasury contribution to the joint memorandum suggested that Thatcher should say in Madrid that the time for British membership was 'ripening'. Then, before or during the next summit, in Strasbourg six months later, she should harden that commitment to membership by July 1990. Kerr and Lankester counselled against pressing for a date. Kerr suggested the use simply of the word 'ripening', without mentioning a time-frame. The final formula, with its three-year target, was a much-discussed compromise.

The officials were aware that their political masters were playing with fire. The drafts were classified 'secret', and only a handful of senior officials had access. Terence Burns added his voice to those counselling discretion, writing cautionary notes in the margin of early drafts. At another point, Kerr was heard to remark that, if Howe and Lawson did not tread with extreme caution, 'They will both be gone by the end of the year.' And so it was. Howe was moved from the Foreign Office in July; Lawson resigned in October.

The memorandum was delivered on 14 June. Lawson signed the final draft while waiting for the start of a cabinet meeting. The submission was now a statement of the political rather than the economic case for membership. Thatcher was scathing: 'It was a typical Foreign Office paper which Nigel Lawson in his better days would have scornfully eviscerated,' she said later.[14] Kerr had anticipated her reaction, but in their haste the officials overlooked the Foreign Office's internal references on the final version sent to No. 10. The initials 'JOK' in the bottom corner marked out Kerr as the guilty man. For some time afterwards he told colleagues he expected his next overseas posting to be as third secretary in a minor embassy somewhere nasty south of the Sahara. Ever unpredictable, Thatcher instead gave him the most important, if not the most glamorous, job in the diplomatic service – head of the UK permanent representation in Brussels.

The document became the subject of two stormy meetings at No. 10. During the first, on 20 June, Thatcher was immovable. She offered an ever-lengthening list of objections, making no secret of her conviction that the time might never be right to take sterling into the mechanism. The meeting was followed by a note to Lawson and Howe from Charles Powell which removed all reference to a date and added new conditions. Sterling could enter the mechanism only when the ERM had shown itself capable of withstanding the removal of all capital controls and the full operation of the single market. The requirements were framed by Alan (now Sir Alan)Walters, who had returned as a part-time adviser to the prime minister the previous month. Before his return Walters had sent Thatcher a still longer list of suggested hurdles. Among them was the requirement that all domestic banking systems and financial markets should first be deregulated – a condition framed to defer indefinitely any decision.

Howe concluded that Thatcher's response was 'calculated to produce exactly the wrong answer' from her European counterparts. The two ministers sent a second joint minute on 23 June in which they again stressed the risk of Britain being sidelined at the summit.

Lawson's view that there was a good chance of breaking the link between the first and later stages of the Delors blueprint had been reinforced by his discussions at an informal meeting of finance ministers in the Spanish town of S'Agaró. So too had his opinion that Britain would first have to demonstrate good intent. After much pressure from both ministers, Thatcher agreed to a second meeting. It took place on 25 June, hours before she and Howe flew to Madrid.

Two days earlier, during a Foreign Office briefing, George Jones, the political editor of the *Daily Telegraph*, had sensed the impending shift. The newspaper led its front page with a story that Thatcher was bowing to pressure from Howe and Lawson.[15] She was furious, suspecting (incorrectly) a deliberate leak to weaken her position in advance of their second encounter. She first tried to insist she would see them separately, but they demanded a joint meeting. When they gathered in 10 Downing Street on the Sunday morning of 25 June the foreign secretary went through the arguments again. Then he threatened resignation if Thatcher did not budge. The chancellor said he too would have no option but to leave the government. She refused to set a date for sterling's entry to the ERM. Later she was to remark of the deadlock, 'They left, Geoffrey looking insufferably smug. And so the nasty little meeting ended.'[16] On the plane to Madrid, prime minister and foreign secretary did not speak. 'She was blazing,' Charles Powell would remark. Nor did Thatcher tell the foreign secretary in advance what she would say at the opening session of the summit.

Her statement to the European Council on the morning of 26 June was an admission that she had lost. Thatcher would insist that she gave no ground, because there was no mention of a deadline for ERM entry. As the original Howe–Lawson document had remarked, however, tone of voice is often more important than detail at such meetings, and no one at Madrid could escape the change in her tone. The official note of her intervention records that Thatcher described as 'valuable' much of the analysis in the Delors report. Britain was prepared for the twelve to embark on stage one of economic and monetary union in July 1990. Finance ministers should begin preparations urgently. Sterling would enter the exchange rate mechanism – 'I can reaffirm today the United Kingdom's intention to join the

ERM' – but the British government must be free to decide the timing. It would be linked to progress in bringing down inflation and, in Europe, to the successful abolition of exchange controls and progress towards the completion of the single market. Thatcher added that the House of Commons would not accept stages two and three of the Delors map for a single currency: these proposals would require further study. Behind her statement was the calculation that she could not prevent Kohl and Mitterrand calling an intergovernmental conference to revise the Treaty of Rome, but she could veto proposed changes to the treaty. She then announced that Britain planned to present its own proposals for closer monetary cooperation. Typically, she made this last commitment without any advance consultation with the Treasury.

For all the caveats it was impossible to miss the concessions. An open-ended and vague commitment to put sterling into the ERM when the time was 'ripe' or 'right' had been replaced by a much clearer pledge. Thatcher had constructed in Madrid the framework which would make it impossible for her to resist sterling's entry fifteen months later. Howe recalled later the applause he received from Delors: 'Congratulations, Geoffrey, on having won the intellectual argument within the British government.'[17]

The prime minister sensed her defeat. Her press conference at the end of the summit lacked the usual bravado and the deep black of her outfit matched her mood. She was defensive, seeking to hedge her new position with additional terms. At one point she sought to extend the list of what would now become the 'Madrid conditions'. Two days later, reporting on the summit to the House of Commons, her discomfort was obvious. Her prepared opening statement, agreed with the Foreign Office, was almost apologetic. The heads of government, she said, had indeed reaffirmed the objective of economic and monetary union, but 'no definition of it was agreed in Madrid'. Under subsequent questioning she came close to disowning her own position at the summit. She told MPs she had not been elected to see Britain coerced into handing its control over taxation and spending to a federal Europe. The lifting of exchange controls in 1990 might also deliver a severe shock to the mechanism.[18] 'She's blown it again,' one official from the Foreign Office commented wearily after the tirade had ended. In fact her visible fury served only to confirm the reality of defeat. Margaret Thatcher had been cornered; now she would exact revenge.

The atmosphere of crisis in the inner councils of the cabinet was seeping out almost constantly to a wider world. Thatcher's aides made little secret of her antipathy to Howe. Colleagues reported that she could barely stand to be in the same room with him. Her anger at his 'betrayal' was amplified by his public admission before the Madrid summit that he had not given up hope of one day leading the party. 'I wouldn't hold out much chance of that,' Bernard Ingham had replied when pressed by journalists for a response. The prime minister herself was inclined more and more to allow her private thoughts to burst into the public domain. Her careless phrases about 'bucking the market' had wrecked Lawson's attempts to stabilize the pound a year earlier. She returned to the subject during a BBC interview in May 1989. Confronted on the same day with the news that inflation had reached an annual rate of 8 per cent, she repeated in public what she had said in private to Ruud Lubbers: 'That's where we picked up inflation actually – by shadowing the Deutschmark.'[19] In a single, brief sentence, she had disowned her chancellor. Lawson, on his way to the S'Agaró meeting of European finance ministers in Spain, revealed later he had threatened resignation. Thatcher persuaded him to stay by apologizing, but that was almost irrelevant. It was clear to observers, if not yet to the participants themselves, that the breach was irreparable.

If any further evidence was needed it came on 22 May, at the start of the campaign for the European elections. The Conservatives, Thatcher declared at the opening press conference in Central Office, 'believe in a Europe of independent sovereign states cooperating freely in a climate of economic liberty'. There followed the inevitable barrage of questions about the ERM. With Howe alongside her, she launched into an unrestrained attack on fixed exchange rates in general and the ERM in particular. 'No one' thought Britain should join until it had got down its inflation rate, and maybe not even then. That was the policy of *the government*. Howe winced, and added that sterling would join the ERM when the time was right, and in any case it was a collective decision, to be taken by the cabinet as a whole.

Thatcher, however, had set the tone for a Gaullist campaign: only the Conservatives, declared the election posters from Saatchi & Saatchi, would save Britain from a 'diet of Brussels'.

Lawson's voice would not be stilled. Within two days of Thatcher's press conference he was telling a BBC interviewer that 'obviously there is a strong case for membership'.[20] On 12 June he used an appearance before the Treasury and Civil Service Committee to establish that case in detail, disclosing in advance of his confrontation in No. 10 the terms Britain should set out for entry at the Madrid summit. He defended the system's record against the criticisms of Alan Walters, arguing that it had helped to deliver both low inflation and exchange rate stability in Europe. As for British membership, the precise timing, he remarked pointedly, would be for 'the government as a whole' to decide.[21]

The public rows were followed by staged reconciliations designed to limit the damage. The financial markets expect governments to put policies before personal pride. By now the problem was not sterling's strength against the Deutschmark but its incipient weakness. The ever more public dispute over economic management compounded the damage done by rising inflation and a strong dollar. The bubble of confidence in sterling had finally burst, despite a widening gap between British and German interest rates. On 24 May Lawson was forced to push up interest rates to 14 per cent – the highest level since January 1985. A week later the pound, below DM3.10, was at its weakest for more than a year. Rumours of Lawson's imminent resignation swept the City. Sterling's fall was threatening still higher borrowing costs. On 7 June, Thatcher cut short a European-election tour to join Lawson on the front bench in the House of Commons in a contrived show of unity. He spelled out the government's policy in a statement which they had negotiated in advance: 'Our overriding objective is to bring inflation down. To do that we will keep interest rates at whatever level is necessary for as long as necessary . . . And we will not allow the firmness of our monetary stance to be under-mined by a depreciation in the exchange rate.'[22] The position, he added, was perfectly clear. No one believed him. Six days later the two were side by side again on the government front bench. She promised him 'full, unequivocal and generous backing'.[23] The aim was to reassure the financial markets, but the truce between prime minister and chancellor was too obviously contrived. Treasury officials conceded privately that she had refused to include in her carefully scripted statement explicit support for Lawson's efforts to stabilize sterling. This marriage had reached that stage when neither protagonist can bring themselves to take the extra step which might, just might, bring reconciliation instead of divorce.

It was the same at the closing press conference of the European elections campaign on 15 June. Here Thatcher foreshadowed the final breach with Lawson later in the year. The chancellor's anger at the return to No. 10 of Alan Walters was an open secret. She rejected, however, suggestions from her inquisitors that the only way to heal the rift with Lawson was to sack Walters. Later the same day Bernard Ingham poured salt into the wound by dismissing as 'nonsense' the idea that Walters's presence could be divisive. The disarray was exploited ruthlessly by John Smith. He taunted Lawson about Walters's influence. Smith, a master of the political insult, took to referring to Lawson as the 'nominal chancellor' – a man whose decisions were carelessly overruled by a part-time adviser. The jibes took their toll.

Predictably, the results of the Strasbourg elections, announced on Sunday 19 June, were disastrous. The stridently nationalist approach upon which Thatcher insisted had inflamed divisions within her own party. Her rows with Lawson over the exchange rate had been mirrored by an equally bitter dispute with her predecessor, Edward Heath, over the general direction of Britain's European policy. The electorate, angered by the sharp rise in borrowing costs and presented with an image of a government racked by divisions, repaid the Conservatives by handing a handsome victory to Neil Kinnock. Fresh from its spectacular win two months earlier in the Vale of Glamorgan by-election, Labour secured forty-five seats compared to the Conservatives' thirty-two – an exact reversal of the 1984 poll. The swing against the government was 9 per cent. More significantly, the 34 per cent share of the vote won by the Conservatives was the lowest they had received in a nationwide poll this century. Sir Anthony Meyer, a Tory back-bench MP hitherto rarely mentioned in the public prints, launched an outspoken attack on the prime minister. The campaign had been 'disgraceful'. The defeat was 'entirely' her fault. Sir Anthony would soon play a bigger role. Barely a month after the tenth anniversary of her first election victory, the myth of electoral invincibility which surrounded Thatcher had been punctured.

There was another element in this explosive chemistry: Michael Heseltine. A multimillionaire with a burning ambition to become prime minister, he had never seen his departure from the cabinet during the Westland crisis as the end of his political career. Instead, from the back benches, he executed a campaign to be the first politician since Winston Churchill to return from the wilderness and lead his party. The MP for Henley set about the task with ruthless and ingenious efficiency. His strategy was to persuade the party faithful that, despite their differences, he was not seeking to undermine Thatcher. However, he devoted all of his energies to framing an alternative manifesto against the day when she left 10 Downing Street – willingly or otherwise. Heseltine would be the loyal pretender.

He was conspicuously successful. Four or five appearances a week among party activists in the shires were combined with a steady stream of lectures, speeches and books. He cultivated his colleagues on the back benches and in government with the same assiduousness with which he had made his personal fortune in the publishing business. Tory MPs were the electorate who would choose the next party leader. If they needed a favour – perhaps a guest speaker at their annual association dinner, or a celebrity to open the summer fête – Michael Heseltine was always on hand. His contacts with journalists ensured that, while many in cabinet struggled for space in the newspapers or time on the airwaves, the thoughts of Michael Heseltine would always find an audience. For those who said he wanted to replace Thatcher in 10 Downing Street there was the feigned weariness of an intricately phrased response: 'I have always said I do not foresee the circumstances in which I would challenge the prime minister. I expect her to lead the Conservatives into the next election and that we will win.' By the time he challenged her, of course, those unforeseen circumstances had materialized.

The endless flow of ideas which tumbled from Heseltine's self-consciously modest office in Victoria Street contained two ever-constant drumbeats: the promise of a new capitalism to restore

Britain's industrial strength and a commitment to build its future in Europe. As the row between the prime minister and her two most senior ministers gathered momentum, Heseltine saw his opportunity. He had set out an economic manifesto in his 1987 book *Where There's a Will*. This called for the aggressively free-market approach of the government to be tempered by an infusion of cooperative capitalism. The British government should match the efforts of its German and Japanese counterparts in creating partnerships with industry, developing its own national champions to compete in the new global economy.[24] In 1989 he turned his attentions to Europe. As the cabinet divided, he made the link between the interventionism at home needed to sustain economic revival and the *sine qua non* of active engagement in Europe. The ERM was a powerful symbol of that link. British industry wanted currency stability: industry must not be left by the government on the sidelines while others shaped Europe's economic future.

The Challenge of Europe: Can Britain Win? was the carefully chosen title of the book Heseltine published in the summer of 1989. The title reflected his patented brand of patriotic Europeanism: Britain should back closer European integration because it was in the national self-interest. The choice was between isolation and decline in the second tier of a two-speed Europe or a leading role in shaping the future. To those who bridled at any further transfer of power to Brussels, Heseltine offered a simple image. A man alone in the desert was sovereign; he was also powerless.[25]

Thatcher's allies responded with a show of support. Within days of the publication of Heseltine's book more than 100 back-bench MPs had signed a House of Commons motion under the heading 'The Right Approach to Europe'. Sponsored by John Redwood, then a back-bench MP but later to join the so-called Eurosceptic 'bastards' in John Major's cabinet, it defended Thatcher's vision of a Europe of 'independent sovereign states'. The motion was a precursor of those tabled three years later by the Eurosceptics at the start of their war with Major over the Maastricht Treaty. In 1989, however, the wind was blowing in the direction of the pro-Europeans. In the Madrid memorandum Lawson and Howe had sown the seeds of their own and of Thatcher's destruction. Heseltine waited to reap the harvest.

CHAPTER SIX

FAREWELL

THE PRIME MINISTER'S decision to move Geoffrey Howe from the Foreign Office in July 1989 and Nigel Lawson's resignation three months later carried an air of painful inevitability. The ultimatum delivered by her two most senior ministers before the Madrid summit had given her a choice. She could leave them in place and submit; or she could seek to break the alliance and reassert her supremacy. It was true to her character that she chose the latter course. It was to be expected also that Lawson would conclude that he had nothing to gain from remaining at the Treasury. The relationship between prime minister and chancellor is the essential hinge of any government. That between Margaret Thatcher and Nigel Lawson had snapped. She failed to realize, however, that in re-establishing the outward form of her authority she would destroy its foundations. Howe and Lawson in their different ways had been the architects of Thatcherism – they had given intellectual shape and substance to her powerful instincts and undoubted courage. Once they had gone, she would be alone. No one could have guessed that within eighteen months John Major would have succeeded all three of them in turn.

As war raged in the cabinet, the economic outlook darkened. The ratcheting up of interest rates that had begun a year earlier had at last halted the house price spiral. All the other economic indicators reinforced the evidence of overheating. Lawson and his advisers had badly underestimated the strength of the boom. The decision the previous year to raise interest rates only in small, half-point, steps had proved a miscalculation. Turning the economy around required shock treatment. As it was, it would take longer, and involve much greater pain, than the Treasury had bargained for – this would be the hardest of landings. The inflation rate had jumped to 8.3 per cent by June 1989, and the Treasury unceremoniously abandoned its Budget forecast of three months earlier that the rate would be down to 5.5 per cent by the end of the year. When the distortions caused by higher interest rates were stripped out, the picture was slightly better. But the annual increase in underlying inflation was still above 6 per cent – higher than at any earlier point during Lawson's chancellorship. If inflation was the judge and jury of his policies, then the verdict was against him. The labour market offered further evidence of an unsustainable boom. Unemployment fell to a recorded 1.7 million – 6 per cent of the workforce – in September 1989. The cumulative drop since a peak of 3 million in mid-1986 was 1.4 million. But the fall brought with it the all-too-familiar pressure on wages. The trade unions had been tamed, but the British disease of wage-push inflation had not been cured. Settlements in manufacturing industry were running at 7.5 per cent a year. Earnings far outstripped productivity growth, pushing up industrial costs at a much faster rate than those of Britain's competitors. The Treasury forecast in the March 1989 Budget that the current-account deficit would stabilize at £14.5bn. It continued to increase, and the foreign exchange markets' love-affair with the pound came to an abrupt end. Lawson's futile attempts to hold sterling below DM3.00 had poisoned his relationship with the prime minister. In the event the pound reached a high of DM3.29 in February 1989 before beginning its long and painful decline. The previous DM3.00 ceiling would soon become an uncertain floor as investors retreated from the darkening economic clouds and the gathering political storm. Lawson had been right when he said that the pound's rise in 1988 was unsustainable, but that was little consolation now.

The manner of Geoffrey Howe's departure from the Foreign Office provided public testimony to the irreparable breach in Margaret Thatcher's cabinet. Throughout July 1989 there was speculation among fellow ministers and MPs at Westminster that either Howe or Lawson would be moved. Colleagues, unaware of the Madrid *démarche* but sensing the deepening conflict at the top of the cabinet, saw Howe as the most vulnerable. Her insulting treatment of her foreign secretary during ministerial meetings was an open secret among Tory MPs. Howe received assurances from David Waddington, the chief whip, that he was secure. Bernard Ingham in Downing Street appeared content to nudge along a spate of press and television reports that Thatcher had decided to keep in place her most senior ministers. A few years earlier Ingham had foreshadowed John Biffen's dismissal from the cabinet by describing him as 'semi-detached', but this time Thatcher would act without warning. Howe's confidence was reflected in a decision to return to the subject of Europe in a speech just days before the reshuffle which Thatcher had scheduled for the last week of July. Howe took head on those opposed to any further transfer of power to Brussels. Sharing sovereignty was 'about giving ourselves a bigger say in the future by accepting that we cannot always have things exactly our own way'. The alternative was 'unique control over a destiny that is diminishing and receding'. He warmed to the theme. It was impossible to see Europe as 'anything other than the necessary vehicle, the central fulcrum, the basic lever for Britain to exercise the influence it wishes to exercise in the world'.[1]

It was not the language of Bruges, but Thatcher's insistence on 24 July that he must move from the Foreign Office none the less came as a brutal shock. Their respective accounts confirm that the prime minister had determined after Madrid never again to allow her foreign secretary and chancellor to hold a gun to her head. She offered Howe the choice of the leadership of the House of Commons or the Home Office. He toyed with the idea of resigning, but temperamentally he was an insider. He still harboured hopes, albeit dwindling, that he might yet succeed her. After several hours of deliberation he accepted the post of leader of the House of Commons – with the proviso that he be also nominated deputy prime minister. The title had been held until 1987 by Lord Whitelaw but had since fallen into abeyance. John Major was catapulted from the number-two slot at the Treasury to replace Howe at the Foreign Office. Kenneth Baker, the smoothest of political operators, was the predictable choice as party chairman. Chris Patten joined the cabinet as environment secretary. His appointment was intended as a symbol of Thatcher's willingness to find room for talented ministers who had never been ideological allies. His principal task, however, would be to keep afloat her flagship – the poll tax. Norman Lamont at last reached the cabinet table, as chief secretary to the Treasury.

Within hours, the attempt to give the cabinet a fresher, softer, image had fallen apart in a welter of recriminations. All reshuffles are messy; this one, remarked a shrewd Conservative MP, had left blood on the walls as well as the carpets. Thatcher's aides made no effort to discourage the inevitable speculation at Westminster that Howe had been deliberately demoted. His allies bridled at his treatment. The day after the reshuffle it was disclosed that Thatcher had offered Howe the Home Office without reference to the incumbent Douglas Hurd. It was also said that Howe was deeply disappointed at the loss of Chevening, the foreign secretary's official country residence. Howe and his wife, Elspeth, had made it a home. Thatcher gave him instead Dorneywood, a smaller country house which she had allocated only a year earlier to Lawson. Both now had been punished for Madrid. Kenneth Baker remarked afterwards that depriving Howe of Chevening was 'an unnecessarily spiteful act which Margaret was to regret'.[2] He might have said the same about Lawson's loss of Dorneywood.

The most destructive revelation, however, came from Bernard Ingham, who disclosed that the title of deputy prime minister conferred on Howe carried with it no additional authority or status. The unambiguous implication was that the honour had been extracted against Thatcher's wishes. Ingham later would insist that he had simply been stating accurately the constitutional position – there is no formal place in the British system for a deputy to the prime minister[3] – but the journalists who gathered for the 11 a.m. briefing in his No. 10 office on the morning after the reshuffle did not miss Ingham's meaning. Howe had been accorded a 'courtesy' title. There was no guarantee that he would deputize if the prime minister was indisposed. In layman's terms, Thatcher was irreplaceable and Howe had been humoured. It was the truth, but deeply damaging for being said so publicly.

Thatcher offered private reassurance to Hurd that his position as a senior minister remained secure. No slight had been intended, she said, in offering his job to a colleague. Hurd was phlegmatic; Thatcher owed him. 'Its fine,' he said a few days later – 'I've got credit in the bank.' Others were not so sanguine. The newly promoted Chris Patten thought Thatcher's handling of the reshuffle had been disgraceful. Conservative MPs fired a warning shot across her bows: when Howe appeared for the first time in his new role as leader of the House of Commons he was loudly cheered from the Tory back benches. Labour's lead in the opinion polls meanwhile had widened to more than 10 per cent – small by subsequent standards, but a cause then for considerable alarm. The cracks in Margaret Thatcher's government were widening.

There was one person whose antipathy towards the ERM was as great as that of Margaret Thatcher. Alan Walters had been a curious choice as her first and only personal economic adviser. He had made a name for himself as a transport economist before joining the eclectic band of monetarists who advised Thatcher first in opposition and then in government. Of distinctly humble origins – his father was a manual worker in Leicester – Walters subsequently had been a lecturer at Birmingham University, the London School of Economics and Johns Hopkins University in the United States. He met the future prime minister in the 1970s when the free-market Institute of Economic Affairs provided a focal point for the monetarist challenge to the Keynesian consensus.

His appeal to Thatcher came from a passionate belief in liberal economics and a shared preference for simple truths. A senior official who worked closely with him during the 1980s put it thus: 'Walters provided the algebraic equations for her flat-earth economics.' During his first spell as her adviser in No. 10, between 1981 and 1983, his relations with the official Whitehall machine were relatively harmonious. An intuitive rather than an intellectual approach to economics brought occasional conflicts with the self-consciously methodical approach of the Treasury, but such clashes were contained within the inner circle of Nos. 10 and 11. Some officials mocked his approach to the complexities of macro-economic management. 'He's a bloody good transport economist,' they would say. His considerable influence meant he could not be ignored, however, and Peter Middleton kept him within the Whitehall machine by appointing Rachel Lomax, then one of the Treasury's rising economists, to work alongside him during these early years.

Alan Walters was sometimes right. He played an important role in persuading Thatcher to relax the monetary squeeze of the early 1980s despite the government's repeated failure to hit its chosen target for the money supply. He played a part (though not one as significant as he would later claim) in shaping the 1981 Budget. His opposition

to fixing the exchange rate was well known, but during the early
Thatcher years there was no serious debate on the issue. In 1983 he
returned to Johns Hopkins University in Baltimore and to an advisory
role at the World Bank in Washington. Later Walters was to fall into
the familiar adviser's trap of exaggerating his own influence, but most
who worked with him during this first spell at No. 10 found him
charming and unassuming, if irritatingly obstinate.

The conflict with Nigel Lawson started well after Walters had left
the No. 10 payroll. Thatcher valued his loyalty and his instincts and
kept closely in touch. To the irritation of Treasury officials, she
routed confidential cabinet papers to him via the British Embassy in
Washington. The apparent breach of official secrecy was justified on
the basis that he was an unpaid adviser. By 1985 he was supplying in
return the ammunition Thatcher needed to block Lawson's early
attempts to take sterling into the ERM. Over the succeeding years,
Walters never budged from his opposition to the mechanism. Despite,
or perhaps because of, his link to No. 10, he denounced in a stream
of articles and interviews any move to link sterling to the Deutschmark in a system of what he liked to call 'pseudo-fixed' exchange
rates. It was no accident that Thatcher chose the summer of 1988 –
the height of her row with Lawson over the exchange rate – to ask
Walters to rejoin her as a paid, if part-time, adviser. Lawson protested
strongly at the decision, but Thatcher was immovable.

The timing of Walters's eventual return – May 1989 – served only
to add fuel to the conflict. Lawson and Howe were preparing their
memorandum on the negotiating position at the Madrid summit.
Walters was on hand to resist them. By now Nicholas Ridley had
been co-opted to all the cabinet committee discussions on Europe.
He sent a series of detailed papers to No. 10 designed to show that
the ERM had failed to bring any measurable benefit to the rest of
Europe. With scant regard for the shifts in exchange rates during the
postwar period, he attributed the economic success of Germany and
Japan to the 'competitiveness' of their currencies. Britain, by contrast,
had been saddled with an 'overvalued' exchange rate. The fact that
both the yen and the Deutschmark had done nothing but appreciate
against sterling did not deter him.

At Westminster, John Smith was ever more mocking of Lawson's
subservience to the whims of an adviser. Several incidents intensified

the friction. Walters opposed the rise in interest rates to 14 per cent in the summer of 1989 which the Treasury deemed essential to stabilize sterling. There were persistent reports that he was criticizing Lawson's policies at private lunches. Walters said later that on his return to London he had approached the chancellor and suggested a thorough private discussion on the ERM to clear the air. Lawson had declined, telling Walters instead to steer clear of the media. As it was, his return reinforced the damaging suspicion in financial markets that the relationship between chancellor and prime minister was beyond repair.

Kenneth Baker, newly installed as party chairman, sought to paper over the cabinet cracks before the autumn party conference. He took as his cue Thatcher's unprecedented statement after the July reshuffle that there would be no more cabinet changes before the next general election. With unabashed disregard for the real world, he set as the conference theme 'The Right Team for Britain's Future'. When the press gathered at Conservative Central Office at the end of September for a preview of the conference, Baker was fully prepared for the questions about Thatcher's autocratic leadership. Her role, he insisted, was that of the captain of a formidable and united team. Cabinet colleagues marvelled at his audacity. 'She won't like that,' one offered a few hours later. Within weeks the careful slogan was shattered by Lawson's departure.

The Bank of England was intervening heavily, buying sterling to hold it above DM3.00. In July, Thatcher, on Walters's advice, had resisted the Treasury's suggestion of another rise in interest rates to slow the still-rapid pace of credit expansion. But publication two months later of an even worse set of trade figures – the monthly deficit had jumped to £2bn in August – and an increase in German interest rates forced her hand. On Thursday 5 October, just four days before the opening in Blackpool of the party conference, Lawson raised borrowing costs to 15 per cent. The government was back where it started, with interest rates at their highest level since November 1981. Treasury officials, lamely, said the government had not promised a soft landing for the economy after the previous year's overheating. Lawson conceded that the increase was awkward, but insisted that the government was determined to 'err on the side of caution' in the fight against inflation. Thatcher had agreed the interest rate rise with great reluctance after Walters had strongly opposed it. Her adviser declined to deny his dissent after it was reported prominently in the *Sunday Times* on the eve of the conference.[4] When Lawson arrived in Blackpool on the following day he was besieged by reporters asking whether he intended to resign. The newspapers gave him what he later described as 'the worst press of my life'. On the financial markets, the pound slid below DM3.00 for the first time since the spring of 1988.

The atmosphere in Blackpool was as brittle as at any such gathering since the ugly confrontation over economic policy between so-called Tory 'wets' and 'dries' in 1981. That conference had seen Thatcher declare that the lady was not for turning. Lawson then had been her staunchest ally. In a speech to the right-wing Selsdon Group he had derided the cabinet's wets as the purveyors of 'cold feet dressed up as high principle'. Blackpool 1989 should have been a celebration of ten triumphant years, but instead the representatives were bewildered and disgruntled. The simple truths which had delivered three election victories had lost their certainty. Thatcher sought comfort in the government's repayment of national debt, telling a dinner for party agents on the Monday evening, 'Because of Nigel and his sound finance we have a budget surplus more firmly based than at any time in our history.' The gossip among ministers shuffling between receptions in the Imperial Hotel, however, was about how long Lawson would stay. Many sympathized with his plight, but such was the fragmented nature of Thatcher's cabinet that none seemed willing to risk his own position in Lawson's defence. In public Baker offered a stream of reassurance, but he privately warned Thatcher that another rise in interest rates to defend the pound would be disastrous. He had written to the prime minister a week earlier, urging her to allow sterling to fall rather than increase borrowing costs to 15 per cent.[5] In the Empress Ballroom, the baroque centrepiece of Blackpool's Winter Gardens, Baker evoked Shakespeare's Henry V: 'He which has no stomach to this fight, let him depart.' The chancellor would be the first to take his advice.

Michael Heseltine strode effortlessly into the spotlight. During his years in the cabinet he had been a conference favourite. A natural and passionate orator, with little time on such occasions for the subtleties of politics, he invariably put himself at the head of the crusade against socialism. He no longer had a place on the conference rostrum, but his lunch-time fringe meeting at the adjacent Grand Theatre was overflowing. Saying what he knew Lawson could not, he asserted that the government could secure the cuts in interest rates needed by industry and home-owners alike only if sterling were put into the ERM. His message was carefully scripted for the small businessmen and -women who populate Conservative conferences: government aid for industry should be increased; education and training should be improved. There was a sideswipe against Lawson's claim that the current-account deficit would look after itself. The trade gap showed that Britain was not paying its way in the world – any housewife knew that. Here was a man who offered answers instead of exhortation; Heseltine's campaign was running.

By Thursday, the party faithful had rediscovered their loyalty. The chancellor insisted without irony that 'The Conservative Party never has been and never will be the party of devaluation.' He received a standing ovation. The following day Thatcher nodded in the same direction: 'As Nigel Lawson made clear yesterday, industry must not expect to find refuge in a perpetually depreciating currency.' The remarks, once again the subject of careful advance negotiation, made no mention of the ERM.

The proximate cause of Nigel Lawson's departure two weeks later was Alan Walters. The chancellor presented the prime minister with a choice: he would go unless she sacked her adviser. In the event, both departed. Walters was by now the symptom not the cause of the malaise. Lawson said later that had Thatcher dismissed her adviser he would have stayed; in truth his position was untenable.

The trigger for the explosion came in an article in the *Financial Times*. Walters provided Simon Holberton, the paper's economics correspondent, with a copy of a paper on exchange rates he had written for an American academic journal. The piece had been completed many months earlier, but Walters said it remained a faithful summary of his views. A news report, including Walters's description of the ERM as 'half-baked' and his dismissal of sterling's membership as lacking a 'minimum level of plausibility', duly appeared in the newspaper on 18 October.[6] Lawson summoned a meeting of officials to discuss the provenance of the report. Had Holberton been the instigator, or had the initiative come from Walters? The consensus was that the fault lay with Walters. The paper supplied to the *FT*, Lawson would comment after his resignation, was one of the least serious of Walters's transgressions, but 'It represented the tip of a singularly concealed iceberg, with all the destructive potential that icebergs possess.'[7] It was a gift to the opposition. John Smith ridiculed the chancellor during Treasury questions in the House of Commons on the following day. He reserved his most caustic scorn for a debate on the economy scheduled for less than a week later.

Smith's performance during the debate on 24 October was a bravura display of his rhetorical skills. He laughed at Lawson's claim only a year earlier that Britain had matched West Germany's postwar economic miracle. He mocked cruelly Walters's authority: here was 'an unelected, unappointed, alternative, chancellor'. With unintended prescience, Smith urged Lawson to confront the prime minister with a simple demand: 'Back me or sack me.' Lawson crumpled. Only three of his cabinet colleagues had turned up to sit alongside him during this torture. Some Tory back-benchers publicly endorsed Lawson's criticism of Walters. Their support, and his own attempt to dismiss his rival as a 'part-time adviser', served only to betray the chancellor's weakness.

Thatcher returned from the Commonwealth conference in Malaysia on the following day, Wednesday 25 October. Lawson had sought to alert her to his anger a few days earlier by summoning Mark Lennox-Boyd, her parliamentary private secretary, to his office. In his subsequent message to Kuala Lumpur, Lennox-Boyd had failed to convey the urgency of the situation. Anyway, Thatcher had ignored similar representations during the preceding weeks from senior Conservative MPs, including Cranley Onslow, the chairman of the back-bench 1922 Committee. Cabinet colleagues were conscious of Lawson's mood but not of his intentions. On the Monday before his resignation Lawson shared a platform with Geoffey Howe at a celebratory dinner to mark the tenth anniversary of the abolition of exchange controls. Lawson had remarked earlier on the same day that he could see little point in continuing, but Howe had not taken the words literally. On the afternoon of Thatcher's return Lawson raised his concern with her. His disquiet was brushed aside.

The two met three times during the following day, but both had made up their minds during the first encounter at 9 a.m. Lawson put to her the choice she had to make. If Walters were to go, Thatcher replied, 'That would destroy my authority.'[8] Later the same day Thatcher tried persuasion by reminding Lawson that she had once indicated he could take over from Robin Leigh-Pemberton as governor of the Bank of England. Surely he did not want to give up that prospect? Even before that offer, Lawson had told his ministerial colleagues and offficials at the Treasury that he would be leaving. Norman Lamont, the chief secretary, pleaded with him to stay, arguing that the ERM was not important enough an issue to sacrifice his career. Peter Lilley, the economics secretary, assumed that they would all be departing: Peter Thorneycroft's team had done so when he had resigned as chancellor in 1958. It was explained to Lilley that the world had changed: loyalty was out of fashion.

Lawson's officials regretted his departure. Not all of them liked him, but nearly all respected him. He was a chancellor who understood economics. He was arrogant but, usually, willing to listen. His influence in the government had restored the Treasury to its traditional pre-eminence in Whitehall. Most concluded that his departure was inevitable, however. Middleton had been dismayed by the warfare between Nos. 10 and 11. Views in the Bank of England were mixed. Eddie George had been horrified by the relaxation of monetary policy in 1988, and was dismayed that Lawson had failed to entrench the low inflation of the mid-1980s. Others in Threadneedle Street resented Lawson's interference in the market operations which had long been the preserve of the Bank. Lawson's intellect and his grasp of economics, however, attracted considerable respect. In earlier years Lawson had treated Robin Leigh-Pemberton with undisguised condescension. Latterly the two had become, albeit unequal, allies. Leigh-Pemberton, by now entirely out of sympathy with Thatcher's approach to Europe, regretted the resignation. His response also revealed a certain affection. Lawson had long since sold his London house, leaving him nowhere to stay in the capital once he moved out of No. 11. Risking Thatcher's wrath, Leigh-Pemberton offered him the loan of the Bank's flat in the City's New Change. In the event the former chancellor found lodgings elsewhere.

The exchange of letters which on 26 October came with the official 6 p.m. announcement of the chancellor's departure laid bare the rift between Lawson and Thatcher. The first two sentences of Lawson's letter encapsulated the essential point: 'The successful conduct of economic policy is possible only if there is, and is seen to be, full agreement between the prime minister and the chancellor of the exchequer. Recent events have confirmed that this essential requirement cannot be satisfied so long as Alan Walters remains your personal economic adviser.' Thatcher's reply was a flight from reality: 'There is no difference in our basic economic beliefs, and Britain's economy is vastly stronger as a result of the policies which you and I and the government have planned and pursued together.' Kenneth Baker adopted the same tack. It was a question of personalities not policies, he explained on the evening news bulletins. However, the party chairman told the prime minister that Walters also would have to depart. Baker telephoned the adviser in the United States with a suggested resignation statement.[9] Walters agreed. He would return occasionally the following year as, in Thatcher's words, a 'family friend', but Lawson's departure had robbed him of influence.

Nigel Lawson's resignation speech a week later stilled the House of Commons. He offered a powerful exposition of the case for sterling's participation in the ERM. The exchange rate was an essential element of financial discipline: 'There is nothing novel, of course, in any of this. The House will recall the classical period of the gold standard, before the First World War; the Bretton Woods system after the Second World War; and, of course, over the past ten years, within the European context, the EMS.' For Britain, linking the pound to the Deutschmark would 'signally enhance the credibility of our anti-inflationary resolve'. So too would an independent Bank of England. On both counts he had tried, and failed, to persuade the prime minister. ERM membership would also provide the political influence needed to promote Europe's future as a community of freely cooperating nation-states. 'Within that context, it is vital that we maximize Britain's influence in the Community so as to ensure that it becomes the liberal free-market Europe in which we on the Conservative benches so firmly believe.'

The most telling section, however, was the indictment of the way that Thatcher had come to run her government. It had long been said in private that she had come to regard dissent as synonymous with disloyalty. Now her former chancellor told the House of Commons, 'For our system of cabinet government to work effectively, the prime minister of the day must appoint ministers whom he or she trusts and then leave them to carry out the policy. Whenever differences of view emerge, as they are bound to do from time to time, they should be resolved privately and, whenever appropriate, collectively.'[10]

Few of those who remained at the cabinet table disagreed. The advice went unheeded by Margaret Thatcher, but she would soon understand what she had lost. Lawson had worked with her for fifteen years in opposition and in government. If the row over the exchange rate was put to one side, there remained a shared vision of Britain's future: an enterprise economy; free markets; lower public spending, taxes and borrowing; and the primacy of the individual over the state. Lawson's influence stretched well beyond economics. She listened to him on privatization, the trade unions, the shape of the welfare state, reform of the health service, education policy, and much else. There were not so many allies left.

Nigel Lawson believed that history would be kinder than his contemporaries in its judgement of his chancellorship, commenting in his resignation speech, 'As for my own record I have no doubt that I have made my share of mistakes; but I am content to be judged when the passage of time has provided a greater sense of perspective than is possible today.' Two front pages of the *Daily Mail* catch the breathtaking collapse in his reputation. The first, on 16 March 1988, pronounced that his tax-cutting Budget had placed him 'among the great political entrepreneurs of all time'. The second, eighteen months later, on 10 October 1989, declared simply 'This bankrupt chancellor'. Such is the sand on which political fortunes are built.

Lawson's reputation was a victim of his own rhetoric. His record is much better when measured against the back-cloth of the real world than against the proud boasts of his chancellorship. If he had not claimed so much, the subsequent criticism would have been similarly measured. As it was, 'the Lawson boom' joined 'the Barber boom' as a term of disparagement in the lexicon of Britain's economic history. The chancellor was too eager to proclaim, and to believe in, a permanent transformation in Britain's economic performance; too dismissive of the evidence of an old-fashioned spending boom. He was right to abandon the malign neglect of sterling of the first Thatcher term, but wrong to become transfixed by a particular rate against the Deutschmark.

Lawson the intelligent politician tempered ideology with realism. An obsessive quest for a simple set of policy rules was matched only by his capacity to ignore such self-imposed constraints. He sought to contain inflation rather than extinguish it, and he did so with some success until 1988. In 1985 the chancellor had told the Treasury and Civil Service Committee, 'I do not believe that there is any salvation for this country through progressive depreciation of the currency.' [11] Then oil prices tumbled and Lawson allowed a 25 per cent devaluation of the pound against the Deutschmark. A depreciation was both necessary and inevitable if Britain was to repair the damage inflicted on industry during the first Thatcher recession, but a weaker pound required a discipline in fiscal policy and a degree of self-restraint which Lawson found impossible.

It is possible, though far from certain, that, had Thatcher given way in November 1985, ERM membership would have sheltered the economy from the subsequent storms. Lawson certainly identifies the 1986 devaluation as responsible for the subsequent upsurge in inflation two years later. By his account, the Treasury's own post-mortem into the boom indicated that both the exchange rate and interest rates should have been higher from 1986 onwards. The Treasury had underestimated the extent of the fall in the savings ratio which underpinned the consumer boom, and had also not foreseen a surge in investment spending. Interest rates should have been on average 2 per cent higher and the exchange rate 10 per cent higher in 1987/88.[12] It was also true that the failure of Treasury economists to grasp just how fast the economy was growing in early 1988 played a significant role in the subsequent mistakes. Sterling's depreciation was, however, only part of a more complicated picture. Lawson deregulated and liberalized the economy and then badly underestimated the scale of the spending and house-price explosion which the reforms unleashed. Personal pride replaced objectivity in his dispute with Thatcher over the ERM. The ratcheting-down of interest rates in 1988 and the tax cuts in that year's Budget were unforced errors.

Lawson's supply-side reforms present a more enduring legacy. Their later struggles over the exchange rate belied his pivotal role in forcing through Thatcher's revolution. He was influential or instrumental in the abolition of exchange and credit controls and in a radical liberalization of the financial services industry. He was the principal architect of a privatization programme which redefined the boundaries between state and private sector, a tax-reformer as well as a tax-cutter, and one of the firmest advocates of curbs on the power of trade unions. Soon after he had gone, Thatcher protested that Nigel Lawson had been 'unassailable'. That was true for about a year after the 1987 election. Then he took his eye off the ball, and, as one cabinet colleague was to remark, the prime minister promptly kicked it away.

CHAPTER SEVEN

Too Late

GIVEN THE MANNER of his predecessor's departure, it was no surprise that John Major's appointment as chancellor was marked by a sterling crisis. The pound, which had been weakening throughout the autumn, dropped sharply on the news of Lawson's resignation. The new chancellor was virtually unknown outside Westminster, so many saw in his appointment the transfer to 10 Downing Street of the principal levers of economic management. The prospect that sterling would enter the ERM appeared to have receded, and the damaging expectation in the City was that the pound henceforth would be allowed to find its own, inevitably lower, level. As it happened, the currency traders misjudged the new chancellor and underestimated the pressures which were now building on the prime minister.

Major was pleased to return to the Treasury. He insisted that he had enjoyed his brief sojourn as foreign secretary, but he had seemed ill at ease with the self-confident diplomats of King Charles Street. His humble background jarred with the Oxbridge self-assurance of his officials. For their part the mandarins had seen in the sacking of Geoffrey Howe a decision by Margaret Thatcher to conduct foreign policy from No. 10. They feared a destructive collision with Britain's European partners, a return to impotent isolation. During the summer months of 1989 and at the Kuala Lumpur Commonwealth summit in early October, the influence of Charles Powell was daily more visible. One senior diplomat remarked caustically that he had instructed his office to refer all important decisions to No. 10: 'After all, Charles is running the show now.' So the appointment in Major's place of the Old Etonian former diplomat Douglas Hurd was greeted with scarcely disguised relief by the Foreign Office establishment. Thatcher's behaviour during the July reshuffle had not dented Hurd's standing. To his many admirers, his patrician calm marked him out as one of a dwindling band of cabinet ministers with an authority independent of the prime minister. A former diplomat, an erstwhile lieutenant to Edward Heath during the early 1970s, and an avowed pro-European, Hurd had always wanted the Foreign Office: 'Douglas has kept the key in his waistcoat pocket for the last thirty years,' a ministerial colleague said at the time. Most importantly, his instincts and temperament promised to act as a check on Thatcher's rising hostility to all things European.

John Major's remarkable political ascent had begun two years earlier, with his appointment after the 1987 election as chief secretary to the Treasury. Thatcher, ever in search of potential successors who would not threaten her own position, had been impressed by his performance as a junior social security minister. He had entered parliament as the MP for Huntington only in 1979, but he quickly established himself as a maker of influential friends. With a natural aversion to ideological debate, he had rarely displayed any doubts about the Thatcher revolution. She had decided that her eventual successor would be chosen from the next generation. In her mind was the thought that, if Major indeed emerged as the leading candidate, his chance would not come for five or perhaps ten years. She would leave 10 Downing Street at a time of her own choosing. Her assessment of her protégé was wrong: she would discover too late that his views on Europe, the economy and social policy were not her own but instead those of the one-nation centre.

As his understudy at the Treasury, Major had respected Lawson's powerful intellect, but he had considered the chancellor remote from the small platoons of Conservatism. Lawson had no time for the aspiring young couples or the thrifty pensioners who were Major's kind of Tory. The young politician from Brixton considered that the tax cuts in the 1988 Budget had been unfairly skewed towards the 'have-lots'. After his own Budget in 1990, he was heard remarking of his predecessor, 'He has never known what it is like to run out of money on a Thursday.'

As chief secretary, Major had proved himself an astute negotiator. His political skills and an easy grasp of detail served him well in the annual bargaining over public spending. Kenneth Clarke was an early admirer of Major's willingness to banish officials from negotiations with his cabinet colleagues so as to strike a political deal. This period also revealed another important clue to Major's political outlook.

Most of his predecessors had been concerned only to reduce the level of public spending. Major took a different approach, insisting that the Treasury's limits on Whitehall budgets should not be an excuse for shoddy public services. He saw the scope for a revolution in the way the public sector was managed, exposing it to market disciplines and to private-sector skills. The seeds of the Citizen's Charter were sown in a speech he gave in June 1989.[1]

Returning as chancellor in the autumn, Major had two priorities: to reassure the financial markets of his resolve to bring down inflation and to avoid if possible another increase in interest rates. He was serious about inflation. Breaking with the price spirals of the 1970s had been a recurring theme of his political career. In Major's mind rising prices were as socially corrosive as they were economically damaging. The victims were the thrifty and the elderly. So in his first speech as chancellor he was unequivocal: 'All aspects of policy will be directed to bringing inflation down. Reducing it is never easy, but it is absolutely necessary.' Coining what was to become an oft-repeated phrase, he added, 'The harsh truth is that if the policy isn't hurting it isn't working.' And, for the benefit of the currency dealers, 'A declining exchange rate pushes up prices so I favour a firm exchange rate. The budgetary position and the present level of interest rates are such as to keep the exchange rate firm. And our tactics in the foreign exchange markets are designed to check fluctuations which are of no economic significance.'[2]

Margaret Thatcher, however, did little to allay the speculation that she, rather than the new chancellor, would decide policy towards the exchange rate. Appearing outside No. 10 on the day after Lawson's resignation, she was unrepentant: 'We have an excellent new team. It will be business as usual and we shall go steadily forward,' she declared. The succeeding weekend brought a cacophony of discordant notes. During an unrepentant, at times surreal, television encounter with Brian Walden, the prime minister affected to be bemused by Lawson's resignation. It was obvious, she insisted, that Alan Walters had had the status of a mere adviser, while Lawson had been 'unassailable'. As to sterling's membership of the ERM, that depended on whether Britain's European partners met their commitments to liberalize their capital markets: 'We shall go in when it's fair,' she told her inquisitor. 'Never,' she might have said, as she recited a list of conditions which betrayed her disdain for the entire European project. Her colleagues could not fail to notice that throughout the interview she referred not to the European Community of the 1980s but to the Common Market that the Conservatives had applied to join in the 1960s.[3]

Douglas Hurd, using some of the credit he had banked after the summer reshuffle, responded by asserting his own authority. As foreign secretary, he remarked, his relationship with the prime minister would be 'loyal and cooperative but not subservient'. Geoffrey Howe was less restrained, warning in a speech in Bath that it was essential that the government 'stuck in good faith' to the Madrid commitment to the ERM if it was to retain the confidence of the rest of Europe.[4] Thatcher later referred to Howe's speech as an act of 'calculated malice', but the deputy prime minister had been careful to clear his words in advance with both Hurd and Major. There was also visible concern on the back benches about the prime minister's autocratic style. Cranley Onslow, the chairman of the powerful 1922 Committee of back-bench MPs, was deputed to deliver a warning to the prime minister. During a Downing Street lunch on 30 October, Onslow and his colleagues on the 1922 executive called for a more transparently collective approach to decision-making. Only hours later, however, Bernard Ingham was abruptly dismissive of the suggestion, telling political journalists at Westminster that Thatcher would continue 'leading from the front'. Robin Leigh-Pemberton meanwhile made a rare television appearance in an attempt to reassure the financial markets: 'I must emphasize that I am not easy about a fall in the pound.'[5] The traders, however, ignored his warning that the Bank would resist any further speculative attacks on sterling.

The new chancellor's first appearance in the House of Commons on the following day was overshadowed by the eloquent dissent of his predecessor's resignation speech. After hurried meetings with Thatcher and further warnings from the Bank, it was decided that Major would stress a commitment to a 'firm exchange rate'. The agreed text said that the defeat of inflation remained the government's priority, but sterling would participate in the ERM once the conditions laid down at Madrid had been met. The ERM was no panacea,

Major insisted, and the circumstances would have to be right if it was to be in Britain's interests to join. That meant respecting the Madrid decision: 'We will join the ERM when the level of UK inflation is significantly lower, there is capital liberalization in the Community, and real progress has been made towards completion of the single market . . . But there should be no doubt: when these conditions are met we will join.'[6]

After a short respite, however, sterling faced a renewed battering. Confidence was collapsing as a threatened challenge to Thatcher's leadership reinforced the impression in the financial markets that the malaise in her government might prove terminal. At the beginning of 1989 sterling had stood at DM3.28, but by late December it had slumped by 17 per cent to DM2.72. The devaluation decisively undercut the Treasury's remaining hopes of a rapid downturn in the inflation rate. Major attempted to calm the storm when he presented the Autumn Statement in mid-November. The Treasury forecast painted as much optimism as credibility would allow on the darkening economic canvas. It suggested that the economy would slow sharply in 1990, but that a recession would be avoided. Inflation, then at 7.7 per cent, would fall to below 6 per cent within twelve months and the current-account deficit would begin to shrink. It was an implausible scenario. The back-bench Treasury and Civil Service Committee listened to the chancellor and his officials with knowing scepticism. In its subsequent report on the Treasury's view of the economic outlook, the committee put its previous inflation forecasts side by side with the actual out-turns over successive years. The predictions had consistently proved over-optimistic, prompting the MPs to comment drily, 'Repetition in the face of failure has not added credibility to this forecast.'[7]

Treasury officials could hardly complain, since they also were decidedly less sanguine than they would admit publicly. Even before the ink was dry on the Autumn Statement forecast, they told the chancellor he might have to raise interest rates again. When sterling's slide resumed in late December, Peter Middleton and Terence Burns urged Major to respond. Some believed he should have acted even sooner. Andrew Tyrie, a special, or political, adviser, was among those who thought that rates should have been raised to 16 per cent, or even to 17 per cent, immediately after Lawson's resignation. The departure of Lawson could then have been blamed for the increase, and Major would have taken the credit for the subsequent reductions. The Treasury's anxiety was shared by the Bank of England, and by early January Major was under intense pressure to accept the advice of his officials. Thatcher, however, promised fierce opposition. The message from No. 10 was that she would allow the Treasury to use the foreign currency reserves to support the pound, but she had had enough with Nigel Lawson of being forced to put up interest rates every time sterling fell. Her influence was apparent in Major's speech in the House of Commons at the end of the Queen's Speech debate in late November. By then sterling had fallen by 4 per cent in as many weeks, but the chancellor's text made no mention of a commitment to defend the exchange rate. Nor did he display any optimism about the prospects for membership of the ERM: there was 'much to be done' before the Madrid conditions could be met, he told MPs.[8] Amid consternation at the Treasury and Bank at the policy shift, his officials blamed No. 10.

Major would later assert that common sense, not weakness, had been behind his decision not to tighten the monetary squeeze. Here was a political chancellor, closely attuned to the mood at Westminster as well as that in the dealing-rooms of the City. He took the view that another rise in borrowing costs would have intensified the panic on the Conservative back benches, further undermining the fragile stability of the government. That in turn might well have triggered a much deeper crisis of confidence in sterling. Doing nothing offered a better prospect of restoring calm. He was fortunate – the pressure on sterling abated and the gamble paid off. The experience had scarred him, though. Before returning to the Treasury he had been a bystander in the battle between Lawson and Thatcher over the ERM. Now he had seen at first hand the destructive potential of the foreign exchange markets. It would not be long before he too would be seeking a shelter for the pound.

There are moments in history when the right decision appears so blindingly obvious that it requires neither debate nor analysis. The consensus becomes fixed, circumstances are ignored. So it was with sterling's entry to the ERM. For the previous eight years the exchange rate had been damagingly disruptive. The speculative storms on currency markets had frustrated the government's political ambitions and derailed its hopes of defeating inflation. An administration committed to sound money had presided over a progressive devaluation of the currency. Fixing sterling's value against the Deutschmark seemed the obvious answer. There seemed little point at this stage in stopping to consider whether the time was right.

John Major's approach in persuading Margaret Thatcher would prove an instructive harbinger of the political style he later would bring to 10 Downing Street. Uncomfortable with intellectual abstractions, Major is a natural problem-solver. His habit at the start of a meeting is to draw a line down the centre of a single sheet of paper. As the discussion progresses he will mark the 'pluses' on one side and the 'minuses' on the other, making his own decision only after a careful weighing of the balance on either side of the line. As he turned his attention to the ERM in early 1990, politically he was in a strong position. Thatcher had survived the demotion of Howe and the departure of Lawson, but she could not risk the loss of Major. He would capitalize on that calculation, though in his own quietly persistent way. Lawson and Howe had been driven to confrontation with the prime minister over sterling; Major would work with Douglas Hurd to bring her round gently. Peter Middleton noticed Major's powers of persuasion early on, telling Whitehall colleagues that the new chancellor was 'good at getting his way in cabinet'. Eddie George was also an admirer, remarking that Major was 'the clearest-thinking politician I have met'.

The credit squeeze imposed by high interest rates was hurting but not yet visibly working. It was clear by 1990 that the process of disinflation would be more painful and protracted than Major had realized. It did not take him long to conclude that the ERM offered the only real prospect of reconstructing a credible economic policy. On his return to the Treasury he had asked for a review of the alternatives, but by late January it was obvious that all faced serious obstacles. Lawson's resignation had removed any possibility of an exchange rate target independent of the ERM. Nor could Major resurrect the money supply targets which his predecessor had abandoned five years earlier. The City would be incredulous, and in any event Major had no time for monetarist ideology. He was initially attracted to the idea of direct controls on credit as a possible substitute for high interest rates. But, despite the clamour at Westminster for a less painful remedy, he was persuaded that such measures would be ineffectual. The Treasury view was that in the new world of liberalized financial markets quantitative controls on credit would work only if they raised the price of money – in other words, through higher interest rates. The more obvious answer, as Ian Gilmour urged, was to increase taxes. A tighter fiscal policy would have allowed a relaxation of the monetary squeeze. This was not the moment, however, for Thatcher's government to admit that it had been wrong in 1988. She, after all, had described the swingeing tax reductions in that year's Budget as 'brilliant, brilliant, brilliant'.

During his final year, Lawson had explored another option – he had pressed Thatcher to grant independence to the Bank of England. He had argued that the transfer of control over interest rate policy to the Bank would provide an alternative to the ERM as an anchor for the government's anti-inflation strategy. The government would buy itself precious credibility by signalling that henceforth there would be no political interference in the setting of interest rates. Thatcher had rejected the proposal outright as humiliatingly defeatist. Major, conscious of a widening rift in the Conservative Party over economic policy and Europe, was not convinced that she would change her mind. He also had serious doubts of his own, voicing scepticism that it would be possible to secure effective parliamentary accountability over an independent Bank.

For a time he looked at one other possibility – the publication in the March 1990 Budget of a formal target for inflation. During the 1980s the government had sought to hit a series of 'intermediate' targets such as the money supply or the exchange rate. But, if the object was low inflation, why not set a specific goal for prices? The proposal met several objections – not least the fact that the Treasury would be obliged to set the target initially at an embarrassingly high level in order to have any hope of meeting it. Major's officials also advised that a domestic inflation target would not sit easily alongside a fixed exchange rate if he did succeed in taking sterling into the ERM.

So all routes took the chancellor back to winning over the prime minister to ERM membership. Inflation was rising and the pound was falling – if the government retreated from the commitment made in Madrid it would exacerbate both trends. And Major saw other, quite separate, advantages in a stable pound. He had been uncomfortable with Lawson's view that the service sector of the economy offered the best opportunities for growth and employment. Intuitively, he saw the widening trade deficit as a reflection of the weakness of Britain's manufacturing industry. The decision to allow the pound to appreciate so rapidly in the early 1980s, which had brought with it the first ever deficits in Britain's trade in manufactures, had been a mistake. Major was attentive to the demand from leading industrial companies for a stable exchange rate environment in which they could plan their investment and export programmes. Such stability would be achievable only within the ERM. Lawson's reliance on interest rates had seen him mocked as a 'one-club golfer'. His successor felt like the player who arrives at the first tee clutching a putter.

A gradual recovery in sterling's value during the first months of 1990 provided scant consolation. The pound was still 10 per cent lower than a year earlier, and inflation would soon defy the forecast in the Autumn Statement that the worst had passed. The annual rate reached 8.1 per cent in March and would not peak for another six months, when it reached 10.9 per cent. It was clear that, unless the government came up with a credible anti-inflation strategy, sterling would soon reappear in the speculators' sights.

Major set out in earnest to win the argument with his Downing Street neighbour after his first and only Budget, in March 1990. Apart from one or two personal touches, such as tax relief for small savers, the Budget was essentially a holding operation. The Medium Term Financial Strategy (it was still published each year, even if its original monetarist *raison d'être* had long since disappeared) proclaimed in its first sentence that its central objective remained 'the defeat of inflation'. In a hollow echo of those early certainties a decade earlier, it added, 'Action to maintain the soundness of the currency remains a prime duty of government.'[9] But a prolonged homily on the destructive and capricious nature of rising prices and a new target for the narrow money supply measure M0 could hardly disguise the absence of an economic policy.

It was clear to Major that, if the Madrid conditions were interpreted literally, sterling would have to remain outside the ERM for at least another year. So he began the process of redefining the terms – focusing above all on the condition that Britain's inflation rate should first be close to the level of the average of the rates of its European partners. Treasury officials began to signal that the conditions should not be interpreted rigidly. The relevant comparison was not between Britain's retail price index (RPI) and the recorded inflation rates elsewhere in Europe. The RPI was distorted by the inclusion of mortgage interest rates, so, in assessing progress towards meeting the Madrid criteria, the Treasury would look instead at the lower 'underlying' rate of inflation, which excluded housing. Over the following months, this formula was to be further modified when officials indicated that it might not be necessary to wait until Britain's performance matched that of its European partners. Instead it could be sufficient for the respective inflation rates to begin converging. Later in the summer the original terms were stretched to breaking-point – the prospect rather than the reality of such convergence might well be enough to satisfy the conditions.

The chancellor worked closely with Douglas Hurd. The two had lunched together occasionally when Hurd was at the Home Office. Now they established a routine of private working breakfasts in the foreign secretary's residence in Carlton Gardens. Hurd put a compelling foreign policy case for an early decision. At the Strasbourg summit in December 1989 Thatcher had tried vainly to prevent the other eleven governments from calling an intergovernmental conference to negotiate the changes to the Treaty of Rome needed for a single currency. The overwhelming view in the Foreign Office was that, as long as it stayed outside the ERM, Britain would be without influence in the future monetary arrangements of Europe.

Hurd was also anxious to begin repairing relations with Bonn. The process of reunification which had begun with the fall of the Berlin Wall in November 1989 had drawn out the worst of Thatcher's paranoia about a resurgent Germany. With studied disregard for German sensitivities, she had repeatedly insisted that the four Berlin powers retain a powerful say in the terms of reunification. She had further angered Chancellor Helmut Kohl by publicly demanding a new treaty to guarantee Poland's borders. Thatcher sought President François Mitterrand's backing for her stance, arguing that a new Franco-British axis was an essential counterpoint to a resurgent

Germany. At one meeting in Paris, she produced for Mitterrand a map showing the various configurations of Germany over the previous century. The map offered little reassurance for the future, she told the French president.[10] To Hurd's irritation, Mitterrand would occasionally play up to her, half-promising to take a similarly robust stance in his dealings with Kohl. Once again, however, she underestimated the Franco-German alliance. And, like George Bush and Mikhail Gorbachev, Mitterrand knew that the tide of history could not be halted. Hurd found it hard to conceal his dismay at Thatcher's intransigence. Like most in her government, he considered it essential to lock the new Germany into the European Community and into NATO. If there were dangers, they lay in an approach which would encourage Germany to rediscover its nationalism, to look eastwards rather than westwards. Kohl wanted a European Germany, but Thatcher feared a German Europe.

In March 1990 Hurd travelled to Bonn to repair some of the damage. His comment afterwards that the two governments had put behind them a 'substantial patch of misunderstanding' was directed as much towards Thatcher as to the outside world. Michael Heseltine meanwhile exploited the obvious tensions within the cabinet by launching a lightly coded attack on the prime minister. In a speech devoted to the implications of German reunification, he argued that the dramatic changes which had followed the fall of the Berlin Wall demanded closer not looser ties within the Community. 'In this time of dramatic change,' he told an audience in Brussels, 'we all need to reaffirm our commitment to the European purpose.' His answer to the fast-changing political landscape was to call for an acceleration of the monetary and political integration which Thatcher was now determined to block.[11]

For all these concerns about political isolation, Hurd counselled Major to press the economic rather than the political case for the ERM: after Madrid, anything that bore the imprint of the Foreign Office would not get a hearing in No. 10. Major embarked on a tour of European capitals to establish personal relationships with his counterparts. He carefully explored their views on sterling's participation in the ERM and sought to gauge the extent to which they might accommodate London's views on monetary union. The perspective he brought back to London confirmed Hurd's assessment:

outside the ERM Britain would not have a voice in the forthcoming intergovernmental conference on monetary union. Equally obvious was the fact that a 'competing currencies' plan for monetary union, drawn up by Nigel Lawson as an alternative to the Delors blueprint, had little if any support elsewhere in Europe.

Among Treasury officials the economic case for the ERM was obvious – too obvious. The late 1980s boom had destroyed the government's anti-inflation strategy. It needed an anchor for policy which would restore its credibility. By 1990 most of the options had been explored or discarded. The Treasury had been exhausted and distracted by the power struggle between Thatcher and Lawson. So, once Major had decided that sterling should be put into the ERM, that basic judgement was not seriously questioned. In retrospect, some officials would see that as a grievous mistake. When the idea had first been seriously mooted, in 1985, the expectation had been that sterling would join the mechanism at a point when inflation was low and economic growth steady. It had also been assumed that the British and German economies would be at roughly the same point in the economic cycle. Now the Treasury was planning entry at the point when inflation was unusually high and the economy was heading for recession. There was also a looming divergence between the German and British economies: reunification in Germany would drive up interest rates, while the impending recession in Britain would within a year demand a progressive relaxation of the monetary squeeze imposed by Lawson. The Treasury was not oblivious to such conflicts. Andrew Tyrie was among those who spelled out the potential obstacles, arguing that the moment for Britain to fix the exchange rate was at the start of an economic upswing not while it stood on the threshold of a downturn. It should also wait until the anchor of the system – the Deutschmark – was relatively stable.

Collectively, however, the Treasury was caught in the mind-set of the moment. The political imperatives pointed to membership, and the economic case against did not appear compelling. Peter Middleton took the view – as he had done in 1985 – that politics demanded a decision on whether economic policy could be conducted effectively within the ERM. The answer he gave was yes. Terence Burns offered roughly the same assessment. 'The politics were such that, provided the risks were not too great, it was worth joining,' Middleton was to comment later. And, if membership carried risks, there were also considerable hazards in standing aside. Were the foreign exchange markets to sense vacillation in Whitehall, the pound could go into free fall. The choice then would be yet higher interest rates or another surge in the inflation rate. So the Treasury was carried along by what seemed the logic of events. As one of its senior officials would remark ruefully, 'We made the classic error. When you are totally focused on doing something you forget to ask yourself whether it is the right thing to do.' A fellow official showed unintended prescience when he remarked in the summer of 1990 that 'Everyone agrees. So we must be wrong.'

Opinions in the Bank of England covered a wider spectrum, but the prevailing view corresponded with the Treasury's. Robin Leigh-Pemberton was persuaded of both the economic and the political case for the ERM. In the spring of 1990 he made no secret of his position. In evidence to the Treasury and Civil Service Committee after the Budget, the Bank governor offered a deliberately upbeat assessment of the speed with which the Madrid conditions could be met. Apart from the 'predominant consideration' of a reduction in inflation, the other criteria were details. He then spelled out the reinterpretation of the Madrid formula which would allow early entry. The requirement was not to reduce Britain's inflation rate to the level prevailing in other ERM countries. Instead, 'The way the trend is going would justify us joining ... the very act of us joining would probably give a degree of impetus to confidence and therefore, ultimately, to continuing downward pressure on the inflation rate.'[12] Eddie George, by now appointed deputy governor, was less enthusiastic. Wary of investing too much credibility in an exchange rate target, George would still have preferred an economic policy based on discretion rather than rules. He believed that interest rates should be set with regard to a range of monetary and economic indicators, rather than tied to a single lodestar. He had been dismayed when Lawson subordinated interest rate decisions to the effort to shadow the Deutschmark. Nor was he an enthusiast for European integration. In mid-1990, however, he did not openly oppose ERM entry. Instead he accepted grudgingly that it was a fair risk when set against the political capital the government required in the forthcoming negotiations on a single currency.

This broad if uneven consensus was shared in the wider world of business and politics. Industry, looking forward to the opportunities which would come from the single European market, was fearful of British exclusion from the single currency project. There was no shortage of metaphors to illuminate the risk that Britain might be about to repeat the historic mistake that it had made when it had stood aside from the founding of the Community at the Messina conference thirty-five years earlier: the government would once again miss the European train; Britain would be trapped in the slow-lane of a two-speed Europe, relegated to the Community's second division. The Confederation of British Industry never tired of reminding the government that, as boom once again turned to bust, industry needed the assurance of a more stable economic environment. In the City, banks and other financial institutions voiced fears that London's pre-eminence as a financial centre would be jeopardized. The opposition Labour Party fell under the same spell. Neil Kinnock saw in a commitment to a stable pound the potential to banish fears that a Labour administration would embark on an inflationary spending spree. And, as long as the Thatcher government did not join, the ERM could be exploited by the opposition to prise open the divisions in the Conservative Party over Europe.

Thatcher's conversion was anything but smooth. In their regular discussions in No. 10, Major found the prime minister alternately reasonable and irrational. For every step forward there was always the risk of her taking two steps back. One such occasion came in February 1990. A senior Treasury aide briefed selected journalists that the initiative had now passed from prime minister to chancellor: Thatcher would no longer resist if Major pressed the issue. This analysis was premature – a calculated attempt by one of Major's aides to 'bounce' Thatcher. Its appearance in the press prompted a strong denial from Bernard Ingham, who told political journalists that German reuni-fication might well be so disruptive of the foreign exchange markets that there would be no ERM to join. Nicholas Ridley, now the trade and industry secretary, sought to keep alive the prime minister's hostility. He was appalled that he had been overlooked for the Treasury in favour of Major, and told colleagues that the new chancellor was an intellectual lightweight with little real understanding of economics. He saw Hurd as the symbol of Foreign Office appeasement in Europe. During the spring and summer of 1990 he bombarded Thatcher with admonitions to ignore the advice of the chancellor and foreign secretary. Alan Walters did likewise. Though no longer employed as an adviser, he would see the prime minister during his occasional visits to London. He set about writing a book to dramatize the risks of linking sterling to the Deutschmark. John Redwood, the former head of her No. 10 policy unit and now a middle-ranking minister in Ridley's department, was among a handful of others who counselled against any attempt to buck the markets.

Thatcher's position was weakening, however. Her strident anti-Europeanism was fuelling the unrest on the Conservative back benches. There were many who concurred with her hostility to the grand ambitions of France and Germany. Among the older generation at Westminster it was not difficult to find those who shared her nightmare of a monolithic European superstate dominated by a resurgent Germany. But at this point the centre of gravity in the Conservative Party tilted towards the realists – those who favoured engagement over confrontation. The fall of the Berlin Wall had removed the old certainties. While Thatcher still spoke in glowing terms of the transatlantic alliance, George Bush and Helmut Kohl were talking of a new special relationship. The telegrams from Washington told the Foreign Office that Britain's influence in the White House would depend henceforth on a leading role in Europe. As the NATO alliance moved to hold out the hand of friendship to the erstwhile Communist states of central and eastern Europe, it was clear that the shape of the new Europe was being decided in Washington and Bonn. In the Conservative Party there were zealots on both sides, but 'We may not like it but we have to be part of it' provided the most apt description of the balance of opinion towards Europe. As the cracks began to show, Douglas Hurd deployed his formidable diplomatic skills to dampen talk of renewed confrontations within the cabinet. But he was not shy of staking out his own ground, remarking in the spring of 1990, 'I see the prime minister very often and I think that we work together very well. But neither of us dictates the other's phraseology. I think that is as it should be.'[13]

This gathering storm over Europe was accompanied by a growing anger among the electorate with the government's policies at home. Mortgage rates were stuck firmly at 15 per cent and house prices were falling. The introduction of the poll tax at levels twice those promised just a year earlier was producing an unprecedented public backlash. Cabinet ministers were admitting freely that scrapping the property-based domestic rating system in favour of a flat-rate local government tax had been a ghastly mistake. Some thought the answer was for the Treasury to pour billions of pounds into additional funding to allow the local authorities to reduce the bills. Others, even at this early stage, judged the position irrecoverable. Chris Patten, the environment secretary, defended the tax with a heavy heart while demanding more cash from the Treasury. Major was sympathetic but constrained by the worsening economic outlook. Thatcher helped neither. 'If only she would just go away for a few months we could sort the damn thing out,' Patten told a colleague at the time. Another cabinet minister spoke bluntly: 'She's mad, mad,' he exploded after the latest in a series of fruitless cabinet committee meetings had failed to find an escape route.

Labour reaped the electoral rewards. Through the spring and summer its opinion lead went from fifteen to twenty and, for a time, to twenty-five points. In March it scored its biggest by-election success since 1935, capturing the prosperous Midland seat of Mid-Staffordshire on a 21 per cent swing against the government. Cabinet ministers reported that, elsewhere, Conservative Party workers were being abused by once-staunch supporters. As if to emphasize the *fin-de-siècle* atmosphere, two of Thatcher's longest-serving ministers – Norman Fowler and Peter Walker – left her cabinet to spend more time with their families and business interests. Rumours swept Westminster that Thatcher would face a leadership challenge in the autumn. Michael Heseltine kept them alive with a steady stream of speeches warning that Britain must not forsake its European destiny. His demand that the government listen to industry and take sterling into the ERM became a constant theme. So too did his warnings that, unless it acted soon, Britain would once again be excluded from the Franco-German project which would decide the future of Europe.

Faced with a rising chorus of demands from outside the government and the persistent pressure from within, Thatcher began to shift her position. By the end of March the chancellor felt confident enough to declare that the prospect of lower inflation had brought closer the prospect of ERM entry. There had been 'encouraging' progress towards meeting the Madrid conditions.[14] On the same day Geoffrey Howe reiterated that there could be no going back on the commitment to join. The message from 10 Downing Street had been that German monetary union might so disrupt the ERM as to significantly delay Britain's entry, but Howe was unequivocal: 'There is no suggestion that German monetary union has altered things either for ourselves or for the Community . . . The sooner we are able to create the conditions [to join] the better.'[15]

By now the ERM was the most frequent topic of conversation at Major's weekly bilateral meeting with Thatcher. Quietly persistent, he stressed that the mechanism would provide the framework in which the government could bring down interest rates while maintaining the squeeze on inflation through a firm exchange rate. Later she would accuse him of sounding like Nigel Lawson's 'cracked record', but his technique proved effective.[16] The most significant breakthrough came in May, when Thatcher addressed the annual conference of the Scottish Conservative Party in Aberdeen. Never once had she mentioned the ERM at such a gathering. Now, accepting the Treasury's reinterpretation, she volunteered that the Madrid conditions were closer to being reached than the performance of the retail price index suggested. The appropriate comparison was between Britain's underlying inflation rate of 6.5 per cent and the average of 5 per cent elsewhere in Europe. 'If you compare like with like, we are not so far above Europe's average for inflation,' she said.[17] This was the public preparation for retreat.

Within the Treasury the strategic decision to join was formally confirmed during a meeting in early June. According to those present, the potential risks – the strains threatened by German reunification and the disjuncture between the British and German economies –

were considered. But, as officials munched on the Marmite 'soldiers' which Major had ordered from the Treasury kitchen, the obstacles did not seem insuperable and the risks of inaction appeared more dangerous. A few days later one of the chancellor's closest aides passed on an account of the meeting to the *Financial Times*. The aide said that Major wanted to be sure that sterling would enter the system at a relatively high exchange rate in order to protect his anti-inflation strategy. Predictably enough, the newspaper's report of the meeting, mentioning September or October as the most likely dates for entry, provoked a sharp rise in the pound's value.[18] It was presumably no accident that the report appeared just a day before the critical meeting between Major and Thatcher on 13 June. The prime minister found that her room for manœuvre had been removed: if she refused the chancellor the government would face a sterling crisis and, quite probably, another rise in interest rates. So, when the two met at 10 Downing Street, she finally agreed that Britain would, rather than might, join. She now had too few allies to resist. She was insistent, though, that sterling would enter the system with the wide 6 per cent bands of fluctuation enjoyed by Spain, and that the government would change its parity if the pound came under pressure. Even at this point she refused to accept that interest rates would be determined by the performance of sterling. However, it was not in the Treasury's interest to dispel that illusion, and Major and his advisers now began to mark off possible dates for entry. The chancellor took care also to ensure that the prime minister could not recant. In early July he declared publicly that the Rubicon had been crossed. Britain would join. Binding Thatcher, he stressed, 'That is not just my idiosyncratic view, that is the view of the British government. It is our agreed policy.'[19] For a brief period, sterling's appreciation took it through DM3.00 for the first time since the previous autumn.

The chancellor had hoped to press his advantage and persuade Thatcher to join the mechanism during July. The pound's entry then would have coincided with the dismantling by other European governments of their remaining foreign exchange controls – the establishing of a free market in capital which had been among the original Madrid terms. Thatcher, however, was not yet ready to give way. She insisted he wait until the autumn. So Major completed his recasting of the Madrid conditions, by stating that sterling could join the system once underlying inflation was 'proximate' to that elsewhere in Europe. It was a formula which allowed the Treasury maximum flexibility.

Alan Walters refused to accept that the battle was lost. During early 1990 he still visited the prime minister occasionally. She provoked hilarity in the House of Commons when, under questioning from Neil Kinnock, she revealed that he had now the status of a 'family friend'.[20] Walters presented a public warning with the publication in July of *Sterling In Danger: The Economic Consequences of Pegged Exchange Rates*.[21] The book blamed the upsurge in inflation on Nigel Lawson's attempts to shadow the Deutschmark. The ERM was characterized as a tool of the Bundesbank, with a dismal record in promoting the exchange rate stability it promised. Walters drew on Spain's experience to warn of the risks posed by the removal of capital controls. When Spain had joined the ERM, a year earlier, the peseta had risen sharply despite the country's high inflation rate. Walters concluded that large short-term flows of speculative capital into high-inflation countries (Britain in this context was bracketed with Spain) would make it harder for such countries to bring down their inflation rates. So too would the equally large outflows from those countries which would precede the inevitable subsequent devaluation of their currencies. So, as he had asserted in the paper which acted as the catalyst for Lawson's departure, the ERM was indeed 'half-baked'. Elements of this argument were taken seriously in Whitehall. The removal of foreign exchange restrictions across Europe was recognized as a new source of potential instability. Governments had hitherto protected weaker currencies by imposing direct restrictions on speculative flows.

Walters's second concern – that an immediate consequence of sterling's membership would be an influx of capital which could force premature cuts in interest rates – also had some validity. It was for that reason that the Treasury wanted sterling to enter the mechanism at a 'demanding' exchange rate. But the world had moved on, and Walters's eccentric alternative to the Delors plan – the creation of a new commodity-based currency, which he called the 'ECOM' – did nothing to enhance the credibility of his polemic. The ECOM was acidly dismissed in the Treasury as 'quarter-baked'.

Thatcher meanwhile understood that she could not again allow

Walters to provoke conflict with her chancellor. On her instructions, Bernard Ingham disavowed the Walters thesis, pointing out for good measure that Thatcher had not seen him during the previous two months. Journalists were told also that Robin Butler, the cabinet secretary, had insisted that some sections of an earlier draft be excised and that the title be changed. Walters's original title had been *The Economic Consequences of Mr Lawson* – an attempt to recall the powerful onslaught by Keynes on Winston Churchill's return to the gold standard in 1925. It was perhaps fitting that, just as the book was published, Thatcher received from Charles Powell, her most loyal aide, a lengthy and confidential memorandum on the ERM. The political case for membership could not any longer be resisted, Powell concluded. She should join.

There was a second strand to this bargaining between chancellor and prime minister – the strand which would fatally bind the economics of the ERM to the politics of Europe. As the British cabinet agonized over whether it should take the first step of joining the ERM, the rest of Europe was planning to enshrine in the Treaty of Rome the plan for economic and monetary union. The Rome summit in December 1990 had been set as the occasion to begin negotiations on the necessary amendments to the treaty. France and Germany had signalled that they wanted stage two of the Delors project to begin in January 1993. President Mitterrand and Chancellor Kohl had also agreed that the conference on monetary union should be accompanied by a parallel drive to closer political integration. The 'political union' sought by the two countries, and backed strongly by their smaller neighbours, was only vaguely defined. Germany wanted to give democratic substance to the new union by greatly enhancing the authority of the European Parliament and extending the competence of the Community into defence and home affairs. France's overriding objective was economic and monetary union – the abolition of the hegemony of the Bundesbank – but, standing outside the military structure of NATO and ever suspicious of the US, it also wanted to add a new European dimension to foreign and security policy. Belgium and The Netherlands sought much greater use of majority voting in the Council of Ministers as the basis for an essentially

federal political structure. The common thread was that every suggestion was calculated to incur the wrath of Margaret Thatcher. What
she called the 'conveyor belt to federalism' was running at full speed.
She regretted now the concessions she had made to secure the single
market, and she determined that she would allow no more British
sovereignty to be lost to Brussels.

At the Madrid summit in June 1989 she had announced that Britain
would produce alternative proposals to the Delors blueprint. Lawson's
immediate response to the central bankers' report had echoed his
earlier speech to the Royal Institute of International Affairs at the
start of the year. He attacked in particular the presumption that a
single currency would require binding central rules on national
budgetary policies. 'What is suggested in the Delors report is that
individual member countries would not have the budgetary or fiscal
freedom which individual states of the United States have,' he told
the Treasury and Civil Service Committee. His comments were
echoed in the MPs' own conclusions: 'The power of the House of
Commons over centuries has depended fundamentally on the control
of money, both taxation and expenditure. This would be jeopardized
by the form of monetary union proposed by the Delors report which
would involve central undemocratic direction within Europe of
domestic budgetary policies.'[22]

So, at Thatcher's direction, Lawson drew up a scheme for a system
of 'competing currencies' in which each of the twelve national
currencies would be granted legal-tender status across the European
Community. The theory was that, as in a more conventional market-
place, the strong would drive out the weak. Businessmen and,
eventually, individuals would discard the weak currencies of high-
inflation countries in favour of the strong currencies of those with
sound monetary policies. Eventually, the choices made in the market-
place might (and here the conditional tense was vital) lead to a single
currency. Completed just before his resignation, it was a typically
ingenious Lawson plan and Thatcher was attracted to the idea as a
market-based alternative to the *dirigisme* of Jacques Delors. There
would be no requirement at the outset to establish a European central
bank or to transfer to Brussels control over domestic monetary and
fiscal policy. More importantly, the prime minister was convinced
that it would not lead to a single currency: sterling would be saved.

Given a choice, the good burghers of Grantham would always prefer the pound sterling to the Deutschmark or the franc. The proposal, which Thatcher had cleared in advance with Nicholas Ridley, was approved by the cabinet just days after John Major returned to the Treasury in October 1989. Introducing it in the House of Commons early the following month, Major insisted that the Delors plan was only one possible route to the economic and monetary union to which the Community had been committed since the 1970 Werner Plan. Competing currencies, he argued, would avoid the 'bureaucratic and centralized' approach of the Commission president. It was not 'a matter of compelling either party to use any particular currency: the aim is to reduce restrictions limiting their joint freedom of choice. This enables currencies to compete.'[23] The proposal attracted a brief flurry of interest, but was soon seen elsewhere in Europe as a delaying tactic. Even within the Treasury, officials showed little enthusiasm. It was, said one of the Treasury officials who had helped draft it, 'just another of Nigel's clever ideas'.

By early 1990 the search was on for a more convincing alternative. It came via one of Thatcher's former Foreign Office advisers. Sir Michael Butler had been Britain's permanent representative in Brussels during the early 1980s. He had sat beside the prime minister during the interminable summits at which she had fought 'to get our money' back through a rebate on Britain's contributions to the Community. Retired from the Foreign Office, Butler was working as a director at Hambros Bank. He also chaired the European Committee of the British Invisible Exports Council, the organization whose task it was to ensure the pre-eminence of the City of London among the world's financial centres. In this latter role, Butler worked with Paul Richards from Samuel Montagu to develop a more convincing scheme. He used his contacts at 10 Downing Street to persuade Thatcher to give it at least a fair hearing. Once that was done, he was given informal but significant help from officials in the Treasury and the Bank of England. Separately, Major's advisers looked at ways in which the plan could be modified with the aim, if that was any longer possible, of making it both attractive to the prime minister and plausible in Europe.

The nub of the Butler thesis was that there was a pragmatic alternative to the 'Big Bang' proposed by Delors in which national currencies and central banks would be replaced with a supranational 'Eurofed' issuing a single currency. Governments should concentrate instead on developing the existing European Currency Unit – the unit of account representing a basket all EC currencies. The ecu already had a significant role in official transactions between central banks and was the unit they used for lending and borrowing within the EMS. Though outside the ERM, Britain already held 20 per cent of its foreign exchange reserves in ecu in the European Monetary Cooperation Fund. More broadly, the government was encouraging the development of a private capital market in ecu in the City of London. Butler's idea was to develop the ecu as a common currency and, crucially, to allow a new European Monetary Fund (EMF) to put ecu notes into circulation. This 'hard ecu' would be so defined as to ensure it could never be devalued against any of the Community's twelve national currencies. The newly created EMF would issue financial instruments denominated in ecu in return for national currencies. Central banks would be obliged to redeem their own currencies for ecu on demand. Eventually the EMF could develop into an embryonic central bank and the ecu into a single currency. The appeal to Thatcher, though, was in the conditional tense – the 'could' lead to a single currency rather than 'would' or 'should'. As in the competing-currencies scheme drawn up by Nigel Lawson, the outcome would not be prescribed at the outset.

Major tried a different tack – the approach he would eventually adopt as prime minister in the negotiations ahead of the Maastricht Treaty. He had been struck during his conversations with other European finance ministers at how committed they were to the Delors blueprint. There was no appetite to abandon the exhaustive analysis produced by the central bankers on the Delors committee in favour of a British proposal. The Paris and Bonn governments had already invested too much political capital in economic and monetary union to see a firm commitment to a single currency replaced by the vague possibility that the markets might one day throw up something similar. So, during a meeting with Thatcher in April 1990, Major suggested that at the forthcoming intergovernmental conference the government should be ready to agree the treaty changes necessary to implement the Delors plan – with one key safeguard. Britain would insist on an 'opting-in' mechanism which would allow each government to defer a decision on whether to participate until the moment when a single currency became a real option. Major said this would leave to a future Parliament the decision on whether Britain should scrap sterling. In a paper sent to the prime minister the following month, Major underlined the warning that France and Germany were prepared to see Britain isolated and press ahead with a new treaty of the other eleven EC states. Thatcher would have none of it, recalling subsequently her disappointment with Major. She had been 'extremely disturbed that he had swallowed so quickly the slogans of the European lobby'. She added, 'Intellectually, he was drifting with the tide.'[24]

She was similarly scornful of Douglas Hurd's efforts to put a positive gloss on Britain's negotiating stance for the intergovernmental conference on political union demanded by Mitterrand and Kohl. For all Thatcher's suspicions, Hurd was not a federalist, but history told him that the government could not stand by and watch the rest of Europe unite on terms over which Britain had no influence. Thatcher was a pre-Suez politician, certain that Britain could stand alone (or at least alongside the Americans) on the world stage. Hurd understood the harsher realities of postwar decline. The end of the Cold War added another dimension. The removal of the Soviet threat would force a re-evaluation of the role of NATO and, inevitably, produce pressure for a more distinct European foreign policy and defence identity. Britain could not leave it to others to dictate the shape of arrangements so vital to its own national interest. So Hurd developed a range of modest but practical ideas to signal the government's willingness to reform the Community's institutions. Among them were proposals to strengthen the Strasbourg Parliament's oversight of the Brussels Commission and enhanced authority for the European Court to enforce Community directives. He also pressed the principle of 'subsidiarity' – the notion of a much clearer dividing line between issues dealt with in Brussels and those which should remain the preserve of national governments. More importantly, he began to develop the concept of a 'pillared structure' for the Community. This would separate those areas like the single market and external trade which were under the umbrella of the Treaty of Rome from a new, strictly intergovernmental, set of arrangements for closer cooperation in areas like foreign and interior policies. This proposition would provide the basis for the later British negotiating stance at Maastricht.

Hurd told the Scottish Conservative conference in May 1990 that Britain must not be 'prickly, defensive or negative'. It was not faced with 'a plot to destroy national institutions' and would not be isolated unless 'we isolate ourselves by shutting ourselves off, raising the drawbridge of argument, acting as if we were a beleaguered island'.[25] Knowingly perhaps, the foreign secretary was offering an apt description of the prime minister's mood. Geoffrey Howe continued to press the same argument, offering strong support to Hurd's conciliatory approach when the planned conference on political union was endorsed at the Dublin summit in the summer of 1990. Risking Thatcher's wrath, he used a lecture at the London School of Economics to confront those arguing that European integration was a threat to British sovereignty. Howe told his audience that sovereignty should be seen as divisible – exploitable in partnership with other nations. 'Sovereignty is not like virginity – now you have it, now you don't.'

Thatcher fumed at Howe's interventions but bowed to the advice of her chancellor and her foreign secretary. She retained enough contact with the world outside No. 10 to realize she could not disavow her two most senior ministers. Just days before the Dublin summit in late June, she agreed that Major should publicly unveil the plan for the hard ecu. At an early-morning meeting in No. 10 on 19 June, she also gave approval for Hurd to press forward with his negotiating strategy for the conference on political union. She could not hide her resentment, however. Robin Leigh-Pemberton promptly described the hard ecu as an intermediate step which might lead to the full monetary union proposed by Jacques Delors. In the House of Commons on 21 June the prime minister was certain that that would not happen. She departed, once again, from the carefully worded script prepared by her officials and in another few careless seconds seriously damaged her own government's position. She would not abolish the pound sterling: 'Those who wish to use the ecu in place of their own currency may. I do not believe we shall,' she told MPs.[26] At the Dublin summit a few days later, she struck the same note of disbelieving and resentful acquiescence. She championed the cause of a European confederation of sovereign states, bluntly telling her partners that a single currency might be something to be considered in twenty years or so. Major and Hurd were downcast. They had won yesterday's battle over the ERM, but the rest of Europe was already moving on.

During the late summer another use of the conditional tense had crept into the gossip in the corridors and bars of Westminster. For the first time since 1979, senior ministers questioned whether Thatcher would survive to contest another term. 'If she fights the election' was a phrase now heard with increasing frequency from some around her cabinet table. This dark possibility had first been raised the previous autumn. Until then few outside Westminster had heard of Sir Anthony Meyer. The old-Etonian baronet was the Conservative MP for Clwyd North-West. A gentle and a genteel man, he had a consuming passion – to preserve Britain's place and influence in Europe. A vice-chairman of the Tory back-bench committee on Europe, he had come to public attention after the Conservative defeat in the Strasbourg elections, describing Thatcher's campaign as 'disgraceful'. At the end of November he decided to challenge her for the Tory leadership. The party's rules allowed for a leadership contest each year, but there had not been one since Thatcher's defeat of Edward Heath in 1975. Meyer had no hope of winning, not much more of delivering even a bloody nose. He was determined, however, to galvanize the discontent that Thatcher's authoritarian leadership style and her Gaullist view of Europe had produced among a swathe of centre-left back-bench MPs. He would comment later that the departure of the chancellor had raised deep constitutional issues and 'it was not right to allow Lawson to be buried in a forest clearing late at night'.[27]

More sympathized with the challenger than eventually voted for him. Ian Gilmour struck a chord well beyond her enemies when he commented in Cambridge that 'The British people like strong government at home and abroad but centuries ago they rejected divine right.'[28] In the weeks after Lawson's resignation the occasional signals that the prime minister was ready to adopt a collegiate style of leadership had come to nothing. The final sentence of her television encounter with Brian Walden had revealed her true position. 'Strong leadership will continue,' she had declared. During the following months, others considered provoking a leadership contest. Geoffrey Howe flirted briefly with the idea, and there was a brisk trade in rumour and speculation in the tea- and smoking-rooms at Westminster. As well as Michael Heseltine, several cabinet ministers were considered potential successors if Thatcher fell. Howe, Kenneth Baker, Douglas Hurd, John Major and Chris Patten all featured on the lists, but none of them would challenge her directly.

When the votes were counted on 5 December 1989 Thatcher had received 314 and Meyer 33. Another 27 MPs had abstained. Some ministers admitted that they had been torn between honour and instinct: membership of her government carried a moral obligation to support Thatcher, but they could no longer say it was the right thing to do. Her friends dismissed the contest as a passing squall. Others were not so sanguine. Tristan Garel-Jones, the deputy chief whip, had helped organize her campaign. A firm pro-European and a close friend of Chris Patten, he was no ideological ally of the prime minister but he warned her that the refusal of sixty MPs to support her had set a dangerous precedent. The number could rise sharply in a future contest. Meyer had broken the spell.

Nine months later she had lost completely her equilibrium. The Thatcher government worked during the 1980s through a curious but vital marriage between conviction and constraint. She was forever fighting to extend the boundaries of her revolution; colleagues and civil servants were forever checking her more extreme ambitions, persuading her to opt for the possible rather than the ideologically pure. During her third term she broke out of the straitjacket. The poll tax was the most important moment. She no longer needed the pragmatists, the faint-hearted – or so she thought. By 1990 her isolation was near complete; her domination of the machinery of government had become a weakness rather than a strength. Many of her cabinet colleagues were treated as outsiders and she relied more and more on the advice of her courtiers in 10 Downing Street. Thatcher had never been liked – had never much wanted to be. But now the undoubted admiration which she had once evoked was giving way to resentments. Chris Patten was overheard making the point in early May: 'After eleven years everything is geared to her, everyone second-guessing what she will say. Just at the time she needs advice, the whole Whitehall structure is operating in the other direction.'

But Nicholas Ridley, her last real ally around the cabinet table, stiffened her resolve. He stirred her fears of a German Europe and told her that fixing the exchange rate against the Deutschmark would subjugate British policy to the whims of the Bundesbank. The images in the kaleidoscope, however, were moving on. In July 1990 Ridley's paranoia about Germany surfaced in the pages of the *Spectator* and forced his resignation from her cabinet. And it was too late now for her to find an escape route in the compromises with Europe which she so detested.

CHAPTER EIGHT

NEMESIS

THE TREASURY ANNOUNCEMENT at 4 p.m. on 5 October 1990 that Britain was joining the exchange rate mechanism was greeted with palpable relief within Margaret Thatcher's government. Most in her cabinet hoped that ERM membership would allow a steady fall in interest rates before the general election. It seemed also to hold out the prospect of a cabinet truce over Europe. The prime minister was unconvinced. This was a defeat at the hands of the federalists. Even as she gave way, Thatcher could not disguise the resentment which burned in her heart.

She was determined to dictate the precise terms in which the world would hear of her surrender. The Treasury press notice issued on 5 October under the name of the chancellor of the Exchequer contained two announcements: sterling would participate in the ERM at a central rate of around DM2.95 from the following Monday morning, subject to the approval of Britain's European partners, and interest rates would be reduced from 15 per cent to 14 per cent. It was this second, scarcely sensational, piece of news that the prime minister and first lord of the Treasury insisted take precedence. The heading of the press notice – 'UK reduction in interest rates and entry to ERM' – carried the emphasis, while in the text below the significant news was relegated to the final two sentences:

> To reinforce our framework of monetary discipline, we have decided that the UK should now join the Exchange Rate Mechanism of the European Monetary System. We have proposed, therefore, to our European Community partners that, as part of the common procedure, we should join the ERM on Monday morning with a central exchange rate at around Deutschmark 2.95 and initially with 6 per cent margins.[1]

That Friday afternoon Thatcher was preparing her speech for the following week's Conservative Party conference in Bournemouth. Just before 4 p.m. she broke off and walked to the Reuters monitor in her private office. News of the interest rate cut flashed first across the top of the screen. Sterling's entry to the ERM came seconds later. The prime minister nodded with satisfaction before returning to work on her speech. The interest rate cut had been the essential concession she had extracted in this moment of defeat. It was a mistake – opposed by officials in the Treasury and by the Bank of England. So too was the decision to announce in advance of consultations with other governments the exchange rate at which sterling would join the system. The rules said the rate was a subject for negotiation. As she had remarked at the start of 1989, however, Thatcher had no intention of giving the Belgians a say in the value of the pound. Sir Nigel Wicks, the official who had replaced Geoffrey Littler as head of the Treasury's international division, was sent to Brussels that weekend with the tightest of negotiating briefs. Sterling had been fluctuating around DM2.93 during the previous few days. Wicks was told its ERM rate should be fixed at DM2.95 or DM2.96; he was not authorized to agree a parity above or below those levels. Both decisions would contribute to sterling's later troubles, but in October 1990 they seemed a small price to pay to put behind the government so many years of conflict.

Throughout the previous summer the Treasury and the Bank of England were never quite certain that Margaret Thatcher would honour the pledge she had made to John Major in June. Her mood was unpredictable. She revealed her doubts in Aspen, Colorado, at the beginning of August. It was here that she would admonish George Bush against 'wobbling' in the face of Saddam Hussein's invasion of Iraq. But the main purpose of her speech, marking the fortieth anniverary of the Aspen Institute, was to define her unflinching Atlanticism. In Europe she saw central control and its associated bureaucracy, the risk of protectionism, and a threat to the nation-state. In the US, she told her audience, she saw enterprise and individualism, liberal economics, and world leadership. 'I am', she said, 'an undiluted admirer of American values and the American dream.'[2] More than once over succeeding weeks she hinted publicly at her unease over trying to 'buck the market' by placing the pound in a European straitjacket. On each occasion that her hesitation showed, sterling dipped on the currency markets. Gus O'Donnell, Major's press secretary, spent much of his time in careful counter-briefing – reassuring journalists and, through them, the financial markets that the chancellor would prevail.

In August the chancellor received backing from the Paris-based Organization for Economic Cooperation and Development, which warned that the government had still to regain a grip on inflation. 'Full membership of the EMS and ruling out periodic exchange rate realignments would force both sides of industry to face the long-standing problem of inflationary wage settlements.'³ But Major was obliged several times to personally restate the commitment to ERM membership in order to steady the nerves of currency traders. At the beginning of September he announced, 'As soon as I think there is a window and we have credibly met the conditions that we have set out, then into the mechanism we will go.'⁴ Two weeks later, on 21 September, a flurry of speculative pressure on sterling forced a stronger statement, negotiated in advance with his Downing Street neighbour: 'The prime minister and I have made it clear that it is our policy to enter the ERM at the earliest sensible date,' Major said. A few days later, at the annual meeting of the IMF in Washington, he repeated the pledge yet again, adding of the Madrid conditions on relative inflation rates, 'What matters here is less the difference between headline figures, which measure what has happened over the last twelve months, than the prospective movements of price levels from now on.'⁵

The mood of anxious expectation in the Treasury was reinforced by the tortuous progress of the behind-the-scenes negotiations. Major's public assurances were accompanied by a detailed minute to Thatcher pressing her to sanction entry to the mechanism in early October. The minute was the subject of a series of agonizing meetings. Thatcher knew she could not resist, but was reluctant and resentful of the prospect of admitting defeat. For his part, the chancellor was determined to maintain the pressure. In a second note delivered to the prime minister, on Tuesday 2 October, he proposed that sterling should join the system on 12 October. Twenty-four hours later, during a meeting in No. 10, Thatcher finally announced her retreat when Major warned her that outside the system it would be impossible to announce an early reduction in interest rates. Even then, however, Major could not be certain that she would stick by the commitment. He immediately arranged a much larger gathering for the following day to tie in the prime minister to the timetable. 'We have got the key in the lock,' he told an official. 'Now we have to ensure it is turned.'

The team of Treasury and Bank officials who joined Thatcher and Major in 10 Downing Street on Thursday 4 October were still not completely sure of her response. Major was accompanied by Peter Middleton, Terence Burns and Nigel Wicks. The Bank was represented by Eddie George. Robin Leigh-Pemberton, preparing to leave for an official visit to Japan, learned of the decision only later in a telephone call from the chancellor. 'We're going in,' Major told him with an understandable sense of triumph. The meeting rehearsed the economic arguments. Papers and charts spelled out the outlook for relative inflation and interest rates and for the trade gap. The Treasury admitted that, strictly interpreted, the Madrid conditions had not been met: the British headline inflation rate of 10.9 per cent compared to a European Community average of 5.5 per cent and a German rate of 2.6 per cent. But there was now irrefutable evidence that Britain's inflation rate would shortly turn downwards and begin to converge with that in the rest of Europe. Major explained that the increased confidence on financial markets which would follow participation in the ERM would provide a framework for the interest rate reductions that the prime minister so desperately wanted. The Treasury had already decided that a cut in rates to 14 per cent was possible, but only if it could be certain that it would not undermine confidence in the pound. Outside the ERM such a reduction might be interpreted as a deliberate attempt by the government to drive down the value of sterling. The calculations produced by the Treasury's economists suggested that a rate of DM2.95 would impose a firm anti-inflation discipline without seriously damaging industry's competitiveness. The rate was in line with the average of the previous few years, and analysis of the main price and productivity indicators in Britain and Germany seemed to suggest it was competitive.

The Treasury's original plan had been to announce membership at the end of the following week, on 12 October, but now Major sought to pre-empt any last-minute doubts. He pointed out that the prime minister's speech on the same day at the end of the Conservative

Party conference in Bournemouth would complicate matters. She would speak immediately after lunch, but nothing could be said about the ERM until 4 p.m., the official close of European foreign exchange trading. Her speech would be overshadowed by the announcement. Then there was the risk that the decision would leak if entry was deferred for more than a week. That could cause havoc in the markets. Unspoken was the thought that she might change her mind. So Major pressed for the announcement to be made the next day, 5 October, with entry taking effect on the following Monday, 8 October. The Treasury had already confirmed that Mario Sarcinelli, the Italian chairman of the European Community's monetary committee, would be available at the weekend to chair the required negotiations.

The officials present could see that Thatcher was beaten, but at times the discussion seemed unreal: 'There we were, cutting this wretched Gordian knot, and all she was worried about was the press release,' one recalled. Thatcher had established in her earlier talks with Major that the pound would enter the mechanism with a 6 per cent margin of fluctuation either side of its central parity. The Deutschmark, the French franc, the guilder, the Belgian and Luxembourg francs, the Danish krone and the lira were bound by more demanding 2.25 per cent margins. But the peseta was still in the wider band, and there was general agreement that, initially at least, sterling would require the same room for manœuvre.

This consensus did not extend to the proposed reduction in interest rates. Bank and Treasury officials wanted to wait until sterling was actually in the mechanism. After all, the purpose of joining was to demonstrate the government's anti-inflation resolve. If Thatcher waited, the foreign exchange markets would force an interest rate reduction within a matter of days by driving up the value of the pound towards its ERM ceiling. Taking this 'dividend' in advance would signal that the government attached more weight to lower interest rates than to the defeat of inflation. Eddie George, in particular, was incensed at the prospect of sacrificing one of the principal benefits of the decision to join for the sake of a few days. Major, however, did not regard the issue as one of critical importance. The main point, he would remark later, was that the Treasury had already decided that lower borrowing costs were justified by the inflation outlook.

Such arguments were academic, however, as Thatcher would not wait even a day longer. She asked George whether he could give an absolute guarantee of a reduction in interest rates once sterling was in the system. He responded that it was a virtual, but not an absolute, certainty. That was not enough. As Kenneth Baker recounts in his memoirs, *The Turbulent Years: My Life in Politics*, lower interest rates were her vital justification for her retreat, her fig-leaf. Baker says he tried to dissuade her from joining the system. She replied, 'Kenneth, I have secured a 1 per cent cut and when we join we will be able to adjust the value of sterling. I have been assured that we will have that flexibility.'[6] The prime minister could not even now acknowledge the logic of a decision which had made the exchange rate the centre-piece of economic policy. She would write later, 'I for my part was determined to demonstrate that we would be looking more to monetary conditions than to the exchange rate in setting interest rates.'[7] That statement was entirely divorced from the reality. Once the exchange rate was fixed against the Deutschmark, the level of interest rates would be decided by the value of the pound.

The other area of important subsequent controversy – the precise rate at which Britain joined – was a dispute with implications on two, interconnected, levels. Its consequences at the time seemed limited, but in the run-up to Black Wednesday, two years later, it would assume a more damaging significance. The rules of the system specified that the parity at which a currency entered should be agreed by all the system's members. Each of Britain's partners would take on an obligation to defend the chosen exchange rate. In return, they were all entitled to a voice in determining that parity. The Bundesbank, responsible for the anchor currency in the system, had a particular interest. The Treasury and the Bank, however, took the view that it was impracticable to join at anything other than the prevailing market rate. They were also conscious of Thatcher's refusal to contemplate a role for any other government in determining the value of *her* currency. So the Treasury sought to pre-empt the discussions of the monetary committee by stating in advance its preference for DM2.95. Anticipating that the decision might cause problems, Nigel Wicks telephoned John Kerr, now the Foreign Office permanent representative in Brussels, on the day before the announcement. Kerr advised that the finance ministry and central bank officials on the monetary committee would certainly protest. He calculated, however, that the inevitable irritation among the EC's technicians would be more than offset by the broader political welcome for sterling's entry in the main European capitals. Kerr was half right. Telephoned by Major on the following day, Karl Otto Pöhl offered hearty congratulations. The government could be certain of the Bundesbank's public support.

During the weekend talks in Brussels, however, the Bundesbank raised objections to the unilateral decision to fix a rate of DM2.95. In part it was a matter of principle: Britain's partners should have been consulted first. But German officials also pointed to the current-account deficit as evidence that the rate might be unsustainably high. Pöhl said subsequently that he had considered a level of DM2.60–2.65 more realistic. In fact Hans Tietmeyer, the senior German representative on the monetary committee, pressed for a much more modest adjustment, to about DM2.90. As it happened, French officials took the opposite view, voicing concern that Britain might steal a competitive edge even at the exchange rate it proposed. After discussion with one of his colleagues, Wolfgang Rieke, Tietmeyer decided not to press the argument. Rieke thought the difference between DM2.90 and DM2.95 too small to provoke a serious dispute. He had his own reservations, but considered that later developments and policy decisions would determine whether the rate was correct. Rieke also pointed out that, as the country entering the mechanism, Britain could expect the benefit of any doubt. None the less, it did not bode well that, from the moment of entry, the Bundesbank had doubts about sterling's parity.

Another strand in the later controversy related to the behaviour of the Treasury and the Bank of England in the months before October. In April 1990 sterling stood at about DM2.75, but the speculation about the ERM then triggered a steady appreciation. The chancellor's aides nudged the process along with upbeat briefings on the likely timing of entry. The Bank publicly applauded the pound's rise, commenting in the August issue of its *Quarterly Bulletin* that it was a welcome reinforcement of the government's anti-inflation stance.[8] In one respect this approach was readily explicable. The annual inflation rate was heading towards the peak of 10.9 per cent which it would reach in September and October. The impact of the monetary squeeze which had begun eighteen months earlier still looked uncertain. If sterling's parity was set at too low a level, interest rates might have to be cut too far and too fast in order to prevent the pound breaching its ERM ceiling. Many in the Bank, for example, wanted a still higher rate than DM2.95, with the consensus favouring DM3.00 and some suggesting DM3.10.

Today's economic policy is more often than not an overreaction to yesterday's mistake. The bias in favour of a high exchange rate during the summer of 1990 was unsurprising as a response to the inflationary boom of the late 1980s but was far less attentive to the looming recession. It missed the potential conflict between the short-term imperative to curb inflation and the longer-term requirement to close an unprecedentedly large trade gap. In 1989 the current account, which measures transactions in services and financial flows as well as imports and exports of raw materials and manufactured goods, showed a deficit of more than £20bn. The Treasury had half persuaded itself that the deficit was not a serious problem. The doctrine developed by Nigel Lawson and Terence Burns and expounded at the annual meeting of the IMF in September 1988 held that it would be self-correcting. In the interim, high interest rates and the dismantling of capital controls around the world seemed to offer assurance that the shortfall would be readily financed by overseas investors. This was a patently flimsy argument. The persistence of such a large deficit as the economy moved into recession suggested that, whatever the Treasury's calculations of relative competitiveness, sterling was over-valued. The problem was compounded by the weakness of the dollar. In the autumn of 1990, joining the ERM at DM2.95 translated into a painfully high rate against the dollar of nearly $1.90. The Bundesbank was not alone in its concern: the Treasury's strategy of 'talking up' the pound during the summer of 1990 prompted serious disquiet among some of its own officials.

The prime minister paid no heed to such debates, as she had decided to change sterling's parity if it came under pressure. There would be no repeat of the massive intervention which occurred during the period when Lawson had been shadowing the Deutschmark. At the end of the No. 10 meeting Thatcher called back Peter Middleton. 'Will it be all

right?' she asked. Middleton replied that the decision would be universally applauded, but, if there were problems subsequently, all those
who had supported it would claim that the government had chosen the
wrong rate. Middleton concluded that she was wise not to invest too
much faith in DM2.95 – after all, it had taken the French several
realignments during the early 1980s to get right the level of the franc.
At this point Major was also ready to admit the possibility of realignments. He had told the Treasury and Civil Service Committee in July
that, while the stability of the system had increased, it 'doesn't have
the rigidity that some claim'.[9] Treasury officials agreed that there was
no certainty that the initial parity would stick. Burns was among those
surprised at how readily sterling settled at DM2.95 in the following
months. Once that happened, however, the government began to
invest in that particular exchange rate a dangerous significance.

Whatever the original intention, the ERM which Britain joined in
October 1990 was profoundly different from the system established
more than eleven years earlier. The drive towards economic and
monetary union had reinforced the trend among other European
governments to treat the ERM as a fixed rather than as a fixed-but-
adjustable, or pegged, exchange rate grid. Seven of the twelve parity
changes within the system had taken place in its first five turbulent
years. The subsequent adjustments had been relatively modest, confined typically to the Danish krone or the lira. The last general
realignment had been in January 1987. France was determined not to
risk the prize of a single currency by changing the parity between the
franc and the Deutschmark. The presumption in the rest of Europe
therefore was that Britain was likely to stick with the rate at which it
joined.

For different reasons, the Bank of England took the same view.
Despite his scepticism about the ERM, Eddie George believed that,
once sterling had joined, a realignment would be a last resort. Robin
Leigh-Pemberton made the point publicly in a speech in Tokyo on
8 October. Sterling's entry to the mechanism was 'a great event in
our economic life. It is something I have looked forward to for a very
long time.' The ERM's value, he added, lay in the discipline that a
stable exchange rate imposed on both sides of industry. But the
discipline would work only if there was a presumption that the

exchange rate would not be adjusted to accommodate inflationary pay awards.[10]

The immediate reaction when the foreign exchange markets reopened on Monday 8 October was favourable. As her advisers had warned her, Margaret Thatcher's decision to demand in advance a reduction in interest rates cast a shadow, but the pound looked safe enough in its new ERM range. The 6 per cent margin of fluctuation around its central rate meant that sterling could move as high as DM3.1320 or as low as DM2.7780. During these first days the pound rose to DM3.08. Most in the City, in industry and in the press applauded John Major's decision, though in terms slightly less effusive than those of Robin Leigh-Pemberton. Neil Kinnock, anxious to persuade the electorate of the Labour Party's conversion to financial orthodoxy, did not quarrel with sterling's new ERM parity. John Smith, the shadow chancellor, said the terms on which sterling entered the mechanism amounted to a 'humiliating U-turn' by Thatcher, but he did not dispute the actual decision.[11] The discordant notes struck initially by some MPs on the right of the Conservative Party – Nicholas Ridley prominent among them – appeared to have much more to do with their distaste for Europe than with the economic arguments. Some commentators saw the dangers. William Keegan wrote in the *Observer* that the rate against the Deutschmark had been fixed too high. He added prophetically, 'I cannot for one moment believe that the exchange rate will hold for more than two years and advise the Labour party and Thatcher's potential successors to be wary of making commitments that they will be unlikely to be able to honour.'[12] Elsewhere the media's response tended to follow the cabinet's cue by emphasizing the politics rather than the economics. The front pages focused on a potential window of opportunity which might restore to the Conservatives the possibility, if by no means the certainty, of a fourth election victory. The *Sunday Times* called this 'the golden scenario'.

There were warning signals, however. After an initial burst of confidence, the mood quite quickly began to change. Reports of the split between Thatcher and the Bank over the timing of the interest rate cut unsettled the financial markets. By the end of October sterling had lost its initial gains and had drifted back to DM2.95. There were also signs of unease on the back benches when, during a debate in the House of Commons on 23 October, Nigel Lawson lamented the decision to tie sterling's entry to a reduction in interest rates: 'This is no small point, because the conjunction of the two has sadly led to a degree of cynicism in financial markets, for which we will have to pay a price.' Noting that Thatcher, who sat grim-faced only a dozen paces in front of him, was now committed to 'shadowing the Deutschmark at a rate not very far from three marks to the pound', Lawson said it was a tragedy that Britain had not joined five years earlier.'[13] Thatcher declined to reply to Neil Kinnock in the debate, leaving Major to defend the policy he had forced upon her. But, in an earlier exchange on the same day with the Liberal Democrat leader Paddy Ashdown, she underlined once again her implacable opposition to a single currency. Eleven Conservative MPs led by John Biffen voted against the government at the end of the debate. They included Tony Favell, who had resigned two weeks earlier as Major's parliamentary private secretary in protest against the ERM decision. The rebels represented only a tiny minority, but many more were deeply hostile to the Delors plan. The golden scenario had already been tarnished.

Long after Margaret Thatcher had left 10 Downing Street, Nicholas Ridley was certain of the cause. He recalled the words of Mary Tudor: 'When I am dead and opened, you shall find Calais lying in my heart.' Lamenting the departure of a prime minister who had inspired and then disappointed him, Ridley continued, 'When Margaret Thatcher is dead and opened it will be those three letters ERM that will be lying in her heart.'[14] During the previous two years the dispute over sterling had torn apart her cabinet and diminished her leadership. Now, just at the moment when she had given way, it was a final reassertion of her will that would load the gun pointed at her premiership.

The Bournemouth party conference followed hard on the heels of ERM entry. The prime minister offered grudging tribute to John Major. Her speech was vintage Thatcher, threaded with the certainties that she would never surrender. The economy's troubles were temporary – a challenge rather than a cause for despair. She could not resist quoting a survey of European companies. Of the fifty most successful, two were German, eight were French; twenty-eight were British. Her government needed no lessons in economics from Europe. The chancellor's decision – for it was his – to tie sterling to the Deutschmark would 'reinforce our own financial discipline'. This was as far as she could be expected to go in support of a policy of which she so violently disapproved. Her speech contained a warning as well as the admission of defeat: she had given ground on the ERM, but she would stand and fight on the bigger issue of a single currency. Her government would never agree to the imposition of a single currency: 'That would be entering a federal Europe through the back-Delors.' She would not bow to those who saw the European Community as a way to rob Britain of its independence. 'Our Parliament', she declared with the scorn she reserved for the younger democracies across the Channel, 'has endured for 700 years and has been a beacon of hope to the peoples of Europe in their darkest days.' Each time in the past that she had compromised in Europe more had been demanded; this time she would not allow the ratchet to move another notch.[15] The party faithful – and despite everything they were still faithful – loved it.

The divisions in her cabinet, however, were transparent. Geoffrey Howe and Douglas Hurd had both given speeches earlier in the week urging a constructive approach to the debate on a single currency. Hurd insisted there was no future in 'a sulky, defeatist, fog-bound membership of the Community'. Howe, whose conviction that Britain must keep its place at the top table of Europe was by now a mirror image of the prime minister's disdain, offered a reminder that the Conservatives had signed up to the idea of monetary union as long ago as 1971. Borrowing a phrase, Howe remarked with some mischief that after the ERM there could now be 'no turning back'. Thatcher, however, was right to fear the ratchet: sterling's entry into the ERM had not frozen the grander ambitions of Germany and France.

Major and Hurd also had moved on. Neither was an admirer of the Delors vision, but Hurd thought it more important to understand than to loathe the French president of the European Commission. He saw him as a clever, impressive man, but above all as 'a Frenchman determined to Europeanize the Germans'. Like Major, he gauged that if Britain were to carry weight at the intergovernmental conference its own proposal for economic and monetary union must admit the goal of a single currency, even if it denied its inevitability. The hard-ecu scheme had only the slimmest chance of winning support. It had no chance if Thatcher would not admit that it might, just might, satisfy the aspirations of other European governments. Major had used the requisite phrasing when he had first launched the scheme. The ecu would first be a parallel, common currency. Then, 'In the very long term if peoples and governments so choose it could develop into a single currency.' Thatcher demurred: the ERM was enough.

Such was her mood when she travelled at the end of October to the first of the two summits which would be held in Rome before the end of the year. Her aides would claim later that she had been ambushed at the meeting by her so-called European partners. That was true to the extent that the Italian prime minister and host Giulio Andreotti saw the summit as the moment for a dramatic *coup de théâtre*. But, in common with the rest of Whitehall, No. 10 had advance warning that Andreotti intended to give fresh impetus to the drive towards economic and monetary union by putting in place a firm timetable. Two weeks earlier Chancellor Helmut Kohl had publicly stated his wish that stage two of the plan for a single currency should start at the latest in January 1994. This phase – involving the progressive locking of exchange rates and the creation of an embryonic European central bank – had been identified as a weak link in the framework. The Delors report had sketched out in only vague terms the progression to the third and final stage, but Kohl saw that as no obstacle to establishing a political commitment to maintain the momentum. Nor did other European leaders. For her part, Thatcher was convinced that the Rome summit should be an occasion for Europe to look outwards rather than inwards. The heads of government should break the deadlock which threatened to derail the Uruguay round of world trade talks. They should spell out their determination to drive Saddam Hussein from Kuwait. This was the real world she inhabited.

Predictably she was isolated. The other ten leaders backed Kohl in agreeing that January 1994 should see the launch of the second phase of monetary union. During a meeting reminiscent of the battles a decade earlier over Britain's contributions to the Brussels budget, Thatcher said she would veto any attempt to impose a single currency. She insisted that her view was recorded in the summit communiqué. It read, 'The United Kingdom, while ready to move beyond stage one through the creation of a new monetary institution and a common Community currency, believes the decision on the substance of that move should precede decisions on its timing.'[16] Drafting the note of dissent, her officials had ensured that it was couched in the language of diplomacy. Once the summit had ended, however, Thatcher felt no such constraint.

During her succeeding press conference and interviews Thatcher cast aside the Foreign Office camouflage. To the BBC she volunteered, 'If anyone is suggesting that I would go to Parliament and suggest the abolition of the pound sterling, No ... We shall block things that are not in Britain's interests.'[17] The decision of other leaders to set a date for stage two was dismissed with scorn and mixed metaphors: 'It seems to be putting the cart before the horse. People who get on a train like that deserve to get taken for a ride.' The Italian's handling of the summit had been 'a mess'; her European colleagues were 'living in cloud cuckooland'; she was ready to wield the British veto. It was Thatcher at her very best and at her very worst. Back in London as the summit drew to a close, Geoffrey Howe was being interviewed by Brian Walden. Britain's hard-ecu proposals, Howe said, could indeed lead to a single currency.[18] This assessment reflected the government's collective position, as set out by Major and Hurd before him, but they could no longer pretend it was the policy of the prime minister.

By the time Margaret Thatcher stood up in the House of Commons on Tuesday 30 October to give her report on the events in Rome, her officials had refastened the diplomatic restraints. Her opening statement, handed out in the parliamentary press gallery, bore the mark of Douglas Hurd. Hurd, rarely ruffled, had publicly affected to be entirely relaxed about her performance in Rome. Privately he would remark with patrician understatement that Thatcher was 'always at her most hazardous in moments of excitement'. Now, after their return from Rome, one of his closest cabinet colleagues reported that the foreign secretary considered that Thatcher had behaved 'dreadfully'. The summit had required, in Hurd's words, a 'measured response'. She had given anything but that. As they reviewed the position in London, Thatcher insisted on including in her House of Commons statement on the summit the sentence 'A single currency is not the policy of this government.' Hurd's officials, however, reinstated into her text the assertion, dropped from her Rome interviews, that the hard ecu 'could evolve towards a single currency'.

As so often before, the careful negotiation proved a waste of time. There was no prepared script for her responses to the questions from Neil Kinnock and others which followed the formal statement. The prime minister now spoke her truth. It was a passionate performance. 'If you hand over your sterling, you hand over the powers of this Parliament to Europe.' The Community would 'extinguish democracy'. As for the hard ecu in which her foreign secretary and chancellor had invested so much effort, 'In my view it would not become widely used.' And then again, 'What is the point of being elected to Parliament only to hand over your pound sterling and to hand over the powers of this house to Europe?' Even those Tory MPs on the benches behind her who disagreed profoundly with her views marvelled at the sheer force of her presence. Neil Kinnock was 'Little Sir Echo' in thrall to the bureaucrats of Brussels. For Jacques Delors she had three words: 'No, No. No.'[19] In *The Times* the following morning, Matthew Parris, the newspaper's parliamentary sketchwriter, commented, 'It was a bravura performance and one of Mrs Thatcher's finest.'[20] Never mind that she had torn up her government's European policy. Never mind that she had thrown away her premiership. As they watched her, few had noticed in the quiet expression of Geoffrey Howe how her words had turned his inner turmoil into certain conviction.

Howe's resignation letter two days later sketched out with polite clarity the fault-line exposed by her appearance in the House of Commons. He was no dewy-eyed European, but:

> We must be at the centre of the European partnership – playing the sort of leading and constructive role which commands respect. We need to be able to persuade friends as well as challenge opponents, and to win arguments before positions become entrenched. The risks of

being left behind on EMU are severe. All too much of our energy
during the last decade has been devoted to correcting the consequences
of our late start in Europe.[21]

In her response, Thatcher could not or would not admit the divide.
The differences were not 'nearly as great' as Howe suggested. 'We
have always been the party of Europe, and will continue to be so.'
She could say little else. She was alone – the only surviving member
of the cabinet over which she had first presided in May 1979. Her
premiership now was in peril.

Talk of a challenge for the leadership had ebbed and flowed
through the late summer and early autumn. The poll tax had been
the unmitigated disaster that Nigel Lawson had predicted. Riots on
the streets of London had been followed by the biggest campaign of
civil disobedience in recent memory. Millions, literally millions,
decided they would not pay the new impost. The recession amplified
the sense of injustice felt about a tax which treated dukes and dustmen
as financial equals. The steady stream of ministers departing from
Thatcher's cabinet left a whiff of decay around her administration.
Her remaining colleagues would comment openly on their ever more
infrequent visits to 'the bunker' in No. 10. Michael Heseltine stood
everywhere, never missing from the House of Commons lobby, from
the smoking-room, from the tea-room, from the dining-room. Nor
could anyone forget that he had always – from his days as environment
secretary a decade earlier – been a staunch opponent of the poll tax.
His lieutenants on the Tory back benches – Michael Mates and Keith
Hampson – were quietly collecting pledges from the disenchanted
and disgruntled. Against that, Britain was about to go to war in the
Gulf. Thousands of young men were preparing to confront Saddam
Hussein's war machine in Kuwait. Surely, said a cabinet minister at
the time, this was not the moment for the Conservative Party to
indulge itself by deposing its leader.

In the days that followed Howe's departure, Douglas Hurd played
well the conciliatory role which would later become a central thread
of his foreign-secretaryship. He made a grievous mistake, however, in
echoing the line adopted by Kenneth Baker in the immediate aftermath of Howe's resignation. This held that the differences between
Howe and Thatcher were more of presentation than of substance, of

style rather than of policy. It was an approach which belittled and angered the former minister – one that suggested he had resigned in a fit of pique. A week later Thatcher took up the same theme when MPs reassembled for the new session of Parliament. Neil Kinnock, she said, 'would be very pressed indeed to find any significant policy difference on Europe'.[22] Respecting on this occasion the prepared text agreed in advance with Hurd and Major, the prime minister also adopted a more emollient tone on the prospects for economic and monetary union. Her supporters meanwhile sought to flush out any threat to her position by bringing forward to the following week the deadline for notification of any leadership challenge.

Geoffrey Howe's resignation speech on 13 November transfixed the House of Commons and threw open to a much wider world the conflict which now destroyed Margaret Thatcher. It was the moment that the television cameras, newly installed in the House, had waited for. Denis Healey had once famously remarked that being attacked by Howe was akin to being savaged by a dead sheep. It was an epithet that had stuck. The radicalism of Howe's chancellorship had given way during his time as foreign secretary to the quiet reasonableness which so exasperated the prime minister. He was not a politician without conviction, but in her eyes he had made the mistake of believing that conviction was compatible with consensus. Now he savaged the prime minister with a quiet, chilling ferocity.

With Lawson beside him on the Tory back benches, he disclosed for the first time the ultimatum the two men had delivered more than a year earlier, before the Madrid summit. He dismissed the 'bogus dilemma' which said that Britain must either embrace a United States of Europe or defend to the last its national sovereignty. The real risk for Britain was not the imposition against its will of a single currency but that it might find itself isolated outside, 'with no say in the monetary arrangements that Europe chooses for itself'. Then came the assault on Thatcher's leadership. Her casual dismissal of policies which had been agreed in her cabinet and presented to Britain's European partners was 'rather like sending your opening batsmen to the crease only for them to find, the moment the first balls are bowled, that their bats have been broken before the game – by the team captain'. The cricketing metaphor had been adapted from her own promise at the Lord Mayor's banquet earlier that same week to 'hit all round the ground' the hostile bowling she had faced of late. The tragedy of her attitude, Howe continued, was that Britain would once again be shut out of a European future from which ultimately it could not escape. That her approach undercut the foundations of cabinet government was the same damaging charge which Lawson and Heseltine had laid when they had resigned.

Howe continued that he had left the cabinet because of a conflict of loyalty – of loyalty to the prime minister and of loyalty to what he perceived as the true interests of the nation. As Thatcher sat burning with anger and anxiety in the prime minister's place on the Conservative front bench, he concluded with what seemed a menacing invitation to Michael Heseltine: 'The time has come for others to consider their own response to the tragic conflict of loyalties with which I have myself wrestled for perhaps too long.'[23] Anthony Teasdale, Howe's political adviser, had played a key role in drafting the speech. He recalled later that the final sentence was not written as an explicit invitation to Heseltine. Instead, the words were 'added late in the day and without unambiguous intent. Although it was read as a call to arms to Michael Heseltine ... my own recollection is that it was meant primarily to encourage the cabinet to constrain Mrs Thatcher and enforce a more pro-European policy.'[24] But Howe's intent was no longer relevant: Heseltine took it as an invitation, and accepted.

The leadership battle that followed exposed the turmoil within Margaret Thatcher's soul. Her advisers warned her she must dispose of the idea that she would happily see Britain left behind in a two-speed Europe. Her own burning belief was that the single currency proposed by its European partners would destroy Britain's national identity. It would hand to others the control over economic policy which was an inseparable part of nationhood. Many Conservatives agreed with her – they would make the same point with equal vigour in the struggle over economic and monetary union which later engulfed John Major's government. But Thatcher had made too many enemies. It was not just Europe: there were also the poll tax, her autocratic manner, the recession. Her campaign, at once imperious and inept, served only to underline her isolation. Hurd and Major had signed her nomination papers, but the cabinet was no more than a bystander in this contest. Major retired to Huntington, pleading the need to recuperate after an operation to remove a wisdom tooth. Others spoke for her in the days before the first ballot, but their hearts had long ago been lost. There was a sense that she had outlived her age: Britain had needed the Thatcher revolution, but, as Douglas Hurd would frequently remark, it was not a nation of Maoists.

On Tuesday 20 November she failed to defeat Heseltine in the first ballot. She secured 204 votes to her opponent's 152. Under the complicated rules for the contest, this meant that there would be another round of voting. The next day her cabinet deserted her. The day after that she resigned. She had been in Downing Street for eleven years. She had never been defeated in a general election. Now she had been deposed by her own party. Europe lay in her heart.

For John Major, the victor of the contest that followed with Michael Heseltine and Douglas Hurd, the first task was to restore a semblance of unity to the Conservative Party. He was, at forty-seven, the youngest prime minister for a century. His party was shell-shocked. For all their anger and frustration with Thatcher's leadership, many in the cabinet could not quite believe what they had done. They had sat shamefaced, staring at their feet, during her last, bravura, performance in the House of Commons on the day she resigned. Thatcher loyalists – some, like Michael Portillo, had begged her to fight on to the end – were appalled at the behaviour of their colleagues. In the country, the constituency activists who had loved her for so long could not understand her betrayal by the party at Westminster. They were dismayed by the recession, yes. They disliked, some of them, the poll tax. She had become too imperious. But to depose her – how could they have done that?

Later, during the civil war in his party over ratification of the Maastricht Treaty after the 1992 election, Major's preoccupation with party unity would be seen as a sign of weakness. The line between conciliation and vacillation became perilously thin – he was a whip, a party manager, not a leader, colleagues would whisper. Now, however, he was needed to bind the wounds; he was chosen because of, not despite, his consensual style. Major had defeated Heseltine in the second round of the contest by 185 to 131 votes. Hurd, though backed by the best and the brightest in the cabinet – including Kenneth Clarke, Chris Patten and William Waldegrave from the centre-left – secured just 56. Major was the choice of the Tory right, the supporters of the *ancien régime* who had determined that Heseltine must be stopped at all costs. Thatcher herself, lost in the packing-cases of 10 Downing Street, had telephoned waverers urging them to vote for Major. So too had Norman Tebbit. Norman Lamont, Major's campaign manager and soon to be his chancellor, was a self-declared Eurosceptic. Only weeks earlier Lamont had presented his credentials in a speech to the Bruges Group, the anti-federalist alliance which had sprung from Thatcher's speech two years earlier.[25] A single European currency, Lamont warned, would lead inexorably to a political federation. Peter Lilley, another leading figure in Major's campaign and later to be nominated by the prime minister as one of the cabinet's 'bastards', had even less time for the federalism of Jacques Delors.

To their dismay, John Major's self-chosen allies on the Eurosceptic right would soon discover that he was One of Them rather than One of Us. Major declared at the start of his premiership that he preferred pragmatism to ideology, but his choice of Patten as party chairman sent a clear message as to where his real politics lay. Patten, a European Christian Democrat as much as a Conservative, would soon be the prime minister's closest ally. In the early 1980s he had been one of the most articulate critics of Thatcher's monetarism. Later he had come to embrace a hard-edged approach to the economy. Otherwise, he remained a one-nation Conservative in the tradition of Rab Butler and Iain Macleod. Hurd, a natural patron, saw in Patten the only true intellectual in the cabinet. Major, however, proved an adept conciliator among the discordant voices. If his sympathies lay with Patten, his instincts told him he would also have to retain the allegiance of Kenneth Baker, newly installed at the Home Office, Norman Lamont and Peter Lilley.

Abroad, the new prime minister made the restoration of good relations with Chancellor Helmut Kohl the first priority of his foreign policy. At the second Rome summit, in December, his message was that, while Britain might not share the ambitions of its partners, he preferred compromise to confrontation. Hurd exulted in the conciliatory rhetoric. He saw in Major's premiership the moment for Britain to settle its relationship with its European partners. The language and venue of a speech in the spring of 1991 symbolized Major's approach. Yes, he wanted a liberal, open Europe of nation-states, but he intended to engage in the debate rather than sulk on the sidelines. Britain, he told the Konrad Adenauer Foundation in Bonn, would be 'at the very heart of Europe'. He paid tribute to Germany's 'social solidarity', and said that Conservative and Christian Democrat members of the European Parliament should henceforth work in the same team.[26] As with Margaret Thatcher's Bruges speech, the tone was as important as the content. This was Major's riposte to his predecessor; here was Patten's influence at work.

In the substance of his approach to the intergovernmental conference, however, Major was careful to remain on the ground he had staked out with Hurd during the last months of Thatcher's premiership. He revived the idea of an 'opting-in' mechanism to allow others to lay their plans for monetary union without tying Britain irrevocably to the same goal. Hurd developed the 'pillared' approach to political union – fostering intergovernmental cooperation on issues like foreign and interior policy – which eventually provided the architecture for the Maastricht Treaty. Major also determined on a British 'opt-out' from the social Europe which Jacques Delors saw as an essential adjunct to the single market.

There were difficult moments. For months after the inglorious end to her premiership Thatcher remained in deep shock. When she re-emerged it was to snipe at her successor's European strategy. Once or twice she threatened to topple him from the high-wire of compromise. Nicholas Ridley and Norman Tebbit echoed her warnings. But when the prime minister eventually signed the Maastricht Treaty, in December 1991, only the most Europhobic in his party opposed him. Thatcher offered sullen consent: caught by the television cameras on the doorstep of her London home, she said simply, 'I'm thrilled for John.' Major proclaimed the treaty, with its opt-outs from a single currency and the social chapter, as 'Game, Set and Match' for Britain. They were words which a year later would dissolve in a sea of acrimony within the Conservative Party.

*

For the economy, the eighteen months between Thatcher's departure and Major's election victory in April 1992 was a winter of dark nights and false dawns. With cruel irony, convincing evidence of the depth of the recession into which the economy had plunged during 1990 came only weeks after sterling had been tied to the Deutschmark. As so often happens when governments grapple with turns in the economic cycle, the primacy of the politics had obscured the reality of the economics.

For much of the first half of 1990 the Treasury and the Bank had been puzzled by the apparent failure of the economy to respond to high interest rates. There were signs – later to prove misleading – of a pause in the process of disinflation. Sterling's steep fall during 1989 was making itself felt, reinforcing a stubbornly high level of inflation. During May, the Treasury had been sufficiently concerned to consider another rise in interest rates. Peter Middleton raised the idea during the Treasury's monthly review of monetary policy with officials from the Bank. The Bank found itself in a curious reversal of its traditional, hawkish, role. Fearful of the huge build-up of debt in the economy – and the systemic risk to the financial system of massive loan defaults – Tony Coleby, the Bank's money markets director, advised against any tightening of the squeeze.

Though it was not evident until much later, during the following month the economy, in a phrase popularized soon afterwards, 'fell off a cliff'. National income, or gross domestic product, dropped by nearly 2 per cent in real terms between the first and second halves of 1990. The slide in house prices turned into a collapse, and manufacturing output fell by 5 per cent within nine months. Loaded with debt, consumers and companies alike stopped spending. The unprecedented expansion of credit since the mid-1980s had seen individuals' debt-to-income ratio double. When house prices fell, the bubble burst. Businesses hit a similar credit crunch. Companies had borrowed heavily to finance take-overs and investment, but, once demand started to turn down, so too did their profits.

The government was slow to recognize the speed or the scale of the downturn. The Treasury's statistics were misleading, its forecasts worse. John Major was driven to comment that the poor quality and conflicting evidence from the official indicators left him steering the economy through 'thick pea soup'. By the end of the year, however, it was clear that the government had made the exchange rate the centre-piece of its economic strategy at just the moment when its economic forecasts would once again fail it. 'We were driving blind,' a senior Treasury official remarked ruefully as he reflected on the circumstances of sterling's ERM entry. At the end of October 1990 the Confederation of British Industry published a deeply pessimistic survey showing the largest drop in business confidence since 1980. Major had expected that the economic downturn would be a painful but relatively brief shock. Instead it would prove as prolonged as it was deep.

It was also a different sort of recession. Its principal victims were not the blue-collar workers of the North and Midlands but the middle classes of southern England. The principal beneficiaries of the Lawson boom became its victims. If North Sea oil production was excluded, national output fell for seven successive quarters – twenty-one months – between the summer of 1990 and the spring of 1992. The loss of output in 1991 alone was over 2 per cent. Unemployment jumped from 1.6 million in mid-1990 to 2.6 million in the early months of 1992. The bailiffs began arriving in the leafy avenues of the Home Counties and in the chic new developments of London's Docklands to repossess the homes of Thatcher's children. Norman Lamont, rewarded with the Treasury for his role in Major's leadership campaign, found his predictions of better times ahead overtaken constantly by an economy sinking under the weight of consumer and corporate debt.

It was a period of infelicitous phrases from the chancellor. In May 1991 he provoked uproar among opposition MPs and dismay on his own side when he told the House of Commons that the recession was a 'price worth paying' for the defeat of inflation. He was confident of a return to growth later in the year. The fall in output, he added, would be of the order of 1 per cent – hardly a justification for the 'exaggerated and irresponsible talk of a depression'.[27] The recovery did not materialize. Lamont's first Budget, in March 1991, sought to neutralize the political damage being inflicted by the soon-to-be-abolished poll tax. For a time, the Treasury considered increasing income tax – Terence Burns believed that Lawson's reductions during the 1980s had dangerously eroded the income tax base. In the event

Lamont judged that a U-turn too far. A £140 across-the-board reduction in the level of the poll tax was paid for instead by an increase in VAT from 15 to 17.5 per cent. The poll tax was Thatcher's most damaging legacy, hated by the middle classes as much as by the poor, who now refused in their millions to pay it. Higher VAT, however, was not calculated to rekindle the consumer confidence the economy so badly needed. Nor were moves to restrict mortgage interest relief and to raise the tax on company cars. By July the chancellor faced a censure debate in the House of Commons. The recovery, he promised again, would come in the second half of the year, though by now he was admitting that the loss of output in the recession would be 3 per cent rather than the 1 per cent he had forecast a few months earlier. In the autumn, at a restless Conservative Party conference in Blackpool, the chancellor maintained the façade of optimism: 'The green shoots of economic spring are appearing once again.'

It was inevitable that the ERM would begin to bear the blame for the recession. Lamont, ironically, had never really supported sterling's entry. He had been chief secretary, Major's deputy at the Treasury, but he had not been told of the decision to join until the morning of the announcement. But he appeared content to accept his predecessor's decision. During the first half of 1991 borrowing costs came down in step with inflation. In early October interest rates had stood at 15 per cent and inflation at 10.9 per cent. By July 1991 the respective rates had fallen in tandem to 11 per cent and to 5.8 per cent. But the relaxation of the monetary squeeze had no visible impact on the recession. The Labour Party's repeated calls for still lower interest rates soon found a strong echo from business. The captains of industry were fast losing their enthusiasm for the rigours of the ERM. The National Institute for Economic and Social Research published one of a number of studies suggesting that sterling's rate against the Deutschmark had been set at too high a level. The Institute thought a rate closer to DM2.60 more appropriate.[28]

The prime minister, forced to delay the general election until the spring of 1992, was impatient. Major knew that he could not risk sterling's stability within the ERM with precipitate reductions in interest rates. Nor, however, could he ignore the gloomy message of the opinion polls. At one point he considered seeking devaluation within the ERM to loosen the squeeze. In the autumn of 1991 he asked Sarah Hogg, the head of the No. 10 policy unit, to prepare a paper on the mechanics of realigning within the system. Hogg drew on the principles enunciated by Nigel Lawson several years earlier in his IMF speech on managed exchange rates. She suggested that, to retain confidence, any devaluation should be confined to an adjustment in the pound's central rate within the existing 6 per cent band. But, as Hogg recalls in an account of the period written jointly with Jonathan Hill, *Too Close to Call*, Major decided against pursuing the option.[29] For its part, the Treasury took some comfort from the fact that the gap between British and German rates had fallen to its lowest level for a decade. To most officials this signalled that the government would have been obliged to keep interest rates at comparable levels even had it not joined the ERM. Just as it had underestimated the boom in the late 1980s, however, the Treasury now failed to grasp the intensity of the deflation.

Unfortunately, German borrowing costs were still rising under the impact of reunification. In the autumn of 1991 Lamont managed to shave another half-point off base rates, but they then stuck at 10.5 per cent until the election in April 1992. From the outset, Major had said that sterling would move to the narrow, 2.25 per cent, bands of the ERM at its existing DM2.95 central rate 'as soon as conditions allow'. It was a pledge which Lamont now repeated regularly in order to reassure the currency markets. It was already obvious to both men, however, that such a move would have to await a sustained downturn in German borrowing costs. In December 1991 the Bundesbank pushed up its interest rates again, putting pressure on the Treasury to follow suit. Major, now committed to an election in the spring, was aghast. Inflation was down to 4 per cent, and the economy was mired still in recession. The demands of the domestic economy pointed to lower, not higher, borrowing costs. After some deliberation, the Treasury decided against following the Bundesbank's lead, provoking a flurry of speculation against sterling. The pound by now had dipped to around DM2.85, and some Bank officials thought it had been a mistake not to follow the Bundesbank. As it happened, calm soon returned. But the incident would prove an unpleasant trailer for the conflict between British and German economic policies which would soon wrench sterling from the ERM.

CHAPTER NINE

SLEEPLESS NIGHTS

ON THE EVENING after Black Wednesday, Norman Lamont sipped dry white wine in his spacious wood-panelled office at the Treasury. Opposition leaders were clamouring for his resignation. Conservative colleagues, including many in the cabinet, also expected him to leave the Treasury. That surely was what chancellors did after being forced to devalue the pound. Sunk deep into his armchair, Lamont was unmoved. Asked how he felt after the biggest economic defeat since Harold Wilson had been beaten by the currency speculators twenty-five years earlier, he replied that he was fine. And he had no intention of giving up the chancellorship. Contrary to political folklore, resignation was not obligatory. Stafford Cripps had remained at the Treasury after devaluing in 1949; so would Norman Lamont. Sterling had fallen by 5 per cent since its ejection the previous day from the ERM. Now it had been suspended from the system, however, Lamont no longer felt obliged to chart its fortunes on the flickering Reuters screen in his outer office. 'I haven't had such a good night's sleep in weeks,' he quipped. 'There was no need to stay awake worrying about the pound.'

The sequence of events which led to the catastrophe had been set in train four months earlier, while the prime minister was basking in the unexpected glow of his election victory on 9 April 1992. Against all expectations, the Danish electorate had voted in a referendum on 2 June to reject the treaty which had been signed by European leaders in the small Dutch town of Maastricht six months before. Suddenly the steady progress towards economic and monetary union upon which the stability of the ERM was predicated was in doubt – the financial markets could no longer be certain that the established ERM parities would hold.

This fatal weakening of the glue of confidence was exacerbated by

President François Mitterrand's announcement that France also would hold a plebiscite on Maastricht. Mitterrand saw in a referendum the opportunity to restore his government's battered fortunes, but he had misjudged the mood of the nation. The danger always with a referendum is that the electorate may choose to ignore the question and take the opportunity to humble its government. If that happened in France, the Maastricht plan for a single currency would suffer the same fate as the abortive Werner Plan twenty years earlier. The date set for the French poll, 20 September, gave the markets a focus, a target at which to aim. As Robin Leigh-Pemberton would comment in a speech soon after sterling's ignominious departure:

> We knew through the summer that we were sitting on a grumbling volcano. The Danish rejection of Maastricht caused a detectable tremor by putting in doubt progress towards EMU, and thereby seemingly weakening confidence in the commitment to existing ERM parities; and the uncertainty surrounding the French referendum provided further impetus to the build-up of pressure and a precise focal point for predictions of an eruption.[1]

This new mood of Europessimism exposed the fundamental disequilibrium within the ERM, hitherto submerged in the assumption that member states were travelling in convoy towards the creation of a single currency. The Deutschmark was the anchor for the system, but Germany was sailing in the opposite direction to its European partners. Its domestic economy demanded high interest rates to stifle the inflationary pressures caused by reunification; elsewhere in Europe governments were struggling to pull their economies from recession and inflation was subdued. As long as interest rates in Germany remained high, its partners could not cut their own borrowing costs to stimulate economic expansion.

The tension had its origins in the economic terms for German reunification set in mid-1990 by Chancellor Helmut Kohl. Against the advice of Karl Otto Pöhl, the president of the Bundesbank, Kohl had decided that the new German monetary union would be based on parity between the Deutschmark and its poor relation the Ostmark for all but the largest holders of the East German currency. Pöhl had wanted to contain the risk of an inflationary surge in the German money supply by fixing the rate of exchange at only one Deutschmark for every five Ostmarks. Kohl's bigger mistake, however, was to finance the marriage of the East's backward economy with that of the infinitely more affluent West through a large increase in the German budget deficit. Reconstruction in the East would be paid for not by higher taxes but by additional government borrowing. The inevitable result of the swelling budget deficit was an acceleration in the inflation rate to over 4 per cent – a disaster by German standards. Pöhl, a jealous guardian of his place in Bundesbank history, had foreseen the damaging consequences and had resigned in 1991.

His successor was the conservative academic Helmut Schlesinger. He adopted the classic response of the postwar Bundesbank to profligacy by the Bonn government by ratcheting up interest rates to offset the inflationary pressures of higher government borrowing. The process was still going on in the spring of 1992, despite the sharp tensions it had provoked within the ERM. Schlesinger had never been a supporter of the attempt to stabilize European exchange rates: like many at the Frankfurt headquarters of the Bundesbank, he saw it as a product of politics rather than economics. More seriously, it threatened irritating interference with the Bundesbank's domestic monetary policy. In the last weeks of the sterling crisis it was Schlesinger whom Norman Lamont would try to browbeat at a disastrous meeting of European finance ministers in Bath, and it was the bespectacled, donnish head of the Bundesbank who would utter the few brief sentences which would seal sterling's fate.

The potential conflict between economic imperatives in Britain and Germany had been apparent when Britain joined the ERM two years earlier. The Bank of England had alluded to the dilemma in its *Quarterly Bulletin*. In a world of floating exchange rates, the Bank said, the response to German reunification should be a once-and-for-all increase in the value of the Deutschmark. Such an adjustment would attract the inflow of overseas capital needed to finance the reconstruction of the East German economy. France, however, had blocked that option by refusing to contemplate devaluation of the franc within the ERM. The implication, the Bank concluded, was that other ERM countries would be obliged to drive down their inflation rates to below German levels in order to deliver the necessary appreciation of the Deutschmark's real exchange rate.[2]

Neither the Bank nor the Treasury anticipated that the dislocation would be as large or as prolonged as it now turned out. Terence Burns, the Treasury's chief economic adviser, had told the Treasury and Civil Service Committee as far back as November 1990 that 'Clearly, at the moment, there are some different pressures in Germany than in some other countries, but it is not clear that they need necessarily last for very long. I have every hope that the system will be able to live with that.'[3] Nor did the government foresee that lower interest rates in the US and a consequent steep fall in the dollar's value would deepen the conflict of interest between Germany and its partners. Sustaining the pound's Deutschmark parity would translate into an exchange rate against the US currency of $2 – a ruinously high level for British exporters. It was not until the summer of 1992 that the Treasury and the Bank began fully to appreciate the seriousness of the conflict between German and British policy. The steady fall in interest rates from 15 per cent in October 1990 to 10 per cent in May 1992 might have happened sooner had German rates not been rising. The more serious problem, however, was that the Bundesbank's stance precluded any further reduction in British interest rates.

Lamont had given a dubiously optimistic gloss to the economic forecasts which had accompanied the March 1992 Budget. Nigel Lawson's budget surpluses had vanished and the government's finances were moving rapidly back into deficit as a result of the recession, but the official projections for public borrowing understated the scale of the problem. Against the advice of senior Treasury officials, Lamont announced a modest package of pre-election tax cuts, based on the introduction of a new 20p lower rate of income tax. Predictably enough, once the election had been won the Treasury's forecasts were decidedly less optimistic. Inflation was falling faster than had been expected, and there were signs of a brief surge in business confidence, but everything else was bad. The economic recovery that John Major had promised during the election campaign had not materialized. The Treasury had once again underestimated the damage to consumer confidence from high interest rates and falling house prices. Voters who had believed the government's claim of an economic miracle were discovering it had been an expensive illusion. Negative equity now entered the lexicon of the ordinary British voter.

The juxtaposition of pre-electoral politics and the recession meanwhile had wrought havoc with the government's efforts to control public spending. As spending rose, tax revenues were falling in response to higher unemployment and an abrupt slowdown in consumer spending. The result was an uncontrolled surge in public borrowing: the government's deficit was heading for £35bn, or nearly 6 per cent of national income. In different circumstances the Treasury would have demanded an emergency package of spending cuts. Now, however, it could not afford to risk deepening the recession: the country would not stand for fiscal austerity while interest rates remained so high. Inflation was already down to 4 per cent, and in July it would fall to 3.7 per cent. At the Bank of England there would soon be fears that, if interest rates were not cut over the following year, prices might actually start falling for the first time since the 1930s. The Treasury considered a further relaxation of fiscal policy in an attempt to kick-start economic recovery. Several options, including personal and corporate tax cuts, were examined, but officials decided that even a temporary addition to public borrowing would be unsustainable.

In the weeks immediately after the election the mood in Whitehall was one of growing disquiet rather than serious foreboding. The Bank probed the intentions of its European counterparts, most notably the Bundesbank and the Banque de France. At the Treasury, Alan Budd, who had replaced Terence Burns as the government's chief economic adviser when Burns took over as permanent secretary from the departing Peter Middleton in 1991, was gloomy but not despairing. Andrew Turnbull, now the senior official responsible for monetary policy, explored with the Bank the alternatives to higher interest rates if sterling began to weaken against the Deutschmark. The position looked difficult but not impossible. There were still hopes that the next move in German interest rates would be down rather than up. In the words of one senior Treasury official, 'The aim was to make the ERM work, but to avoid a rise in interest rates. We had to reduce the tension between the exchange rate and domestic monetary policy, to manoeuvre our way through.'

The prime minister was also relatively relaxed. He had just won an election that most of the pundits had expected him to lose. He had escaped from the shadow of his predecessor. For his first eighteen months in No. 10 she had been a constant source of irritation. Lost in her enforced retirement, she had not waited long to display her annoyance with Major's policies. The criticism, public and private, had quickly followed his decision to scrap the poll tax, to sign up to the Maastricht Treaty and to relax the public-spending reins. Now he had won his own electoral mandate and she would soon be ensconced, more safely, in the House of Lords. Major calculated that he had time on his side: if the economic upturn was delayed, there was ample time to realign the economic and political cycles before the next election. His parliamentary majority had been reduced by the election to twenty-one, but there was no inkling yet that the Conservative Party was about to tear open the wounds which had precipitated his predecessor's fall.

During his frequent appearances on the Whitehall cocktail circuit the prime minister could scarcely disguise his exuberance. Yes, he would say, he realized that the promised economic upturn would not be rapid, but he preferred the steady to the spectacular. His sights were on a bigger prize – sustained, non-inflationary growth. The disinflation wrought by the ERM would deliver that prize. Yes, he had heard Thatcher's suggestion that he should devalue to free the British economy from the constraints imposed by high German interest rates, but, no, he would not do so. Instead he would deliver what she had promised but never achieved: permanently low inflation and steady growth. She had abolished socialism; he would rid Britain of the boom-to-bust cycles which drained its economic strength.

Around the cabinet table the studied pragmatism of Major's wider political agenda did not stir great excitement among his colleagues. But most had expected to lose the election. Just being there was a remarkable bonus. 'I'm looking forward to some peace and quiet,' confessed one cabinet minister over lunch a few weeks after the election. Major's collegiate style was seen as a strength rather than a weakness. Only later was his attachment to consensus to be derided as vacillation.

There was also relative calm at first in the financial markets. Despite the steady rise in German interest rates, the Treasury felt confident enough to cut interest rates from 10.5 to 10 per cent on 5 May. Sterling hovered comfortably around the DM2.95 central rate of its ERM band. From the optimists in Whitehall there were whispered hints that Britain might be able to 'decouple' its interest rates from the upward trend in Germany without undermining the pound. Gus O'Donnell, who had moved from the Treasury with Major to replace Bernard Ingham as the No. 10 press secretary, floated the idea more than once at his daily briefings for political journalists. Two years earlier short-term borrowing costs had been five or six points higher than the equivalent rates in Germany; now the gap was only one-quarter of 1 per cent.

As the weeks went by and prospects for recovery receded, however, so there were visible signs of unrest on the Conservative back benches. Europe and the economy were becoming inextricably and explosively entangled. Those on the right of the Conservative Party who had tolerated but never approved of the Maastricht Treaty had started to make a fatal elision between the treaty, the ERM and the recession. This combustible combination would translate the divisions over Europe in the party into the most destructive internal conflict since the split over tariff reform at the beginning of the century.

The Maastricht Treaty, signed in December 1991, had revealed Major's talents both as a party manager and as a negotiator on the international stage. It was a treaty that the British government had not wanted, but which it could not avoid. Its continental partners were determined to translate into a firm timetable the blueprint for a single currency set out in the 1989 Delors report. They also wanted a framework for political integration which would transform the European Community into the European Union. Major's task during 1991 had been to reconcile those demands with the instincts of a party which had rejected Thatcher's Europhobia but remained at best deeply ambivalent about the transfer of any further authority to Brussels. Her defiant isolationism had led to her downfall, but her views commanded sufficient support on the back benches to pose a significant threat to her successor.

During the first year of his premiership Major conducted in effect two sets of negotiations: one with other European leaders and another with his own party. By mid-1991 it was clear that, on the central issue of economic and monetary union, the hard-ecu proposals he had tabled as chancellor commanded no support in other capitals. Against that, a treaty which threatened to subsume sterling in a single European currency and take from the government control of national monetary and fiscal policy would divide his party and cabinet. So Major returned to the strategy that Thatcher had rejected in the spring of 1990 – he would sanction changes to the Treaty of Rome to pave the way for a single European currency as long as Britain retained the right to defer a final decision. Shifting the terms of the debate within his own party, Major stressed that he would never accept the 'imposition' of a single currency: Parliament would have the right to decide the fate of sterling if and when others decided to create an economic and monetary union.

At the Community's Luxembourg summit in June 1991, Jacques Delors told Major he would accept a formula which allowed governments to opt in to the process at the moment a single currency was created. If Major insisted, the European Commission president was also ready to acquiesce in a more specific set of arrangements giving Britain the right to opt out. When the treaty was signed, six months later, Major insisted it include a tailor-made opt-out. The British protocol attached to the treaty had been drafted in London and confirmed as 'watertight' by a raft of Whitehall lawyers. Its opening sentence stated unequivocally that 'The United Kingdom shall not be obliged or committed to move to the third stage of economic and monetary union without a separate decision to do so by its government and Parliament.'[4] After his departure from the government, Lamont would claim the credit both for the opt-out and for the removal from the main text of the treaty of a legal commitment to membership of the ERM. Both contentions were vigorously disputed by the prime minister's aides. None the less, during 1991 Lamont was an important ally. The chancellor's Euroscepticism was then a strength rather than a weakness. By putting his name to the treaty, he reinforced Major's argument that the government had conceded nothing of substance in signing it.

During the months before the Maastricht summit, Margaret Thatcher, still brooding on the back benches of the House of Commons, encouraged rebellion. She let it be known, privately and then over time publicly, that she would oppose changes to the Treaty of Rome to prepare the way for a single currency. If Major agreed such amendments, she would demand a referendum. Never mind that she had denounced as constitutionally corrupt the then Labour government's use of a referendum in 1976. Now she attacked Major just as her predecessor Edward Heath had harried her. 'He should just say no – if the others want a single currency it should be outside of the Treaty of Rome,' she remarked at one lunch in the City during the late summer of 1991. She extended her attack to Major's domestic economic policy at other social gatherings, on one occasion accusing her successor of 'spending like a socialist'. Her views were echoed by Nicholas Ridley, now nursing his resentments on the back benches. The prime minister, Ridley said, gave the impression 'he would agree to everything'. There were also warnings from the anti-federalist Bruges group. William Cash, its spokesman in the Commons, had secured the chairmanship of the party's back-bench European committee as a power-base from which to oppose further integration. Michael Spicer, James Cran and Christopher Gill were among others on the back benches who emerged as powerful critics of any further advances along the road to a united Europe. Teddy Taylor, an unrelenting opponent of what he referred to as 'the Common Market', and Teresa Gorman, a brash Thatcherite, gave a populist edge to the opposition. Major was dismayed by Thatcher's behaviour. He would remind colleagues that her approach to Europe during the 1980s had been first to bang the table and then to give way. She had signed the Single European Act in 1985 – the most significant transfer of national sovereignty to Europe since Britain had joined. 'There is only majority voting in Europe because Mrs Thatcher agreed it,' he was driven to remark at one point.

Publicly, however, he responded to the tensions with a skilful, if frequently inelegant, balancing-act. At one moment he would stress his determination to keep Britain at the 'heart of Europe', only to promise soon afterwards that he would make no concessions to federalism. These perplexing swerves were the catalyst for the early charges that Major was more comfortable in his role as party manager than as leader. In private conversations he endorsed Chris Patten's view that nothing would be more disastrous than Britain's exclusion from the European mainstream. Major would add that, if his rhetoric was sometimes tinged with Euroscepticism, that was because he was speaking to the cause of party unity. He applied the same patient conciliation to divisions within the cabinet. Breaking with the habit of his predecessor, he encouraged lengthy debate on the shape of the treaty, paying close attention to the views of the sceptics. Kenneth Baker at the Home Office, Michael Howard at Employment and Peter Lilley at Trade and Industry were persuaded in turn to sign up to Major's negotiating stance.

Douglas Hurd adopted a similar approach in the parallel negotiations on political union. During countless reassuring appearances in the House of Commons he promoted the cause of closer cooperation, while insisting he could be relied upon to veto the creation of a federal superstructure for Europe. Hurd proposed the intergovernmental pillars – for foreign and security policy and for interior and justice issues – which formed the basis for the treaty amendments at Maastricht. He ensured that such issues as defence and immigration – the touchstones of national sovereignty for Conservatives – remained outside the remit of the Treaty of Rome. Concessions to Britain's partners elsewhere – some extension of majority voting and an enhanced role for the European Parliament in legislative decisions – were camouflaged by the incorporation into the treaty of the principle of subsidiarity. Displaying the serenity of a politician achieving at the Foreign Office his lifetime's ambition, Hurd cleverly presented this ill-defined commitment to devolution of power from Brussels as a new shield for the nation-state – a bulwark against European intrusions into the nooks and crannies of Britain's national life. The exclusion from the final document of the word 'federal' was likewise proclaimed as a triumph for British diplomacy. When the treaty was signed, Hurd claimed, like Major, that it represented a decisive victory for Britain's vision of a Europe of nation-states over the federalism of Jacques Delors. Privately he described the outcome as 'an honourable draw'.

Major completed the negotiations with his own party in late November 1991, two weeks before the Maastricht summit. An intentionally vague House of Commons motion, the subject of a two-day debate, gave him a mandate to keep Britain 'at the heart of Europe' while resisting moves towards a federalist future. Thatcher, speaking from the back benches, demanded a referendum on any move towards a single currency, but she was outflanked by her successor. In an adroit performance, Major obscured the concessions he was ready to make by robustly rejecting those demands he knew his European partners would not press. His promise to excise from the final text any mention of the word 'federal' was enough to win over some doubters. At the end of the debate, fifteen of his party's Eurosceptics defied him, nine abstaining and six voting against. Thatcher this time was not among them.

Major's assured performance at the Maastricht summit in early December – he exploited to the full the rapport he had established with Chancellor Kohl – secured him the best treaty available to the leader of such a divided party. He was obliged to accept a timetable for a single currency, but at either of the proposed starting dates for the third and final stage – 1997 or 1999 – Britain could decide whether to join or to stand aside. Alongside that opt-out, he secured at the eleventh hour Britain's permanent exclusion from the social provisions of the treaty. This social chapter opt-out assured him the support of the sceptics in his cabinet and the acquiescence of most in his party. A week later Norman Tebbit joined six other Conservative MPs in defying Major in a House of Commons vote on the treaty. Thatcher chose to abstain. She knew that to defeat Major over Maastricht before the election due the following spring would be to hand the keys of Downing Street to Neil Kinnock. For his part, the prime minister believed he had at last salved the wounds inflicted by her departure.

Fate, however, was on the side of the prime minister's enemies. A foretaste of the trouble ahead came within weeks of the general election, when the Queen addressed the European Parliament in Strasbourg. Her speech, in the second week of May, was unremarkable – a gesture before Britain assumed the six-months rotating presidency of the Community two months later. Reading from a Foreign Office script, she struck a careful balance between high praise for the European Community's role in preserving the postwar peace and insistence that it must accommodate national diversity. The simple fact of her appearing at Strasbourg, however, provoked outrage among a small group of Europhobes. During her premiership Thatcher had refused to contemplate a visit by the sovereign to an institution she held in contempt. Now she responded to her successor's attempt at glasnost by amplifying the fierce antipathy to closer European integration which she had set out in her Bruges speech four years earlier. This updated version, delivered in a speech in the Hague in mid-May, carried a warning: she would continue the fight against ratification of Maastricht when she took up her seat in the House of Lords.

Thatcher's supporters had begun to gather their forces. On 21 May the legislation to implement the treaty faced its first House of Commons hurdle after the second-reading debate. Major's speech to the House was defensive: 'What we kept out of the Maastricht Treaty is as important as what is in the treaty,' he told MPs. There was no social chapter, no diminution in the power of NATO, no weakening of national decision-taking in foreign policy, no word 'federal', and 'no commitment to a federal Europe'.[5] Labour's decision to abstain in the vote assured the government a comfortable victory, but twenty-two Conservative MPs defied the government and voted against the bill. A handful of others abstained. It was the biggest Tory rebellion over Europe since the party had debated entry to the Common Market twenty years earlier; fewer had voted against the ratification in 1986 of the Single European Act. It marked the emergence into the public consciousness of anti-Maastricht crusaders on the Tory back benches like William Cash, Michael Spicer and Richard Shepherd. A corrosive factionalism which would crack the foundations of Major's government had taken hold.

The decisive impetus, however, came from the outcome of the Danish referendum. Just as it cracked the foundations of the ERM, so the rejection of the Maastricht Treaty by the stubbornly independent Danes destroyed the peace which Major had been painstakingly building in his party. The soon-to-be Baroness Thatcher of Kesteven hailed the result as a triumph for democracy and called for a halt to the British ratification process. When Major indicated that he would press ahead, she put herself at the head of the campaign for a British referendum. Her successor would admit the chasm now between them by denouncing her views as those of 'Little England'. The tide was turning against him, however. In the House of Commons the ranks of the hard-line sceptics were swelled by those who had voted for ratification of Maastricht out of loyalty rather than conviction. Within a day of the Danish vote, seventy Conservative MPs had signed an early day motion calling for a 'fresh start' for the government's European policy. Major had acknowledged that the passage of the Maastricht legislation would have to be delayed, but the MPs' motion went further, suggesting that the treaty should be abandoned in favour of an agenda for Europe which promoted enlargement and the completion of the single market.[6] By 4 June another nineteen MPs had signed the motion. On the terrace of the House of Commons, middle-ranking ministers ostentatiously toasted their Danish cousins.

In the cabinet, Michael Howard, Michael Portillo and Peter Lilley were among those who judged that Major should now consider ditching a treaty that Britain had never wanted. Lamont also warned the prime minister against trying too hard to resist a vote in Denmark which had vindicated his own government's original opposition to further European integration. Lilley thought it perverse for Britain to rescue the treaty. As Treasury chief secretary, Portillo held the most junior rank in the cabinet. He was not yet forty, but he had been marked out on the right of the Conservative Party as the guardian of the Thatcherite torch. He had come to believe that his party's embrace of Europe thirty years earlier had been an historic error. The Conservatives' natural role was as the party of the nation-state, the upholder of British institutions and tradition. The free trade promised by the Common Market was fine; the march towards economic and political integration was anathema. In public Portillo supported ratification of Maastricht; privately he was certain it should be abandoned.

In different circumstances Major too might have disowned the treaty. Despite his conviction that Britain's future lay in the European mainstream, he would have been happier if Maastricht had never been signed, and he had fought hard to win the British opt-outs. Just a day before the Danish vote he had remarked in a speech in Ayrshire that Britain's priority for its forthcoming presidency of the Community would be to roll back interference from Brussels.[7] Now, however, Major would emerge as the champion of Maastricht, using Britain's presidency of the Community during the second half of 1992 to bring Denmark back into the Maastricht fold. Backed by Douglas Hurd, Kenneth Clarke and Michael Heseltine, the prime minister concluded it was better to salvage an imperfect treaty than to confront again the federalist ambitions of Germany and France in a new set of negotiations. Hurd was sure it would be a costly mistake to use the Danish referendum as an excuse to halt the ratification process. Despite the vote, the Copenhagen government had itself indicated that it hoped to find a way to reverse the decision. Hurd acknowledged some time afterwards that he had underestimated the reaction among Conservative MPs to the referendum, but he told colleagues that he would have opposed passionately any attempt by the prime minister to resile from the treaty.

As it happened, Major concurred with the foreign secretary's analysis. At Maastricht he had finessed the dangerous choice between being an actor or a spectator on the European stage. He saw that might no longer be possible if a new treaty was negotiated. The first reaction of most other European governments to the referendum result had been to suggest that Denmark be cut adrift and a new treaty of the other eleven states be negotiated in place of Maastricht. If Britain were obstructive it could just as easily be a treaty of ten. There was also a small question here of pride. Major saw in Maastricht a notable personal achievement on the international stage. Thatcher had thundered and blustered in her negotiations with Europe; he had been reasoned and resolute. He was convinced that he had achieved a better deal than ever his predecessor would have secured. So now he ignored the clamour from the Tory right. 'The treaty itself has not changed and neither has my view of the treaty,' he told the House of Commons in an emergency statement after the Danish vote – adding, 'The ratification and implementation of the treaty is in our national interest.'[8]

The prime minister was obliged to acknowledge, however, that the arithmetic at Westminster had altered. Crucially, John Smith, the Labour leader, had decided to maximize the divisions in the Conservative Party by voting against ratification of the treaty unless Major scrapped the social chapter opt-out. That meant that a relatively small number of Tory rebels could now derail the process. The government had intended to push the Maastricht bill through the House of Commons before the summer parliamentary recess began at the end of July. Now the remaining stages of the legislation would have to await clarification from the Danish government of its strategy and the outcome of the French referendum on 20 September. Richard Ryder, the chief whip, was unequivocal in his advice: any course other than delay would court defeat at the hands of an unholy alliance of Tory rebels and the Labour Party.

Major's opponents meanwhile began to capitalize on the disenchantment among Tory MPs over the economy. The recession seemed to be deepening, and the economic indicators underlined the depressed state of consumer spending, industrial output and business confidence. It was obvious what was needed – a sharp cut in interest rates – but that was not possible as long as sterling remained tied to the Deutschmark in the ERM. And what was the ERM, the sceptics asked, if not the route to the single currency and the federal European state envisaged by the Maastricht Treaty? The conclusion was conveniently manifest: Europe – and more particularly Germany – was to blame for Britain's economic ills. Thatcher made the link just before her elevation to the House of Lords in late June. In a television interview with David Frost she declared bluntly, 'Maastricht is a treaty too far. This is a treaty we didn't need and didn't want.' She then demanded that Major risk devaluation of the pound by cutting interest rates to pull the economy from recession: 'You will not get economic recovery in this country while this interest rate stays this high.'[9] Major's cabinet allies responded by raising the possibility that he was ready to make ratification of Maastricht an issue of confidence in his government.

The first reaction in the financial markets to the Danish vote was awkward but not unnerving. The pound drifted towards the bottom of the ERM grid, but held close to its mid-point against the all-important Deutschmark. The speculators' sights were more firmly fixed on the lira and on the small Scandinavian currencies which had been pegged informally to the European Currency Unit.

The reprieve was short-lived: during the latter half of June the disarray at Westminster – punctuated by calls from the Tory back benches for cuts in interest rates regardless of the ERM – began to percolate through to the trading-rooms of the City. Addressing a restless evening meeting of his party's back-bench finance committee on 16 June, Lamont sought to quieten the unrest with a warning that a precipitate cut in interest rates would throw away the government's hard-won gains made in the fight against inflation. John Townend, the newly elected and right-wing chairman of the committee and a long-standing critic of fixed exchange rates, was unconvinced. Townend would soon join those calling publicly for an ERM realignment – the polite description for devaluation.

The expectation earlier in the summer had been that German interest rates, already at record postwar levels of just under 10 per cent, had reached their peak and that the next move would be a reduction. By late June, however, it was clear that the Bundesbank was still deeply concerned about the rapid growth in the German money supply and was contemplating yet higher rates. By contrast, interest rates in the US had fallen to a thirty-year low. International investors in search of higher returns switched their funds from dollars to Deutschmarks, intensifying the strains in the ERM. The pound began to slide against the German currency, falling at the end of June to below DM2.90 for the first time since the general election. By the beginning of July the nervousness in the Treasury had turned to serious anxiety.

The concern was shared in 10 Downing Street, where Maastricht and sterling now dominated John Major's agenda. During their regular meetings, the chancellor voiced his fears of another rise in German interest rates. More than once Major spoke directly to Chancellor Helmut Kohl to underline the risks to the ERM and to request that the Bonn government put pressure on the Bundesbank to avoid any further increase. The Treasury's contacts with the French government had confirmed that Mitterrand would not contemplate a devaluation of the franc; the Italians also were anxious to avoid an ERM realignment. As the strains in the mechanism intensified, the prime minister asked Lamont to prepare a detailed Treasury presentation of the options.

Other members of the cabinet privately voiced alarm at the grisly evidence of rising unemployment, soaring bankruptcies and falling house prices that confronted them during visits to their constituencies. There was no serious discussion within the cabinet about the chancellor's strategy, however. Twenty-five years earlier Harold Wilson had all but banned discussion of the exchange rate. As Denis Healey was to remark, Wilson regarded the sanctity of sterling as absolute, allowing only one cabinet debate on the issue between the

1964 election and devaluation three years later.[10] There was no such formal bar in Major's administration but nor was there any real discussion. Even the sceptics within the cabinet seemed to doubt that the government could break free. Over lunch in late June one of Major's senior colleagues voiced his horror at how quickly the mood of the nation had soured after the election. He saw parallels with the 1980s, when the last deep recession had divided the Conservatives into so-called 'wets' and 'dries'. Now he was driven dolefully to evoke Margaret Thatcher's famous phrase in defence of the ERM. 'There is no alternative,' this minister said – 'is there?'

This sense of impotence extended to the Treasury and the Bank. Their analyses of relative inflation and productivity rates suggested that an exchange rate of DM2.95 was not wildly out of line with economic fundamentals. Lamont concurred, remarking after sterling's ejection from the ERM that 'Even if a different rate had been taken I do not believe that we would have avoided being under siege in the foreign exchange markets.'[11] There was general agreement, however, that sterling's rate against the dollar was unsustainable and that interest rates were too high.

It was at this point, in June 1992, that the government made the critical judgement which locked it into the course which then led inexorably to Black Wednesday. It ruled out devaluation except in the highly unlikely and unexpected circumstance of a revaluation of the Deutschmark against all other ERM currencies. From the starting-point that the economy required above all lower interest rates, the Treasury concluded fatefully that devaluation within the ERM would lead to higher rather than to lower borrowing costs. The reasoning was straightforward if contentious. By the summer of 1992 British interest rates were only about 0.25 percentage points higher than those in Germany. This small 'risk premium' for investors in sterling was lower than at any point in the recent past. During the 1980s the differential was frequently four or five percentage points, and in October 1990, when Britain joined the ERM, it had been as high as 6.5 percentage points. This gap reflected the demand from investors in sterling for a higher interest rate return to set against the expectation that the currency was likely to depreciate over time against the Deutschmark. The Treasury believed the gap had closed by mid-1992 only because investors now accepted the government's commitment to hold sterling steady against the German currency within the ERM.

The conclusion drawn by the Treasury was that if sterling was devalued – unilaterally or alongside other weak currencies like the lira and the peseta – the government would lose this essential credibility. A depreciation of, say, 5 or even 10 per cent within the ERM would lead investors to doubt the government's commitment to a strong pound and, perversely, to anticipate a further depreciation. In those circumstances they would demand a higher interest rate, or risk premium, to hold sterling in preference to Deutschmark assets. Since German rates stood at about 9.75 per cent, a devaluation of the pound against the Deutschmark would necessarily be followed by a rise in British rates from the then level of 10 per cent to, perhaps, 11 or even 12 per cent, otherwise sterling's new, lower, central rate in the ERM would quickly come under pressure. So, far from providing an escape route, a unilateral devaluation would lead to higher interest rates or still further pressure on sterling.

This analysis – set out in detail in a Treasury paper written by Alan Budd and endorsed by Terence Burns – was reinforced by a second assumption. The conventional wisdom in the Treasury was that the theoretical benefit in terms of international competitiveness of a fall in the pound's value would be strictly temporary. Higher import prices would quickly feed through into increased costs for domestic producers. Those would translate in turn into accelerating domestic inflation, wiping out the initial competitive gains from devaluation. This pessimism had been shaped by events in Nigel Lawson's chancellorship. A weak pound, and in particular the large devaluation of 1986, was blamed for fuelling the inflationary boom of the 1980s. The ready-reckoners developed at the Treasury during that period indicated that a 5 per cent fall in the exchange rate would add more than a percentage point to inflation two years later. As it happened, the analysis would very soon be proved wrong by events: the competitive gains of the devaluation which followed the pound's departure from the ERM were not in fact dissipated in higher prices. That had not, however, been the experience of the 1980s.

Alan Budd's paper did include two qualifications to the assertion

that devaluation inside the ERM would be followed automatically by
higher interest rates. The first applied if the fall in the exchange rate
within the ERM was sufficiently large, say 15 or 20 per cent, to
persuade investors that the next move in sterling's value was more
likely to be up than down. In those circumstances the financial
markets might subsequently accept a fall in British interest rates to
below German levels. The same might be true if the pound's central
rate against the Deutschmark was lowered as part of a realignment in
which the German currency was revalued against all other ERM
currencies, including the French franc. After such a realignment,
investors might well believe that sterling would stabilize at its new
Deutschmark rate. The Treasury, however, assumed that a large
devaluation would be vetoed by its European partners and, in any
event, would reignite inflation. The French government, meanwhile,
appeared determined to avoid the devaluation of the franc upon which
a general realignment would depend.

The occasional dissenting voice was heard in Whitehall. Chris
Riley, a senior Treasury economist, and Andrew Turnbull were
among those said to believe that the government should keep open
the option of devaluation within the ERM. Such officials were sceptical
of the orthodox view that a lower exchange rate would lead inexorably
to higher inflation. Riley was heard to argue for the possibility of a
'real' depreciation of sterling, while Turnbull was certain that, if the
pound managed to stay in the mechanism until after the French
referendum, the only option then would be to devalue. Rachel Lomax
was similarly open-minded. Meanwhile the Treasury's assumption
that other European governments would refuse a large devaluation
was not universally shared. John Kerr, the permanent representative
in Brussels, thought it might have been possible to negotiate a change
in the Deutschmark parity of between 10 and 15 per cent.

The more pessimistic view, however, was echoed in the Bank of
England. Eddie George told colleagues he saw only two options:
holding the present Deutschmark rate or withdrawal from the ERM.
'There were two mutually exclusive conditions for a successful
devaluation,' another senior Bank official said later, 'we had to devalue
by no more than our partners would allow, and we had to persuade
the markets we had done enough.' A senior Treasury official agreed:
'We took the view that a very large fall in the exchange rate would be

necessary to get interest rates down. That would have led to higher prices and we would have lost the counter-inflationary battle.'

This consensus at the top of the Treasury was reflected in a speech given by the chancellor to the European Policy Forum on 10 July. This speech was the definitive text for the next few months, setting out in public the conclusions of the Treasury's private analysis. Budd, Burns, Turnbull and other senior officials worked on the speech over several weeks. Its obstinate rejection of devaluation would return to haunt the chancellor. At the outset Lamont indicated that he was an agnostic in the theoretical debate about the relative advantages of fixed or floating exchange rates. Sterling, however, was in the ERM, and he was content to defend the record since October 1990. Inflation had fallen from nearly 11 to under 4 per cent; interest rates had been cut from 15 to 10 per cent; the interest rate differential with Germany had fallen to only 0.25 per cent, and Britain's trade performance had shown a sharp improvement. 'I cannot believe we could have achieved all this outside the ERM.' As chancellor, he was determined to deliver the permanently low inflation which had eluded Britain during the 1980s. The exchange rate mechanism, he insisted, 'is not an optional extra, an add-on to be jettisoned at the first hint of trouble. It is and will remain at the very centre of our macro-economic strategy.' He then went through the options proposed by the government's critics, one by one, dismissing them in turn as flawed or out of reach.

The first was a sharp cut in interest rates within the ERM to stimulate output and pull the economy from recession. Such a move, Lamont told the European Policy Forum, would lead ultimately to higher rather than lower borrowing costs: 'Foreign exchange markets do not expect a weak and falling currency, with low interest rates, to bounce back up again. They expect it to carry on falling and they sell it, forcing interest rates up.'

To the second option, that of a general realignment of the ERM based on a revaluation of the Deutschmark, the chancellor took a different approach. Though it judged the prospect unlikely, this was a possibility that the government wanted to keep open. So, instead of rejecting it outright, Lamont said simply it was 'not on the agenda'. Britain's European partners were not prepared to 'sacrifice their hard-won credibility by allowing their currencies to be devalued against the Deutschmark'.

Turning to the third possibility – devaluation within the ERM – Lamont drew heavily on the analysis produced by Budd and Burns, commenting that it was 'patently absurd' to suggest that devaluation would allow lower borrowing costs, because currency markets would expect a further depreciation and demand higher interest rates in compensation. A unilateral devaluation 'could only put interest rates up, not down'.

The fourth option was to cut interest rates sharply and leave the ERM – the course being urged on the government by its Eurosceptic critics on the Conservative back benches at Westminster. Lamont, echoing the conventional wisdom in the Treasury, said that such a move would shatter the credibility of the government's anti-inflation strategy: 'The result of leaving the ERM, combined with large cuts in interest rates, would be a fall in the pound probably unprecedented in the last forty years. It's the cut and run option: cut interest rates and a run on the pound.'

Finally there was the suggestion that the government could leave the ERM and reintroduce domestic monetary targets to determine the right level of interest rates. Lamont drew on the frustrating experience of the 1980s, when the government had tried and failed to find a stable domestic anchor for policy and had discovered that it could not ignore the exchange rate. It was no surprise, he said, 'that most interest rate changes in the 1980s were associated with move-ments in the exchange rate'.

Lamont's conclusion was unequivocal: the easy alternatives peddled by the government's critics were a plea for a free lunch. 'Sadly there is no such thing. As the Russians say, only mousetraps have free cheese.'[12]

This was the speech which bound Lamont's own reputation to the mast of the ERM. He believed he could have done little else. The foreign exchange markets have never tolerated circumlocution. When speaking about the value of sterling, a chancellor cannot show a shadow of self-doubt. As James Callaghan reflected of his troubles with the currency markets, 'Confidence is the surest guarantee of stability for a currency. The biggest enemy is doubt; rumours can all too often turn a flurry into a hurricane.'[13]

A few days later Major echoed his chancellor's certainty, telling the House of Commons that his commitment to sterling's place in the ERM was '100 per cent'. Gus O'Donnell reinforced the message in his briefing for Westminster's political correspondents. The cabinet, he said, had been reminded by Major that membership of the mechanism had never been a 'short-term' option. The prime minister, O'Donnell added, had received 'complete' backing from his colleagues. Sterling's DM2.95 rate was 'non-negotiable' and, if necessary, Major would order an increase in interest rates to defend it. The growing dissent on the right of the Conservative Party, however, was mirrored in a letter to *The Times* from six leading monetarist economists. Headed by Alan Walters, the economists warned of a 'serious risk' that recession would be deepened and prolonged well into the following year. The government should leave the ERM and return to a 'properly constructed regime' of money supply targets.[14]

Such nostalgia for the early 1980s was not calculated to win allies in Whitehall. But there were those in the Treasury who questioned the government's wisdom in slamming shut quite so publicly the potential escape routes. By now the policy and the rhetoric had become dangerously self-reinforcing. The truth was that it was impossible to declare with certainty that a devaluation of sterling alongside, say, the lira and the peseta would be counterproductive. Once Lamont had delivered the European Policy Forum speech, however, the internal discussion became circular. The die had been cast. The atmosphere in the upper echelons of the Treasury tended to stifle debate. It was an insular world, populated by clever insiders. Officials were not encouraged to think the unthinkable; instead their judgements tended to be mutually reinforcing. As one explained, 'There was nothing to be gained from rocking the boat.' Terence Burns had watched with dismay the upsurge in inflation during the late 1980s. To devalue unilaterally – or even alongside the Italians and Spanish – would be to jeopardize the painfully expensive progress made in rebuilding credibility. In any event, Burns believed that fresh options could open up after the French referendum if the government kept its nerve. 'Terry', a colleague would remark later, 'believes in keeping shoulders to the wheel.'

Prone to bouts of melancholy, Lamont was deeply pessimistic about an early end to the recession. He relied heavily, however, on the advice of the Treasury establishment. His temperament – a curious mix of amusing self-confidence and intellectual insecurity – reflected his long, arduous climb to the top of the political ladder. After years in the shadow of Nigel Lawson, he never quite believed he had made it. Handed an early draft of the Budget speech in early 1991, he had thrown it back with the words 'Lawson would not have put it like that.' Lamont's careless working habits – he preferred Westminster's social circuit to the overnight boxes full of briefing-papers – greatly annoyed his officials, but on important questions of economic policy he strayed only rarely from the consensus in the Treasury.

Around the same time, the analysis for the European Policy Forum speech formed the basis for the Downing Street presentation which had been requested by the prime minister. Accompanied by Burns and Budd, and joined by Eddie George and Sarah Hogg, Lamont offered a gloomier assessment of the position than he had delivered publicly. Pessimistic about the outlook for German interest rates and the prospects for an upturn in the economy, Lamont discussed with Major for the first time the possibility of suspending sterling's participation in the ERM. Those present, however, recall that the chancellor dismissed the option as quickly as it was raised. Departure from the mechanism would be politically and economically devastating, he remarked. For all the present strains, the ERM had succeeded in bringing down inflation. More significantly, there were clear signs that it had succeeded in breaking once and for all the inflationary wage culture which had for decades dogged British industry.

Major and Lamont agreed that, for the reasons set out in the European Policy Forum speech, unilateral devaluation offered no escape. There was no guarantee that a single, limited, adjustment of its ERM parity would ease the pressure on sterling; it was more likely that it would lead to higher interest rates. Equally, it was impossible to cut interest rates within the ERM without precipitating a devaluation. As for a general realignment, it was still not on offer. The Rome government was keen on a revaluation of the Deutschmark, because the doubts sown in the foreign exchange markets by the Danish vote had already forced two increases in Italian interest rates. France, however, was still implacable in opposing any change in the franc's exchange rate. So, if Britain pressed for a comprehensive realignment, sterling would be bracketed with the 'weak' currencies like the lira and peseta.

The conclusion was that, for as long as France vetoed a Deutschmark revaluation, the only real choice for Britain was between remaining in the system and leaving it. No one at the No. 10 meeting demurred. 'Lamont said we should tough it out. Major agreed,' one of those present said. The Bank was instructed to accelerate its work on a strategy to defend the pound against the gathering storm. George was charged with building the defences. From this point onwards the focus would be on sustaining sterling's position until after the French referendum on 20 September. If the government held the line until then, something might turn up.

Another option, which went largely unspoken in the public debate, was to raise interest rates to defend sterling – to accept a still fiercer monetary squeeze in the short term as the price for long-term credibility in the financial markets. This possibility hung in the background between June and September, but it never reached the stage of a serious proposal. At one point during the summer Eddie George broached the subject directly with Major. He needed to know whether the Bank could count on the prime minister if it concluded that an interest rate rise was essential to protect the pound's ERM parity. Major's reply was that, if the alternative was devaluation, George could include higher borrowing costs in the Bank's armoury against the speculators. Until it was too late, however, there was never a real prospect that the weapon would be used.

Watching from the sidelines as sterling fell, Nigel Lawson could not understand the inaction. At one point he telephoned Alex Allan, once his Treasury private secretary and now serving Major in No. 10, to voice alarm. Lawson said the government must raise interest rates pre-emptively. It should also support sterling in the markets before it hit its ERM floor. This 'intramarginal' intervention was a technique that had been deployed successfully by the Banque de France to defend the franc. His advice went unheeded.

Politics, of course, spoke powerfully against piling more agony on to an anguished electorate. Higher interest rates would have heightened the rebellion on the Conservative back benches, drawing still tighter the dangerous thread between the recession and the Maastricht Treaty. By early July the sniping against the prime minister had spread from the back benches to within the ranks of government. A handful of middle-ranking ministers were openly contemptuous of his stance on Europe. Maastricht was fast becoming a fault-line as the pain of the recession was linked directly to the prime minister's commitment to Europe.

The Treasury and the Bank would argue subsequently that higher interest rates could not anyway have saved the pound. Instead, officials believed an increase would have served only to heighten the tension between the domestic economy and the ERM. The financial markets would have recognized an increase as an act of desperation. In the words of one Bank official, 'There was a huge overkill even with base rates at 10 per cent. Increasing rates would have been incredible.' The Bank's concerns extended beyond the general misery of the recession. Asset price deflation had exposed the imprudent lending policies of banks and building societies. If the squeeze were tightened, the banking system would be at risk. So, in the words of another senior official, 'By July we had arrived at the conclusion that raising rates for an indeterminate duration would have invited massive speculation against the currency.' Lamont concurred, commenting subsequently, 'I think that most people would have judged that that was a pretty desperate thing to have then done, and would have been difficult to sustain, and I suspect it would have undermined rather than strengthened our position.'[15]

The case against increasing interest rates was indeed persuasive, but the Treasury was to make the damaging mistake of revealing the weakness of its position. At the beginning of July, National Savings had issued a new high-interest bond. The First Option Bond, with a guaranteed return of more than 10 per cent, was an immediate success, but it infuriated the building societies, which were struggling to attract funds. The Cheltenham & Gloucester led a high-profile campaign against the new bond. Its chief executive, Andrew Longhurst, warned that the society would increase its mortgage rate unless National Savings cut its rate. On 20 July the Treasury gave way and ordered a reduction to 9.7 per cent. The decision provoked dismay among officials, however: the Treasury had given a clear signal to the financial markets that it could not accept a rise in mortgage rates. Henceforth, any threat to defend the pound with higher borrowing costs would be recognized as a bluff. Shaking his head in disbelief at the inept handling of the incident, one senior official was to remark, 'We had run up the white flag.' Thus, by mid-July, John Major's government had closed off two of its possible escape routes from the humiliation which would soon follow. It had rejected any possibility of an orderly, managed, devaluation of sterling; and it had acknowledged that it could not use its most powerful weapon in defence of the exchange rate.

The event which set the seal on sterling's fate occurred on 16 July. By an unkind coincidence, the meeting that day of the Bundesbank's eighteen-strong ruling council coincided with an end-of-term party hosted by the prime minister. Parliament had broken for the summer recess and, as the guardians of German price stability gathered behind the austere concrete of the Bundesbank in Frankfurt, John Major chatted to journalists in the elegant first-floor reception rooms of 10 Downing Street. The pound had fallen to below DM2.85 – a level last seen just before the April election – and Major was anxious to emphasize his determination to stick to the ERM parity. He had made the same point to his colleagues two days earlier at the last cabinet meeting before the summer break. Gus O'Donnell had told reporters after that meeting that the cabinet had given the prime minister 'unequivocal backing': even if the French decided to devalue, sterling's DM2.95 central rate was sacrosanct.

Major reminded his guests that he had not listened to the siren voices calling for sharp cuts in interest rates before the April election and he had been proved right. Why should he pay attention to the critics now? The prime minister then went further, raising eyebrows among his guests by musing that in five, maybe ten, years' time sterling would be among the world's strongest currencies – stronger perhaps than the Deutschmark. It was a fanciful proposition: twenty years earlier a pound had bought nine Deutschmarks; now it bought fewer than three. Major, however, was unabashed. Soon afterwards he would repeat his confident prophecy at a dinner hosted by the *Sunday Times*. He would come to regret the banner headline that followed.

There was a mixture here of wishful thinking and bravado. The prime minister knew that to show the smallest chink in the government's resolve would be to court defeat at the hands of the speculators; even in private he could not leave the slightest doubts. But the occasion also provided a glimpse of the conviction that clouded judgement. When he had entered Downing Street two years earlier, it had been as a self-declared pragmatist. The ideological certainties of the Thatcher era were to give way to a Conservatism which listened rather than lectured. There had always been one fixed point, however, in Major's political firmament: an abhorrence of inflation. The preoccupation was rooted in the Conservatism of Worcester Park, the London suburb in which he had grown up before hard times had forced a move to Brixton. Inflation – the subject of his maiden speech in the House of Commons – was a social as well as an economic evil. It robbed the vulnerable of hard-won savings, and destroyed the hopes of those on modest fixed incomes. Conservatives were the guardians of little platoons such as these; now the ERM was their shield. Parallel to inflation, the inexorable fall in the external value of the pound had been a potent symbol of Britain's postwar decline.

Major's words betrayed the perilous trap into which his government now fell. Sterling's exchange rate against the Deutschmark had become a badge of national pride. Other European governments had come to treat the ERM as a fixed-rate mechanism largely because of their commitment to the goal of a single currency. Its opt-out from Maastricht freed Britain from that obligation. By mid-1992, however, John Major's administration had voluntarily accepted the constraints seen by other European governments as the necessary price for a single currency. As Leigh-Pemberton subsequently was to admit to the House of Commons Treasury and Civil Service Committee, it had become 'mesmerized' by the shift to a fixed rather than flexible ERM.[16] A senior Treasury official put it rather more bluntly: 'We had walked into a trap of our own making. We had pinned the credibility of our anti-inflation policy on holding an exchange rate which was never meant to be fixed for all time.'

Willing a strong pound would not be enough. Even as Major spoke during the July reception, Alex Allan and Gus O'Donnell could be seen darting to and fro between the guests and the Reuters screen in a downstairs office. Eventually the Bundesbank's decision was telephoned directly from Frankfurt to one of No. 10's private secretaries – it had left its internationally important Lombard rate unchanged at 9.75 per cent, but had raised its Discount rate by three-quarters of a point to 8.75 per cent. The reaction was initially muted, but it was soon apparent that the decision had changed the psychology in the foreign exchange markets: speculators concluded that the Lombard rate also might soon rise, drawing still more funds into Deutschmarks. Other continental European countries followed the Bundesbank's lead. And, just at the moment when the Deutschmark's appreciation gained momentum, falling US interest rates delivered a further downward push to the dollar. Later the same day Virginia Bottomley, the health secretary, hosted another Whitehall reception. The serious talk was of the economy and sterling rather than of the state of the National Health Service. A middle-ranking minister sensed a looming crisis as he questioned the wisdom of Major's public commitment to the exchange rate. His musings were at once disloyal and prophetic: 'I wonder whether he will turn out to be another Wilson.'

The pressures on sterling were reinforced by polls of French public opinion. The Maastricht Treaty had been a triumph for President Mitterrand. It had been the key which would fix a united Germany into a western-European landscape and bring an end to the hegemony of the Bundesbank over Europe's economic policy. Now the opinion polls suggested that the French people, disgruntled and disillusioned with Mitterrand's domestic policies, might vote against the treaty. If there was no future for economic and monetary union, the financial markets concluded, the ERM would crack.

By the end of July the pound had fallen dangerously close to its lowest permitted point level of DM2.7780 in the ERM. Parliament had broken for the summer recess, but the unease among Conservative MPs was all too apparent. It was already clear that the Maastricht ratification process would have to be delayed at least until after the

Edinburgh summit in December. Even among pro-European Tories, faith in the ERM was turning to frustration. Sterling continued to weaken in the first weeks of August, falling beyond the ERM 'divergence' level which, under the rules of the system, created a presumption that the government would act to defend the currency. There was no move to raise interest rates: the Treasury could no longer disguise the intensifying conflict between its exchange rate policy and the economic recession. To avoid a rise in mortgage rates, Lamont bowed for a second time to pressure from the building societies and lowered the interest rates paid to investors in National Savings. Helmut Schlesinger would later point to what he saw as the Treasury's failure of nerve as an invitation to the speculators against sterling. The Treasury's reasoning was reflected in a study published by the Bank of England in the August edition of its *Quarterly Bulletin*.[17] Negative equity in the housing market now amounted to a massive £6bn; the market would not withstand still higher mortgage rates. From the unforgiving perspective of foreign exchange markets, however, the government had raised the white flag for the second time in as many weeks.

The Bank meanwhile began building alternative lines of defence. Eddie George travelled to Frankfurt to secure Schlesinger's approval for the British government to denominate in Deutschmarks half of a 10bn ecu credit which the Treasury planned to raise on international capital markets. The credit would be announced in early September as part of a last-ditch strategy to support the pound. George also finalized the Bank's tactics in the event of a sudden speculative assault on sterling. The first phase of this classic central bank defence involved large but covert purchases of the pound. If that failed to stabilize the currency then the Bank would respond with massive, open intervention on the foreign exchange markets. The third and final line of defence – the last resort – would be an interest rate rise. George discussed the details with Sarah Hogg, the head of the Downing Street policy unit. Major and Lamont, both abroad on holiday, signalled their approval in a series of mid-August telephone conversations.

Weakening by the day against the Deutschmark, sterling was still rising against a falling dollar. The two-dollar pound brought noisy protests from industry, but there could be no relief without a devaluation against the Deutschmark. Calls for such a realignment from Sir Denys Henderson, the chairman of ICI, and Brian Pearse, Midland Bank's chief executive, attracted a terse rebuff. Downing Street briefed reporters that the prime minister was ready to endure a 'bitter autumn' of unpopularity as the price for sticking with the present exchange rate; Lamont used an article in the *Daily Express* to denounce devaluation as 'fool's gold' – a phrase later picked up by Major. The forces ranged against them, however, were strengthening; three concerted attempts during August by European central banks to ease the tensions in the ERM by intervening in support of the dollar failed to reverse the decline of the US currency. The Deutschmark rose pitilessly.

Committed to holding the line until the French referendum, the government's attention turned increasingly to the two remaining, narrow, avenues of escape. The first was to persuade France to accept the general realignment, or revaluation of the Deutschmark, which Lamont had referred to in his European Policy Forum speech before dismissing it as an option which was not on offer. The second was to prevail upon the Bundesbank to begin reducing interest rates. Both possibilities were remote, but these were desperate times.

More than once Major sounded out Pierre Bérégovoy, the French prime minister, on the strength of his commitment to the franc's parity against the Deutschmark. Lamont did likewise in his contacts with the French finance minister, Michel Sapin. Unsurprisingly, their reaction was less than encouraging. A devaluation of the franc would add to the growing mood of doubt in financial markets about the prospects for monetary union – the essential prize of the Maastricht Treaty. Abandonment of the *franc fort* policy which Mitterrand had pursued for the previous nine years would be an open admission of political failure, an invitation to the French voters to reject the treaty. The reaction was not unexpected, but the Treasury did not regard the contacts as entirely fruitless. The groundwork might be useful if the French electorate indeed voted no. And it was possible, if not likely, that the foreign exchange markets might force the hand of the Paris government before the referendum.

In its decision to apply pressure to the Bundesbank, however, the government embarked on a course which at first proved misguided and then positively dangerous. It was a strategy which brought Norman Lamont into fatal conflict with Helmut Schlesinger. It also illuminated the political naïvety in Whitehall and at Westminster about the Europe to which Britain now belonged. In their contacts with Bonn, the prime minister and chancellor had several times voiced their growing alarm about the tensions caused by high German interest rates. Each time Chancellor Helmut Kohl and finance minister Theo Waigel had given the same response. They were sympathetic: for their own, domestic, political reasons they resented the vigour with which Schlesinger was applying the monetary squeeze. Inflation in Germany had fallen from 4.7 per cent in March 1992 to 3.3 per cent in July. The Bonn government was as keen as its European partners that interest rates should fall. It could not, however, interfere with the Bundesbank's constitutional right to set an independent monetary policy. After several conversations in which he warned that Germany risked 'busting' the ERM, Major was left with the impression that Kohl, a broad-brush politician, understood neither the detail nor the urgency of the situation.

For the Bundesbank, the primacy of price stability in Germany's domestic economy was inviolate. It was a principle also that the central bank considered to be to the long-term benefit of its European partners. The Deutschmark was the anchor of the ERM because its external value was buttressed by internal stability: it could only act as the gold standard for the rest of Europe if Germany refused to compromise its own anti-inflation policy. Seen from Frankfurt, the ERM worked not in spite of this subservience to domestic German policy but because of it. Schlesinger made the point succinctly in an unapologetic interview with *Fortune* magazine after Black Wednesday: 'Our policy for a stable currency is not only good for us, it is good for our neighbours ... There must be some countries that show how a stable currency and stable prices enrich a country and a population.'[18] France had grasped this point after its successive devaluations during the early 1980s. The *franc fort* policy was predicated on the assumption that, until the authority of the Bundesbank was dissolved into a new European central bank, France would remain on the side of the strong currencies.

The Bundesbank, it was true, had in the past made small concessions to other governments – notably during the period of the
Plaza and Louvre accords and in its acceptance of adjustments to the
intervention arrangements in the ERM. Karl Otto Pöhl had been an
astute politician who could see the benefits of occasional deviations
from Bundesbank orthodoxy. But the essential asymmetry in the
ERM – placing the prime responsibility to respond to exchange rate
tensions on those governments with weak currencies – was non-
negotiable. With Schlesinger at the helm, there was never any serious
possibility that the Bundesbank would bend to pressure from Britain.
The unshakeable self-belief of the sixty-eight-year-old central banker
underpinned his view that sterling's ERM parity against the Deutschmark had been set at too high a level. The Bundesbank saw in
Britain's current-account deficit – estimated at more than 2 per cent
of national income even while the economy was in deep recession –
clear evidence of an overvalued currency. In private conversations
with British officials and journalists during the summer of 1992,
Schlesinger was heard asking more than once, 'Why don't you
devalue?'

Major believed that circumstances had changed since the conflicts
over the ERM between Germany and France during the early 1980s.
Germany had been in the forefront of those pressing for the Maastricht Treaty. Kohl saw closer European integration as the historic
mission of his chancellorship. The ERM was the precursor to the
single currency which lay at the heart of Maastricht. Germany now
bore a heavy responsibility to ensure the mechanism's survival. This
was a logical but flawed assumption, for Kohl's European vision was
not shared in the Bundesbank. As an institution, it had always had
reservations about the ERM and could never endorse a monetary
union which had as its central objective the destruction of Bundesbank
independence. Schlesinger was among the most hawkish. His colleagues believed he would be quite happy to see the splintering of the
ERM and the fracturing of plans for a single currency.

By 14 August sterling had fallen to its lowest ever level in the
mechanism. At DM2.8150, it was just 3 pfennigs above its ERM
floor. The message from Downing Street, conveyed again by

O'Donnell – that the government would resist devaluation in all circumstances – went unheeded by the speculators. Ten days later Terence Burns was concerned enough to return early to London from his Welsh holiday cottage. Major and Lamont, holidaying in Spain and Italy respectively, were also back by 24 August.

Burns had just read a draft of Nigel Lawson's memoirs. He was incensed by Lawson's version of some of the most critical decisions of the 1980s, believing the former chancellor had unfairly laid the blame for mistakes on his officials. Burns had also pressed for Lawson to remove references to the so-called 'devaluationist tendency' in the Treasury – this was not the time for a former chancellor to suggest publicly that senior officials might welcome a devaluation of the pound. Burns took one idea from Lawson's manuscript, however. On his return to London, he reviewed a plan drawn up by Geoffrey Littler seven years earlier. This was the proposal for sterling's temporary suspension from the ERM during a general election campaign. It had been drawn up in 1985 to assuage Margaret Thatcher's fears that ERM membership would threaten interest rate rises, a devaluation or both in the immediate approach to polling day. The Littler proposal had remained in the Treasury's files after Thatcher had rejected Lawson's pleas to put sterling into the mechanism. The circumstances now were entirely different, but the position was becoming desperate. Burns thought the idea of temporary withdrawal from the mechanism worthy of reconsideration. It was already clear that sterling's suspension might be unavoidable if the pressures intensified.

CHAPTER TEN

HUMILIATION

THE COUNTDOWN TO Black Wednesday began on the bright summer morning of 26 August. Reporters and television crews were summoned at 8 a.m., to record an extraordinary press statement on the steps of the Treasury. Standing alongside a highly polished brass plaque carrying the inscription 'HM Treasury', Norman Lamont explained that he wanted to remove any 'scintilla of doubt' about the government's intentions towards the pound. 'We are going to maintain sterling's parity and we will do whatever is necessary,' the chancellor declared.[1] His statement was followed by ostentatious intervention by the Bank of England to support the currency. More than $1bn was sold from the reserves. Despite its own substantial foreign currency reserves, the Bank chose to activate a 'swap' agreement with the Bundesbank to finance the operation. The swap had been negotiated by Nigel Lawson in 1986 but had then never been used. It had the advantage of being 'invisible' to the outside world: the foreign currency borrowed from the Bundesbank would not show up in the Bank of England's published reserves at the end of the month.

Later that same day, Norman Lamont travelled to Paris for emergency talks with his French, German and Italian counterparts. Such was the secrecy surrounding the meeting that the chancellor flew to Orly from the RAF base at Northolt. On arrival he was whisked by car to the Place de la Concorde in the centre of Paris. Here the cloak-and-dagger arrangements became comical as Lamont boarded a small boat to take him the short distance along the river Seine to the French Finance Ministry at Bercy. There he entered through a small entrance opening directly to the river bank. 'The Traitor's Gate,' one official would joke afterwards.

The finance ministers and central bank governors had met previously on 7 January of the same year in the wake of the strains on the system created by the previous month's rise in German interest rates. That gathering too had been secret because of the concern to prevent turbulence on the financial markets. The slightest hint that governments were discussing the possibility of a realignment would provoke a torrent of speculation. But the four also wanted to avoid leaks to other European governments. They were meeting outside the normal Brussels procedures and, in a sense, pre-empting decisions in which other European colleagues had an important legitimate interest. The mere fact of such a gathering would prompt strong protests from some smaller countries. In the event the January meeting was entirely inconclusive; Pierre Bérégovoy, then the French finance minister, was clear at the outset that his government was not prepared to devalue. So too was Guido Carli, the Italian finance minister. Lamont replied with some acerbity that, in those circumstances, a change in sterling's parity would hardly amount to the realignment. The three finance ministers pressed for a cut in German interest rates, but were rebuffed by Helmut Schlesinger, the Bundesbank president. Theo Waigel, the finance minister, indicated that Bonn was not pressing for parity changes. But Schlesinger remarked that exchange rate adjustments would represent the 'classic response' to the pressures in the system.

This second meeting in August was called at least in part at the chancellor's instigation. Falling US interest rates and a weakening dollar were intensifying the strains between European currencies. There was talk in advance that the four might agree a joint demarche to Washington. Lamont reaffirmed that the government had publicly committed itself to using any means necessary to defending sterling's parity, including higher interest rates. But the chancellor's subsequent confidential minute to the prime minister recorded that he had noted also that a small rise in borrowing costs might anyway fail to ease the pressure on sterling. In any event, he had continued, the depressed state of Britain's domestic economy argued for lower not higher rates. Nor did he think there was much point in waiting for the US authorities to ease the strains on the ERM by acting to strengthen the dollar. The presidential election was looming. All the evidence pointed to the need for Germany to relax its monetary policy.

On this occasion Waigel was accompanied by Hans Tietmeyer, the Bundesbank vice-president. They argued that the level of interest rates did not risk tipping the German economy into recession. The blame for the tensions in the ERM rested with lax monetary policy in the US and policy mistakes made by Washington during the 1980s. The Bundesbank had no immediate plan to raise its rates further but equally it would not pledge a reduction. Lamont's note said that the Bundesbank had not been pressing for sterling's immediate devaluation, but Tietmeyer had questioned whether the existing 'distortions' in exchange rates could be sustained in the longer term. The Germans, however, took away a somewhat different impression from the meeting. They were convinced that they signalled that the escape route from the crisis lay not with the Bundesbank but with those whose currencies were under siege.

Summing up, Michel Sapin, who had replaced Bérégovoy as French finance minister, noted the two opposing views, but suggested the Bundesbank might at least signal its intention not to raise rates further. The four also agreed that Lamont would co-ordinate a joint statement of all European finance ministers stressing their determination to defend existing parities. Finally, the central banks would activate the Basle-Nyborg arrangements which provided for Bundesbank intervention in support of weaker currencies before they reached their lowest permitted ERM levels. After dinner Lamont returned to London. Empty-handed.

The financial markets were unimpressed by Lamont's earlier statement outside the Treasury. Large corporations had joined the fund managers and speculative investors betting on a sterling devaluation. (Among those who reaped the rewards was George Soros, the Hungarian-born arbitrage specialist whose Quantum Fund was later reputed to have made a $1bn profit from Black Wednesday.) The British government's determination to avoid an increase rate increase was ever more apparent. And even as the finance ministers and central bankers met in Paris, expectations of a realignment were reinforced by some careless remarks from Reimut Jochimsen, a member of the Bundesbank Board. His comments, later qualified, suggested there was the 'potential' for further ERM parity changes. The Bank of England's intervention had been wasted. The opening sentence in an editorial in the *Financial Times* summed up the consensus in the markets: 'Words are cheap. Deeds may yet be required.'[2] An air of desperation was now enveloping Whitehall. James Callaghan had offered similar, worthless assurances twenty-five years earlier. Ter-

ence Burns thought the chancellor's early morning appearance had
been 'over the top'.

On 28 August, the lira, sterling and the French franc were hit by a
wave of selling as the Deutschmark rose to the top of the ERM.
Britain had held the rotating European Community presidency since
the start of July, so it fell to Lamont, as chairman of the finance
ministers' council, to issue the statement which had been drafted in
Paris. It said that European finance ministries would defeat the
speculators. In the jargon beloved of finance ministers and central
bankers, it declared that 'A change in the present structure of central
rates would not be an appropriate response to the current tensions.'[3]

A few days later Norman Lamont added substance to sterling's
defences. The 10bn ecu credit which Eddie George had discussed
with the Bundesbank during the late summer was announced with a
deliberate fanfare on Friday 4 September. Half would be raised
immediately in Deutschmarks and would then be swapped for sterling
in the foreign exchange markets to underpin demand for the pound.
The rest would be held in reserve. The message was that the Bank
had plenty of ammunition to resist a devaluation. The initial reaction
to the initiative was favourable, and sterling edged above the immediate danger zone of its DM 2.7780 floor in the mechanism. Eddie
George was optimistic, informing Sarah Hogg in 10 Downing Street
that he was greatly encouraged by the response.

Lamont travelled on the same day to Bath for what was to prove a
calamitous meeting of European Community finance ministers and
central bank governors. The talks, held in the spa town's elegant
eighteenth-century Assembly Rooms, had been scheduled as the
opportunity for an informal review of the world economy ahead of
the IMF's annual meeting later in September. After the opening
dinner on the Friday evening in the Georgian splendour of the Royal
Crescent Hotel, the chancellor decided to scrap the agenda for the
following day. Over post-prandial drinks with Nigel Wicks, the
Treasury official responsible for international policy, and Jeremy
Heywood, his principal private secretary, he hatched an alternative
agenda. He would use his chairmanship of the meeting to browbeat
the Bundesbank. If the German central bank would not cut its interest

rates immediately, Helmut Schlesinger could at least be pressurized into declaring that there would be no further increase.

Here Lamont and Wicks made an elementary error. Schlesinger, *primus inter pares* on the Bundesbank board, had neither the inclination nor the authority to alter the Bundesbank's policy. Meetings of European finance ministers and central bankers were not the occasion for fresh changes in German monetary policy. Interest rate decisions are not made by the bank's president but collectively by its board. The rows which had punctuated the Bundesbank's relationship with the US administration during the mid-1980s had provided ample testimony of its intransigence in such circumstances. Nigel Lawson had warned James Baker, the US Treasury secretary, on more than one occasion of the futility of attempting to pressurize the German central bank: the one thing calculated to bring out its stubborn independence was criticism of its policies by its international partners.

The chancellor won some support, however, in a series of bilateral conversations with other finance ministers early on Saturday morning. The Italians and Spanish were equally anxious that their currencies might soon be picked off by the speculators. Italy had raised its interest rates to 15 per cent and had announced a new round of cuts in its budget deficit, but had failed to stem the speculation on the lira. But while Piero Barucci, the Italian finance minister, saw in the Bath meeting the opportunity for a realignment, Lamont was determined not to be drawn into a discussion which might lead to pressure for sterling's devaluation. Michel Sapin had a similar priority. Just two weeks before the Maastricht referendum, his government was as uncertain as ever about the outcome. An enforced devaluation of the franc would be fatal.

From the outset, Lamont's strategy went badly wrong. As chairman, his responsibility was to search for consensus rather than to press a particular case. Instead, the meeting turned into an ugly and fruitless confrontation with Schlesinger. In an atmosphere as sour and angry as anyone could recall at such a gathering, the Bundesbank president was pressed four times by Lamont to pledge a reduction in interest rates. Schlesinger considered that his first refusal should have been sufficient. If some of his colleagues sympathized with Lamont's objective, they were shocked by his persistence. In the words of another finance minister, the chancellor 'broke all the rules' by seeking to mobilize the meeting against Germany. Recalling the rows between Paris and Frankfurt before Mitterrand adopted the *franc fort* policy, the minister added, 'He [Lamont] made the mistake the French had made – the Bundesbank does not respond to threats.'

Others feared that the meeting would break up in open disarray as Lamont launched into a lengthy critique of German policies. The Bundesbank, he said, was misguided in interpreting the rapid expansion of the broad money supply measure, M3, as a justification for interest rate increases. Britain's experience had shown that the very fact of high interest rates tended to distort the signals from that particular measure. Lamont then turned his attention to the Bonn government, directing at Theo Waigel, the finance minister, criticism of the subsidized credits used to finance reconstruction in East Germany. Historically high borrowing in Germany – the federal deficit had reached about 4 per cent of national income – was contributing to the credit squeeze. As the atmosphere darkened, the governor of one European central bank was seen shaking his head in disbelief. Another was to comment afterwards that it was 'the most-ill tempered meeting I had ever attended'. Furious, Schlesinger considered walking out of the room; Waigel restrained him.

After several hours of fruitless discussion interspersed with huddled talks among smaller groups in corners and corridors, Lamont's private secretary was sufficiently concerned to alert Terence Burns to the deadlock. Burns, reached on his mobile telephone on the golf course, abandoned his clubs and drove to Bath. With the press and the financial markets waiting for the outcome, it would be disastrous if the ministers and central bankers failed to agree a joint statement.

Burns's arrival in mid-afternoon marked the start of serious efforts to draft a communiqué which would reassure the markets without compromising the Bundesbank's independence. Schlesinger finally assented to the use of an ambiguous phrase which indicated that the central bank had no plans to increase its interest rates. The finance ministers then restated their public if not their private conviction that an ERM realignment would not restore calm to the currency markets. The full statement read as follows:

In the face of the tensions in the exchange markets the following decisions have been taken. The August 28 agreement not to proceed

to a realignment in the European Monetary System has been confirmed. The central bank governors stand ready to intervene in the
exchange markets to counter tensions in those markets, exploiting as
fully as necessary the means and instruments provided under the EMS
for member states. The ministers and governors have also examined
the present economic situation in the Community and in this context
they emphasized the importance of early and full implementation of
strict convergence programmes, in particular to consolidate fiscal
positions and to keep under control wage and other cost pressures.
They particularly welcomed the recent policy decisions by the Italian
government, and its firm commitment to achieve a substantial primary
budget surplus in 1993. In the light of a slowing of the growth
prospects of their economies, and in so far as the disinflationary process
allows it, they have decided to take advantage of any opportunity to
reduce interest rates. They welcome the fact that the Bundesbank in
present circumstances has no intention to increase rates and is watching
closely the further development of the economy.[4]

Lamont interpreted this last sentence as a signal victory, telling a
press conference at the end of the talks that it marked the first time
that Schlesinger had given such a commitment 'openly and publicly'.
Lamont's hope was that the statement would change expectations in
the financial markets: the Deutschmark's appreciation had been
underpinned by the perception that the Bundesbank's Lombard rate
might be increased. Sapin too told the waiting press that there had
been a change of mood during the meeting. And, as far as sterling
was concerned, Lamont was uncompromising, hinting again that he
was ready, if necessary, to raise interest rates: 'I have made it clear
again and again that we will do whatever is necessary to defend the
value of the pound. If that necessitates a change in interest rates then
we will do so.'

The statement was the hollowest of triumphs. Schlesinger, whose
anger with Lamont was apparent from the countenances of the two
men as they stood in the hotel foyer during the following morning,
considered he had made no policy concessions. The statement that
Germany had no plans in present circumstances to increase its interest
rates was an affirmation of the obvious – it did not preclude such a
rise if circumstances changed. Schlesinger, however, was annoyed by
the subsequent gloss which had been given to the communiqué. His

mood could not have been improved by some casual remarks of one of the British drivers assigned to the German delegation. Wrongly assuming that Schlesinger spoke no English, the driver complained loudly about the complicated travel schedules demanded by the security arrangements for the German visitors. The Bundesbank president made his position clear in an interview with the BBC. Questioned by Graham Leach, the BBC's Brussels correspondent, he remarked bluntly of the communiqué, 'This is no change in our policy.' Challenged about Lamont's very different interpretation, he replied simply, 'Well, this is his judgement on the situation.'[5] Nor would the Bundesbank president defend the section of the communiqué ruling out an ERM realignment. Schlesinger was to repeat the sentiment at a meeting of central bank governors in Basle two days later. Lamont had failed. More seriously, he had alienated and angered the most powerful banker in Europe.

Bath was a missed opportunity – the last occasion before the French referendum for finance ministers to discuss the orderly realignment of the ERM which might, just might, have deflected the approaching storm. But Lamont was determined not to allow such a debate lest sterling find itself categorized with the lira and the peseta. It is true that the varying accounts of the participants paint a complex picture. Some undoubtedly chose to recall later those incidents which suited their own preconceptions. The criticism of Lamont's chairmanship, however, was near unanimous; even the interpreters who provided the simultaneous translation of the discussions were startled by his approach. But he was not alone in failing to explore the possibilities for an agreement which would have balanced a reduction in German interest rates with a revaluation of the Deutschmark. As one finance minister was to remark afterwards, 'The [German] delegation hinted at an interest rate cut in return for a realignment, but there was no formal offer on the table. France would not hear of a devaluation, while Lamont would not move without the franc.' Ruud Lubbers, the Dutch prime minister, made the same point: realignment was not discussed because 'England had its pride and France said it could not be done because it was facing a difficult referendum and they could not discuss it, and the English said the Bundesbank should do something first.'[6]

Lamont was to emphasize afterwards that no one in Bath had called for the pound's devaluation or suggested it would be followed by a cut in German interest rates in return. 'No proposal was made for a realignment related specifically to the pound sterling,' he said.[7] That was correct in the narrow sense that Schlesinger did not formally press the case for a change in sterling's parity. Lamont had departed from the etiquette of such meetings by pressing the Bundesbank to cut interest rates. It would have been a far more serious breach had Schlesinger openly requested that Britain devalue. 'These things cannot be said in public,' one finance minister would remark. For the same reason there was no formal German offer on the table to respond to a realignment of parities with lower interest rates. There was, however, an unspoken understanding. Several of the ministers and central bankers sensed from their huddled conversations in the corridors that a deal could have been struck. If Britain, Italy and Spain had suggested devaluation, Schlesinger could and would have pre-empted the Bundesbank council and offered to reduce interest rates. Robin Leigh-Pemberton detected the opening during separate talks between the central bankers. The Bank of England governor was later to regret that he had not sought to stimulate a wider discussion when they rejoined the finance ministers. At the time, however, he judged the political atmosphere too charged. As the sole representative of the Bank, he also felt vulnerable: Lamont would not thank him for appearing to question sterling's ERM parity. But Leigh-Pemberton was not alone in regretting that so much had been left unsaid.

The outcome also brought criticism of Nigel Wicks. His Treasury colleagues were surprised that he had not restrained Lamont. Instead, the archetypical Whitehall civil servant, Wicks appeared to encourage the chancellor in the enterprise, returning to the Treasury on Monday morning in dangerously optimistic mood. Perhaps Lamont's conviction that responsibility for the crisis lay with the Germans was infectious; perhaps the stakes were too high for so senior an official to offer even the merest hint that Britain might shift its position. In any event, neither man seemed to appreciate the strategic error. Others in Whitehall were appalled at the outcome. Schlesinger, these officials realized, might hold sterling's fate in his hands. John Major, enjoying an afternoon's cricket at Lord's, was informed of the outcome in the starkest terms: 'No realignment, no interest rate cut, lots of bad blood.'

The Bath weekend revealed a more serious weakness in the way that Whitehall conducts its business. The Treasury, its power-base built firmly on unchallenged control of public spending and taxation, is a quintessentially British institution, as insular as it is self-confident. In joining the ERM it transferred into the joint control of Europe one of the most important levers of economic strategy, but its culture remained stubbornly British. It was true that small groups of officials travelled regularly to meetings in Brussels, Washington, Paris and Bonn. Burns, for example, knew Schlesinger from meetings of the Economic Policy Committee, run by the Paris-based Organization for Economic Cooperation and Development. The contacts with other finance ministries and central banks, however, rarely went beyond these formal meetings. There was no real intelligence, no network of personal relationships to inform the government of the private thinking elsewhere in Europe. Britain's membership of the ERM was not followed by a coordinated attempt to make friends among those upon whom the government might well soon have to rely. In the summer of 1992 an imperious manner could not disguise the absence of reliable allies. As one Treasury official was to lament, 'We were never much good with foreigners.'

There were technical shortcomings too. Whitehall's contacts with the Bundesbank were conducted indirectly through the Bank of England. Andrew Crockett, the Bank director responsible for international affairs, was an experienced and astute official, but the Treasury was at one remove from the thinking in other central banks and yet had long been reluctant to rely too much on the Bank's assessments. The secret intelligence services provided occasional reports on developments behind the scenes in the Bundesbank's Frankfurt headquarters, but their reports added little to what appeared in the public prints.

For his part, Schlesinger was the archetypical German banker. His predecessor, Pöhl, had combined the conservatism appropriate to his position with a capacity for deal-making. He would defend the Bundesbank's prerogatives, but he was conscious of the advantages of occasionally striking political compromises. Schlesinger, by contrast, epitomized the monetarist orthodoxy the Bundesbank had been established to defend: he had been on its policy-making council for twenty years and had served as its chief economist for seven before his appointment as president in 1991. A reputation as an unapologetic German nationalist did not endear him to all of his European colleagues. An academic rather than a markets expert, he was also insensitive to the weight his words carried in the financial markets.

John Major believed sterling could survive the storm. On 8 September, at a Foreign Office reception hosted by Douglas Hurd, the prime minister reacted indignantly to suggestions that his policy was misguided. Life, he said, would be even rougher outside the ERM – witness the turmoil engulfing the Scandinavian countries which had tied their currencies informally to the ecu. Sweden had been forced to raise its interest rates to unprecedented levels to halt a run on the krona, and the Finnish markka was under siege. At a cabinet meeting two days later, he adopted the same approach, praising Lamont for his defence of sterling and outlining in detail the arguments against devaluation. No one around the table demurred. One later recalled that, as they left the cabinet room, a colleague had muttered grimly, 'I hope it works.' Another minister said that he had realized then that the position was 'tight', but no one seemed to doubt that the government would get through to the date of the French referendum.

The cabinet presentation was a dress-rehearsal for the public defence of his policy that Major delivered to a dinner of the Scottish branch of the Confederation of British Industry that evening. This was the moment when the prime minister finally nailed his own political reputation to a parity for sterling of DM2.95, when the exchange rate became an icon. Of course Major was obliged at such a moment to state unequivocally that sterling would not be devalued – to have done anything else would have invited an immediate onslaught from the speculators. But his language, as lurid as it was forceful, carried him too deeply into those perilous waters where personal pride displaces political pragmatism. 'All my adult life,' he said, 'I have seen British governments driven off their virtuous pursuit of low inflation by market problems or political pressures. I was under no illusions when I took sterling into the ERM. I said at the time that membership was no soft option. The soft option, the devaluer's option, the inflationary option, would be a betrayal of our future; and that is not the government's policy.' A realignment of sterling's parity, he continued, would bring 'rising import prices, rising wages, rising inflation, and a long-term deterioration in Britain's competitiveness which would offset any short-term gain'. The road to stable prices would not be easy, but 'we must bite the anti-inflation bullet or accept that we will be for ever second-rate in Europe'. Tempting fate, Major recalled Harold Wilson's devaluation in 1967: 'The pound was devalued by 14 per cent. Did this lead to a sustained improvement in the UK's competitiveness? It did not. A brief flurry only. Retail price inflation doubled over the following year, and any improvement in competitiveness swiftly ended. No greater competitiveness and doubled inflation: what sort of bargain is that?' Warming to the theme, Major also called in aid Keynes's remark that 'There is no subtler, no surer means of overturning the existing basis of society than to debauch the currency.'[8] The prime minister had nailed himself to the mast of a sinking ship. Sarah Hogg saw the risks: she had advised Major that he could tone down the language without casting doubts on his commitment to defend the pound. The prime minister acknowledged as much in an interview with one of his biographers, but added that the financial markets would have seen through any equivocation.[9] Other Whitehall officials, however, concurred with Hogg's assessment. John Kerr queried whether it was essential that the wording be so uncompromising. One official said later that Kerr regretted deeply that he had not been more forceful in making the point. Peter Middleton, a veteran of past sterling crises who now watched the drama from the sidelines of the City, was appalled at the way the prime minister had been allowed to put himself squarely in the front line.

Major was right, though, that it was no defence against the speculators to be outside the ERM. The first victim to be claimed by the markets was Finland, which had pegged the markka to the ecu and was now forced to break the link. The markka dropped by 15 per cent. The Swedish krona, also tied to the ecu, resisted the pressure only after the country's central bank pushed overnight interest rates to levels as high as 500 per cent. By the time of Major's speech the speculators had the Italian lira in their sights. The Rome government announced that it would take emergency powers to forestall a collapse of confidence in the economy. But, with the lira at its lowest permitted level against the Deutschmark, the Italian and German central banks were committed to unlimited intervention to sustain its parity. As reserves drained from the Italian central bank and the Bundesbank was obliged by the rules of the ERM to pour tens of billions of Deutschmarks into the Frankfurt money markets, Schlesinger determined to seek a realignment. The obligation to intervene in such huge amounts was undercutting his attempts to rein back the expansion of the German money supply. Schlesinger asked the Bonn government, whose responsibility it was to initiate any realignment, to seek Italy's agreement to devaluation. Chancellor Kohl travelled to Frankfurt to meet personally with the Bundesbank president on the afternoon of Friday 11 September. Schlesinger indicated that, in return for a devaluation of the lira, the Bundesbank would agree a small cut in interest rates to ease the pressures on other ERM currencies. If other governments were willing to devalue as part of a broader realignment, the Bundesbank would be ready to make a steeper cut in rates to balance the corresponding appreciation in the value of the Deutschmark.

Subsequently much effort was devoted to discovering whether the British government was urged that weekend to join the Italians in a broader adjustment of the system. If an orderly devaluation of the pound had led to a larger reduction in German interest rates, the humiliation of Black Wednesday might have been avoided. The answer is more complicated than the question. It is clear that the Bundesbank wanted a broad realignment, including at least the lira, sterling and the peseta, and probably also the franc. But, as during the Bath meeting, mutual awareness of entrenched positions, communication breakdowns and calculated self-interest ensured that the possibility was never properly explored.

Two senior German officials – Horst Köhler from the finance ministry and Hans Tietmeyer from the Bundesbank – travelled to Rome on Saturday 12 September. First, however, they broke their journey in Paris to explain their plan to Michel Sapin, the French finance minister, and Jean-Claude Trichet, director-general of the French Treasury. Trichet was chairman of the Community's monetary committee, the group of senior European officials responsible for coordinating ERM realignments. After protracted discussions in which the French officials reaffirmed their determination to maintain the franc's parity, Köhler and Tietmeyer left Paris convinced they had none the less conveyed their preference for a shake-up of the mechanism extending beyond the lira–Deutschmark rate.

Trichet did nothing until he was informed later that day that the Rome government had agreed to a 7 per cent devaluation of the lira in return for a 0.25 point cut in the German Lombard rate and a slightly larger 0.5 point reduction in Germany's money market rates on the following Monday. Only then did the French official call his counterparts on the monetary committee to seek their agreement, making no mention of the possibility of a wider realignment. The contacts normally would have been made by Andreas Kees, the Dutch secretary of the committee, but he was on holiday, so it was Trichet rather than Kees who telephoned Nigel Wicks on the Saturday night to ask for British approval. Crucially, the French official did not suggest a meeting of the committee to discuss the possibility of more far-reaching parity changes. Nor did he convey Germany's hopes of such a realignment. European officials were to reflect later that had Kees coordinated the discussions he probably would have done both things, and Trichet was criticized for what was seen as a deliberate manœuvre to avoid a meeting. His motivation was obvious: an open discussion among finance ministers and central bankers might have led to an ERM realignment which left the franc in the firing-line. Trichet, however, insisted that he had behaved properly – it was not his role to broker a devaluation of sterling or of any other ERM currency.

Terence Burns heard of the Italian devaluation in a telephone call from Nigel Wicks on the Saturday evening. Burns, attending an anniversary party in a school sports pavilion in Dulwich, south London, had been tracked down by the legendary operators who staff the Downing Street switchboard. As it happened his host was Andrew Turnbull, the Treasury colleague responsible for monetary policy, celebrating that night his twenty-fifth wedding anniversary. Lamont was told later the same evening, after returning home from the Last Night of the Proms at the Albert Hall. He met with Treasury and Bank officials early on Sunday morning. Major, staying with the Queen at Balmoral, had been alerted to the Italian devaluation by telephone.

During the discussions in the chancellor's office on Sunday morning, Burns raised the possibility that sterling might also be realigned. But this was a rhetorical question, not the cue for a serious discussion. Once Lamont had rejected it, the idea was put to one side. 'It was raised and dismissed,' said one official. Major gave the same response when he was telephoned at Balmoral by Giuliano Amato, the Italian prime minister. Major and Lamont confirmed the position by telephone, both voicing hopes that the German interest rate cut might alleviate the immediate pressure on sterling. Some of the officials at that Sunday morning meeting, however, were far less sanguine. The lira's devaluation would leave sterling in the speculators' sights, and the last opportunity for a negotiated realignment had been lost.

Major would later declare that the possibility of a larger reduction in German interest rates in return for a more extensive shake-up of the mechanism had never been on offer. Pressed on the issue a few days after Black Wednesday, he would state, 'No, there was not [any offer], formal or informal.'[10] Schlesinger confirmed that there had been no direct contact between Frankfurt and London, remarking that it was not the role of the Bundesbank to inform the British of its intentions. Tietmeyer, however, clearly thought a general realignment was a real possibility. When he returned to Frankfurt from Rome on the Sunday morning, senior Bundesbank officials were put on standby to fly to Brussels for a meeting of the monetary committee which, in the event, never took place. For their part, senior British officials doubt that events would have turned out differently even if Trichet had conveyed the information he received from Köhler and Tietmeyer: Major and Lamont were determined not to devalue as long as France refused to do likewise.

A few days earlier the Treasury had belatedly realized the need to persuade the Bundesbank that sterling's ERM parity was sustainable. After a chance conversation between Nigel Wicks and Horst Köhler, Alan Budd from the Treasury and Mervyn King, the chief economist at the Bank, were despatched to Frankfurt. Their secret mission, subsequently disclosed by Samuel Brittan, the economics commentator of the *Financial Times*, was to convince the Bundesbank that a rate of DM2.95 was consistent with the two countries' relative economic performance.[11]

The two men arrived on Monday 14 September and met with

Otmar Issing, the Bundesbank's economic adviser and a member of its board. Drawing on the work which had been done in the Treasury during the previous few months, Budd and King argued that sterling's parity was consistent with the main economic indicators. The two men produced analyses of export performance, productivity and wages in an attempt to demonstrate that sterling remained 'competitive'. They insisted that the current-account deficit was readily financeable from overseas savings. The Treasury had realized that the Bundesbank was likely to offer much stronger support to France than to Britain in the event of a serious crisis on the currency markets, so the visitors stressed also that sterling's exchange rate against the franc was well-aligned. Budd and King, however, had been told in advance not to be drawn into any discussion of changes in the present constellation of exchange rates. Issing and his colleagues appeared unconvinced. Assuming apparently that his guests would know that Germany had sought a realignment extending beyond the lira's devaluation, Issing said that parity changes in ERM were the responsibility of the Bonn government. Twenty-four hours later Schlesinger would disclose the central bank's true position.

Two days before Black Wednesday, Norman Lamont and John Major discussed seriously the possibility of sterling's withdrawal from the ERM. Their meeting, which remained a close secret among just a handful of senior Whitehall officials, was the basis upon which Lamont would later assert in his resignation speech that he had realized that sterling's position in the mechanism was unsustainable but that the prime minister had resisted any suggestion of withdrawal. In fact, Whitehall accounts of the discussion paint an ambiguous picture. And, in any event, nothing considered on that Monday evening would have avoided the hurricane which swept away the government's economic strategy two days later.

Major and Lamont met in 10 Downing Street after the prime minister's return earlier that day from Balmoral. Lamont was accompanied by Terence Burns; Major was joined by Sarah Hogg and Alex Allan. The purpose of the gathering was to review the contingency plans being laid in Whitehall for the following Sunday, when France would vote in its Maastricht referendum. At this point there was no immediate alarm about sterling. The financial markets that day had been relatively subdued in the wake of the lira devaluation and the parallel reduction in German interest rates. The Bank of England had been obliged to intervene to stabilize sterling's new rate against the Italian currency, but the pound had edged up slightly against the all-important Deutschmark. But the outlook was sufficiently disconcerting for Major to cancel a planned visit to Seville later in the week. The official excuse was pressure of work; the reality was that he realized he could not take the risk of leaving the country in the last critical days before the French referendum.

The initial focus of the meeting on Monday evening was on the likely reaction to the referendum. The opinion polls still suggested that it might well be a no vote, threatening immediate turmoil in the ERM. Helmut Kohl had told Major that, even if the outcome was negative, the Bonn government wanted to salvage the Maastricht Treaty. Kohl believed that France's European partners should declare the treaty 'suspended'. Major and Lamont rejected the analysis and agreed that it would be impossible to secure ratification at Westminster if France joined Denmark in rejecting the Maastricht blueprint: the treaty would be effectively dead. If the French voted yes, however, then Major would hold to the position established after the Danish referendum.

Much more difficult was to predict the reaction in the financial markets. Major and Lamont were obliged to acknowledge the growing conviction among officials that the cherished Deutschmark link could not be sustained indefinitely. The Treasury and the Bank of England were laying plans against the possibility of an extensive ERM realignment immediately after the referendum. Senior Bank officials had been told to be at their desks on the Sunday evening in case the outcome forced immediate parity changes. European finance ministers would be in Washington for the annual gathering of the IMF and would meet if necessary to negotiate any changes. Guarding against all eventualities, Treasury officials had arranged for the dispatch to Washington of the sophisticated computer software necessary to recalibrate exchange rates after a realignment.

Eddie George had concluded that a change in sterling's parity was unavoidable. The principal purpose of sustaining the existing position until the French referendum was to secure subsequently either an orderly realignment or a temporary suspension of sterling. Terence Burns considered that if the government held out until the result of the referendum several escape routes might open up. Rejection of Maastricht by the French voters – and by implication repudiation of the treaty's blueprint for a single European currency – might fracture the ERM. In the resulting upheaval sterling could be set free with minimum political cost. If France endorsed the treaty by a narrow margin (as it indeed turned out), the Paris government might none the less be obliged to abandon the *franc fort* policy and sterling's parity might be adjusted as part of a general revaluation of the Deutschmark. There was a third, more optimistic, scenario in the bundles of policy papers piled high in the Treasury. A yes vote might just persuade the foreign exchange markets that the existing ERM parities were credible. Sterling would win a breathing space, German interest rates would fall during the winter, and the British economy would move into the long-awaited recovery. This was an expression more of hope than of expectation.

It was against this background that Major and Lamont reviewed the outlook on the Monday evening. Both knew that the government might have no option but to accept a revaluation of the Deutschmark. It was then that Lamont suggested that the government should also consider suspending sterling's membership of the ERM. It could not accept indefinitely, he said, the deflation involved in maintaining sterling's parity against the Deutschmark. Lamont was deeply pessimistic about the economic outlook, fearing that, without a cut in borrowing costs, recession might turn to slump. He said that, if German interest rates did not fall over the coming months, the government would have to reappraise the commitment to the ERM. The mechanism had done its job in bringing down inflation; the risk now was of dangerous overkill. The Treasury's forecasts indicated that, without a cut in British interest rates, the economy would be locked into 'zero' growth indefinitely. If that was still the case after Christmas, then the prime minister must consider taking sterling out of the system. Devaluation within the ERM would not provide the room for the cuts in interest rates the economy so badly needed.

It was clear, in the words of one aide, that the chancellor was 'putting down a marker' rather than pressing for an immediate decision. There are differing accounts, however, of Major's response.

One of those present recalls that the prime minister appeared sceptical. Only a few days earlier he had staked his government's reputation on preferring the ERM parity. With unintended prescience, Major now observed that this was not a conundrum which could be solved by setting out timetables and deadlines in advance: it was much more likely events in the financial markets would dictate the outcome. The Downing Street note of the meeting, however, also records another reaction which suggests that Major was alive to the damage being inflicted on the economy. If there was no easing of the tensions in the system, he is reported as saying, the government might well be obliged to act 'a good deal before' the Christmas deadline suggested by the chancellor. The discussion would prove academic. Sterling would not last until midweek.

On the following evening, Tuesday, Lamont summoned his senior advisers to his Treasury office. Pressure had built up on sterling throughout the afternoon, and heavy intervention by the Bank had failed to make a visible impact. Sterling had ended the day's trading in London only a fraction above its DM2.7780 floor in the ERM. The financial markets, belatedly, appeared disappointed with the small reduction in German interest rates which had followed the Italian devaluation. Eddie George warned that a further attack on the pound was likely the following morning, and sought approval to step up the scale of intervention. However, the situation did not seem critical until the meeting was interrupted by news of reports being carried that evening on German news agencies. Helmut Schlesinger had remarked that the weekend ERM realignment would have been more effective had it been more extensive. His words carried the clear implication that sterling should have been devalued alongside the lira. Schlesinger had been interviewed that afternoon by journalists from *Handelsblatt*, the German business newspaper, and the *Wall Street Journal*. He told the newspapers that 'The tensions in the EMS are not over. This will only happen when there is a comprehensive realignment. Further devaluations are not excluded. There may still be pressure on other currencies. There could have been a better solution if there had been a more complete realignment.'[12] The gist of his remarks was released by *Handelsblatt* to local news agencies.

The first the British authorities knew of the story was when the Bank of England was asked for its reaction. John Footman, the press secretary, was sufficiently alarmed to telephone the Treasury. Ian Plenderleith, a senior Bank official, was summoned from the chancellor's office to answer the call. When Plenderleith took the news back into the meeting, the chancellor reacted furiously. It was obvious that Schlesinger's comments would be interpreted as a signal that the Bundesbank was ready to leave sterling to its fate. Within hours it would fall beneath its DM2.7780 floor during trading in New York's financial markets. Lamont demanded that Leigh-Pemberton telephone Schlesinger to insist upon a retraction. He then released his own statement in an attempt to calm the situation: 'There has never been any question of sterling being realigned or devalued and at no stage did anybody else suggest we should move with the Italians.' But Terence Burns and Eddie George were not alone among those who now considered the battle lost.

Lamont was left with a handful of possibilities. One was to withdraw from the system if the pressure on sterling had not abated by the following morning. George and Burns later mused that they might have given more thought to the option. The politics, however, dictated otherwise. If Britain had withdrawn without showing serious resistance it would have been accused of wrecking the ERM. Sterling's departure would have left the franc exposed only days before the Maastricht referendum. Perfidious Albion would stand accused of sabotaging the future of Europe. In any event, such a momentous decision would have to be agreed by the cabinet. Kenneth Clarke, Michael Heseltine and Douglas Hurd – all strong Europeans – would have insisted that the government attempt to ride out the storm. More likely than not the prime minister would have taken the same view.

There was another suggestion that the Bank should put up interest rates before the financial markets opened the following morning, in an attempt to turn the tide. It was not followed up. The discussion that evening lacked a precise focus. It was clear that the position was now critical, but there was no enthusiasm for a radical rethinking of the previously agreed strategy. Instead the officials would reconvene early the next morning. In the meantime the Bank would step up its intervention in the markets. Covert purchases of sterling would be followed by massive open intervention. Only then would the government consider raising interest rates.

Lamont left the Treasury with his wife, Rosemary, to attend a dinner hosted by Ray Seitz, the US ambassador. Richard Lambert, the editor of the *Financial Times* and a guest at the same dinner, fell victim to the chancellor's thunderous mood. Lamont, alerted to the fact that the *FT* was carrying Schlesinger's remarks, said the news agency reports were erroneous: the Bundesbank president had been misquoted, and the reports of his remarks were being corrected. The *Financial Times*, he warned, could do serious damage to sterling. Lambert checked back with his news desk and was told the story was accurate. The Bundesbank had indeed put out a statement, but it had not denied the substance of the reports. Lamont received the same message when he spoke by telephone to his private office: Schlesinger had agreed to say that the quotations were 'unauthorized' and incomplete, but not to deny them.

The chancellor now demanded that Leigh-Pemberton seek a stronger retraction. Tracked down for a second time, the Bundesbank president appeared contrite. Leigh-Pemberton gained the impression that he had indeed made the damaging remarks, but had intended them to be off the record. Schlesinger had told his interviewers that any direct quotations must be referred to the Bundesbank before publication. *Handelsblatt*, however, had circumvented those terms by paraphrasing his remarks. As it turned out, some of Schlesinger's other comments were more supportive of sterling. He had remarked, for example, that 'The pound is in a different situation from the lira. The UK has plenty of currency reserves to support it. The Italians have run out of money.' It was too late for clarification, however, and by the time that the authorized text appeared sterling had been engulfed.

For those who spent Wednesday 16 September 1992 in Admiralty House as sterling was driven out of the ERM, the overwhelming emotion was of disbelieving impotence. This was a convulsive experience – the most devastating of their political careers. It was a bright, sunny day, Douglas Hurd would later recall, but the mood of John Major and his senior ministers had never been darker. Robin Leigh-

Pemberton would later tell friends that he had been overwhelmed by a terrible sense of failure – the greatest sense of defeat he had ever experienced. James Callaghan, beaten by the speculators in 1967, well understood how they felt. He had described the scene in his memoirs, *Time and Chance*: 'In all the offices I have held I have never experienced anything more frustrating than sitting at the chancellor's desk watching our currency reserves gurgle down the plughole day by day and knowing that the drain could not be stopped.'[13] The only difference now was that the reserves were pouring out minute by minute rather than day by day. Kenneth Clarke and Michael Heseltine, the most activist of politicians, were stunned by their helplessness. Hurd was outwardly calm, but acutely aware that his carefully crafted European policy was being demolished alongside the government's economic strategy.

For a short time afterwards, everyone blamed everyone else. In Whitehall, the Bank was censured for its handling of sterling's defence. The politicians were criticized by officials for taking too long to face up to reality. The politicians blamed that favourite enemy, the Germans. But, once the initial shock had passed, the recriminations were subsumed in the recognition of collective failure. Still later it would be said that nothing could have been done – that the government was no more than a victim of events. Among senior officials at the Bank who had confronted the speculators there was also a curious feeling of release and escape.

Some kept memories of the faintly comic circumstances of the defeat. The prime minister had moved to Admiralty House, an eighteenth-century porticoed building directly overlooking Whitehall, while building contractors strengthened Downing Street's defences against terrorist attack. But this temporary base had no telephone switchboard, no Reuters monitors, no computer network. So, during the worst moments of the day, officials and ministers found themselves scouring the building for additional telephone lines. Eddie George carried a pocket Reuters screen to keep track of the speculators, but, when he returned to the Bank, Major's officials had to dart to and fro to 10 Downing Street to check the monitor in Gus O'Donnell's office. At one point during the day three of the government's most important ministers – Hurd, Heseltine and Clarke – found themselves sitting idly in an ante-room without even a television set to follow events in the financial markets. Richard Ryder, the chief whip, set off to search in vain for a radio. There was also occasion for gallows humour – as the reserves poured out of the Bank of England, the pro-European Clarke was heard remarking that the lesson was that governments should establish a single currency 'pretty damn quick'.

Newspaper reports afterwards included speculation that Major had 'wobbled' – that he had had a breakdown at the height of the crisis. No one who was there, including Norman Lamont, has substantiated the reports. Aides deny them vehemently. 'It is absolute junk,' one of the officials present that day in Admiralty House would comment. Sarah Hogg sought to scotch the rumours publicly: 'All that nonsense that is talked about Black Wednesday. I was there the whole way through, and I have never seen anyone in such seriously difficult circumstances, and a very, very fast-moving situation, so calm, so in control, so organized with his colleagues.'[14] As to the source of the reports, Lamont confessed to be as perplexed as the officials: 'I don't know how the rumour started. It started long before I resigned. The twisted and bitter Norman Lamont might, I suppose, have spread it, but not while he was chancellor,' Lamont would say two years later.[15]

It is true that the prime minister was at times visibly angry. He railed against the Bundesbank, seeing in Schlesinger's actions a betrayal of Germany's oft-repeated commitment to European integration. However, he was capable at the same moment of cold political calculation. Even as the pound sank, Major called in Sir Marcus Fox, the chairman of the powerful 1922 Committee, to prepare him for the worst. Sir Norman Fowler, the party chairman, was also summoned, later to be dispatched to defend the government in the television studios. Determined to preserve the façade of normality – and anyway powerless against the tide of events – Major went ahead during the day with a long-planned meeting with a group of Tory back-benchers. Most importantly, he safeguarded his own position by ensuring that his senior cabinet colleagues shared in the disaster. Kenneth Clarke was to recall with some admiration the way that, along with Hurd and Heseltine, he had been locked into every decision. That made it a collective defeat. 'We were there to put our

hands in the blood,' Clarke would say. The No. 10 officials who were
at the prime minister's side for virtually every minute echo the denial
that he broke down: 'It just did not happen,' says one his closest aides.
A cabinet colleague offers the same view: 'I suppose it is just possible
that he burst into tears when he went to the loo – I would have done
– but none of us saw him other than in control.'

The day started with a telephone conversation between Major and
Lamont just before 9 a.m. It was already clear from the early trading
on continental European markets that sterling faced a fierce
onslaught. Lamont told the prime minister that they would have to
put up interest rates. Major, an aide said later with some understatement, was not best pleased. Even if the interest rate rise worked, it
would fuel the mounting rebellion over Europe on the Tory back
benches.

The decision to increase rates from 10 to 12 per cent was endorsed
at a meeting which began soon afterwards at the Treasury. Leigh-
Pemberton and George joined Burns, Turnbull, Budd and other
Treasury officials in the discussion. At 10.30 a.m. Lamont telephoned
Major and secured his approval. Clarke, Hurd, Heseltine and Ryder
had arrived earlier that morning at Admiralty House for a long-
planned meeting to discuss contingency plans for the following
Sunday, the day of the French referendum. Major was accompanied
by Sarah Hogg and Alex Allan. John Kerr had travelled to London
from Brussels for the talks. The ministers were aware that sterling
was under siege on the currency markets, but Major waited to hear
from Lamont before telling them the worst.

The cabinet's big beasts, as Hurd, Heseltine and Clarke were
known, readily endorsed the decision to raise interest rates. They had
no other choice: the Bank had already spent over $10bn from the
reserves in its vain defence of the pound. To one of the officials
supervising the efforts to prop up sterling, the pressure was unprecedented: 'It was an absolute avalanche of speculation, there had been
nothing like it before. As technicians we wanted to get out [of the
ERM] as soon as possible. But it was for the politicians to decide
when we had met our legal obligations.' The Bundesbank and Banque
de France had joined the Bank of England in attempting to keep

sterling above its ERM floor at the start of trading. The intervention had been brushed aside.

Before 11 a.m. Leigh-Pemberton returned to Threadneedle Street from the Treasury for the first of two conference calls that day with his European counterparts on the central banks' private telephone network. He spelled out the scale of the pressure on sterling, now locked at its DM2.7780 floor in the mechanism. He explained the interest rate rise and asked his colleagues if they could do anything to ease the pressure. In his mind was the thought that, even at this late stage, a cut in German interest rates might forestall the crisis. With the lira and the peseta also under attack, the Belgian and Dutch central banks had cut their rates by 0.25 percentage points. Schlesinger said the Bundesbank would meet its legal obligations within the ERM to act as a buyer of last resort for sterling in Frankfurt; it would do no more. Major meanwhile spoke by telephone to Helmut Kohl and Pierre Bérégovoy, informing them he would do everything he could to keep sterling within the system but warning that it might not be possible.

Lamont knew it was over at one minute past 11 a.m. He was by then standing in his outer office at the Treasury, hunched over the Reuters screen. At 11 a.m. news of the interest rate increase from 10 to 12 per cent flashed across the top of the screen. Lamont watched the display below which charted second-by-second movements in sterling's exchange rate. Just before the announcement the pound was on its ERM floor of DM2.7780. The news of the interest rate rise flashed on the screen. Sterling did not move. 'It was over,' Lamont said later.

By now the Bank was buying pounds at the rate of tens of millions every few minutes. Its purchases had ceased to be intervention in the conventional sense of the word. In normal circumstances such operations are an attempt to tilt the balance between buyers and sellers in the markets. On 16 September there were no other buyers of sterling apart from the central banks. Instead every commercial bank, corporate treasurer and fund manager was selling to the Bank of England or the Bundesbank at DM2.7780. The Bank was overwhelmed, its reserves puny against the forces ranged against it. The Bank's total holdings of foreign exchange amounted to only a little over 10 per cent of the average daily turnover of $300 billion in the London markets. The speculators knew that devaluation was inevitable. Within hours they would be able to buy back at a lower exchange rate the pounds they had sold and make a handsome profit at the government's expense.

At mid-morning Hurd, Heseltine and Clarke returned to their offices. Bemused by the government's apparent impotence, Clarke charted the pound's dismal fortunes in his suite at the Home Office via the Ceefax service on his office television. At the Foreign Office, diplomats hurriedly checked the legal procedures for sterling's withdrawal from the ERM. By 12.30 p.m. all three cabinet ministers had been recalled to Admiralty House to put their hands again in the blood.

At 12.45 Major heard Lamont's dismal prognosis before reconvening the larger meeting of ministers and officials fifteen minutes later. The chancellor told this gathering that sterling's withdrawal from the system appeared all but inevitable. Leigh-Pemberton concurred: the reserves were haemorrhaging and there was no sign that the pressure on sterling would abate. Major then set out four options:

- The Bank of England could simply keep intervening until its foreign currency reserves were completely exhausted.
- The government could announce a further, temporary, interest rate rise of 3 per cent.
- The government could seek a realignment of sterling's parity within the ERM.
- The pound's membership of the mechanism could be suspended.

Major told the group that if intervention did not stabilize the currency – and there was little expectation that it would – the chancellor and the Bank favoured the fourth option. He then went round the table to elicit the views of each of his most senior ministers. According to the accounts of those present, Hurd led the argument that the government must observe all the proprieties. In the words of a colleague, the foreign secretary was determined to ensure there could be no accusation that it had 'thrown in the towel at the first squall'. Clarke endorsed Hurd's stance – it would be foolish to admit defeat without at least testing the reaction to another rise in interest rates. If higher rates had no effect, however, the Bank should stop intervening. Clarke had no time for suggestions that Britain's legal obligations meant it must continue to enrich the speculators at least until 4 p.m. – the official close of European trading. Heseltine also backed another interest rate rise, remarking that the government should keep open the option of rejoining the mechanism once calm was restored. Later Heseltine would tell colleagues that the options had been presented only when it was too late to make a real choice between them.

The response of these ministers was greeted less than enthusiastically by the Treasury. It knew the battle had been lost and that, even if it was short-lived, another increase in borrowing costs could do serious damage to confidence. Ministers and officials, however, subsequently gave conflicting accounts of the debate. Treasury officials said they had wanted to suspend sterling's membership even before lunchtime. As well as avoiding another interest rate rise that would have protected what remained of the Bank of England's dwindling foreign exchange reserves. The Treasury also resented the fact that Clarke, Heseltine and Hurd were being given a voice in interest rate decisions. This was a dangerous precedent as, hitherto, only the chancellor and prime minister had determined the level of borrowing costs. Clarke, however, was adamant that, if he were to share in the blame for the fiasco, he would be heard. He also recalled afterwards the apparent confusion over whether the government could halt intervention before sterling had been formally suspended from the mechanism. He thought a second interest rate rise, perhaps futile in terms of sustaining sterling's parity, might none the less staunch the 'flow of blood' from the reserves. Summing up the discussion, Major came down in favour of an increase to 15 per cent. Aware of the opprobrium which would be heaped upon him, the prime minister wanted to be sure he could not be accused of losing his nerve or of reneging on Britain's obligations to its partners: 'It was rulebook stuff,' one of his cabinet colleagues would remark.

The meeting broke up at 2 p.m. and ministers returned once again to their departments. Leigh-Pemberton left for a second conference call with other European central bankers. The governor explained to his counterparts that, if the second interest rate rise had no effect, Britain would have no option but to suspend its ERM membership.

He had little expectation that it would work. At 2.15 p.m. the Bank announced that rates would rise to 15 per cent; the pound once again remained glued to its ERM floor. In fact the announcement contained within it the implicit admission that it would fail. The 15 per cent rate would come into effect only from the following day, allowing the banks to wait before raising their commercial lending rates to the same level. In the event, Lamont announced later that evening that the increase had been reversed. Twelve hours later he would also scrap the first, two-point rise, taking interest rates back down to 10 per cent.

By the time the ministers regrouped at Admiralty House for the third time, at 3.45 p.m., no one had any doubts that the government had lost. The announcement that base rates would rise to 15 per cent had succeeded in blunting somewhat the speculative assault on sterling, but the pound remained under intense pressure and the Bank's reserves were close to exhaustion. Clarke, Hurd and Heseltine had to wait around for an hour before Lamont and Leigh-Pemberton arrived. Alex Allan, Major's principal private secretary, suggested they return later. They stayed, cut off from the news, but unhappily certain that this was a moment too terrible to be missed. The chancellor briefed Major privately in the upstairs flat at Admiralty House before the larger meeting was again reconvened at 5 p.m. and the decision was taken to pull out of the ERM. It was a formality. Nigel Wicks had made the arrangements for the meeting of European monetary officials which would give legal force to the move. Wicks and Andrew Crockett left for Brussels to attend to the formalities. That meeting would endorse also the suspension of the beleaguered lira from the system and a 5 per cent devaluation of the Spanish peseta. It would reject, however, a British suggestion that the entire mechanism be suspended.

At this last meeting of the day it was agreed that Lamont would announce the reversal of the three-point rise in rates. Now that the game was lost, Heseltine and Clarke pressed also for the earlier two-point rise to be scrapped immediately. But the pound had fallen well below its ERM floor, and the Treasury and Bank feared it could go into free fall. After a sometimes heated exchange, it was agreed that a decision would be deferred until the following day. Major returned to the telephone to relay the decision to Kohl and Bérégovoy. Stephen

Wall, his foreign affairs private secretary, informed his counterparts in other European capitals. To the annoyance of Clarke, Treasury officials instructed all of those present that they could say nothing until the meeting of the monetary committee had been formally convened. Only once that had been done could Lamont announce the decision. Norman Fowler would then begin to tour the television studios to pretend that the day had been other than a catastrophe. As the meeting turned its attention to what the chancellor would tell the waiting world, the mood was dire. 'We were all pretty clear that the whole thing had been an unmitigated disaster,' one minister would remark.

During the next few days Clarke was to tell colleagues of his abiding horror at being a helpless bystander as the disaster unfolded. By the time he had become involved, 'The whole thing was taken out of the hands of the politicians by the technicians. We were just there to sign on the dotted line.' The home secretary resolved that henceforth he would take an altogether closer interest in economic affairs. Heseltine, like Clarke a passionate supporter of Britain's place in Europe, could not understand why there had not been fuller discussion of the options before the point of crisis had been reached. Hurd was to admit that he had simply not appreciated the size of the waves which would wash away the government's economic policy.

At 7.30 p.m. Lamont appeared outside the Treasury. His comments had been drafted and redrafted in Admiralty House. With supreme understatement he announced the markets' savage destruction of his economic strategy:

> Today has been an extremely difficult and turbulent day. Massive speculative flows continued to disrupt the functioning of the exchange rate mechanism. As chairman of the Council of European Finance Ministers I have called a meeting of the monetary committee in Brussels urgently tonight to consider how stability can be restored in the foreign exchange markets.
>
> In the meantime the government has concluded that Britain's best interests can be served by suspending our membership of the exchange rate mechanism. As a result the second of the two interest rate increases

that I sanctioned today will not take place tomorrow. Minimum
Lending Rate will be at 12 per cent until conditions become calmer.

I will be reporting to Cabinet and discussing the situation with
colleagues tomorrow and may make further statements then. Until
then I have nothing further to say. Thank you very much.[16]

The Bank of England's intervention on Black Wednesday was by far
the largest ever undertaken, exceeding many times over foreign
currency sales during previous sterling crises. For that reason its true
extent has never been revealed officially. The government instead has
hidden behind obfuscation. One of the worst flaws of the present
arrangements for parliamentary oversight of the nation's finances is
that the Treasury can avoid any serious scrutiny of operations in the
foreign exchange markets. A few million pounds wasted by a hospital
trust or an unusually generous remuneration package for a university
vice-chancellor can attract intense scrutiny by the Public Accounts
Committee, but taxpayers have no way of knowing how many billions
of their money have drained from the foreign currency reserves in the
Bank of England.

The official response says that divulging the scale of intervention
would weaken the government's hand on any future occasion when it
needed to defend the pound. The Treasury also insists that it is
misleading to calculate from any one particular episode the extent of
the losses faced by the British taxpayer: much of the foreign currency
sold on Black Wednesday had been accumulated over several years
and bought at many different exchange rates. Similarly, the rebuilding
of the reserves would take years, not weeks or months, and the value
of sterling would continue to fluctuate, so a simple comparison based
on the cost of buying back reserves spent on Black Wednesday at a
lower exchange rate is dismissed as too simplistic an assessment of the
losses then. The Treasury sums up its position by stating simply, 'No
unambiguous estimate can therefore be made of any profit or loss
made from intervention.' Honest officials dismiss such sophistry: the
arithmetic is not simple, but perfectly respectable calculations of the
losses incurred can be – and indeed have been – made for internal
consumption in Whitehall. The secrecy has one aim – to hide
government defeats.

Taking the Tuesday afternoon and Wednesday together, the Bank sold over $30bn (equivalent at the then exchange rate to about £15bn) from its reserves. According to one official present in Admiralty House, the sales of dollars and Deutschmarks equalled at one stage the $37.9bn which the Bank held in readily convertible currencies. The overall level of the reserves at the start of September had stood at $44.4bn, but $6.5bn of that was held in gold and IMF special drawing rights. The reserves had gone 'negative' once before – in 1976, during the sterling crisis which forced James Callaghan to call in the International Monetary Fund.

Much of the intervention was hidden by the operations of the Bank in the forward foreign exchange markets. As Nigel Lawson explains in his memoirs, the published figures for the reserves at the end of each month relate only to 'spot' or immediate transactions: they take no account of any outstanding liabilities during the following weeks and months.[17] The reserve figures published two weeks after Black Wednesday were artificially inflated by spot repurchases of foreign exchange which were then matched against equivalent sales in the forward market. Nor did those figures take any account of the massive debts the Bank had accumulated with the European Monetary Cooperation Fund. In simple terms, the Bank had borrowed large amounts of foreign exchange to disguise the fact that its own reserves had been all but exhausted.

The official statistics for the reserves at the end of September 1992 showed a drop of less than $2bn, to $42.7bn, although the Treasury did admit an 'underlying' fall of $7.7bn. What it did not say was that its operations – along with the compulsory intervention by the Bundesbank – had left it with a DM33bn ($23.6bn) debt at the European Monetary Cooperation Fund. The government had also spent the 5bn ecu ($6.4bn) credit which it had received in Deutschmarks at the beginning of September, and would be obliged to raise speedily the second tranche of the credit. It had further liabilities to commercial operators in the market. The Treasury's subsequent anxiety – one official called it panic – to conceal the extent of the losses was unsurprising.

Some of the debts were paid off quickly, but the Bank's own, highly selective, statistics show that in 1995 the Treasury still had outstanding liabilities dating from Black Wednesday.[18] During that intervening period, sterling had fallen by about 20 per cent against the dollar and the Deutschmark. The calculation depends on the timing of the foreign currency purchases required to repay the debts, but senior officials do not demur at the suggestion that the overall loss to the taxpayer was at least £3bn and quite likely £4bn – an expensive price tag for twenty-four hours' trading in the foreign exchange markets. By contrast the Banque de France, which spent more than a year defending the franc and was forced eventually to allow it to float in much wider ERM bands, is thought to have made a small profit from its even larger intervention. It exhausted its reserves in 1993, but the French central bank bought back the foreign currency only after the value of the franc had recovered to its original level.

Black Wednesday was more than a defeat for Norman Lamont: it was a failure of government. A pall of gloom hung over Whitehall. The Treasury, the Bank of England and, above all, John Major would share in the opprobrium. The government's economic policy lay in ruins. Major's political reputation was in shreds, his party torn asunder. The failure to hold sterling's ERM central rate of DM2.95 robbed the prime minister of the authority of his office, just as devaluation had undermined Harold Wilson in 1967. After his enforced departure the following year, Lamont would charge that the government now behaved as if 'in office but not in power'.[19] To the extent that was true, the pound's exit from the ERM was responsible.

But there was no serious post-mortem within Whitehall into the events of Black Wednesday. Inquests have a tendency to allocate blame, and the government had decided it was blameless. The official story was unequivocal: the dark forces which drove sterling from the exchange rate mechanism had been unpredictable and irresistible. The pound was not alone in falling victim to the storm: Spain, Italy and a clutch of Scandinavian countries suffered the same fate. Less than a year later the system itself almost broke when the franc was driven off its Deutschmark parity. In the government's mind, there were fault-lines in the system and, if there was blame to be assigned, one needed to look no further than the Bundesbank in Frankfurt.

Robin Leigh-Pemberton delivered the authorized analysis a few weeks after Black Wednesday. In a speech drafted by Eddie George, the Bank governor said that the decision to join the ERM had been 'right in the circumstances'; and, 'having joined, we were right to endeavour to stick with it; and, in the circumstances which evolved, were also right to withdraw'.[20] The government, in other words, had been a helpless victim of cruel circumstance. The task of government, however, is to shape events and, if that proves impossible, to choose orderly retreat over ignominious defeat. As John Kenneth Galbraith once put it, 'Politics is not the art of the possible. It consists in choosing between the disastrous and the unpalatable.' In retrospect it is easy to see how the disjuncture between the German and British economies made devaluation irresistible. But Black Wednesday was much more than a devaluation – it was a national humiliation.

The misalignment of German policy with that of the rest of Europe was indeed the fundamental cause of the strains in the system. The Bonn government's decision to finance reunification through higher borrowing and the Bundesbank's refusal to accommodate that policy imposed serious costs on Germany's neighbours. Helmut Schlesinger's Bundesbank was carelessly indifferent to the interests of others in Europe. Then there were the unpredictable Danes. The economic pressures were at their most intense just as the outcome of the Danish referendum on Maastricht undercut the credibility of the existing exchange rate pattern in Europe.

So it became fashionable soon after Black Wednesday to argue that, after ten years of promising to join the ERM when the time was right, the government finally locked sterling into the system just as the time became wrong. Up to a point that was true but the decision was also readily explicable. When Britain joined, in the autumn of 1990, it was distracted by the pressures of the moment. The government had been exhausted by the battle between Margaret Thatcher and Nigel Lawson and feared growing isolation in Europe. It needed to rebuild the credibility of its anti-inflation strategy after the 1980s boom. Some officials felt the DM2.95 rate was too high, while others worried about Britain's inflation rate, but most accepted that the important decision was to join – that the economic problems facing the government would not be any worse within the ERM and there was a chance that membership might help.

Politics pointed strongly in the same direction, and, for many, clinched the argument. Britain was at risk, once again, of being

marginalized in negotiations to shape Europe's future. Outside the
ERM it would have no real voice in the Maastricht bargaining over
economic and monetary union. There seemed no time to assess
whether there would be a better moment to join. And John Major
was in distinguished company. Industry was unanimous in its applause
for entry, as were the big financial institutions in the City. The
Labour Party endorsed it, and so did most of the Conservative Party
– less than a dozen Tory MPs registered a protest in the Commons
vote on membership. Newspapers which later vilified the ERM as the
cause of all of Britain's economic ills judged at the time that it might
speed the process of economic and political recovery.

The real mistakes were made in 1992. By the summer of that year
it was clear that circumstances had radically changed. In 1990 the
government's priority had been to reduce and then contain inflation;
eighteen months later the ERM was imposing too fierce a squeeze on
an economy which risked sliding from recession into slump. The
official statistics now date the start of the economic recovery to mid-
1992, but it is doubtful that it would have been sustained without the
cuts in interest rates which followed the break with the Deutschmark.
Unprecedented levels of consumer debt and the collapse in the
housing market demanded much lower borrowing costs. So too did
sterling's rise to $2.00 – a level which threatened serious damage to
industry. Holding sterling to a Deutschmark parity which had been
established in entirely different circumstances closed off the option of
lower interest rates.

There was also a fundamental – and inexplicable – contradiction in
the government's position. For France and most other ERM
countries, sticking with their existing parities was considered a price
worth paying to secure a single currency. Major had never endorsed
that goal, negotiating an opt-out for sterling at Maastricht. In the
summer of 1992, however, although Major was publicly dismissive of
the short-term prospects for a single currency, his approach appeared
indistinguishable from that of those committed to it. If it was perfectly
understandable for the French government to treat the ERM as a
fixed-rate system, there was no such pressure on Britain. The
government should have explored during the summer the option of a
substantial devaluation, most probably alongside the lira and the

peseta. Instead the Treasury invested everything in an unproven theory – that such a devaluation would have led inevitably to higher rather than to lower interest rates.

At the other end of the spectrum there were a series of tactical errors. If the government was determined, albeit mistakenly, to sustain sterling's parity until the French referendum, it should have been ready to raise interest rates. From the moment it had joined the system, interest rates had been falling. When the pound had come under pressure in December 1991 the government had signalled that it was unwilling to defend it with higher borrowing costs. Its commitment to the Deutschmark parity henceforth lacked credibility. The markets' scepticism was confirmed when the Treasury cut the rates for National Savings in July 1992. The Bank's strategy meanwhile paid insufficient heed to the experience of other European central banks. The scrapping of capital controls had exposed the ERM to the full force of the hundreds of billions of dollars being traded each day in the foreign exchange markets. The Bank mounted its most serious attempts to support the pound only when it had reached its ERM floor; the Banque de France deployed massive intervention well before the franc reached its lowest permitted level. More importantly, the Bank made no attempt during sterling's ERM membership to establish a more sophisticated interest rate structure to defend the pound during bouts of speculative pressure. Other European central banks had developed mechanisms to raise the cost of borrowing in financial markets to levels of 100 per cent and above without immediately affecting the rates applying more widely in the economy. Such techniques allowed them to fight off speculation without hitting the electorate. Sterling had no such defence.

This institutional weakness was apparent also in Whitehall. The decision to join the ERM transferred a large say over Britain's economic policy to other European governments. Whitehall, by instinct parochial and secretive, did not respond by building new alliances and allegiances with other finance ministries. The interdependence of national economies is a constant theme of Treasury pronouncements. As an institution, however, it failed to understand that membership of the ERM blurred the dividing lines between domestic economic management and foreign policy. When the crisis hit in 1992 Britain had no real allies.

The most important error, however, was the elevation of the exchange rate parity into a badge of pride. Winston Churchill learned the lesson to his cost during the late 1920s, when he took sterling back to the gold standard. Fifty years later Harold Wilson made the same mistake and suffered the humiliation of the 1967 devaluation. Major now repeated it, raising the stakes repeatedly, and ensuring that when the defeat came it was devastating. Devaluation is never easy within a fixed or semi-fixed exchange rate system, but it is always much harder and damaging when it comes later rather than sooner. By 1992 the exchange rate had once again become an end of policy rather than a means. During sterling's brief spell in the ERM the politicians and the policy-makers persuaded themselves that a strong exchange rate would provide the key to sustained economic revival. Successive devaluations of the pound had done nothing to reverse Britain's relative economic decline, so the government would force industry to adjust to the chill winds of international competition by pegging the exchange rate.

This analysis displayed a basic misunderstanding. Sterling's steady depreciation over several decades had been a symptom as much as a cause of economic failure. Fixing the exchange rate would not solve the more fundamental structural problems besetting the economy – a weak manufacturing base, a large current-account deficit, low investment, and poor education and training among them. A credible anti-inflation policy – whether delivered by a fixed exchange rate or by a discretionary approach to setting interest rates – is a necessary condition for economic success, but it is not a sufficient one. A free-floating exchange rate rarely provides either the freedom or the benefits claimed by its advocates: witness the damage inflicted on the economy during the 1980s, firstly by too high a pound and then by its precipitate fall. By 1992, however, the pendulum had swung too far in the opposite direction. The government failed to distinguish between the sensible pragmatism of a fixed but adjustable rate for sterling and the danger of investing its reputation in one particular parity. Devaluation was stigmatized as an admission of failure, an act of weakness, rather than seen as a sensible response to changing economic circumstances. The government made the mistake of believing its own rhetoric. History spoke to the fact that political pride and the pound do not mix.

Finally, Black Wednesday provided an object lesson in the dangers of the Treasury's obsessive secrecy. No one outside Nos 10 and 11 Downing Street and the Bank of England was consulted on joining the ERM or on the appropriate exchange rate. Even Douglas Hurd, the foreign secretary, was informed only after the decision had been taken. Then, in the months following the 1992 election, the cabinet was denied any serious discussion on the options. The Treasury's determination to hold all authority to itself led to bad decision-making and, ultimately, to disaster.

There was a small but rather curious postcript to Black Wednesday as regards the Labour party. The opposition was clearly embarrassed subsequently by its failure to attack Major's government for seeking to defend DM2.95. But some time afterwards, Neil Kinnock indicated that, had he won the 1992 general election, the incoming Labour government would have devalued sterling within the ERM at the outset. The statement baffled Whitehall officials because on the very eve of the election one of Kinnock's senior aides, John (later Lord) Eatwell, had met with Terence Burns to agree the text of a press release which would have been issued by the Treasury after an outright Labour victory or in the event of Labour emerging as the largest party in a hung parliament. The draft release, never issued, said that the new Laour government would defend the existing ERM parity, echoing the line which John Smith, the shadow chancellor, had adopted throughout the election campaign. Kinnock's friends, however, insist that the draft press release was a false trail, reflecting their mistrust of the Treasury establishment. Separate talks between Labour officials and a 'trusted' director of the Bank of England had established the need for a realignment. So, if the Labour leader had entered No. 10 Downing Street on 10 April, the release would have never been issued and the new prime minister would have sought a 10 per cent devaluation within the ERM during the following weekend. It is an intriguing story but also, for the Labour party, a convenient one.

CHAPTER ELEVEN

BROKEN PROMISES

THE GOVERNMENT MADE two important promises before the 1992 general election: to reduce taxes and to tame inflation by maintaining sterling's parity in the exchange rate mechanism. It broke both. So it was something of an irony that, together, Black Wednesday and the largest package of tax increases in modern peacetime delivered by accident what so many previous governments had failed to achieve by design – a successful devaluation. What followed the pound's departure from the ERM was a textbook rebalancing of the economy, with low inflation accompanied by an export-driven recovery in output. Debt deflation and higher taxes held down prices while industry successfully exploited a more competitive exchange rate to boost sales in highly profitable export markets. This favourable conjuncture – arguably the best for several decades – offered little political comfort to John Major. The government never apologized for Black Wednesday. Unsurprisingly, the voters chose not to assign to it the credit for what followed.

In the immediate aftermath of 16 September no one dared contemplate such a propitious sequel for the economy. It was true that there were senior officials in the Bank of England who celebrated the escape from the straitjacket of the ERM, but the prevailing mood was of failure. Eddie George's careful defences had been brushed aside by the markets. For all Norman Lamont's easy humour, the Treasury was steeped in gloom. It was not until three weeks later that the government began seriously to remake its economic policy. The first important decisions would be taken in a hotel room in Brighton.

After his departure from the cabinet in 1993, Norman Lamont said that he had offered to resign after sterling's ejection from the ERM. He told the House of Commons:

On 16 September he [the prime minister] made it clear to me in writing that he had no intention of resigning himself and that I should not do so either. Of course I discussed the question with the prime minister subsequently. In all those discussions, he emphasized that he regarded the attacks on me as coded attacks on himself. So I decided that my duty and loyalty was to the prime minister and that I should remain in office.[1]

Senior officials present at the time do not recall the exchanges, and there is no record of such a correspondence in the Whitehall archives. Major has told aides that he has a vague recollection of the conversation and that scribbled notes may have passed between the two men. But, whatever the precise circumstances, it was obvious that Lamont saw no reason to bear the responsibility for the defeat. For his part, Major could not be certain that his premiership would survive. Their fortunes were bound together, so the chancellor would stay. In a series of television interviews twenty-four hours after sterling's departure from the mechanism, Lamont was unequivocal: 'I am not going to resign. I have been operating the policy of the whole government. I know I have the support of the prime minister,' he told the BBC. Later there was an ill-judged echo of Harold Wilson's assertion that devaluation had not affected the pound in the voter's pocket. As sterling's value fell, Lamont told ITN, 'We have not resorted to devaluation. The pound is now floating, and we shall have to see what level it finds.'

Major's decision not to reshuffle his cabinet was a mistake. Lamont would also have fared better had he followed James Callaghan's example by moving to the Home Office. He was adamant, however, that he should not be a scapegoat. It was Major who had taken sterling into the ERM. The chancellor, whose Euroscepticism would now flourish, made it clear that he had never been an enthusiast for fixed exchange rates.

On the morning of Thursday 17 September, the cabinet met for three hours to reflect on the disaster. In a brief statement afterwards, it said that sterling's suspension was a temporary expedient: the pound would be restored to the mechanism once calm returned. Gus O'Donnell was instructed to brief journalists that each and every minister had endorsed this position. In truth the cabinet was dazed. There had previously been occasional allusions in cabinet to the pressure on sterling, but no real debate about the options. Even within the inner circle – Douglas Hurd, Kenneth Clarke and Michael Heseltine – the assumption had been that the government would ride out the crisis at least until the French referendum: 'I only really knew what I had read in the newspapers,' Clarke would remark. Heseltine wondered how much consideration the Treasury had given to a pre-emptive devaluation. He had not questioned the rate at which sterling had joined the system, but, as industry's costs had continued to outstrip those of its competitors, he had wondered if the rate remained sustainable. Such views were not for general discussion, however. Nothing much had changed. The Labour cabinet minister Richard Crossman had been alerted to the impending sterling crisis of 1967 not by the prime minister but by the newspaper proprietor Cecil King.

The cabinet statement on that Thursday morning was economical with the truth. The prime minister and the chancellor had decided in their own minds that sterling would remain outside the ERM for the indefinite future. Major knew on the Wednesday evening that it would be politically impossible to return. The cabinet's Eurosceptics had reached the same conclusion. Michael Howard made the point forcefully during this first discussion. His judgement was shared by Michael Portillo and Peter Lilley, although at this stage they kept their counsel. And there had been reaction enough from Conservative MPs to indicate that the party at Westminster would not accept a return to the exchange rate straitjacket. The sceptics were already talking of 'White Wednesday', to celebrate sterling's release from its European shackles.

The cabinet Europhiles wanted to keep open the option of rejoining. Heseltine and Clarke thought something might be salvaged from the wreckage after the French referendum on the following Sunday. Lamont spoke as if on their side, arguing that the cabinet must emphasize that the pound's suspension was purely temporary. His motivation was tactical, however – sterling had been falling fast on financial markets and was now only fractionally above DM2.60. If the government was seen to abandon the ERM, the pound might go into free fall. Lamont's draft statement was toned down slightly to reflect Howard's intervention and Major's doubts, but the message conveyed to the outside world by O'Donnell remained positive: the pound would be put back into the ERM 'as soon as conditions allow'. O'Donnell also reported that the cabinet had given full backing to Lamont after Major, in a curious phrase, had told colleagues that the chancellor must not be used as an 'air-raid shelter'. As the meeting broke up, Clarke was heard to remark that the government had better start the search for another economic policy 'pretty damn fast'.

The yawning gap in the government's economic strategy left by sterling's exit from the ERM would not easily be filled. John Major had made the defeat of inflation his pre-eminent goal, and maintaining sterling's parity against the Deutschmark had been the essential instrument. The political shock of the pound's devaluation, however, was accompanied by deep uncertainty about the economic outlook. Within hours of the débâcle came the news that unemployment had risen by 47,400 in August – the twenty-eighth successive monthly increase. The jobless total of 2.8 million was the highest for five years – ample confirmation that the anti-inflationary squeeze within the ERM had been too tight. Though quickly reversed, the interest rate rises which had accompanied sterling's exit from the mechanism had delivered a further heavy blow to confidence. A more expansionist policy was necessary. The Treasury, however, was cautious, acutely aware of the case it had deployed against the pound's devaluation over the previous few months. Sterling was still falling – it would reach DM2.50 by the end of September – and the government had insisted that a depreciation would reignite inflation. It had now to pay lip-service at least to its own dire predictions.

Lamont sketched out the barest outlines of a new strategy at the annual meeting of the International Monetary Fund a few days after Black Wednesday. Alan Budd accompanied Lamont to the Washington meeting, while Terence Burns supervised a frenetic burst of activity at the Treasury in London. Lamont, assisted by Nigel Wicks and by his press secretary, Andrew Hudson, worked on the speech into the early hours of the morning at the British ambassador's residence in Washington. The defeat of inflation would remain at the centre of policy, and the Treasury would impose strict limits on public spending and borrowing, Lamont said. Outside the ERM, interest rate decisions would be based on a careful and continuous assessment of a range of economic and monetary indicators. The Treasury, he added, would monitor various measures of the money supply as well as movements in the exchange rate, and it would pay careful attention to asset prices. His speech was, however, little more than a statement of good intent.

From Washington, Lamont returned to London to face an emergency debate in the House of Commons. The recall of Parliament from its summer recess had been successfully demanded by the opposition. The debate, on 24 September, exposed vividly the vacuum at the centre of government. Major offered few clues to the direction of economic policy and a lacklustre defence of his European policy. He promised to delay ratification of Maastricht, but would not abandon the treaty. In his House of Commons début as Labour leader, John Smith poured scorn on the prime minister's assertion a few months earlier that sterling might replace the Deutschmark as the strongest currency in Europe. Major was 'the devalued prime minister of a devalued government'. For his part, Lamont used the debate to shore up his personal position, launching a strong attack on the Bundesbank for its role in the ERM débâcle. Two days earlier he had lowered interest rates to 9 per cent, and now he embraced the opportunity to pursue what he referred to repeatedly as a 'British' economic policy. Lamont knew his political position was deeply exposed, so he pitched his message towards the most vocal of the government's critics – the Eurosceptic right.

For their part, the Conservative MPs summoned back to Westminster from their long summer break were nervous and fractious. They knew that their role on this occasion was to offer a public display of unity but, outside the Commons chamber, few bothered to disguise their dismay. Many urged a rapid ratcheting down of interest rates – a dash for growth. Others called for a decisive break with Europe – the government should ditch the Maastricht Treaty. This was also the moment when doubts over Major's leadership began to solidify. The rumours that he had 'wobbled' on Black Wednesday were retold with some glee by the sceptics. Less committed Tory MPs wondered why Major had not been prepared to face the cameras. During the previous few days it had fallen to the home secretary to tour the television and radio studios defending the government. Clarke was to comment later that the prime minister had made the mistake of retreating into his bunker: 'You cannot sit inside the walls of Downing Street or Admiralty House hoping things will go away.'[2]

By the time the Tory faithful gathered in Brighton for the party's annual conference on 5 October, Norman Lamont had still to enunciate an alternative economic policy. His speech to the conference would not be the occasion for a recital of the finer points of macro-economic policy. The party's activists wanted to be cheered, not lectured, and Lamont needed the reassurance of a standing ovation. The financial markets, however, were impatient for signs that a new strategy had emerged from the ashes of the ERM. Lamont's answer was to combine a populist speech to the party faithful with a separate detailed statement of the government's new economic policy. This latter was contained in a letter, dated 8 October, to John Watts, the Conservative chairman of the Treasury and Civil Service Committee.

On the opening day of the conference, senior Treasury officials were summoned from London to confer with Major and Lamont in the Grand Hotel overlooking the Brighton seafront. The hotel was the conference headquarters, long rebuilt since the IRA had bombed Margaret Thatcher and her cabinet there in 1984. The officials arrived without fanfare and went unnoticed by the television crews as they gathered in an upstairs suite. The Treasury delegation, headed by Lamont and Terence Burns, sat along one side of the long table. Facing them, Major and a team of officials from No. 10 looked down through the windows towards the beach. A knot of protesters gathered opposite on the promenade; another group travelled along the seafront in a bus equipped with loud-hailers. As Major and Lamont debated the new strategy, the amplified demands of the demonstrators drifted into the room. 'Cut interest rates now' was one chant. 'End the recession' was another. If only they knew, thought one of the officials – the prime minister and the chancellor were musing at that very moment as to how best to meet the demonstrators' demands.

The approach agreed in Brighton marked a return to the pragmatism of the mid-1980s, to the relatively brief period between the unthinking monetarism of Margaret Thatcher's first term and Nigel Lawson's decision to shadow the Deutschmark. Eddie George, soon to realize his ambition to succeed Robin Leigh-Pemberton as governor of the Bank of England, looked back with nostalgia to this period. He believed the combination then of low inflation alongside steady growth had demonstrated that a discretionary approach to management of the economy could work. He blamed Lawson for throwing away the achievement during his struggle with Thatcher over the exchange rate. Now the route to low inflation would once again be via a variable mix of monetary and fiscal policies rather than through the pursuit of a single money supply or exchange rate target. Turning back the clock, however, would not be quite that simple. After its defeat at the hands of the currency speculators, the Treasury knew that it could no longer expect to be taken entirely on trust. Mervyn King, the chief economist at the Bank and an influential voice in the internal debate which followed Black Wednesday, was prominent among those pressing for a framework which would rebuild the confidence of financial markets.

At the heart of the strategy set out in Lamont's letter to John Watts was a formal target for the inflation rate. During the remainder of the Parliament the Treasury would contain the annual rate of increase in the underlying inflation rate (the retail price index minus mortgage interest payments) to a range of 1 to 4 per cent. By the end of the Parliament, in other words by mid-1997 at the latest, the rate would be in the lower half of the range, or below 2.5 per cent. This marked the first occasion since 1979 that the government had committed itself to a specific objective for the rate of price increases. Previously it had expressed its ambition with deliberate ambiguity, talking in terms of permanently low inflation or, occasionally, of stable prices. More precise targets had been reserved for intermediate objectives such as the money supply or the exchange rate. Other industrial nations, however, had long operated with direct inflation targets. In the case of West Germany, the unstated, but well-understood, goal of the Bundesbank was to contain the annual rate of price increases to 2 per cent or less. Lamont mentioned the same figure in his letter to Watts as a long-term ambition for Britain. New

Zealand and Canada had recently announced similar targets. As chancellor during 1990, Major had considered doing the same, but had dropped the idea in favour of the ERM.

Now the object was to provide a foundation-stone for policy outside the mechanism. The details had been the subject of considerable debate within the Treasury and the Bank. Colleagues would recall that Eddie George was initially reluctant to see the ill-fated attempt to fix the exchange rate replaced immediately with another close-fitting straitjacket. After the experience of shadowing the Deutschmark and of the ERM, he was suspicious of staking too much credibility on a single target. The Bank initially suggested a series of annual ranges which would chart a declining path for inflation over several years. This idea, however, reawakened memories in the Treasury of the missed money supply targets set out a decade earlier in the Medium Term Financial Strategy. Treasury officials then proposed a single band of 1 to 5 per cent. The underlying inflation rate had fallen to just below 4 per cent by September 1992, but officials feared that the devaluation could push it temporarily higher in early 1994. Lamont, however, decided that an upper limit of 5 per cent represented too loose a commitment. As luck would have it, the actual inflation rate remained firmly within the chosen, lower, range.

The weakness of the new guideline lay in the fact that inflation is a lagging indicator of economic policy. The rate of price increases at any particular moment usually reflects events and policy decisions two years earlier. So there would be an obvious temptation for the government to delay necessary but unpopular increases in interest rates until too late. Financial markets would demand reassurance that it would be ready to act well in advance of any new inflationary threat. As Eddie George was to remark during a later dispute with the Treasury over the level of interest rates, 'given the long lags before policy changes have their full effects, it may be many months before anyone can be certain of the outcome'.[3]

Lamont's response was to inject greater transparency into official deliberations on the level of interest rates, and to extend the influence of the Bank. His letter to the Treasury and Civil Service Committee, promising a 'conclusive break to low inflation', foreshadowed a series of initiatives detailed three weeks later in his speech at the annual Mansion House dinner. He announced then that the Treasury would publish a regular report after the chancellor's monthly meeting with the Bank governor, setting out in detail the basis upon which policy judgements were made. At Mervyn King's suggestion, the Bank was charged with producing a separate *Inflation Report* alongside its *Quarterly Bulletin*, with a remit to assess the government's progress in meeting its inflation target. All interest rate changes would be accompanied by the release of a detailed analysis of the elements which prompted the decision. Finally, Lamont established a group of seven independent economic advisers, soon to be dubbed 'the Wise Men', to supplement the Treasury's forecasts of the economy.[4] Leigh-Pemberton welcomed the initiatives, commenting that confidence required 'a willingness to be open in explaining, to Parliament and to the public at large, the influences on inflation and our responses to them'. But, like many in the Treasury and Bank, he believed more needed to be done. In January 1993 Lamont did take a small further step, to coincide with the appointment of Eddie George as governor-designate. A Treasury statement said that the chancellor had 'made clear to the new governor that his central responsibility should be to support the government in our determination to bring about a lasting reduction in the rate of inflation'. This was a presentational device, however, and, in the eyes of the financial markets, the new inflation target remained an uncertain aspiration.

Some senior officials believed that sterling's exit from the ERM should have been followed by a rapid rebalancing of economic policy. One suggestion at the Bank was for an immediate and large cut in interest rates, accompanied by sizeable tax increases to reduce public borrowing. As it turned out the government eventually adopted that course – but hesitantly, over two years, rather than as an immediate, positive, response to Black Wednesday. The Treasury meanwhile stressed that the pound's departure from the ERM did not mark a return to neglect of the exchange rate. It would no longer set a specified objective for sterling or seek to shadow the Deutschmark, but, as Lamont put it in his letter to the Treasury and Civil Service Committee, 'I do not propose to adopt a policy of setting interest rates in relation to domestic criteria and then letting the exchange rate go where it will. The lesson from the 1980s is that exchange rates can move a long way, upwards or downwards, if markets come to believe the authorities do not care.'[5] The test henceforth would be whether any fall in the pound's value posed a threat to the government's inflation objective. The speed of any depreciation might be as important as the extent. This was a statement that Nigel Lawson might have issued in 1983 or 1984.

The prime minister and the chancellor were certain that sterling would not return to the ERM. Within days of the cabinet's upbeat statement on 17 September, Lamont shifted the position. A confidential Treasury briefing-note, headed 'ERM: New Line to Take', was circulated on the following Monday to senior ministers. Its tone implied a significant hardening of the conditions for re-entry. Economic growth was now the first priority. Kenneth Clarke and Michael Heseltine saw in the note a deliberate departure from the spirit, if not the letter, of the earlier cabinet accord, but John Major quickly endorsed the chancellor's stance. In an article in the *Evening Standard* on 21 September – his first public utterance since Black Wednesday – the prime minister indicated that there was no question of sterling's return until the system had been reformed. With some understatement, he said that sterling's ejection had been a 'set-back'. But 'last week's tensions exposed the fault-lines in the way it is run. We shall not go back into the system until the flaws have been put right.'[6] Three days later he again hardened his position by telling the recalled House of Commons, 'I do not believe that we shall be able to go back into the mechanism soon, or go back into the same mechanism we left.'[7]

At the morning cabinet meeting on the day of the debate, Heseltine and Clarke had argued for a more conciliatory tone. By now, however, Lamont had regained sufficient confidence to press the case for indefinite suspension. Politics and economics were on the chancellor's side. The recall of Parliament had seen more than seventy Conservative MPs sign a House of Commons motion calling on the government to abandon any thought of a return to the mechanism. More names were being added daily. It was modelled on the earlier motion demanding a 'fresh start' for European policy after the Danish referendum. That motion had marked the beginning of the back-bench revolt over the Maastricht Treaty. Now the Eurosceptics offered a warning that to contemplate re-entry to the ERM would be to stoke the fires of rebellion. The new motion stated bluntly that 'This house welcomes the government's decision to leave the ERM; and urges a fresh start to economic policy, in particular the abandonment of fixed exchange rates and a commitment to sound finance, stable money and the right climate for steady growth.'[8] Facing a bitter struggle over ratification of Maastricht, the prime minister now knew that sterling must take second place to economic recovery. So, by the time the Conservatives had gathered in Brighton for the party conference, even the cabinet's most committed Europeans realized there was little purpose in pressing the case for early re-entry. Lamont told journalists at the conference that it was a 'dead issue'. Michael Portillo and his allies on the right indicated they would quit the cabinet if there were any attempt to revive it.

An unfortunate postscript to the ERM débâcle reinforced Major's resolve. The prime minister and the chancellor had made no secret of the fact that they blamed the Bundesbank for Black Wednesday. Major saw in the Bundesbank's 'selfish' refusal to lower its interest rates the fundamental cause of the catastrophe. Schlesinger's unguarded comments had provided the catalyst. Major's resentment intensified during the days after the French referendum. The narrow vote in favour of Maastricht was followed by a tidal wave of speculation against the franc. This time Helmut Kohl applied pressure on the Bundesbank to assist its European partner. It extended virtually unlimited lines of credit to the Banque de France, and the franc's parity was maintained. No such assistance had been offered to the Bank of England. But Schlesinger, annoyed at his treatment during the fateful Bath meeting, responded with a detailed rebuttal of the British charges. His statement, sent to the German ambassador in London, was intended as a private briefing-note. Instead, on 30 September, it was passed by the embassy to Peter Norman, the economics editor of the *Financial Times*.

The document said that Schlesinger had not undermined the pound and rejected suggestions that the Bundesbank had failed to support sterling in the markets or had afforded preferential treatment to the French franc. To the dismay of the Treasury, it pointed out that the Bundesbank intervention in support of the British currency had been 'the largest compulsory intervention ever'. The high level of support for the pound was 'primarily due to the fact that the UK monetary authorities seem to have been prepared to allow sterling to

fall to its lower intervention point. The Banque de France, by
cnntrast, concentrated on keeping the franc above its intervention
point.'⁹ Still more damagingly, the Bundesbank president hinted that
Major had turned down the option of a general realignment when the
lira was devalued on the Sunday before Black Wednesday.

The release of the statement sparked an extraordinary public row.
Major put his name to a Treasury press notice accusing the Bundesbank of breaching confidential communications between the two
governments. The Treasury then offered its own point-by-point
rebuttal of the Bundesbank case. Referring to Schlesinger's remark in
the interview with *Handelsblatt* on 15 September that the tensions in
the ERM would have been eased by a wider realignment the previous
weekend, the Treasury stated, 'against a history of reports emanating
from the Bundesbank, this was inevitably interpreted as a reference to
sterling'. Lamont insisted on a flat denial of the damaging suggestion
that he had turned down the offer of a wider realignment: 'No request
was made by the German authorities to the United Kingdom on that
weekend that it too should realign.'¹⁰ To remove any doubt as to the
government's anger, Douglas Hurd's name was added by 10 Downing
Street to the statement. On the very same day Hurd had travelled to
Bonn for a meeting with his German counterpart, Klaus Kinkel. The
foreign secretary's original intention, now derailed, had been to mend
fences with Bonn. Major did not let the matter rest. In a letter the
following day to John Smith, he stated unequivocally that 'The
German authorities made no request to the United Kingdom that
sterling should realign.'

The Bundesbank council meanwhile chose to underline its proud
independence by once again resisting pressure from its European
partners to lower interest rates. Even outside the ERM, sterling could
not escape Schlesinger's influence – on 2 October sterling dropped to
the latest in a succession of record lows. At DM2.43 it was more than
15 per cent below the central ERM rate of DM2.95 which only weeks
earlier the government had pledged to defend to the last. Sterling's
trade-weighted value was now at its lowest point since the election of
the Thatcher government in 1979.

*

There was no consensus within the government over how far and how fast to switch the emphasis of economic policy from containing inflation to promoting economic recovery. The pound's depreciation reinforced the Treasury's innate caution. The deepening economic gloom and the intense political pressures on the prime minister argued for a decisive gesture. It took another dreadful mistake to force the government's hand. Michael Heseltine's announcement in mid-October of the government's plans to close more than thirty of British Coal's mines provoked a wave of public outrage. A government that had just seen its economic strategy disintegrate was proposing now to sack 30,000 miners in the midst of a recession. Another one-point cut in interest rates – taking them to 8 per cent – did nothing to assuage the anger. The miners, vilified only a few years earlier as the unacceptable face of trade-union power, returned to the streets as popular heroes. The closure announcement crystallized discontent across a broad swathe of the Conservative Party at Westminster and in the country. Facing a growing rebellion on the Tory back benches, Heseltine was forced into an ignominious U-turn. He was sure of the economic judgement behind the closure plan – and indeed the pits eventually would close – but the government had seriously misjudged the mood of the nation. The miners would keep their jobs pending a lengthy review.

The episode stirred Major's frustration with what he saw as the Treasury's timidity. Alongside the back-bench rebellion over Maastricht, the coal dispute represented another grievous blow to his authority. There had also been a row with Lamont over the timing of a reduction in interest rates to 8 per cent. The furore over the coal closures erupted just as Major was hosting an emergency summit of leaders of the European Union (as the European Community would become after Maastricht) in Birmingham. The Treasury agreed that there was scope for a reduction in borrowing costs, but wanted to delay until the following week. The prime minister overruled the chancellor and insisted that the cut coincide with the opening of the summit on 16 October. His hope that it would secure at least one day's good headlines was in vain. Major now faced a constant barrage of invective from the traditionally Tory press. *The Times* and the *Sunday Times* joined the tabloids in an unremitting onslaught against his leadership. The *Sunday Telegraph* inveighed each week against his European policy, demanding the abandonment of the Maastricht Treaty. In a particularly damaging article, *The Times* portrayed Major as a lonely, isolated figure suffering from visible weight loss and stress. It also gave prominence to the rumours that he had 'wobbled' on Black Wednesday.[11] Six months earlier the mass-circulation *Sun* had claimed the credit for the government's re-election; now it was merciless in its daily ridicule. No prime minister had faced such a barrage since Harold Wilson had made the same mistake of gambling his credibility on the exchange rate. As had happened with his Labour predecessor, an angry rift would now open up between the press and prime minister.

On 20 October Major made his decision. Senior political journalists were summoned to his room at the House of Commons for an extraordinary, unscheduled, briefing. As the journalists crowded around the large table in the elegant oak-panelled office, the prime minister laid out his plan for political survival. Henceforth the government would pursue a 'strategy for growth'. His objective, he said, was an 'early and strong recovery'. The disinflation already in the pipeline and the favourable international outlook meant that the new strategy would not rekindle inflation. Major, who had avoided the press during the previous few weeks, now signalled his intention to listen to the clamour in the country for an end to the recession. The public-spending targets in the Treasury's Autumn Statement in November would be tough, he said, but he had decided that White-hall's large capital-investment programmes would be protected. And the private sector would be given a bigger role in the financing of public-sector infrastructure projects, to boost confidence and employ-ment. Major's briefing set the scene for a series of staged television interviews later the same evening: 'A strategy for growth is what we need. A strategy for growth is what we are going to have,' Major told Michael Brunson, the political editor of ITN.

The Treasury was caught unawares. Andrew Hudson, Lamont's press secretary, at first responded by insisting that there had been no change in the direction of economic policy. Within hours, however, senior Treasury officials realized they had been 'bounced' by the prime minister. The differences were still apparent the following day. Lamont denied that there had been a policy U-turn, but in his routine briefing for political correspondents Gus O'Donnell underlined once again the prime minister's message. He was dismissive of the Treasury's caution and stressed instead that the strong disinflationary pressures in the economy – the weak employment market, unprecedented falls in house prices, and depressed consumer confidence – would more than offset any upward pressure on prices from a lower exchange rate. Major had decided that rebuilding shattered confidence could not wait for a careful assessment of the impact on inflation of the devaluation of sterling. He wanted further reductions in interest rates. He could also draw support from the Bank of England, which was increasingly alive to the risk that debt deflation would stifle recovery. The November issue of the Bank's *Quarterly Bulletin* was sanguine about sterling's depreciation, suggesting that the high level of spare capacity in the economy and the depressed state of the labour market would limit the impact on prices.[12] So the government's policy now saw deflation rather than inflation as the greatest threat to the economy. For the time being, the exchange rate could find its own level.

This was a strategy for political survival. The prime minister knew he would have no hope of containing the looming rebellion over Maastricht if Tory MPs suspected that interest rate cuts had been delayed to keep open the option of rejoining the ERM. The Autumn Statement, on 12 November, confirmed his approach. Interest rates were cut by another percentage point to 7 per cent – the lowest level for nearly fifteen years – and the Treasury announced a package of measures to boost business and consumer confidence. They included a £750m plan to allow housing associations to buy 20,000 empty houses, a relaxation of controls on local authority spending, and an additional £700m of credit cover for exporters. The tax on new car purchases was scrapped, and public-sector pay awards were restricted to 1.5 per cent to allow £1.5bn to be shifted to public-sector capital projects. Lamont emphasized at every turn that this was a 'British' policy.

Behind the scenes another conflict was developing in Downing Street. Lamont shared the view of Bank officials that the new inflation target

and the promised transparency of decision-making did not provide a
strong enough anchor for economic policy. He had been irritated by
Major's decision to force the timing of the interest rate cut in mid-
October and the pre-emptive announcement of an economic growth
strategy. Later, Lamont would accuse the prime minister of weakness,
of being driven to take the wrong decisions by bad newspaper
headlines. Now, in the autumn of 1992, he considered that the
government could best rebuild an anti-inflation policy by transferring
responsibility for interest rates to the Bank.

As the point of contact between the government and the financial
markets, the Bank traditionally had enjoyed considerable influence in
monetary policy. It was influence, however, rather than authority.
The 1946 Bank of England Act, under which the Bank had been
nationalized, made it clear that real power rested with the government, stating that 'The Treasury may from time to time give such
directions to the Bank as, after consultation with the Governor of the
Bank, they think necessary in the public interest.' As Robin Leigh-
Pemberton discovered during Nigel Lawson's chancellorship, this
meant that a powerful chancellor had no difficulty in imposing his
will. Lawson gave his view of the balance of power in an unguarded
remark to the Treasury and Civil Service Committee in the spring of
1988: 'We take the decisions but they [the Bank] do the work.'[13]

The Conservatives, however, had raised the idea of greater autonomy for the Bank while in opposition during the 1970s. *The Right
Approach to the Economy*, the economic manifesto published by Margaret Thatcher in 1977, included the suggestion of a 'more independent role for the Bank of England'.[14] Control of inflation might be
easier if interest rate decisions were 'depoliticized'. The idea remained
in abeyance until Lawson resurrected it in the autumn of 1988.
Thwarted by Thatcher over the ERM, Lawson deputed three Treasury officials – Rachel Lomax, David Peretz and Michael Scholar – to
draw up a plan for Bank independence. The scheme, disclosed
publicly only in Lawson's resignation speech a year later, had been a
last throw in his conflict with Thatcher.

By the autumn of 1988 inflation was rising strongly, and Lawson
saw in an independent Bank of England a second-best option to the
ERM. Typically, he was unblushing about the apparent contradiction

with his earlier, cavalier, treatment of the Bank. At the end of
November 1988 he delivered a five-page memorandum to Thatcher.
The objective, as Lawson put it, was to 'be seen to be locking a
permanent anti-inflationary force into the system, as a counterweight
to the strong inflationary pressures which are always lurking'. A new
statutory framework for the Bank would impose an explicit obligation
to achieve price stability and give it direct authority to set short-term
interest rates and monetary targets. The governor of the Bank would
be directly accountable to a select committee of the House of
Commons, and his colleagues on the Bank's court would be appointed
subject to the committee's approval.[15] Predictably, Thatcher rejected
the proposal, judging that to grant the Bank independence just as the
inflation rate was rising would be a stark admission of failure. The
Treasury officials who had drafted the memorandum had not expected
otherwise. They were accustomed by now to Lawson's restless search
for policy frameworks. In the circumstances of the time, one senior
official regarded the exercise as a rather curious joke – 'something for
the history books'. Another wondered whether Lawson was planning
his departure – seeking independence for the Bank before replacing
Leigh-Pemberton as governor.

When John Major replaced Lawson as chancellor in October 1989,
the proposal remained in the Treasury archives. Major's energies
were directed towards the ERM, and anyway he had never seen a
strong case for strengthening the Bank's powers at the expense of the
Treasury. The idea was revived, however, by Norman Lamont soon
after he became chancellor in November 1990. Lamont was an
unashamed admirer of Lawson. He had been intrigued by Lawson's
resignation speech, and asked his officials to reactivate the proposal.
He also raised the idea with Major on several occasions, but found
him unresponsive. With the general election approaching, Lamont
did not press the issue. After Black Wednesday, however, he again
revived the idea. The Treasury establishment was understandably
opposed, but, on Lamont's instructions, several possible models of
independence were studied. Lawson's plan had been an adaptation to
British circumstance of elements of the different legal frameworks for
the Bundesbank and the US Federal Reserve. The form of independence granted to those institutions, however, had been designed to fit

the federal political systems of Germany and the US. There were obvious difficulties in grafting them on to the British, unitary, system of government.

Lamont was attracted to the New Zealand model. The 1989 Reserve Bank of New Zealand Act had given that country's central bank operational independence while retaining for the government a right, in exceptional circumstances, to override its decisions. Under an explicit contract with the government, the central bank was obliged to pursue a policy of price stability – defined as an inflation rate of between zero and 2 per cent – but it remained accountable to the elected government and to Parliament. The combination of operational autonomy for the central bank and the retention by the government of ultimate political control had obvious appeal. The officials also explored the possibility of establishing a Bank of England Council which would discuss openly interest rate decisions and be accountable to Parliament. Lamont thought that a White Paper proposing autonomy for the Bank could be made the centrepiece of his 1993 Budget, with legislation following in the next session of Parliament. The gains which the government had made against inflation would by then be permanently entrenched. But Major, like Thatcher before him, rejected the idea. Lamont, emulating Lawson once again, later disclosed his plan in his resignation speech to the House of Commons.

Major spelled out one of his principal objections in June 1993, when he told MPs that:

> The very real concern that I have always faced is one that I believe is spread widely across the House: the need for accountability to Parliament for decisions on monetary policy matters. Were a way to be found to get the benefits of an independent central bank without the loss of parliamentary accountability, my views would be very close to those of my right honourable friend [Lamont].[16]

Privately he offered a list of other obstacles. Interest rate changes in Britain were much more politically sensitive than elsewhere, because of the high proportion of home-owners with variable-rate mortgages. That was doubly so in the midst of the worst housing slump in living memory. Any proposal to give independence to the Bank would also stir the anti-Maastricht rebellion – it would be interpreted by the sceptics as the precursor to sterling's return to the ERM and eventual participation in a single European currency, because the Maastricht Treaty provided specifically that the national banks from which a European system of central banks would be created should be autonomous. According to one senior aide, Major had another, overriding, objection – one which, curiously, reversed the logic of Thatcher's rebuff to Lawson. She could not accept the idea of handing control to the Bank at the moment inflation was accelerating. Major, by contrast, had beaten inflation; he did not want to hand the credit to the Bank.

For two weeks after the 1967 devaluation the then chancellor, James Callaghan, would return to 11 Downing Street to find a group of young Conservatives gathered on the pavement opposite. 'Traitor,' they would jeer. 'Resign.' As Callaghan recounts in his memoirs, *Time and Chance*, after several nights of this the young men appeared to tire of the ritual. As he entered the door of No. 11 the noisy abuse would tail off, to be followed by a rather gentler 'Good night, Sir.'[17] The heavy wrought-iron gates installed at the entrance to Downing Street after the Brighton bombing meant that Norman Lamont could not suffer the same indignity. Lamont, however, remained at the Treasury. Had he followed Callaghan's example and moved to another cabinet post, his career might have survived the devaluation. But this chancellor had no interest in running the prisons. The result was an unremitting campaign of vilification by the media and by some in his own party. Lamont – never the most adept of political communicators – was to prove one of his own worst enemies.

A few years earlier Lamont had all but given up hope of cabinet office. Like John Gummer, Kenneth Clarke and other contemporaries among the Tories' Cambridge mafia, he had chosen politics as his career at the outset. For much of the 1980s he had fretted on the fringes of the cabinet as younger rivals had secured preferment, and his time had almost passed when Nigel Lawson persuaded Thatcher to make him Treasury chief secretary. He had seen his real chance a year later, during the last days of Thatcher's premiership. A Treasury official recalls that Lamont reacted instantly to Geoffrey Howe's devastating resignation speech – from that moment he was certain she was finished. His reward for running Major's campaign was the most important office outside 10 Downing Street, but the new chancellor was uncertain. Prone to bouts of deep pessimism, his self-doubt was carefully concealed beneath an insouciant manner. Moments of pressure would often be met with an amusing quip. In the days after Black Wednesday he cheerfully admitted to journalists that his wife, Rosemary, had noticed he had been singing in the bath. There was a similar display of careless confidence during the Newbury by-election the following spring. Then, he borrowed the words of Edith Piaf to tell an angry electorate, '*Je ne regrette rien*.' This was not the moment, however, for dry humour.

Lamont's rediscovery of his Eurosceptical instincts in the aftermath of Black Wednesday proved a flimsy shield. He had, after all, been a signatory to the Maastricht Treaty. Cabinet colleagues let it be known that he had been less than forceful in pressing the sceptics' case in the negotiations which preceded the treaty: Michael Howard, Kenneth Baker and Peter Lilley had made the stronger case against further entanglement with Europe. More dangerously, the 'British' economic policy the chancellor now promised would take time to yield results. Public borrowing was rising at an unprecedented rate, and Lamont would soon be obliged to announce large tax increases. The invective in the tabloid press spread well beyond the realms of economic policy, and editors demanded his resignation. The Labour Party exploited the disclosure that the government had contributed £4,700 to the legal expenses Lamont had incurred in evicting a self-styled 'sex therapist' who had rented his house in Notting Hill. An alleged purchase of cheap champagne and cigarettes in a notorious area of Paddington was given extensive coverage. The report was false, but none the less further damaged his public image. There were other, threadbare, stories about allegedly unpaid hotel and credit card bills in what was to become an unrelenting campaign. Lamont, who had never had an easy relationship with the media, became ever more reluctant to give radio and television interviews. When he did appear in the studios, he found it difficult to contain his anger at the constant barrage of criticism.

There were also strains in his relationship with the prime minister. The two had never been close, and in the run-up to the 1992 general election their relationship was described as cordial rather than warm.

During the election campaign itself there had been disagreements. Lamont considered that Major's frequent campaign promises of tax cuts 'year by year' were rash. Major was irritated by Lamont's pessimism and his disregard for the presentation of policy: if the chancellor looked glum, the electorate could hardly be expected to have faith in the government's promises of economic recovery. The strains re-emerged after Black Wednesday. The prime minister's instinct was to 'talk up' recovery to help rebuild confidence. His government by now was under fire on all fronts. Within weeks of sterling's exit from the ERM, David Mellor, one of Major's closest cabinet allies, had been forced to resign in the wake of disclosures about his private life. Only a month later the government was rocked by allegations that ministers had colluded before the Gulf War in the secret relaxation of the embargo on arms sales to Iraq. Major's decision to set up an independent inquiry under Lord Justice Scott did little to deflect the multiplying charges of sleaze which were engulfing his administration. Above all else, the prime minister needed good news on the economy.

The chancellor, however, found it difficult to disguise his melancholic temperament. He knew that the unprecedented level of consumer borrowing (the ratio of personal-sector debt to disposable income had more than doubled from 55 per cent in the early 1980s to 115 per cent in 1990) and the collapse in house prices would make for a painfully slow recovery. Alongside the row over independence for the Bank of England, there were also the disputes over interest rates. Lamont acknowledged in his resignation speech that he and Major agreed on the substance of policy, but he thought the prime minister too eager to accelerate interest rate cuts in order to counter bad news. In late January 1993 the fourth successive one-point cut in rates, which took borrowing costs to a twenty-year low of 6 per cent, sparked a dispute similar to that of the previous October. Lamont told friends that the prime minister was forever 'snatching' at rate reductions, risking the medium-term stability of policy in the hope of a good headline.

By early 1993 his cabinet colleagues were adding fuel to the speculation at Westminster that Lamont would be moved from the Treasury in a summer reshuffle. Conversations over lunch with senior ministers rarely ended without a discussion of the rival claims of potential successors. Kenneth Clarke was the clear favourite. Michael Howard, the environment secretary, was the preferred choice of the right. John MacGregor was spoken of as a possible compromise candidate. After the March Budget, senior Whitehall officials who had earlier said that the chancellor retained the full support of the prime minister were suddenly noncommittal. Lamont had lost the confidence of a broad swathe of the party at Westminster, and his credibility in the City had never been lower. In a delayed reaction to Black Wednesday, opinion polls pointed to a dramatic collapse in the government's popularity. By March 1993, less than a year after its general election victory, the government was fifteen points behind Labour in the opinion polls, and the gap was widening each month.

The Budget that month, with one of the largest packages of tax increases in living memory, did not help. The recession – reducing tax revenues and bringing unavoidable increases in social security benefits – had fatally undermined the government's commitment to sound public finance. The public-sector borrowing requirement, ignored before the election, had escalated to £35bn in the 1992/93 financial year. Worse, it was projected to rise still further to a staggering £50bn in 1993/94. The financial markets had taken fright, and by early March sterling had fallen to DM2.35 and $1.43. Measured by the sterling index, against the Deutschmark or against the yen, the pound had never been worth less. Overall, sterling had lost 15 per cent of its value in only six months.

Lamont's Budget package was a skilful attempt to sustain confidence in the fragile economic recovery while persuading the financial markets that the government would restore its grip on the public finances. A series of changes in corporation tax, capital gains tax and stamp duty offered immediate relief for business and the housing market. The much larger increases in direct and indirect taxation were deferred. The pain – a total of £10.3bn in tax and National Insurance increases – would not be felt by the electorate until the spring of 1994, and the measures would not bite fully until the following year. The view of Whitehall insiders was that Lamont had made the best of a fairly appalling task. No recovery would be sustainable if the government borrowed nearly 8 per cent of national income, and, by putting in place now a 'wedge' of tax increases, the government could hope to start cutting income tax again before the general election.

It was a Budget of broken promises, however. The voters, left sore and disillusioned by the recession, were outraged. Most of the additional revenue was to come from increases in taxes on income – most notably higher National Insurance contributions and the scaling-back of income tax allowances – but the Budget also included plans for the staged imposition of value added tax on domestic fuel. Major had said before the election that there were 'no plans and no need' for an extension of VAT. Aware that the pledges would be thrown back at him by the opposition, the prime minister had initially been opposed to the Treasury's proposal. But the revenue had to be raised, and an alternative suggestion to introduce VAT at a lower rate on a wide range of zero-rated goods was judged even more likely to provoke a popular backlash. As it was, the government could not escape the fact that it had chosen to tax one of the most sensitive items in the household budget. For all the promises of compensation, the poor and the elderly were the victims. Like the pit closures, VAT on fuel provided a focal point for the anger of the electorate. The opposition parties reacted furiously, and Rupert Murdoch's *Sun* once again led the tabloid onslaught.

The Newbury by-election and the local council elections on 6 May 1993 gave the electorate the perfect opportunity for revenge. In Newbury the 28 per cent swing against the Tory candidate which handed the once-safe seat to the Liberal Democrats represented the worst by-election defeat since 1979. In the local elections, the loss of nearly 500 Conservative seats left the party with control of only one of England's shire councils. In the ensuing panic, Lamont was the most obvious target. Kenneth Clarke's frank acknowledgement that the government was in a 'dreadful' hole did not help. Senior members of the cabinet – and John Major's aides in Downing Street – no longer defended Lamont. The two most precious commodities for any chancellor are the confidence of the City and the trust of the prime minister. Lamont had lost both.

On 12 May, during his speech to the Scottish Conservative conference, he made a last bid to keep his job. In a searing attack on the media's distortion of his remarks during the Newbury campaign, he told his audience, 'I do have regrets. I regret that inflation got out of control at the end of the 1980s. I regret the hardship that getting down inflation has caused. But I do not regret taking the tough but necessary decisions to get inflation down.'[18] It was the start of a two-week fight for political survival.

Behind the scenes, Lamont embarked on a frantic campaign to enlist the support of leading figures on the right of the party and called on his critics in government to keep their nerve. Major consulted widely on whether he should reshuffle his cabinet. Norman Fowler, the party chairman, told him that Lamont had lost the confidence of Tory activists and voters in the country. Fowler believed the most powerful weapon deployed by the victorious Liberal Democrats in Newbury had been a simple slogan: 'A vote for the Conservatives is a vote of confidence in Norman Lamont.' Richard Ryder, the chief whip, said that the chancellor's position among back-benchers was tenable but far from strong. Soundings among Conservatives with strong connections in the City revealed a near-unanimous view that Lamont should be replaced. Douglas Hurd, the foreign secretary, backed the appointment of Clarke, as did Lord Wakeham, the leader of the House of Lords. Lord Whitelaw, the party's elder statesman, shared that judgement. Whitelaw considered the previous twelve months the worst endured by any government during the postwar period.

Others warned Major that his own position was in peril – he could well face a formal challenge to his leadership in the autumn unless the government recovered its balance. To do that it needed a new chancellor. As one cabinet minister said on the eve of Lamont's departure, 'Nothing could be more dangerous than the status quo.' Among Major's advisers in 10 Downing Street there was increasing frustration at Lamont's apparent unwillingness to preach the gospel of good news. Officials said that Sarah Hogg, the linchpin and frequent mediator in relations between the prime minister's office and the Treasury, believed the relationship had broken down. Chris Patten had become Governor of Hong Kong after the loss of his Bath seat in the 1992 general election, but he was still closely consulted by the prime minister. He agreed that Lamont should be moved.

On 27 May, at the start of the Whitsun parliamentary break,

Lamont was asked by Major to leave the Treasury. The prime minister offered him John Gummer's place at the Department of the Environment. It was a serious offer, and Major hoped he would accept. Unsurprisingly, though, Lamont chose to leave the cabinet rather than accept what would have been an obvious demotion. The only post he was prepared to consider seriously was that of foreign secretary, and there there was no vacancy. Norman Lamont did not depart quietly. His resignation was followed not by the traditional, polite, exchange of letters with the prime minister but by a terse statement in which he conspicuously failed to pledge his future loyalty. He felt betrayed, and among friends he made no secret of his determination to exact revenge. There followed a bitter public display of acrimony between Lamont and Fowler. Michael Heseltine caught the mood in a disarmingly frank remark. Politics, he said, had always been 'a ruthless business'.

Nigel Lawson's resignation speech had eclipsed John Major's first appearance as chancellor in the House of Commons. Norman Lamont likewise overshadowed Kenneth Clarke. The former chancellor accused the prime minister most damagingly of failing to offer leadership. As the bitterness seeped through his twenty-minute speech, Lamont revealed that Major had refused to grant independence to the Bank of England, and he attacked his interference in the timing of interest rate cuts. He said the prime minister had told him not to resign after the ERM débâcle. By staying at the Treasury he had provided a shield for Major. The most vitriolic and wounding criticism, however, was reserved for Major's leadership:

> The government listens too much to the pollsters and the party managers. The trouble is that they are not even very good at politics, and they are entering too much into policy decisions. As a result, there is too much short-termism, too much reacting to events, not enough shaping of events. We give the impression of being in office but not in power'.[19]

The speech lacked the sheer force of those delivered by Nigel Lawson and Geoffrey Howe, but it exploited brilliantly the growing feeling among Conservative MPs that the government had been drifting without direction from the top, that Major was a leader at the mercy of events. Lamont would continue to beat the same drum for years with the single-mindedness which only revenge can inspire.

The appointment of Kenneth Clarke as chancellor caused little surprise. In a cabinet with less than its fair share of political heavyweights, Clarke had emerged in the months since Black Wednesday as keeper of the government's collective nerve. Confident and combative he had toured the television studios to insist that the government would recover. His temperament was that of the self-confident Midlands barrister, sometimes dangerously blunt in acknowledging the government's weaknesses, but essentially optimistic. The principal obstacle to his appointment was his avowed pro-Europeanism. Closer European integration had been a constant thread in his career. As a student at Cambridge in the early 1960s he had been a committed admirer of Harold Macmillan's attempts to negotiate Britain's entry to the Community, and he had spoken to that ambition at a Conservative Party conference as long ago as 1963. But, as his biographer Malcolm Balen records, Clarke's passionate Europeanism left room for realism.[20] By the spring of 1993 he knew there was no prospect of sterling's early return to the ERM and he began to temper his enthusiasm. This was a signal to the right of the Conservative Party that he could be trusted at the Treasury. Just two weeks before Lamont's departure, he stated publicly that he saw little prospect of sterling rejoining the mechanism ahead of the next general election.

Clarke's arrival at the Treasury promised, for a time, a revival in the government's political fortunes. When Terence Burns appeared on the steps of the Treasury to greet the new chancellor, some took it as a sign that the officials had decided that they henceforth would be running economic policy. The reverse was true. Clarke was no economist, but in mid-1993 he was the most powerful, self-confident politician in the cabinet. His pugnacious style had won him admirers even among those who deeply suspected his pro-European instincts. Though his political fortunes would later decline, in the summer of 1993 Clarke was seen as the clear favourite to succeed to No. 10 should Major fall. He was, a friend would remark, Rab Butler with rough edges. The Treasury, demoralized by the failure of the previous

September, welcomed the arrival of a politician who promised to restore its influence.

Clarke himself was slightly irritated by media comment on his lack of formal training in economics: rather lamely, he would remind journalists of his time as the trade and industry minister. But, as it happened, his common-sense approach to economics matched the mood of the moment. The nation had had enough of the intricacies of money supply and exchange rate targets. His first significant comments as chancellor – delivered, appropriately enough, at a lunch hosted by the parliamentary press gallery – struck the right note. Of course he would take no risks with inflation, and he was as determined as his predecessor to bring down public borrowing. His main concern, though, was to strengthen the real economy: 'That's the point of the whole thing – growth and employment.'[21] This was a political chancellor, and his first appearance at the House of Commons dispatch-box, later on the same day, offered an effortless exhibition of the political skills his predecessor had lacked. For the first time since Black Wednesday, Gordon Brown, the shadow chancellor, found himself facing an opponent with the self-confidence to fight back.

The new chancellor did not disguise an instinctive preference for managed rather than floating exchange rates. His constituency was the manufacturing industry of his Midlands political base; it wanted a stable pound. However, he understood the political realities. A firm supporter of economic and monetary union, he had also begun to doubt whether the ERM was any longer a viable route to a single currency. Attending his first meeting of European finance ministers, in Luxembourg in early June, Clarke pointed to the continuing strains in the system caused by high German interest rates. He told journalists afterwards, 'Conditions in Germany are so far out of line at the moment that the conditions are not there for anyone to talk about rejoining the ERM.' A few weeks later he offered the same verdict in a lengthy newspaper interview. He still believed managed rates had real advantages, but 'For every conceivable reason we are not going back to a fixed exchange rate system for some years to come.' In those circumstances, he would not be mesmerized by day-to-day movements in the pound's value. Nor would he seek to emulate Nigel Lawson: 'Nigel's experience of shadowing the Deutschmark, whilst noble at the time, I think he would accept did not succeed.'[22] Privately his views were more complex. He accepted that economics and politics militated against sterling's re-entry to the ERM, but he was as sure as he had ever been that Britain must retain the option of participation in a single currency.

Events were initially to spare him any serious conflict between these short-term realities and medium-term ambitions. The monetary committee of European finance ministry officials and central bank experts had launched a thorough review of the ERM in response to John Major's charge that the events of 16 September had exposed fault-lines in the system. Two reports – one by the finance ministry officials and the other by central bank governors – concluded, to Major's chagrin, that the system was fundamentally sound.[23] At the core of the government's complaint was the asymmetry in the mechanism. This meant that, although German policies had provoked the tensions, it fell to other governments to respond. The experts disagreed, concluding that Black Wednesday had resulted not from inherent flaws in the system but from the refusal of governments to realign their currencies in response to the pressures caused by German reunification. In May 1993, European finance ministers endorsed a recommendation for tighter surveillance of exchange rates to ensure more timely realignments, but they backed the overall assessment that the events of 16 September had been triggered by the mistakes made by governments.

The financial markets were not quite so sanguine. The essential tension within the system – between the Bundesbank's determination to rein back German inflation and the squeeze this imposed on the economies of other ERM members – remained. In the early months of 1993 the speculators returned to the attack. In February it was the turn of the Irish punt to be devalued, and in May that of the peseta and the escudo. The French franc then faced the brunt of the onslaught once more. For a time in July the Bundesbank again gave the Paris government the massive support on foreign exchange markets that it had denied to Britain nine months earlier. By the end of the month, however, the pressure was irresistible. Finance ministers were summoned to an emergency meeting in Brussels on 1 August. The Bundesbank refused to lower its interest rates to bolster the franc. In the early hours of 2 August the mechanism was saved from complete destruction only by an unprecedented widening of the permitted margins of fluctuation from 2.25 per cent to 15 per cent – to all intents and purposes currencies now floated within the system. The tension between Germany and the rest of Europe had all but broken the system. Emerging from the meeting, Clarke told the waiting press with more than a hint of satisfaction that others have discovered the fault-lines in the ERM which the British have been pointing out'.[24] Understandably perhaps, the chancellor did not mention his own role during the lengthy debate which had preceded the eventual decision. Some of his fellow finance ministers had argued that the whole mechanism be scrapped. Clarke had been in the forefront of those pressing for it to be salvaged.

John Major drew greater satisfaction from the outcome. Here was evidence that sterling's exit was not an isolated British failure but part of a wider phenomenon which had now claimed even the franc. The acrimony between the Paris and Bonn governments and the further evidence of the Bundesbank's readiness to sacrifice currency stability across Europe to its domestic policy seemed a vindication of sterling's withdrawal. A month later the prime minister declared the ambition of a single European currency effectively dead. Writing in the *Economist*, he said that a single currency was 'not realizable in present circumstances, and therefore not relevant to our [Europe's] economic difficulties'. Looking ahead to the European summit the following month, he added, 'I am not prepared to sit down in Brussels in a few weeks' time and pretend that Humpty Dumpty is whole and well. I care too much about the European Community to pursue Sellotape policies – patching together the unmendable – or to play the politics of illusion – pretending it was never broken.'[25] It was an understandable, but premature, prediction.

Norman Lamont was to complain with some justification after his departure from the Treasury that his successor would reap the rewards of the tough decisions which had led to his own downfall. In part, it was true. But Kenneth Clarke also made his own luck and took his own tough decisions. Nor did the Treasury bring political rewards. Like Roy Jenkins, the Labour chancellor who had succeeded James Callaghan in 1967, Clarke would discover that the right policies are rarely popular. The balanced economic recovery of the following two years impressed economists, but did little to recapture the support of the electorate.

Clarke's first important judgement during the summer of 1993 was that his predecessor had not done enough to curb public borrowing. The projected government deficit for 1993/94 was 7.75 per cent of national income – higher than the shortfall which had confronted Geoffrey Howe in 1981. November 1983 had been set as the date for the first of a new system of unified Budgets in which tax and spending decisions would be brought together once a year in a single package. That meant that Clarke had an immediate opportunity to build on the tax increases which Lamont had unveiled in March. So he announced a £10bn cut in the government's spending targets over the following three years and an additional round of tax increases which would add nearly £5bn to the government's revenues in the 1995/96 financial year – in addition to the £10.3bn of tax increases put in place by Lamont. Taken together, the two 1993 Budgets imposed the largest tax increases ever seen in peacetime. Critically, they also allowed Clarke to forecast that the public-sector borrowing requirement would fall from a projected £50bn in 1993/94 (in the event the out-turn was £45.4bn) to near balance by the end of the century. The chancellor was forced by a back-bench revolt a year later to abandon the second stage of the introduction of VAT on domestic fuel, but by then a fresh round of spending cuts had been put in place to help reduce the government's deficit.

The tax increases would have been needed even if the pound had not been forced from the ERM, for Nigel Lawson's tax cuts in the late 1980s had badly eroded the Treasury's revenue base. Blinded by the benign, but strictly temporary, impact on its finances of the economic boom, the government had also loosened the public-spending reins. Higher taxes were a price that had to be paid and, in strictly economic terms, the timing could not have been better. By holding down the growth of incomes, higher taxes would dampen the risk that a lower pound would reignite inflation. The inflation profile during 1993 confirmed the earlier suspicions of the Bank: if Britain had remained in the ERM, retail prices might well have fallen during 1993 for the first time since the 1930s. Even after the sharp relaxation of monetary policy which followed Black Wednesday – sterling fluctuated in 1993 between DM2.35 and DM2.55 and interest rates were reduced to 6 per cent – the annual inflation rate fell steeply. As measured by the retail price index, it dropped to 1.2 per cent in June 1993 – its lowest for thirty years – before rising gently to around 2 per cent at the end of the year. The slight upward drift continued during 1994, and by mid-1995 the underlying rate hovered just below 3 per cent. Given the strength of the recovery – output rose by 4 per cent in 1994 – that represented the best performance since the early 1960s. The government's dire predictions before Black Wednesday that devaluation would be followed by a prices and wages spiral were confounded.

The slack in the economy left by the recession provided another powerful countervailing force to the impact of sterling's depreciation on prices. Output had fallen by nearly 4 per cent in the two years from the summer of 1990. The housing market remained in deep depression, with prices in 1994 on average more than 30 per cent lower than at the start of 1990. The sharp rise in unemployment to nearly 3 million in early 1993 was followed by a succession of monthly reductions which reduced that total by nearly 700,000 during the following two and a half years. Employment insecurity, however, emerged as one of the most potent economic forces of the 1990s, acting as a powerful restraint on pay awards – the annual growth of average earnings decelerated to between 3 and 4 per cent during 1993 and 1994. Industry's unit costs held steady in real terms. Subdued domestic demand and a 15 per cent improvement in international competitiveness offered an ideal backdrop for the export-driven economic upturn which followed. National output rose by 2 per cent in 1993 and by 4 per cent in 1994. More importantly, the volume of exports increased at nearly twice those rates. Against all past experience, Britain's trade position improved rather than deteriorated as the economic recovery gathered pace. The picture would darken somewhat in 1995 but during 1994 the massive current-account deficit which had built up during the 1980s was all but eliminated. This was not, however, an economic recovery calculated to win back the support of the electorate. Virtue in economics rarely wins votes. The corollary of tax increases was a strong squeeze on real disposable incomes. This was a recovery without the feel-good factor. The benefits were not felt where they count in politics – in the voters' pockets.

*

Another important decision taken by Clarke was to strengthen further the authority of the Bank of England. In the autumn of 1993 he announced that, once a decision to adjust interest rates had been taken, the timing of the subsequent announcement would be left to the Bank. He gave further substance to the Bank's role as guardian of the government's inflation conscience by ending the Treasury's advance vetting of the new *Inflation Report*. The decisive initiative, however, came in the spring of 1994. The chancellor announced that the minutes of his monthly interest rate deliberations with the Bank governor would henceforth be published – albeit with a delay of six weeks.

This last, superficially innocuous, decision involved a large shift in the balance of power between Whitehall and Threadneedle Street. The chancellor retained the option of rejecting the governor's advice, but, if he did so, the conflict would quickly be exposed to the scrutiny of the financial markets. Eddie George was thus given an unprecedented level of influence, if not direct control, over interest rates. Like his predecessor, Clarke would have preferred a more complete transfer to the Bank of authority over interest rates. Looking back at the experiences of Lawson and Lamont, he saw the danger of political interference from No. 10 in interest rate decisions. The all-party Treasury and Civil Service Committee had taken the same view. After an extensive investigation of monetary policy in Britain and abroad, in December 1993 it recommended legislative changes to enshrine 'price stability in statute as the primary objective of monetary policy and a transfer of responsibility for determining the level of interest rates from the Treasury to the Bank'. The Bank, though, should be made accountable to Parliament, and 'The government should have the power to override the Bank's objective of price stability temporarily and in exceptional circumstances. This should require parliamentary approval and be for a period of six months, renewable for a further six months.'[26]

The prime minister, however, was determined that the level of mortgage rates would remain under political control. Major was reluctant even to allow publication of the minutes of the meetings between the chancellor and the Bank governor. The resulting shift in the balance of power had implications for the occupants of both 10 and 11 Downing Street. One effect was to weaken the relative position of the chancellor vis-à-vis the Bank governor. Another, as Clarke had fully intended, was to remove much of the influence of No. 10 on interest rate decisions. A transparent process of decision-making would make it harder for the prime minister to manipulate interest rates for short-term political gain. Clarke's favourite phrase was that good economics would in the end prove to be good politics. Major gave his consent to publication, however, only after the production for several months of 'shadow minutes' of the monthly meetings. Even then it took what one of the participants described as a 'robust debate' with the chancellor to finally persuade him.

George, installed as governor in July 1993, was quick to exploit the Bank's new role, stressing from the outset a personal commitment to price stability. By now he made no secret of his long-held scepticism about attempts to target the exchange rate. In September 1993 he drew a lesson from the near break-up of the ERM. Convergence of domestic economic policies should come before efforts to set exchange rates. Stable currencies were necessary if Europe was to derive the full economic benefits from the single market, but 'without domestic policies within member countries directed to stability, stable exchange rates will be an illusion'.[27] Nine months later he developed the argument. During the era of the gold standard and subsequently, under the postwar Bretton Woods arrangements, exchange rate targets had represented the substance of monetary policy. Now it was the role of central banks to ensure that 'the cart of exchange rate stability should not be put before the horse of domestic stability'. The recent past had demonstrated that well-balanced domestic policies offered a more reliable route to a stable exchange regime than artificial attempts to peg the nominal value of currencies.[28]

Taking up their respective responsibilities within a month of each other in mid-1993, the governor and the chancellor established an easy relationship. George was fifty-five, Clarke fifty-three. Both had studied at Cambridge, but had prospered on the basis of ability rather than privilege; both were plain-speaking. In one of their first conversations, Clarke told George that he would never seek to censor his pronouncements, but if he disagreed with the Bank he reserved the right to say so publicly. George readily agreed, but with a proviso – the right of reply, he told the chancellor, must be reciprocal. There were early disagreements. In November 1993 George supported a decision by the chancellor to edge down interest rates from 6 to 5.5 per cent. In February 1994, however, the Bank governor opposed the further quarter-point reduction ordered by the chancellor. Reports of the disagreement over the interest rate cut soon surfaced in financial markets. Clarke blamed Bank officials, and would later remark that the incident had strengthened his determination to secure publication of the minutes – the Bank's advice would then be exposed to public scrutiny.

George described the move to publication as a 'terrific decision', but it did not take long for the inevitable tensions to emerge. In September 1994 the Bank urged the chancellor to announce the first in a series of rises in interest rates designed to hold inflation within the official target range. Clarke, a skilful politician, would later claim the decision was proof positive of the Treasury's rare determination to safeguard economic recovery by acting pre-emptively to contain inflation. In truth, Whitehall officials recall that his first reaction to the Bank's recommendation was one of dismay. He waited two days before accepting the advice, and only then decided it could be turned to political advantage.

The more significant conflict arose in the spring of 1995, when sterling began to demonstrate again its potential to disrupt the management of the economy. Caught, as it was so often during the 1980s, in the crossfire of a falling dollar, the pound fell to a record low of DM2.20. The fall came amid evidence that the growth rate in the economy remained strong and that the government's target of an inflation rate below 2.5 per cent by the spring of 1997 might well be missed. The Bank's analysis, based on its assessment of the price, cost and capacity pressures in the economy, pointed strongly to an overshoot unless corrective action were taken. For all his determination not to be mesmerized by the exchange rate, George believed that sterling's depreciation threatened the credibility of the government's anti-inflation stance. So, at his meeting with Clarke in early May, he called for a half-point increase in interest rates to 7.25 per cent. His demand carried a warning that, if the government did not act, it might soon be confronted with a full-scale sterling crisis. As the subsequent minutes recorded his comments, 'There was an immediate market risk that the exchange rate would fall, perhaps sharply, if the expected interest rate rise was not forthcoming ... the authorities could be faced very quickly with a loss of credibility and a very difficult market situation.'[29]

Taking an enormous gamble, Clarke rejected the Bank's advice. His meeting with George came just a day after the government's worst-ever defeat in the May local government elections. Major's hold on the premiership looked increasingly threatened. Labour's lead in the opinion polls was stuck firmly at thirty points. There were warnings of a backlash among Conservative MPs if interest rates were increased. Clarke deployed none of those objections during his meeting with George. Instead he pointed to the clear evidence of a deceleration of the growth rate of the economy. Implicitly, he rejected also the Bank's relatively pessimistic analysis of the underlying potential of the economy to expand without generating inflation. Clarke's decision ran against the advice of his own officials as well as that of the Bank: the consensus within the Treasury was that the balance of risks favoured an interest rate rise. But the chancellor did not take his decision lightly – officials were later to recall that the brief period between the break-up of the meeting and his appearance at a hastily summoned press conference marked the first time they had seen him visibly unnerved.

The struggle with George continued during the following three months – with the Bank pressing for higher rates and Clarke rejecting the advice. Luck or fate was on the side of the chancellor. As the summer progressed the economic indicators appeared to confirm his predictions of a more sustainable economic growth rate. Sterling stabilized and inflation remained subdued, if just above the official target. The conflict, however, underlined the flaws inherent in the new institutional arrangements. If the chancellor refuses too often the advice of the governor, he risks undercutting the credibility of his anti-inflation strategy. If he accepts the Bank's word against his own best judgement then he invites a political backlash at Westminster. The governor cannot be called to account by parliament for his advice, but can be discredited by his mistakes. It is not a pattern of relationships which promises long-term stability.

By autumn 1995 sterling had fallen about 25 per cent from its ERM parity of DM2.95. Its depreciation against the dollar during the previous three years had been slightly less, at about 20 per cent. The deflationary shock inflicted by membership of the ERM spared the

economy the surge in domestic prices which might have followed
such a large depreciation. The government now celebrated a 'competitive' rather than a strong pound. Those with memories of the 1980s,
and particularly of the 1986 devaluation, were not quite as sanguine.

CHAPTER TWELVE

A SOVEREIGN POUND

IT IS POSSIBLE to imagine that in different circumstances John Major's administration might have recovered its balance after Black Wednesday. The near-break-up of the ERM in the summer of 1993 gave some substance to the claim that, whatever the British government's mistakes, sterling had been the victim of an unprecedented upheaval on international currency markets. The pound's ejection from the mechanism was, however, the catalyst for another, more destructive, crisis. The fault-lines which Major had identified in the ERM tore open the divide in his own party over Europe. This corrosive breach, reminiscent of the split over the Corn Laws 150 years earlier and that over tariff reform at the start of the twentieth century, eroded the foundations of Major's government. At the centre of the divide were the future of sterling and the Maastricht plan for a single European currency.

The process of ratifying the Maastricht Treaty after the 1992 election had always threatened to stir the unrest in the party over the process of European integration. Major's parliamentary majority of only twenty-one – compared to the 100-plus enjoyed by Thatcher for most of the 1980s – left his administration badly exposed to rebellion. It needed only a dozen Eurosceptics to threaten the government's stability, and there were many more than that. There were some who burned still with resentment at the way that Thatcher had been toppled because of her unashamed defence of British sovereignty. On her advice, they had supported Major for the succession, only to discover that he preferred consensus in Europe to isolation. The new intake of MPs at the 1992 election tilted the political balance on the back benches further towards the Eurosceptic right. Many had been drawn into political careers or selected as candidates during the triumphant years of Thatcherism and arrived at Westminster full of her past certainties. A vocal minority were proud to style themselves Eurosceptics. Others on the back benches were drawn to the anti-Brussels cause by the impact of economic recession and by the humiliation of Black Wednesday. There were still vocal enthusiasts for Europe – Edward Heath had never lost the passionate conviction which had led him to negotiate Britain's entry to the Community – but much of the support was passive. Many Conservative MPs – a majority – would admit that participation in Europe was vital to the nation's prosperity and security, but far fewer were prepared to trumpet its virtues.

Major himself, pragmatic but positive during the first two years of his premiership, became increasingly disillusioned after Black Wednesday. He could not forgive Germany for its role in the sterling crisis. He would stake his premiership on ratification of Maastricht, but doubts replaced enthusiasm in his dealings with other European leaders. He would not close the door on the possibility of a single currency, but he became convinced that Britain was unlikely to join one in the foreseeable future. He understood the political realities which demanded that Britain maintain its influence in Europe, but party management took precedence.

The political backlash triggered by the Danish referendum in June 1992 took Major and his colleagues by surprise. Douglas Hurd would later admit that he had badly misread the mood on the back benches. He did not change his view, however, that Britain had no option but to proceed with ratification. He believed that if the government had reneged on the deal it would have been left alongside Denmark on the sidelines. In such circumstances, Hurd would have quit the Foreign Office. It anyway still seemed plausible that the treaty could be ratified without an irrevocable split in the Conservative Party. The Copenhagen government had immediately indicated its wish to return to the Maastricht fold. The terms needed to convince the Danish electorate to reverse its decision would go with the grain of the British government's thinking. The principle of decentralized decision-making, or subsidiarity, which the government had insisted be included in the original treaty, would be reinforced as part of a strategy to pave the way for a second Danish referendum. Major hoped that in the process all but a few die-hard anti-federalists on the Conservative benches at Westminster would be won over.

Black Wednesday extinguished such optimism. Defeat at the hands of the Germans gave momentum to the back-bench revolt which had taken shape during the summer. Devaluation had robbed the prime minister of authority. If Denmark's rejection of the treaty had lit the fuse of rebellion, sterling's departure from the ERM on 16 September was the explosion. Now that the pound had floated free of the Deutschmark, the sceptics demanded that the government also reject the Maastricht blueprint for a single currency. Their resolve was strengthened by the perilously narrow margin – 51 per cent to 49 per cent – by which the voters of supposedly federalist France had ratified the treaty on 20 September.

The parliamentary struggle that followed during the next ten months was one of the most remarkable of modern politics. The divisions frequently spilled over into the cabinet. The Conservative Party emerged bitter and divided, the prime minister weak and exhausted. At times a party which had once boasted unity as its most potent weapon was gripped by a collective madness hitherto seen only on the extreme left of the Labour Party. The bitterness it would engender was apparent within days of Black Wednesday. When Norman Lamont arrived in Washington for the annual meeting of the IMF, he found that Lady Thatcher was already in town. Speaking at a conference on world economic development, Thatcher exulted in sterling's departure from the ERM. Recalling the phrase that had symbolized her conflict with Nigel Lawson, she declared once again that 'If you try to buck the market, the market will buck you.' Apparently oblivious to the fact that she had been prime minister when Britain had joined the ERM, she then resumed her onslaught on Maastricht. 'If the divergence between different European economies is so great that even the ERM cannot contain them, how would they react to a single currency?' she asked.[1]

The party conference in Brighton a few weeks later was the occasion for an extraordinary public rift between Major and his predecessor. She had promised a brief, uncontroversial, appearance on the conference platform. She ensured it was otherwise by delivering a scathing condemnation of Maastricht in an interview with the *European*. 'It is time to get our priorities right,' she said. 'The government must recognize that Maastricht, like the ERM, is part of the vision of yesterday. It is time to set out the vision of tomorrow.'[2] Her comments drew a curt response from the prime minister, who insisted that ratification of Maastricht had 'the cabinet's complete and unanimous support'. Privately he seethed, telling colleagues that his predecessor had still not come to terms with the indignity of her departure from 10 Downing Street. Kenneth Clarke's blunt comment caught Major's private mood: 'How can a former prime minister come along and attack her successor about a decision in which she was the senior partner?' he asked.

Amid scenes reminiscent of the Labour leadership's battles with the Militant Tendency during the early 1980s, the newly ennobled Norman Tebbit sought to destroy what remained of Major's authority with an unashamedly populist attack from the conference floor on all things European. 'This conference', he declared, 'wants policies for Britain first, Britain second, and Britain third.'[3] Tebbit, involved later in the week in an acrimonious exchange with Clarke at a late-night party hosted by Jeffrey Archer, won a standing ovation and came close to winning over the conference. Only a confident and condescending riposte from Douglas Hurd restored a calmer mood. Hurd would now look forward to spending the next three years at the Foreign Office in an arduous effort to prevent his party from either detaching itself from the European mainstream or splitting irrevocably over the issue. It was a role he would fill with considerable political skill and no small measure of intellectual dexterity. It was one which would leave him accused alternately by Tory anti-federalists of appeasing Brussels and by enthusiastic pro-Europeans of bowing to his party's nationalists. As the years passed, Hurd's unabashed insistence that the vast majority in his party embraced his own pragmatic Europeanism began to stretch the credulity of his audiences. But now he warned that the siren voices of Lord Tebbit and his allies would leave Britain stranded on Europe's sidelines: 'Let us decide to give that madness a miss.'[4]

The prime minister was determined to press on. Maastricht had been his success: to abandon it now would be to deny the victory he had so loudly proclaimed in December 1991. Like Hurd, he saw it as a compromise which had kept Britain in the European mainstream while preserving its national identity. The treaty was far from ideal, but it would not smother the open, free-market Europe which the government was determined to promote. Once sterling had been devalued, Major also knew that to disown Maastricht would be to sacrifice what remained of his already battered authority. He had staked out his position in the House of Commons in late June 1992, when he declared, 'I have no intention of breaking the word of the British government ... and wrecking this country's reputation for plain dealing, honest dealing, and good faith.'⁵ By the time of the October conference he was ready to offer more in the way of rhetorical concessions to the anti-federalists, but the basic message remained the same: reneging on Maastricht would mean 'breaking Britain's future in Europe'.⁶

A month later Major revealed the streak of frequently reckless determination with which he would now force the treaty through the House of Commons. He staked his premiership on a single vote to allow resumption of the ratification process. At the Birmingham summit in mid-October European leaders had agreed to reinforce the subsidiarity provisions of Maastricht as part of a strategy to return Denmark to the fold. There was also a commitment to speed up the process of enlargement. Those pledges persuaded Major to raise the stakes in his confrontation with the sceptics in his party. The Maastricht bill had received its second reading in the House of Commons before the Danish referendum, but the prime minister had promised another full-scale debate before MPs moved on to line-by-line consideration of the bill in its committee stage. This so-called 'paving' vote was not essential to the passage of the legislation. Nor was the government required to table a substantive motion for debate. Major, however, was determined to force the issue. During a trip to Egypt in late October he horrified close colleagues by indicating to the accompanying journalists that, if he lost the vote, he was ready to resign and force a general election. A few days earlier the cabinet had agreed to set 4 November as the date for the debate, but Richard Ryder, the chief whip, had argued that it should be a low-key event, to minimize the risks of defeat. So too had Lord Wakeham, the leader of the House of Lords. The threat of an election destroyed that possibility. Some in the cabinet thought Major had put pride before reason. Others blamed Gus O'Donnell, the No. 10 press secretary, for careless briefing of the press.

In any event, John Smith's Labour Party now had the excuse it was looking for to vote against the government. Maastricht presented Labour with a dilemma. Smith, a long-standing European who had defied his own party's opposition to membership of the Community during the 1970s, had to strike a careful balance. His objective was to weaken the government by maximizing at every turn the internal dissent on the Tory back benches. But Labour had retreated during the 1980s from its anti-Europeanism. Smith himself had pressed the case for still stronger engagement, opposing the opt-out from the treaty's social provisions and accusing Major of appeasing the sceptics. To wreck the ratification process would be to undermine fatally the credibility of Labour's conversion to the European cause. No such objection could be raised, however, if the future of the government rather than of the treaty was at stake.

The outcome of the debate was as finely balanced as any faced by Conservative governments since 1979. Fearful that the prime minister would resign if defeated, Lord Wakeham arranged in advance for a group of senior colleagues to be on hand immediately after the vote to persuade him to stay. Major, himself unsure whether he would win or lose, opened the debate with a stark warning that Britain would be left 'scowling in frustration' on the fringes of Europe if it abandoned Maastricht: 'The essential question is simple: are we or are we not in this country to play a central role in Europe's development.'[7] Despite this warning, twenty-six Tory MPs voted with the opposition. The rebels were dismissive of the threat of a general election and indifferent to the possibility that they might force Major's resignation. When MPs filed into the House of Commons division lobbies at 10 p.m., the government survived by the nerve-rackingly slim majority of three votes. Even then, it had been obliged to depend on the support of Paddy Ashdown's ardently pro-European Liberal Democrats.

Six weeks later Major hosted the Edinburgh summit of European leaders. Displaying the diplomatic skills which he frequently deployed in European negotiations, he secured agreement on the terms for the Danish government to hold a second referendum on Maastricht. Other governments formalized the commitment to treat seriously the subsidiarity provisions in the treaty. Jacques Delors tempered his federalist rhetoric and agreed that enlargement of the Community to include the Nordic countries and Austria should take priority over any further institutional upheaval. Together with some other specific assurances to the Copenhagen government, in May 1993 this would be enough to persuade the Danish electorate to reverse the result of the first referendum. There was no reward for the prime minister, however. His very success at the Edinburgh summit condemned the government to eight months of trench warfare in the House of Commons.

Between December 1992 and July 1993 the debate on the European Communities (Amendment) Bill absorbed more than 170 hours of parliamentary time spread over twenty-five days as the government battled to secure ratification of Maastricht. When earlier debates were included, the treaty consumed more than 200 hours of parliamentary time. There had been nothing comparable since the parliamentary battles over devolution which had so distracted and weakened the Callaghan government in the late 1970s. Each hour of the Maastricht debate sapped the authority of John Major's administration.

Between twenty-five and thirty Conservative MPs consistently voted against the treaty, and another twenty to twenty-five regularly abstained. Up to forty others supported the government only reluctantly and under great pressure. The rebels, with their own organization and whips, broke with all past precedent by colluding openly with the Labour Party to maximize the chances of defeating the government. With by-election defeats beginning to erode his parliamentary majority of twenty-one, Major relied on the European commitment of the Liberal Democrats to deflect more than 600 amendments. John Smith, who had pledged not to prevent ratification of the treaty, none the less ruthlessly exploited the Tory divisions by making his party's support conditional on the scrapping of Britain's social chapter opt-out – a condition Major could never accept.

In the event, the prime minister secured the passage of the legislation only after again threatening his party with destruction at a general election. George Robertson, Labour's European spokesman, led a skilfully disruptive campaign which harried the government at every turn. Richard Ryder and his colleagues in the government whips' office could never be sure when they might be defeated. The constant rebellions on the back benches soured and divided the party at Westminster. Then, on 22 July 1993, a revolt by twenty-three Tory MPs led to a humiliating defeat on a Labour amendment to remove the social chapter opt-out. During a tense late-evening cabinet meeting in his room at the House of Commons, the prime minister secured the agreement of his colleagues to make the issue one of confidence in the government. If his administration could not secure the support of Parliament for an international treaty which had been freely negotiated and signed, it would resign. A second motion was tabled for debate the following day as cabinet ministers toured the lobbies of Westminster to issue the unprecedented threat.

By now the government was lagging twenty points behind Labour in the opinion polls – the rebels understood that the choice was between supporting ratification of Maastricht and certain defeat at a general election four weeks later. Major won the confidence vote comfortably – even the most extreme among the sceptics were not at this point prepared to put their principles before the loss of their parliamentary seats. It was a Pyrrhic victory, however, achieved at immense further cost to the prime minister's authority. A senior cabinet colleague remarked only hours afterwards that it offered a 'respite not a reprieve'. A few days later the government's unpopularity was underlined once again by a crushing by-election defeat. Technically the government's fifteenth-safest seat, Christchurch was lost with an unprecedented 35 per cent swing to the Liberal Democrats.

Nor did ratification of the treaty close the wounds on the back benches. Major found himself leading a bitter and demoralized party. Henceforth he would be haunted by threats of a leadership challenge, by speculation about plots to remove him. His precarious balancing-act during the succeeding months and years undermined his standing among allies as well as enemies. Frustrated outbursts against the rebels and threats of a general election were all too often followed by the rhetoric of appeasement. Opposition accusations that he had put party management before principle, that he had sacrificed leadership to survival, found echoes in his cabinet. The swings in the prime minister's mood frequently vexed Douglas Hurd and baffled other colleagues. As one minister was to remark, 'To survive, he [Major] must show that he is in charge of the government and that the government is in charge of the country.' For more than two years he did neither.

The prime minister's own resentment had surfaced during an off-the-record conversation with Michael Brunson, the political editor of ITN, in the hours after his victory in the final Maastricht vote. His remarks, picked up by a stray microphone, revealed a deep frustration at the charges of weakness but also an acknowledgement that he was a prisoner of the divisions within his party:

> What I don't understand, Michael, is why such a complete wimp like me keeps winning everything. The way people who oppose our European policy go about it is to attack me personally. Think of it through my perspective. What happens if they resign? Where do you think most of the poison has come from? It's coming from the dispossessed and the never-possessed on the back benches. Would you like three more of the bastards out there?

The unnamed 'bastards' were the sceptics in Major's cabinet – Michael Portillo, Peter Lilley and John Redwood. There had never been any secret about their disenchantment with Maastricht; others had heard the prime minister use much stronger language. But now the division had been made public it was also that much deeper.

There was a similar outburst a few months later. During a trip to Tokyo in September, Major found once again that his off-the-record remarks had been recorded by the accompanying press. Earlier he had demanded publicly that the sceptics end their 'stupid internecine squabbling'. But the private comments, published in the *Independent* by the newspaper's political correspondent, Colin Brown, revealed a much deeper angst. He was determined, he said, to confront his critics at the forthcoming party conference. And of those who attacked his leadership, he commented, 'I could name eight people. Half of those eight people are barmy. How many apples short of a picnic?'[8] Publication of the remarks served only to fan the flames of speculation at Westminster. By the time Major returned to London a few days later, Kenneth Clarke, Michael Howard and Michael Portillo were being openly discussed as possible successors.

The struggle over Europe brought a wider paralysis. Mesmerized by internal divisions, the government lost a sense of purpose – policy-making was abandoned in favour of crisis management. In the aftermath of Black Wednesday, policy U-turns became as familiar as the stream of ill-fated initiatives with which the prime minister sought to rebuild his authority. There were exceptions. Major pursued the cause of peace in Northern Ireland with rare and brave determination. He remained adamant that the gains which had been made against inflation during sterling's ERM membership should not be thrown

away in an unsustainable boom. But, a pragmatic rather than a
conviction politician, he was buffeted by events much as Harold
Wilson had been after 1967.

Misfortune bred misfortune. A lurch to the right in the autumn of
1993 with the launch of an ill-judged and short-lived 'Back to Basics'
campaign was followed by a string of resignations as successive
ministers fell victim to charges of sleaze and moral laxity. Each by-
election defeat was followed by still-greater panic, each ostentatious
display of party unity by fresh evidence of divisions. Major's leadership appeared under constant threat, bringing further echoes of the
1960s. 'What's going on? I'm going on,' Wilson had told his party
conference to dispel speculation about his leadership.[9] 'I am fit, and I
am well. I am here. I am staying,' was how Major would put it.[10] He
would be forced to repeat the same sentiment again and again during
the following two years.

There were, however, occasional glimpses of a character trait much
underestimated by his enemies. Between the mood swings – the
anxiety to secure consensus and the all-too-frequent outbursts –
Major began to display the stubborn resilience which would confound
his opponents. However much they attacked him, it seemed, he would
be yet more determined not to be pushed from office. It was as if, one
cabinet colleague would comment, the prime minister looked each
morning in a Downing Street mirror and told himself simply, 'I'm
staying.'

Some of his most visceral critics represented no more than the
flotsam and jetsam of the Thatcherite era – failed ministers, disinher-
ited courtiers and never-promoted populists. Others on the back
benches saw in Brussels a convenient scapegoat for the recession, an
opportunity to deflect the storm of dissatisfaction with the government. The conflict over Maastricht, however, exposed deeper currents
both in the Conservative Party and in the country. Not all of the
opponents of the treaty were motivated by malice or prejudice. Many
Conservative MPs instinctively shared the hostility to European
uniformity which the treaty appeared to impose. The blueprint for
economic and political union spoke too much to a continental rather
than a British political tradition. Sensible, pragmatic pro-Europeans
began to wonder whether Maastricht had not been a treaty too soon
if not too far. To understand that Britain could not sulk on the fringes

of Europe was not necessarily to enjoy the experience of engagement. The European tide which had swept away Margaret Thatcher began to ebb almost as quickly as it had flowed. It was clear also that, across the Channel, the grand vision of the continent's political élites had run ahead of the popular mood. Battered and bewildered by their unpopularity, many Conservatives who had proudly declared themselves members of the party of Europe thirty years earlier began to huddle beneath the Union flag. The changing mood was given vivid expression at the party conferences, in the enthusiastic receptions that demoralized representatives offered to the cabinet's 'bastards'. Michael Portillo, fast emerging as Thatcher's heir apparent, and Peter Lilley, the most sceptical in the cabinet, were now the ministers guaranteed noisy standing ovations.

Maastricht had been ratified, but the issue which defined the divide in the Conservative Party and in John Major's cabinet was at the heart of the treaty. Economic and monetary union – the future of sterling – became the emblem of the conflict between those who saw in Brussels a plot to destroy the nation-state and those who believed that Britain could retain influence only as a partner in Europe. There was no question of the pound's early return to the ERM but, to the anti-federalists, the threat was far greater – sterling might be subsumed in a single currency.

Pro-European Conservatives admitted the possibility of serious practical objections to early participation in EMU. In Germany and France also there were signs, albeit shortlived, of waning enthusiasm among the élites who had promoted the vision of a federal Europe. The issue was as divisive in the cabinet as on the back benches. Kenneth Clarke and Michael Heseltine led those determined that the government should not prejudge the issue. Michael Portillo was most prominent among those certain the door must be slammed shut.

The provisions of the Maastricht Treaty were clear. The first stage of the move to economic and monetary union had begun, with Margaret Thatcher's assent, in July 1990. It involved closer coordination of economic policies, strengthening of the ERM and the role of the European Currency Unit, and an extension of the remit of central bank governors. The second stage, with a starting-point of

January 1994, involved the establishment of the forerunner of the European Central Bank, the European Monetary Institute. The EMI was charged with coordinating policies to achieve price stability and the technical preparations for EMU. Stage three was scheduled by the treaty to begin in January 1997 or January 1999. This would be the moment at which a European System of Central Banks would be established to oversee the interest rate policy for those countries joining a single currency. Eligibility for EMU would be based on a set of strict economic convergence criteria – for inflation rates, interest rates, public-sector deficits and debt, and currency stability. Maastricht envisaged that a single currency would be created by the irrevocable locking of exchange rates in 1997 if a 'critical mass' – seven out of the then twelve countries – met the convergence criteria. If not, the third stage would begin in January 1999 for those countries, however few, which met the economic conditions. It was at this point that Britain's opt-out gave it a choice whether to participate or to stand aside.

For a time after the near-break-up of the ERM in August 1993, John Major considered that this was a choice which would probably not have to be made. The speculative hurricane which destroyed the relative stability of ERM currencies pointed to an indefinite delay – just as the Werner Plan had been blown off course in the early 1970s by the breakdown of the Bretton Woods system. Major knew that there was little enthusiasm in Germany for the surrender of the Deutschmark, and a decision by that country's constitutional court would require a new parliamentary vote before a single currency was created. It was soon apparent, however, that the Bonn and Paris governments would not shelve their ambitions. While sharp divergences in economic performance meant that 1997 was no longer a serious option, Germany, France and the Benelux countries still saw 1999 as a realistic target. Stage two of the process began in January 1994 with the establishment of the European Monetary Institute. Senior finance ministry and central bank officials began the detailed technical work necessary to map out the precise route to a single currency. The prime minister was obliged to fall back on the logic of the Maastricht opt-out – the government would decide its position only when the economic and political circumstances were clear. Meanwhile it would use its place at the negotiating table to shape the arrangements under which a single currency would be created. Britain could not allow those countries which went ahead to impose penalties on those which remained outside. Sir Leon Brittan, whose departure from Margaret Thatcher's cabinet had been followed by his appointment to the European Commission, warned of the dangers. 'We must play our full part in these preparations, as we have the right to do so, even though we are not ourselves committed to joining,' he said in the autumn of 1994. 'Otherwise EMU will be cast in a mould which would be wholly contrary to our interests whether we ultimately join or stay out.'[11]

The sceptics demanded that Major abandon this awkward neutrality in favour of declaring that, whatever its partners decided, Britain would retain sterling – and with it sovereign authority over its domestic monetary policy. Their case – made in the cabinet as well as on the back benches – echoed Nigel Lawson's warnings in early 1989, when the Delors committee was finalizing its blueprint for EMU. A single currency would lead to the permanent transfer to an unelected European central bank of control over domestic economic policy. The inescapable implication was that Britain would surrender to the European Union an essential pillar of self-government. Most obviously, within a single currency, the government would lose the safety-valve of devaluation if Britain's industrial costs exceeded those of its European partners. The result would be higher unemployment. Inevitably, large disparities in unemployment rates would lead to a progressive extension of the European Union's control over fiscal policy. Large budgetary transfers would be necessary to even out economic performance. Parliament would thus lose the right not only to set the level of interest rates but also to determine spending and taxation. So this analysis saw in a single currency a constitutional rather than an economic choice. There was no reason to wait until the economic circumstances were clear to decide that Britain would not accept the destruction of parliamentary sovereignty. As Margaret Thatcher put it in the second volume of her memoirs, *The Path to Power*, EMU 'would be a fundamental and crucial loss of sovereignty and would mark a decisive step towards Britain's submergence in a European superstate'.[12]

Michael Portillo, ever more confident of his position as leader-in-waiting, broke cabinet ranks to underline his opposition to a single currency during a controversial television interview in May 1994. Asked if he supported the ambition, he replied simply 'No.' The British people had 'the most extreme doubts' about EMU, because centralizing economic decision-making in Europe would undermine national sovereignty, he added. 'No British government can give up the government of the UK. That's impossible.'[13] The comments, breaking with the agreed cabinet position, prompted a public rebuke from the prime minister. Senior Downing Street aides made no secret of his annoyance, disclosing that No. 10 had struck out similar sentiments from early drafts of Portillo's speeches. The truth, however, was that Portillo's stance was shared by several members of the cabinet, including Michael Howard, Peter Lilley and John Redwood. Jonathan Aitken, soon to be promoted to the cabinet, took the same view. Others, like Gillian Shephard, did not count themselves in the sceptics' camp, but saw little prospect of a Conservative administration joining EMU without breaking the party at Westminster. Outside the government, Norman Lamont and Norman Tebbit joined Thatcher in demanding that, at the very least, Major state publicly that sterling would never be scrapped without a referendum.

In the opposing camp, Kenneth Clarke insisted that the option of participation must be sustained. He had long backed the idea of a single currency as a way to entrench the benefits of economic integration and as a potent symbol of the postwar political settlement in Europe. Alongside Michael Heseltine, he believed that, if Germany and France went ahead, standing aside could inflict severe damage on Britain's economic prospects. Clarke's view was that a single currency was a natural extension of the single market in goods and services in the Union. Exchange rate instability and uneven inflation and interest rates were the last obstacles to genuine free trade. The globalization of capital and goods markets had already transferred to international bond and currency traders much of the control over economic policy once held by governments, so the transfer of sovereignty involved in the creation of a single currency was far smaller than the sceptics claimed. The independence that Britain would retain outside EMU would to a large extent be illusory. If it stood aside, the financial markets would draw the obvious conclusion that the government was defending its right to higher inflation and a depreciating currency. They would impose a significant cost in terms of higher interest rates and a weak pound. More fundamentally, Clarke denied that EMU implied a constitutional upheaval. If there was sufficient economic convergence it would be perfectly possible to operate a monetary union without moving to the political union feared by the sceptics. Britain and Ireland had enjoyed a de-facto economic union for fifty years from the early 1920s, but no one had doubted the Republic's independence.

Major's own views coincided with that of Eddie George at the Bank of England. Putting aside the political obstacles (in the prime minister's mind important if not entirely insuperable), there were serious economic objections. George argued that European governments and central banks should give priority to achieving real economic convergence over any timetable for EMU. The Bank governor cautioned that the political aspirations of Britain's partners were running far ahead of economic realities. Pointing to the already high levels of unemployment throughout Europe, he warned that a premature move to a single currency would carry with it 'enormous costs'. Unless it was accompanied by sustainable economic convergence, monetary union would lead to stagnation in some parts of the Union or pressure for large-scale fiscal transfers from rich to poor countries: 'Neither of these possibilities is particularly attractive. Either long-term stagnation in some countries or the rapid expansion of the adjustment mechanisms could become a source of political, as well as economic, disharmony within Europe.'[14]

During the autumn of 1994 Major edged towards the promise of a referendum on EMU. Douglas Hurd – a self-declared agnostic on the issue of a single currency but anxious both to keep the option open and to preserve a semblance of unity within the cabinet – pressed the case. Hurd also suggested that the prime minister could defuse the growing threat to his position from the sceptics by promising a separate referendum on the outcome of another looming set of negotiations on the future shape of the European Union. Maastricht had provided for a second intergovernmental conference in 1996 to resolve those issues left unsettled by the treaty. It was already clear that the more federally minded of Britain's partners expected a further push towards economic and political integration. During several exchanges in the House of Commons, Major came close to offering a referendum at least on the issue of a single currency. Privately, he indicated that it might well be impossible to frame the party's general election manifesto without such a pledge. But he faced opposition from both camps within the cabinet. Clarke and Heseltine saw in a referendum a needless concession to the sceptics. If the anti-Europeans were so concerned to preserve the sovereignty of Parliament, Clarke would say, how could they argue for important decisions to be submitted to a referendum? Portillo, shrewder than many of his supporters on the back benches, saw the risks for the sceptics inherent in a commitment to a referendum. As Hurd knew well, a Conservative government could hold a referendum only if it had decided that Britain should join a single currency. If the cabinet rejected EMU, there would be no requirement for a plebiscite.

In February 1995 the cabinet tensions burst into the open. Clarke, responsible as chancellor for representing the government in Brussels in the practical preparations for EMU, gave a defiant speech in which he denied that participation in a single currency would carry significant constitutional implications. During two tense meetings in 10 Downing Street, Major had asked the chancellor to tone down his address. Rashly, the prime minister had trailed the chancellor's speech a few days earlier, indicating it would set down new conditions for the abolition of sterling. Major had warned that, unless the economic conditions were right, a single currency could 'tear apart' the European Union. More than 100 Tory MPs had responded by signing a House of Commons motion praising the prime minister's seemingly more sceptical stance. Clarke fully acknowledged the need for much greater economic convergence before Europe could contemplate monetary union. But the chancellor was increasingly frustrated by the sceptics, and concerned that a weak prime minister was drifting too far in their direction. He had decided it was time to stake out the positive case for a single currency. When an advance draft of his speech arrived at the Cabinet Office, senior officials suggested several cuts and amendments to align it with the prime minister's public statements. Clarke refused, and during his meetings with Major he argued successfully for the offending passages to be reinstated. He defied also the advice of his own political adviser, Tessa Keswick. She was conscious that such a speech, offering not the slightest concession to the right of the party, could end permanently Clarke's hopes of eventually succeeding Major. Keswick was right, but the chancellor would not be moved.

The speech, delivered at a dinner for the European Movement, began with a call for a 'sensible and informed debate' about monetary union to examine the potential advantages as well as the objections. Clarke agreed that 'an ill-thought-out, ill-conceived monetary union would do Europe harm'. But he reminded his audience that Britain's role in the world 'is not based on our position as a nation of 60 million people on the edge of the continent. It depends crucially on our position as a European power. It depends on our ability to develop as one of the movers and shakers in European Union affairs ... We must not allow Britain to become marginalized in Europe.' Chiding the sceptics, he added that a decision on participation in a single currency must not be clouded by 'political dogma'. Monetary union could secure low inflation and lower, more stable, interest rates over the medium term or, if not sufficiently prepared, could inflict severe economic damage. But the essential point was that the economic issues weighed more heavily than the constitutional ones: 'It is quite possible to have monetary union without political union. It is a mistake to believe that monetary union need be a huge step on the path to a federal Europe.' The debate on whether to join, he added, should be free of the 'ridiculous' suggestion that those who saw real economic advantages in a single currency 'are somehow committed to a European superstate'.[15]

Predictably, the sceptics were enraged. In a staged rebuke to his more senior colleague, Portillo summoned the television cameras to record his reaction as he left home the following morning. The speech, he said, had been 'unhelpful'. Admitting openly the breach at the highest levels of the government, he added, 'I think we all have our opinions about what might happen later, but giving voice to those personal opinions won't help.' The cabinet was now as visibly divided as the Conservative Party at Westminster. Clarke was to acknowledge that he had indeed badly damaged his chances of ever succeeding Major, but he was unrepentant. 'Sometimes you have to stand on your principles,' he told friends.

The prime minister re-established the truce during a tense House of Commons debate on Europe at the beginning of March. Tony Blair's speech in the debate positioned the Labour Party squarely alongside Clarke: important economic conditions must be met, but, if they were met, there would be no overriding constitutional objection to a single currency. Blair, who had won the Labour leadership after the death of John Smith the previous summer, saw a pro-European stance as an essential ingredient in his plan to turn Labour into a mainstream social democratic party comparable to its continental counterparts. In truth, however, Blair saw strong objections to participation in a single currency in 1999. He thought 'remote' the possibility that the first Labour government for twenty years would take such a momentous decision so soon after returning to office. The damage inflicted on the prime minister by the ERM débâcle had not escaped his attention. But Blair was certain that Britain could not afford to exclude itself in advance from a development which would have profound implications for its economic well-being.

For his part, the prime minister was once again obliged to perch uncomfortably across the divide in his cabinet, setting out in public the terms of the compromise he had negotiated with his ministers in private. He refused to rule out the option of economic and monetary union, but he went as far as he could to highlight the obstacles. It could require 'far greater alignment of spending and tax rates'. The changes in fiscal and monetary management would be 'the most sweeping this house, with its history of control of supply, has ever known'. That meant that there were indeed big constitutional issues to be confronted, of a significance which might well demand a referendum. Major reaffirmed for the umpteenth time, however, that the government's policy was not to decide until it had to.[16] The Maastricht opt-out, negotiated as a device to paper over the divisions on the back benches, was now needed to prevent civil war in his cabinet. Few on either side of the argument were persuaded that the truce would hold. The conflict over sterling had become as fundamental as any the Conservative Party had faced during the previous 150 years. The divisions could be patched up, but not wished away.

As the centre of gravity in his party shifted, so also did Major's attitude to the broader debate on the direction of Europe. Before the elections for the European Parliament in May 1994, he led a campaign rooted in the rhetoric if not the ideology of the sceptics. The government was presented as the defender of British sovereignty against further encroachment by the federalists on the other side of the channel. The Labour Party and the Liberal Democrats were cast as willing pawns of Europe, willing to sacrifice Britain's independence to the bureaucrats of Brussels. The social chapter opt-out from Maastricht was exalted as an escape route from the dead hand of continental interventionism. And, in an effort to sidestep the charge that Britain would be isolated, Major campaigned on the theme of a multi-speed, multi-dimensional European Union. This 'variable geometry' – an idea developed by Douglas Hurd – would allow diversity to flourish alongside closer cooperation. The implication was that Britain, which already had opt-outs from the social chapter and EMU, would stand aside if those countries grouped around the Franco-German core of the Union pressed ahead with tighter integration. But there would be ample room for such diversity in a Europe which would soon have fifteen and, within a decade, perhaps twenty-five members. The campaign rhetoric – stressing a commitment to a Europe of nation-states, not a United States of Europe – absorbed much of the substance, if not the visceral hostility, of Margaret Thatcher's position during the late 1980s. At Bruges in September 1988 Thatcher had promoted a vision of a Europe stretching from the Atlantic to the Urals. Six years on, in January 1995, the entry of Finland, Norway and Austria would extend the Union to fifteen. Echoing his predecessor, Major put enlargement to the east – to include the new democracies of central and eastern Europe – at the centre of his agenda. A wider not a deeper Europe was the slogan.

The chauvinism in the Tories' electoral message did not win back the affections of the voters. The June 1994 poll saw only eighteen Conservatives elected to the Strasbourg Parliament, compared to the Labour Party's sixty-two, and the government lost Eastleigh in another crushing by-election defeat on the same day.

The sceptical tone of the campaign, however, did help to ease the immediate pressure on Major's leadership. So too did a staged clash with his European partners over the succession to Jacques Delors. In the spring of 1994 Major had unwisely provoked a confrontation over the operation of majority voting in Brussels after the Union's forthcoming enlargement to include Norway, Finland and Austria. He was determined that the changes needed to accommodate the new entrants should not dilute Britain's ability to block controversial European legislation. In a heated exchange in the House of Commons with John Smith, he raised the stakes in the conflict by deriding the Labour leader as the 'poodle' of Brussels. But this was a dispute that bore all the depressing hallmarks of the Thatcher era – Major's bellicose words could not disguise the reality that he would soon be obliged to retreat. He had misread the weight of opposition in European capitals and was forced into a humiliating and public climb-down when other governments responded with a threat to block enlargement.

The defeat triggered a new crisis of confidence in his leadership. In the House of Commons, the maverick back-bench MP Tony Marlow publicly demanded Major's resignation – the first time in fifty years that a fellow Tory had called in the Commons chamber for the prime minister of the day to stand down.[17] It was a sentiment echoed by many more in the privacy of the bars and lobbies.

Major now needed a confrontation which he could win. So, at the Corfu summit of European leaders two months later, he vetoed the choice of the Belgian prime minister Jean-Luc Dehaene to succeed the retiring Jacques Delors as president of the European Commission. Dehaene, the choice of the other eleven governments, was labelled by Major as too ardent a federalist. Within weeks, however, Major was obliged to endorse the alternative candidacy of Jacques Santer, the Luxembourg prime minister. Santer's views were indistinguishable from those of Dehaene, but Major had decided to make a point. The crude message to the sceptics on the Tory back benches was that he too was ready to exult in isolation.

This more sceptical approach was distilled into a speech at Leiden University in The Netherlands in September 1994. Looking ahead to the 1996 intergovernmental conference on the next stage of the Union's development, Major again said the priority was to widen rather than deepen Europe. The rationale behind the original Common Market had been to entrench the postwar peace in western Europe and to create a united and prosperous counterweight to the Soviet bloc. The Union, Major said, was now outgrowing the concept of its founders: 'Their vision proved right for its age. But it is outdated. It will not do now.' The future lay in enlargement to the east rather than in further institutional upheavals which would stifle the nation-state: 'We now have the chance to entrench democracy across Europe. History will not forgive us if we squander it.' He warned those seeking tighter integration that 'Diversity is not a weakness to be suppressed: it is a strength to be harnessed. If we try to force all European countries into the same mould, we shall end up cracking that mould.'[18]

Such reassurance, however, could not disguise the tension between the realities of Europe and the deep antagonism of the Tory sceptics. Nor could the soothing rhetoric of Douglas Hurd. With painstaking patience the foreign secretary would explain month by month that Britain could be at ease with Europe without sacrificing its nationhood. But, as the cement of unity in the party at Westminster dissolved, scepticism had begun to merge into Europhobia on the back benches. Norman Lamont, still burning with resentment and now a self-appointed leader of the sceptics, capitalized on the mood in a speech to the party conference at Bournemouth in October 1994. At a packed fringe meeting, the former chancellor broke the taboo of the previous thirty years by arguing that Britain might have to consider withdrawal from the Union. Lamont dismissed as 'wishful thinking' the prime minister's assertion that Britain's partners were unlikely to press ahead with the creation of a single currency. Nor was there a 'shred of evidence' that other European governments shared a view of the future of Europe similar to Major's. Britain, he added, 'is on a collision course with its partners unless we find a means of resolving the different aspirations'. The speech went too far for some in the audience, but not for all. 'Rather a good argument', was the comment offered the same evening by one of the sceptics in the cabinet.

The following month legislation came before the House of Commons to implement an agreement at the Edinburgh summit two years earlier to increase the resources available to the Union. The additional cost for Britain was relatively small, but for the sceptics the issue offered another opportunity to harass and harry the government. Expecting a prolonged and debilitating struggle, Major decided to make the vote an issue of confidence. The tactic had first been suggested by Douglas Hurd, who feared a repeat of the protracted anti-Maastricht campaign. The decision to launch a pre-emptive strike was then finalized at a Downing Street dinner attended by an inner circle of ministers comprising Hurd, Kenneth Clarke, Michael Heseltine, Malcolm Rifkind and Michael Howard. The so-called cabinet 'bastards' were informed only once the decision had been taken. Clarke, responsible as chancellor for the passage of the bill, then warned publicly that the entire cabinet would resign if the government were defeated. The result would be the dissolution of Parliament and a general election. With characteristic bluntness, Clarke remarked that 'If anything silly were to happen ... it would be the inevitable consequence of the defeat that the government would fall.'

For some of the sceptics, however, the threat of a general election had lost its potency. Major won the vote on 28 November with the support of the Ulster Unionists, but eight Tory MPs abstained. He had no choice but to suspend them. A ninth voluntarily resigned the party whip. The rebels, who included the voluble Teresa Gorman, the maverick Tony Marlow and the self-styled Powellite Nicholas Budgen, revelled in the publicity bestowed by their expulsion. Six months later it was clear they would not meet the 'good-behaviour' criteria which had been demanded for their readmittance. Facing another humiliating electoral defeat in the local elections in the spring of 1995, Major retreated and allowed the rebels to return uncon-ditionally. To one of his senior cabinet colleagues this was an act of 'abject surrender'. To others it was simply an act of political realism – Major's leadership was under siege, and the effect of the expulsions and of a relentless series of by-election defeats had been to rob the government of its parliamentary majority.

The prime minister would quickly rediscover that appeasement was not an escape route. During the House of Commons debate in which he had set out the terms of the cabinet truce on a single currency, he had also sketched the government's negotiating stance at the 1996 conference. The government would not cede any additional sovereignty to Brussels. It would uphold the British veto by blocking any extension of majority voting. Nor would there be any increase in the competence of the Brussels commission. Such prom-ises were no longer enough. The sceptics' agenda had moved on: they wanted not to hold the line but to win back ground already conceded. The Fresh Start Group, named after the MPs who had called for the abandonment of Maastricht after the Danish referendum, demanded wholesale 'renationalization' of many of the Union's common policies and strict limits on the competence of the European Court of Justice, which, responsible for interpreting European Union law, was increasingly seen by the sceptics as an instrument of Europe's federalists. The like-minded European Foundation and the European Research Group demanded withdrawal from the common agricultural and fisheries policies and the reassertion of Parliament's sovereignty over all European legislation. Together these groups claimed the tacit support of upwards of seventy Conservative MPs. They would now wield the veto in the government's dealings with Brussels.

John Major's decision in the summer of 1995 to flush out a challenge to his leadership was as inevitable as it seemed at the time extraordinary. He had been haunted since Black Wednesday by constant sniping from the right of his party. During the autumn of 1993 the plotting had provoked the extraordinary outburst which had wrecked his trip to Japan. A year later his enemies had come perilously close to raising the thirty-four signatures needed under the party rules to mount a formal leadership challenge. Their strategy was clear – to put up a candidate who would draw sufficient support and abstentions to fatally wound the prime minister and force an open contest. Norman Lamont appeared ever-willing to fill this 'stalking-horse' role.

The corrosive expectation on the Tory back benches and in the media that Major might not survive to fight the general election placed a permanent obstacle in the way of his efforts to restore his authority. His government had been battered on all sides. Multiplying charges of sleaze provoked a steady stream of ministerial resignations. A rebellion on the back benches had forced a humiliating defeat over VAT on domestic fuel. Plans to privatize the Post Office had had to be abandoned. The conclusions of the Nolan committee into standards in public life had incensed many Tory MPs by demanding tough new restrictions on their earnings outside Westminster and Major was blamed for establishing the committee. Lord Justice Scott was promising a damning report into the government's role in allowing arms sales to Iraq in the years before the 1990 Gulf War. The standing of the Conservatives and the prime minister in the opinion polls was at a record low. And, perhaps above all, the divide over Europe had robbed the Conservative Party of discipline and Major of respect. What meagre good news his government could offer was constantly undermined by renewed outbreaks of infighting over Europe.

The prime minister was by now trumpeting his government's defence of the national veto and ruling out further constitutional upheaval in the 1996 intergovernmental conference. But what he referred to as a new 'Eurorealism' was not enough for his critics. The notion of Britain's eventual withdrawal from all but the free-trade dimension of the European Union had gained respectability among a sizeable group on the right of his party. The minimum condition that the government rule out participation in a single currency for the lifetime of the next Parliament was accompanied by demands that the government withdraw from other commitments made at Maastricht. For all his disdain for the grand ambitions of Europe's federalists, Major could not accept the case for disengagement.

It was appropriate, therefore, that the catalyst for his decision to cauterize the wound was an ugly confrontation with the Eurosceptics at a meeting which had originally been intended as a bridge-building exercise. Michael Spicer, the chairman of the Fresh Start Group, had in previous months acted as mediator between the anti-federalists and Major's government. But at 4 p.m. on 13 June 1995 more than sixty MPs arrived in the House of Commons ministerial committee-room for what had been expected to be a much smaller gathering. A few weeks earlier the prime minister had been subject to another barrage of invective from his predecessor. The second volume of Margaret Thatcher's memoirs included a fierce attack on his economic and European policies. She claimed that she had assented to membership of the ERM only because she was isolated in cabinet. And she had never intended the exchange rate to be fixed as a precursor to the creation of a single currency. The tide of federalism in which her successor had been swept along at Maastricht would lead to a European superstate with 'its own flag, anthem, army, parliament, government, currency and, eventually one supposes, people'.[19]

The tone of Major's opening statement to his back-bench critics was conciliatory. He dwelt at length on why he thought the economic conditions for a successful single currency would not be met by the end of the century. He left his audience in no doubt that, even if a small group of other European countries went ahead before then, it was almost inconceivable that Britain would join them. A few days earlier he had said as much publicly in the House of Commons in response to the publication of the *Kingsdown Report*. Ennobled after his departure from the Bank, Robin Leigh-Pemberton had been asked by Kenneth Clarke to chair an independent inquiry into the economic implications of a single currency. The report produced by the now Lord Kingsdown under the auspices of the Action Centre for Europe (ACE) had warned of significant economic costs if Britain stood aside from the enterprise.[20] Lord Howe, now one of the most active figures on the pro-European wing of the party and a patron of ACE, had also inveighed against the government's drift towards the sceptics. But Major had told the House of Commons that, as far as a single currency was concerned, 'arguably the circumstances might not ever be right'.[21]

If the prime minister thought such remarks would assuage his audience at the Fresh Start meeting, he was swiftly disabused. A succession of MPs – among them Norman Lamont, John Townend and Sir George Gardiner – accused him of prevarication. The party and the country wanted a decisive lead. That meant rejecting now a single currency. They were scornful of Major's case that to prejudge the issue so far in advance would rob Britain of influence in every negotiation on the future shape of Europe. It was the tone as much as the content of the criticism which so damaged the prime minister. Instead of respect – the Conservatives had once understood deference – Major found himself treated with open contempt. He left the meeting burning with anger, telling Douglas Hurd that he was now certain of his opponents' strategy – they were determined to imprison him or to destroy him, and were not much concerned which it was.

He had briefly considered a pre-emptive move the previous summer. Now he began to see it as the only escape route. It was certain after this latest encounter that his enemies would find the requisite number of signatures to provoke a leadership challenge in the autumn. His analysis was shared by his enemies. Edward Leigh, the right-wing former minister who had orchestrated the attempt the previous autumn, was confident that Lamont would put himself forward. Within hours of the prime minister's humiliation by his critics, the House of Commons was full of speculation that he would be gone by November. Two days later, in an interview with the *Daily*

Express, Major indicated that he was perfectly prepared for an autumn challenge. But he was already planning to fight the contest on his own terms.

The idea solidified during his trip to the G7 world economic summit in Halifax, Nova Scotia, on the following weekend. A close ally explained his thinking thus. If, as seemed ever more likely, the infighting in the party ensured a massive defeat at the next election, he would be removed within a day of the election. The prime minister could readily accept that reality, but with one essential proviso – he had to be given at least a chance of winning. That chance would come only if he was seen to defeat his opponents. Returning from the summit, Major discussed the plan at length with Douglas Hurd. The foreign secretary endorsed the conclusion that the alternative to a 'sudden-death' contest on his own terms was another summer of damaging rumour and the real possibility of defeat in the autumn. The government had been lagging in the opinion polls by a record thirty points for the past year, but political recovery was impossible while its energies were absorbed in internal strife. Hurd advised that, if Major defeated his opponents now, there was a fair prospect that he could rebuild his leadership and the party's fortunes before the general election.

Hurd, it must be said, also had an ulterior motive. He had decided a year earlier to retire from the government after reaching his sixty-fifth birthday in March 1995. After nearly six years at the Foreign Office he had fulfilled his ambition. He appeared increasingly weary of the constant bridge-building at Westminster and fence-mending in Europe. He had other interests to pursue, including that of financial security for a relatively young family. Hurd was sensitive, however, to the fact that others might see his departure as confirmation that the government was beyond rescue, the fault-line over Europe beyond repair. That would further weaken Major – perhaps fatally. But to leave after the prime minister had fought and won a leadership contest would be logical, safe. It would also remove the pressure on Major to replace him at the Foreign Office with one of the cabinet's sceptics.

On his return from the summit to London at the start of the following week, Major consulted with several other close colleagues, including Ian Lang, Brian Mawhinney and Lord Cranborne. Some were alarmed at the risks, but the objections were outweighed by a broad consensus that to wait until the autumn would be still more dangerous. On Wednesday evening Major told a few others of his decision. The so-called 'bastards' – Michael Portillo, John Redwood and Peter Lilley – would not be informed, however, until just hours before the public announcement on the following afternoon. By then a large and well-resourced campaign team would have been established in a borrowed house in Cowley Street, a few hundred yards from the House of Commons.

Major's announcement came in theatrical if solemn style in the garden of 10 Downing Street at 5 p.m. on 22 June. Christopher Meyer, who had returned from his Foreign Office posting in Washington eighteen months earlier to replace Gus O'Donnell as Major's press secretary, had borrowed the horticultural affectation from longstanding practice at the White House. Major's earlier appearances among the roses had been calculated to promote good news. Now, with his wife, Norma, a few paces away, he explained to the assembled political journalists that he had decided to take a huge political gamble. The leadership speculation, he said, was destabilizing the government and damaging the Conservative Party. Declaring himself 'sick and tired' of the persistent rumours, Major said, 'I am not prepared to see the party I care for laid out like this on the rack any longer.' He was resigning the leadership in the full confidence of winning any subsequent contest, but 'should I be defeated, which I do not expect, I shall resign as prime minister and offer my successor my full support'. It was time for his opponents to 'put up or shut up'.[22] An hour before his press conference, Major had met with the executive of the back-bench 1922 Committee to secure their approval for the contest – and their assurance that the rules would be changed to prevent a subsequent challenge in the autumn. Theoretically there would be another chance for his enemies in 1996, but Major's calculation was that that would be too close to a general election to pose a serious threat.

Major's allies had fully expected the sceptics to pick up the gauntlet. They had also assumed that Lamont would be the candidate. For the next three days that indeed seemed the likely outcome. Edward Leigh, the former chancellor's self-appointed campaign manager, was ever-present on the television news bulletins to promote Lamont's potential candidacy. But, on Monday 26 June, John Redwood pre-empted

Lamont by resigning from the cabinet and announcing his own candidacy. The forty-four-year-old Welsh secretary, one of the original cabinet 'bastards' and a former head of the No. 10 policy unit for Margaret Thatcher, offered publicly the oddest of reasons for his challenge: Major had not consulted him about his resignation (he had been told only by Michael Howard) and he disagreed with the decision. Whatever his motivation, Redwood now offered himself as the Eurosceptic alternative. An intelligent if rather cold politician, he had long been resentful of the assumption that Michael Portillo was the natural heir to Thatcher. During the next week he would stake out his claim to her legacy.

Redwood's hastily drafted manifesto was a curious mix of the populist and the ideological. He promised deep, though apparently painless, reductions in public spending (£5bn could be deducted from Whitehall overheads) to pay for immediate tax cuts, a war against bureaucrats in the health service, tougher action against crime, and a plan to rescue the Royal Yacht *Britannia* from planned decommissioning. But at the heart of his challenge was a simple pledge: that under his leadership the Conservatives would rule out participation in a single European currency. The opening press conference of his campaign, on 26 June, set the tone: 'All the time I was prime minister I would not bring forward proposals to abolish the pound.'

That was a promise that the prime minister could not and would not match, but during the leadership campaign he went as far as he had ever gone in voicing his doubts about participation in a single currency. The Cannes summit of European Union leaders, which coincided with the campaign, had confirmed that there was no longer any prospect of economic and monetary union in 1997 – the first possible date under the timetable laid down at Maastricht. Even among the so-called 'central core' of countries – France, Germany, Austria and the Benelux countries – the economic convergence criteria in the treaty were proving exacting. In France, the newly elected Jacques Chirac had signalled that growth and employment would take precedence over the stability of the franc in the first years of his presidency. None would admit that the commitment to a single currency had weakened, however.

Major reflected that, if a small number of countries went ahead, Britain could well emerge as the leader of those nations outside monetary union: 'Once the decision has been made, if we do have a two-core Europe – an inner core and an outer core – I think the small nations in the outer core will probably look to some of the bigger nations and we might well be that nation,' Major remarked.[23] This olive-branch to the sceptics was accompanied, however, by an unshakeable defence of his decision to keep open the government's options. To close the door prematurely, he told MPs, would be to 'forfeit our influence over the most crucial current issue affecting Europe's future'.[24] During an exchange with William Cash, one of his most persistent critics among the anti-federalists, his frustration boiled over. Cash, he exploded, was talking 'claptrap'. Major knew that to have conceded further ground would have been to lose the support of his allies on the centre-left of the party – most notably Heseltine and Clarke. His premiership now depended on their support in the ballot. He could survive, probably, if the sceptics voted against him. He could not go on if Heseltine's supporters chose to abstain.

The outcome was uncertain until the moment the votes were counted. There was no doubt that Major would secure a technical victory, even under the complicated rules which demanded that he receive more than a simple majority of the votes cast. The question mark lay over whether enough might support Redwood or abstain to fatally undermine his authority. Heseltine and Clarke offered strong public and private support throughout the ten days of campaigning, but some of their supporters had long been frustrated by Major's appeasement of the sceptics. Others saw Heseltine's self-confidence and natural political authority as making him the only leader capable of rebuilding the government's fortunes. This would be his last chance to win the keys to 10 Downing Street. Michael Portillo meanwhile found himself badly outflanked by Redwood's challenge. From within the cabinet Portillo could do nothing but give his public if grudging backing to the prime minister. But his views on a single currency, on rolling back the powers of Brussels and on reinventing the Conservatives as the party of the Union flag were indistinguishable from those of Redwood. Portillo's own doubts that Major would survive were clumsily exposed by the decision of his aides to prepare for his candidacy in a second round of voting: additional telephone lines were installed in a putative campaign headquarters near Westminster. Portillo meanwhile told political journalists at the BBC that he might well be prime minister within a matter of weeks.

Major himself was also unsure whether he would survive. He had fought a gritty and determined campaign, but on the Monday evening before the poll his advisers found him beset by anxiety. If his support fell below 200 votes, there would be an instant clamour for his resignation. But even if he surmounted that hurdle, he could not be certain his position was secure. His campaign team knew that at least 100 MPs would either vote for Redwood or abstain. That left the prime minister with between 200 and 230. If his support was at the bottom end of that range, his position would be in peril. For much of the final twenty-four hours, his campaign team worried that Major might well have fixed in his own mind a threshold of support below which he would quit. Preparations were made to persuade him to stay.

In the event, when the votes were counted at 5 p.m. on 4 July, Major had secured 218 against Redwood's 89. A further 20 MPs abstained. A third of the party had withdrawn their support from the prime minister, but adroit presentation by his campaign team and his own expressed determination to stay allowed him to claim a decisive victory. Within twenty-four hours he had underpinned that authority with a decisive reshuffle of his cabinet.

Major had triumphed because the vast majority of Michael Heseltine's supporters chose in the end to vote for him rather than to abstain. Heseltine would have contested (and probably won) the leadership had the prime minister fallen, but he decided from the outset of the campaign that he would not play any part in promoting that outcome. Heseltine knew that, after his role in Thatcher's downfall, he could not be seen to be anything but completely loyal to her successor. He also doubted whether there would be anything worthwhile left to inherit if Major was defeated. The enforced removal of two leaders within five years would have left the party ungovernable, he told friends.

His reward came in the reshuffle. In a reconstruction of the government which once again defined Major as a politician of the centre, Heseltine was appointed deputy prime minister and first secretary of state. The titles had last been held at the same time by

Rab Butler more than thirty years earlier, and now gave Heseltine the most important role in Major's new cabinet. Hurd, as he had hoped, was replaced at the Foreign Office by Malcolm Rifkind. Clarke remained at the Treasury, and Ian Lang and Brian Mawhinney were promoted respectively to the Department of Trade and Industry and the party chairmanship. Despite his indiscretion during the leadership campaign, Portillo was given notional promotion to the Defence department. But overall the reshuffle provided Major with a cabinet of friends rather than enemies. If his own attitude towards Europe had been hardened by experience, he filled the most important posts in his government with colleagues who preferred engagement to retreat. It was a temporary respite.

CHAPTER THIRTEEN

ALONE

JOHN MAJOR DID not capitalize on his victory. In the choice of his cabinet the prime minister had asserted his political authority. But within weeks the party manager in him resurfaced. His ministerial reshuffle had seemed to suggest that the prime minister now understood that appeasement and authority were mutually exclusive. This had been the point pressed upon him by the departing Douglas Hurd and by Richard Ryder, who had chosen to stand down as chief whip. Free to speak their minds, they told Major it was time to abandon the shifting sands of compromise and concession. He must be his own leader, a strategist rather than a tactician. Instead, he again sought friends among the enemies he had so recently vanquished and the opportunity for strong leadership was lost. A single currency, the issue which more than any other defined the European fault-line in the Conservative party, loomed menacingly.

By the time of the Conservatives' Blackpool conference in October 1995, the Eurosceptics had regained their confidence. John Redwood, who in defeat a few months earlier had pledged loyalty to Major, took to the fringe with the message he had offered in the leadership contest. Europe threatened to stifle Britain's sovereignty. Participation in a single European currency would rob the nation of its prosperity as well as its freedom. Redwood's ambitions had not been stilled – he would fight from the back benches to keep alive his candidature for the leadership. The scepticism spilled over into the conference proper where Michael Portillo, newly-installed as defence secretary, delivered an extraordinary tirade against Brussels. Conjuring up the illusory threat of a British army sent to war by European bureaucrats, Portillo declared that 'The European Court would probably want to stop our men fighting for more than forty hours a week. They would send half of them home on paternity leave.' With less than mature judgement, he then appropriated to his anti-Brussels cause the motto of the army's elite SAS, Who Dares Wins.[1] The

prime minister's reaction displayed his weakness: he had read the
speech in advance and not sought changes. There would be no
reprimand. Instead Major told cabinet colleagues that the jibes had
been made in a spirit of fun. The intention was to titillate the
conference representatives not to rewrite government policy. Others
were not so forgiving of the defence secretary. His speech had
shattered the post-leadership unity on Europe which had been
imposed in the summer. One of the cabinet ministers most prominent
in Major's leadership team declared that it had been a demeaning
event. He wondered why the prime minister had not sacked Portillo
when he had had the chance during the summer. The defence
secretary himself came to realize that his words had been badly
misjudged, not least because the chiefs of staff of the armed forces
made no secret of their disdain. There would be other mistakes over
the following few months, but Portillo was to appreciate that his
claim to lead the right of the party would be better made in a more
demonstrably loyal approach.

The mood at the Blackpool conference confirmed a perceptible
shift in the political centre of gravity within the government. The
newly-elected French president Jacques Chirac for a time offered the
hope of a new Anglo-French *rapprochement* which would slow the
drive towards greater European integration. Britain stood almost
alone in backing a resumption of French nuclear testing in the South
Pacific. Major was still hopeful that the single currency project might
yet founder. At a summit of European leaders in Majorca in late
September, he predicted that only a handful of nations would meet
the tough economic conditions necessary to participate from January
1999. Seeking to exploit a public rift between Bonn and Rome about
Italy's hopes of meeting the deadline, he declared that 'a large number
of countries are simply not going to be economically ready to move
forward'. Other European leaders were unmoved. And the mercurial
Chirac would soon disappoint Major by reconfirming the primacy in
French foreign policy of the Paris–Bonn axis. Euroscepticism, the
French leader remarked at the end of October, was a passing 'fad'.
Such comments served to reinforce the prime minister's increasing
detachment from the ambitions of his European partners. It was the
same elsewhere in Whitehall. Malcolm Rifkind had been Hurd's
choice as his successor, but the new foreign secretary was quick to

strike a more sceptical note than his predecessor. In his first significant speech as foreign secretary, he evoked Lord Palmerston's famous dictum that the only object of foreign policy was the furtherance of Britain's national self-interest. Rifkind declared that henceforth every proposal for further European integration would be tested against this rule. The pursuit of influence would no longer be sufficient cause for Britain to assent to the pooling of sovereignty in the EU.[2] In reality, the distinction between self-interest and influence was beguiling but false. The latter had always been sought as a means of securing the former. Many of Rifkind's officials were privately scornful of the speech. So were most pro-European Tories. But it went down well on the Tory back benches and, for a brief moment, seemed to offer grounds for another truce.

The foreign secretary made no secret also of his grave doubts about participation in a single currency. He was certain that a re-elected Conservative government would not give up sterling during the lifetime of the next parliament. This, after all, was now the majority view in the cabinet. Rifkind found some unlikely allies. Stephen Dorrell, the health secretary, for some time had been seen as among the most promising leadership candidates of the centre-left from the younger generation of cabinet ministers. He had been close to both Kenneth Clarke and Douglas Hurd, sharing their affinity to One-Nation politics at home and engagement with Europe abroad. By the autumn of 1995, however, Dorrell was moving with the tide in his party. To Clarke's annoyance, he floated the suggestion among colleagues that there was nothing to be lost by ruling out participation in a single currency during the next parliament. His judged the replacement of sterling would not win the support of the cabinet, the party or the people. The national mood was running against Europe. Why not capitalize on it?

It was an analysis which dismayed the chancellor. He understood that if the Conservatives fought one election on a platform of preserving the pound, then it would become virtually impossible subsequently to argue the case for a single currency. The shift to an anti-EMU stance would be seen as one of principle. Clarke suspected Dorrell's motives had more to do with his ambitions for the leadership than with cool analysis. But he was facing growing isolation. Rifkind acknowledged that the chancellor would not be forced into abandoning the each-way bet on EMU negotiated by Major at Maastricht. The foreign secretary told friends that, in spite of his own inclination, the issue was not worth a cabinet confrontation. Others thought differently. Michael Howard and Peter Lilley made no secret of their antipathy towards a single currency. And, with Hurd gone, the chancellor was alone in the sights of the ever more vociferous sceptics on the back benches. In cabinet, he could count on the support of Michael Heseltine. This was a formidable alliance, but Heseltine's new role as Major's deputy acted as a powerful constraint on his public pronouncements. He had lost the freedom which comes with running a Whitehall department – in public at least, a deputy must be his master's voice. Others shared the view that the government might as well make a virtue of necessity by ruling out entry into EMU. As one of his senior officials remarked ruefully, the chancellor sometimes seemed more at home with other finance ministers in Brussels than with cabinet colleagues.

That was to exaggerate the extent of the rift. But only slightly. At the Madrid summit of European Union leaders in mid-December 1995, Major and Clarke did not hide their differences. The prime minister seemed unable to recognize the determination of France and Germany to meet the January 1999 deadline for economic and monetary union – even when he was obliged to endorse the decision of the other leaders at last to give a name to the new currency. He believed that France, in the grip of a wave of industrial and popular unrest caused by the government's fiscal austerity programme, would not meet the economic convergence criteria set out in the Maastricht Treaty. In particular, the Paris government would be unable to reduce its budget deficit to less than three per cent of national income. Major told the summit there would be 'chaos right across the community' if governments rushed into monetary union. Clarke, however, recognized the political will which others had invested in the uninspiringly named 'euro'. To the obvious dismay of the prime minister's entourage he declared that the odds were now stacked 60:40 in favour of the project going ahead more or less on time: 'I believe that the strongest northern European states are likely to go ahead . . . pretty well on the present timetable.' The summit leaders confirmed this assessment by endorsing a detailed schedule of preparatory work to ensure the 1999 target date was met. Governments would decide in spring 1998 which countries had met the criteria for participation. EMU would begin on 1 January 1999 with the irrevocable locking of exchange rates and the transfer of interest rate policy to the new European central bank. Governments would begin from that date to issue public debt in the new euro. By 2002 at the latest, national currencies would be replaced by euro notes and coins in those countries which had qualified for inclusion. Major did win from his fellow European leaders an agreement that they would study the impact of EMU on the stability and coherence of the Union and, in particular, the likely relationship between those currencies inside and outside the euro zone. He heralded it as a British triumph but it was no real concession on their part. Within months they would decide that those countries outside the new currency bloc would be expected, though not obliged, to join a remodelled exchange rate mechanism.

The prime minister returned to London to further misery. Reporting to MPs on the summit, he gave a broad hint that if the single currency did go ahead, sterling's participation would be contingent on a referendum. He refused to rule out the option of joining a single currency because, he said, Britain's voice had to be heard in the negotiations on EMU. Whatever its eventual decision, the country would be affected by the arrangements agreed by others. But, urged by Douglas Hurd to keep open the possibility, Major replied: 'For a decision of such magnitude we shall certainly keep in mind the possibility of a referendum if the cabinet were to recommend entry.'[3] Such assurances, however, were not enough to placate the Eurosceptics. A row over the impact of Europe's common fisheries policy on hard-pressed British trawlers saw some of the sceptics join with the opposition parties to inflict a defeat on the government at Westminster. They would be satisfied only with a firm commitment to stay out of EMU. Even without such rebellions, the parliamentary arithmetic had begun to look increasingly precarious. By-election defeats, which had become an awkward fact of life in the preceding few years, were followed by defections. In the autumn of 1995 Alan Howarth crossed the floor of the House of Commons to join Tony Blair's New Labour. His defection was followed a few months later by the departure of Emma Nicolson to the Liberal Democrats. Major had started the parliament with a majority of twenty-one. By the second week of

January 1996 it had fallen to three. Labour meanwhile held a lead of more than twenty points in the opinion polls.

Further problems came in February with the publication of the long-awaited Scott report into the sale of arms to Iraq under Margaret Thatcher's administration. This report would set out in documented detail the extent to which ministers and officials had misled parliament about Britain's willingness to sell military equipment to Saddam Hussein during the late 1980s. Some thought its publication might prove the trigger for the collapse of the government. The careers of at least two members of the cabinet, William Waldegrave and Nicholas Lyell, were at stake. In the week before its publication the prime minister and his senior colleagues decided their response would have a single objective: to prevent the report from forcing any resignations. To that end an elaborate defence was prepared to justify the actions of ministers and civil servants. Robin Butler, the cabinet secretary, had already sought during the inquiry to limit the flow of embarrassing documents to Lord Justice Scott. Now, to the dismay of other senior civil servants, he co-ordinated from the cabinet office a sophisticated effort to put a misleading gloss on Scott's conclusions. The opposition parties were denied access to the report for a week after its arrival in Whitehall. When it was finally published, the accompanying cabinet office press release began with the assertion: 'Sir Richard Scott's report completely exonerates all ministers and civil servants from any sort of conspiracy or cover up in relation to the sale of arms to Iraq.'[4] The statement was technically true but it grossly misrepresented the catalogue of criticisms made of both ministers and officials in the 1,800-page report. As one cabinet minister admitted a few days later, the government had been 'economical with the truth'. But Sir Robin had served his ministerial masters well. Despite a withering attack from Robin Cook, the Labour foreign affairs spokesman, the government won a critical House of Commons division by a single vote. There were no enforced resignations. Minds turned again to Europe and to the fate of the pound.

When the cabinet convened on Thursday 7 March, the formal business before ministers was the approval of a government White

Paper on the Intergovernmental Conference on institutional reform in the EU due to begin the following Easter. Preliminary discussions had already begun with Britain's European partners on the so-called Maastricht II treaty. John Major had made it plain that he would resist most of the demands from other capitals for an extension of the Union's reach into national affairs. The objective of the White Paper, pressed by the foreign secretary Malcolm Rifkind, was to restore a semblance of unity to the Tory back benches by uniting the party around this minimalist stance. In this, the government was anyway over-optimistic. A year or two earlier the ambition of most of the Eurosceptics had been to halt any further integration. But, encouraged by their growing numbers and by the paralysis they had brought to John Major's government, they had ratcheted up their demands. Disputes with Spain over the common fisheries policy and anger at judgements of the European Court had fuelled calls for the government to roll back many of the measures agreed at Maastricht. From some, it brought a more fundamental challenge to the foundations of British participation in Europe. By the spring of 1996, Norman Lamont's suggestion at the 1994 party Conference that Britain might be obliged eventually to withdraw from the Union found an echo in the corridors of power as well as on the Tory back benches at Westminster.

The details of the White Paper, however, had been hammered out without particularly controversy on the cabinet sub-committee for European Affairs, OPD(E). Clarke saw little purpose in publishing such a document and had once or twice tried to block it. But Rifkind was insistent, and there was no serious dispute about the broad thrust. This said that there must be no erosion of the 'three-pillared' structure of the Union established at Maastricht, which kept justice and foreign affairs outside the competence of the supranational institutions. Britain would oppose any extension of majority voting and any significant enhancement in the powers of the European Parliament. It would seek a limit on retroactive judgements of the European Court of Justice and reform of the Common Fisheries Policy. In short, the new treaty would involve only minor tinkering with the existing Maastricht arrangements. Ministers knew that Britain's partners would not accept such an agenda. But they were confident also that the negotiations would not end before the general election due at the latest in May 1997. A hard-line negotiating stance could open up 'clear blue water' between the Conservatives and Labour. In this view, the government could wrap itself in the Union flag as the defender of the British 'veto' in Brussels. The Labour party would be cast as federalists ready to cede control over the nation's destiny to Brussels. Ministers assumed that the voters would side with the government.

There was nothing of substance, however, in the document about plans for a single currency, the issue which aroused most wrath among the Eurosceptics. Even before the cabinet met, voices had been raised in favour of adding to the White Paper a section on EMU. Stephen Dorrell, who had modified somewhat his antagonism after discussions with Kenneth Clarke, backed the promise of a referendum on the issue. If a Conservative government ever contemplated scrapping sterling (unlikely he thought), such a fundamental constitutional change would demand public assent in a plebiscite. There was nothing to lose and much to gain in making that clear well before the election. Others in the middle ranks of the cabinet, like Gillian Shephard and Tony Newton, took a similar view. More sceptical colleagues like Michael Howard, William Hague and Michael Forsythe had long seen the promise of a referendum as inevitable, even if they would have preferred to close the door permanently on the option of abolishing the pound. Rifkind was sympathetic, though still anxious not to provoke renewed turmoil in the cabinet.

During the weeks that preceded the 7 March meeting such ministers made no secret of their views. They found strong echoes from Conservative Central Office and the party chairman Brian Mawhinney. A referendum was also the minimum demand of the increasingly hostile editorials found in the columns of *The Times*, the *Telegraph*, the *Sun* and the *Daily Mail*. The view among the central office strategists preparing for the general election campaign was that such traditional Tory newspapers had to be won back to the cause. The promise of a referendum on EMU would be a useful start. Further impetus came from Sir James Goldsmith's plans to use his formidable political wealth to bankroll a new political party at the general election. Sir James, an Anglo-French financier who was dividing his time between his Mexican estate and the European parliament in Strasbourg where he sat as a French MEP, threatened that his newly-created Referendum Party would field more than 600 candidates at the general election. Its sole objective was to force a plebiscite on Britain's future in Europe. Its candidates would oppose all those MPs, regardless of party, who failed to support its cause. Goldsmith himself would stand against David Mellor in Putney. The steadier politicians in the cabinet dismissed this venture as no more than the latest in a long line of eccentric twists in Sir James's career. They held that his flamboyant tirades against an alleged plot to subvert Britain's independence would gain no credibility beyond the crackpot fringe. Goldsmith had money but no track record. He was also fiercely protectionist. Others had less steady nerves – young researchers in Conservative Central Office calculated that the Referendum Party could draw support mainly from former Conservative voters. Even if he received only a small number of votes, his campaign might put at risk twenty or more Tory MPs in marginal constituencies. His profile was given a further boost by well-publicized attempts by John Redwood to mediate with Sir James. Redwood, still exploiting the freedom of the back benches to stake his claim to the candidacy of the Eurosceptic right in the next contest for the party leadership, saw an opportunity to promote his own demand for a far more aggressive line towards Brussels. Brian Mawhinney told Major that by offering its own referendum, the government could outflank both the Referendum Party and Labour. Sir James, whose immense wealth obscured the absurd contradictions in his party's demands, wanted a more far-reaching test of public opinion on Britain's future in Europe. Blair had been equivocal about the possibility of a referendum on the single currency, but there was a risk Labour might steal a march by stepping in first with such a pledge.

Kenneth Clarke had dropped his guard. There had been widespread speculation in the press and in Whitehall for some weeks that Major would force the issue. In conversations with colleagues, the prime minister made no secret of his own desire for a referendum. Mawhinney told him that local Conservative activists were overwhelmingly opposed to a single currency, but their loyalty could be secured with the offer of a plebiscite. Clarke ignored the signs. He had forestalled the same proposal when Douglas Hurd had promoted it in the winter of 1994/95. He was convinced he could do so again. Clarke argued that Major's public hints on the issue could be interpreted as triggering the referendum option only if and when the government finally arrived at a decision to join. That moment was several years off. Just weeks before the cabinet discussion, the chancellor had made his position clear in private conversations. He could not accept that a referendum was the right way to make such a decision on the single currency. 'I am not going to campaign during the election on that basis. They can stick that,' he was heard remarking. Here was a consistent politician. He had always opposed plebiscites as dangerous politically and subversive of the constitution. They were dangerous because the outcome might be determined not by the electorate's considered judgement on the specific question but by its broader view of the government. A popular government might get anything through. But if the vote happened to fall during an economic downturn, then it could be treated as a glorified opinion poll on the government's overall performance. Those who brushed aside such risks had only to look at President Mitterrand's narrow escape during the French referendum on the Maastricht treaty.

Clarke's view was that a decision to enter a single currency could only be made on the basis of a free vote in the House of Commons. That was how Edward Heath had secured Britain's entry into Europe in 1971. Referendums were also a threat to the constitutional position of parliament. The British system of government had been built on the sovereignty of Westminster. It was absurd that the sceptics, who pretended to be the defenders of that sovereignty, were prepared to undercut it. It was also wrong to announce that a decision as important as that on the single currency would be taken in the wrong way simply to secure a short-term political advantage. In any event, the sceptics would not be satisfied by the offer of a referendum. Once the cabinet had conceded on that point, the opponents of a single currency would immediately step up the pressure on the prime minister to rule out the option for the lifetime of the next parliament. The chancellor had made all these points to Major. He was sure the prime minister would not push it to a vote. Clarke had Michael Heseltine on his side. Other pro-Europeans, like John Gummer, Sir

Patrick Mayhew and George Young, could also be relied on. 'That makes a pretty good start,' he remarked. And the prime minister could not afford to lose another chancellor.

He had miscalculated. Badly. During the cabinet meeting of 7 March, the issue of a single currency was raised by Douglas Hogg, one of the most junior around the table. If the government was setting out in such detail its stance on future European integration could it really ignore the issue of a single currency, Hogg asked rhetorically. The issue had not been on the agenda and Clarke moved to forestall a debate. Major thought otherwise and encouraged contributions from around the table. Within a matter of minutes, the chancellor was on the defensive. His reaction was furious. Hogg's manner and Major's encouragement convinced several of those present that the agriculture minister's intervention had not been coincidental. He had entered the cabinet only the previous summer. And he was spouse to Sarah Hogg. She had left the No. 10 policy unit but remained a close confidant of Major. So Clarke's assumption that he had been deliberately ambushed at the prime minister's bidding was widely shared.

The chancellor could not disguise his fury. Sitting just a few feet away, one fellow minister was stunned: 'I thought he was going to have a heart attack – or he was going to hit someone.' EMU fell within the Treasury's responsibility. It was not for his colleagues to determine policy. Clarke rehearsed the arguments against. A referendum would be a vehicle for protest votes. There was nothing to be gained by offering such a hostage to fortune. He was badly outnumbered. One of those who spoke in favour of the referendum later voiced considerable sympathy for Clarke. 'He absolutely exploded,' this minister said. 'It was clear that he thought he had been ambushed. And I am sure that Hogg was put up to it.' The chancellor also tore into his colleagues for leaking to the press his contributions to cabinet discussions. He suspected Brian Mawhinney and Peter Lilley were among those briefing against him.

Heseltine spoke out in support of Clarke, arguing that EMU was an issue that should be decided in parliament. Referendums did not fit in a representative democracy. The prime minister, however, summed up the discussion as strongly in favour of, at the very least, a thorough review. Malcolm Rifkind was charged with the task of examining the pros and cons. A paper was to be prepared. No one reminded Major how vehemently he had opposed the popular vote on the Maastricht treaty which had been demanded by Margaret Thatcher. He had then quoted Thatcher's own claim during the 1970s that referendums were the device of demagogues and dictators. The mood did not improve when the discussion moved on to 'the line' ministers should take when subsequently asked about the review. Gillian Shephard, the education secretary, was heard to remark pointedly that perhaps the cabinet should agree a line for those ministers who would immediately be asked whether they intended to resign. She disagreed with Clarke, but sympathized with his predicament.

Technically, no firm decision had been taken. The cabinet was to look at the options. But Major knew the outcome he wanted. He left no doubt when he appeared in the House of Commons a few hours later. The Conservative whips had 'planted' a question with Sir Marcus Fox, the chairman of the back-bench 1922 committee. Mr Major's response was well prepared: 'I have made clear to the House on previous occasions that I believe that a referendum on a single currency could be a necessary step. My position has not changed. I still believe that it might be the right course. At present, the government are considering the circumstances in which a referendum might or might not be appropriate. We shall tell the House of our conclusions as soon as we have reached them.'[5] The implication was clear. He wanted a referendum. So did the majority of the cabinet. Kenneth Clarke could not reasonably stand in the way.

News of the cabinet confrontation spread quickly through the Treasury, and Clarke's officials were deeply concerned he might resign. He did nothing to dispel similar fears among his political allies. The chancellor's anger was reinforced by his assessment of Major's motive. When Douglas Hurd had first floated the referendum proposition, Clarke had been opposed but willing to listen. The then foreign secretary had argued that, whatever the general suspicion of plebiscites, the single currency decision was special. It did carry major constitutional implications. And British participation could be made to work only if it commanded the support of the electorate. Clarke disagreed, but respected Hurd's as a principled position. The same could not be said of the prime minister. Time and time again the chancellor had seen Major give ground to the sceptics, only to whet their appetite for more. He saw the offer of a referendum as a further step in the same direction, a decision based not on the requirements of good government but on that of party management.

By the middle of the following week, Clarke's anger had become public knowledge. One of his closest aides confirmed that he was contemplating resignation. The chancellor put out a brief statement denying that he had authorized anyone to speak on his behalf. But he did not deny the substance. When the issue was discussed within the Treasury, he did little to dispel the speculation. He knew that the sceptics would insist next that Major fight the general election as the guardian of sterling. Clarke wanted to draw a line in the sand. But, in quieter moments, he realized also that this was not the ideal issue on which to make his stand. Many in the pro-European wing of his party had doubts about EMU. Like him, they were certain that the government should keep the option to join firmly open. But Hurd was not alone in believing that actual participation would indeed require the direct consent of the electorate.

The chancellor had time to cool down. Fortuitously, on 15 March he left London for a long-planned trip to South Africa and Zimbabwe. His officials at the Treasury thought that the trip probably saved him from resignation. Leon Brittan, now a member of the Brussels Commission and an old friend of the chancellor from his Cambridge days, took the lead in persuading him to stay. Brittan saw in Clarke the most important bulwark against the sceptics. Though he still deeply resented the prime minister's tactics, the chancellor decided he was ready to strike a deal. When the referendum idea had first been mooted in 1994, Clarke had formed a curious alliance. Michael Portillo had opposed the plan as firmly as the chancellor, though for entirely different reasons. Shrewder than most sceptics, Portillo knew that to suggest a referendum was to admit that a Conservative cabinet might indeed contemplate sterling's demise. He did not want Major to admit that possibility. During this second round of discussions, however, the defence secretary realized that the referendum argument was lost. He dropped his objections, further isolating the chancellor.

The issue was resolved on Wednesday 3 April, more than three weeks after the first cabinet discussion. Clarke spent much of the previous day in meetings with Major to hammer out the precise terms, based on a draft prepared by Malcolm Rifkind. Michael Heseltine joined the prime minister and chancellor for the negotiations. Heseltine was still against a referendum. Contrary to the press reports at the time, he did not act as a disinterested broker between Major and Clarke. But he was in a uniquely difficult position. As Major's deputy, Heseltine's first loyalty was to the prime minister. In this respect, he realized that his exalted title carried with it a clear constraint on his freedom of action.

Clarke was determined that the poll offer should apply only during the next parliament, reflecting the special uncertainty which would surround the prospects for EMU at the time of the 1997 general election. He wanted to keep alive the possibility that the Conservatives could fight the subsequent election on a platform in favour of EMU. In those circumstances, there would be no need for a plebiscite. Most importantly, Clarke extracted a solemn pledge from the prime minister that, on this issue at least, no further ground would be given to the sceptics. Major would retain the two-way option agreed at Maastricht through the 1997 election campaign.

A special 45-minute discussion in the cabinet endorsed this deal on the following morning, setting out the position in an agreed statement.

> The cabinet met in political session this morning. We noted that, at the time of the General Election, no one will know for certain whether a single currency may go ahead at all in the next parliament. Furthermore, even if it does, no one will know which countries will be eligible to participate in it or what the circumstances might be at the time.
>
> Britain has an option, negotiated at Maastricht, of deciding whether or not to join a single currency even if others go ahead. Because we will be keeping that option open at the next General Election, we have decided to make a commitment in our Manifesto that, if the government decided to join a single currency during the course of the next parliament, that decision would be subject to confirmation in a referendum.
>
> Cabinet would make the decision whether or not to join. If they decided it was in Britain's national interest to do so, they would prepare legislation to this effect and present it to Parliament. This legislation would include a clause providing that it would not come into effect until confirmed in a referendum.

This would be government legislation, and normal collective responsibility would apply. The referendum would be held as soon as possible after passage of the legislation, and a simple majority of those voting would be taken as confirmation of Parliament's decision.

The wording of the referendum would be a simple, neutral question on the lines 'Should the UK take part in a single European currency as from (the appropriate date)?'

The commitment only applies to the next Parliament. A decision on what if any action would be taken in the Parliament after that would be made before another General Election[6]

Appearing at a press conference at Conservative Central office with Brian Mawhinney and Malcolm Rifkind, Clarke sought to make the best of the deal. Facing sharp questioning from reporters, he declined to deny that he had considered resignation. Nor would he personally endorse the idea of a referendum, telling journalists that 'I have not changed my well-known views.' But the chancellor stressed that the government's pledge had been carefully constructed around a number of common-sense parameters. A poll would take place only after a recommendation from the cabinet that sterling should be part of a single currency. Once the cabinet had decided in favour, all its members would be bound to support that view under the doctrine of collective responsibility. And the referendum would be held only after the cabinet's decision had been endorsed by parliament. Above all, Clarke stressed repeatedly that the two-way bet on EMU now had the unequivocal backing of the cabinet. Rifkind nodded his assent, remarking that there was 'no possibility' other than that the government would preserve the option through the general election: 'The government made clear quite some considerable time ago that we are not going to rule out the possibility of joining a single currency in the next parliament.'

John Major's hopes that the referendum deal would bring peace to his party were quickly dashed by another row with Europe. This time it was mad cows. A week earlier his government had been obliged to admit that the latest scientific evidence pointed to a link between the spread of BSE in the nation's beef herds and several new cases of the fatal Creutzfeldt-Jakob brain disease in humans. Stephen Dorrell at health and Douglas Hogg at agriculture had badly underestimated the public reaction to the announcement. They assured consumers that measures taken to eradicate BSE over the previous six years meant that beef currently on sale was safe. Few believed them. Consumption plummeted within a matter of days. Schools and restaurants banned the sale of British beef. So too did the European Commission, getting the agreement of EU agriculture ministers to ban exports not only to the rest of the Union but also worldwide. The ban extended to beef by-products like gelatin and tallow as well as to the meat. Led by Bonn, several other European governments insisted that it would not be lifted until BSE had been eradicated. The industry was plunged into chaos, the Conservative party into fury. BSE was a British phenomenon, a dismal legacy of the government's failure during the 1980s to impose sufficiently stringent safety requirements on farmers. Several other countries had long before banned imports of British beef. As one member of the cabinet admitted during a private discussion of the crisis: 'It is no use treating Europe as an alibi for our own failures. BSE is not a European issue. It is a British problem. Our partners have responded as independent nation states. And their consumers as consumers. The problem must be dealt with here. The US banned our beef years ago.'

But such was the mood in Major's party that it needed a scapegoat. The Brussels Commission, fearful of the impact of the collapse of consumer confidence on beef sales across the continent, wanted a staged lifting of the export restrictions in tandem with a British programme to eradicate BSE. But it found itself vilified in the House of Commons by the Tory Eurosceptics. Faced with a bill running into hundreds of millions of pounds to pay for the slaughter of much of the nation's cattle herd, cabinet ministers also looked to put the blame elsewhere. Michael Forsyth, the Scottish Secretary, refused to fly the European flag on Scotland's public buildings to mark Europe day. In spite of his pro-European instincts, Michael Heseltine was among the first to suggest that the government might threaten retaliation against its continental neighbours. He soon thought better of the idea, but by then it had been taken up by the prime minister and several other colleagues. The breaking-point came in May. The cabinet had endorsed in principle a few days earlier the idea of retaliation if a meeting of European veterinary experts in Brussels on

20 May did not agree to scrap the export ban on beef by-products. But the decision by the national experts to maintain the prohibition on overseas sales of tallow, gelatin and bull's semen came as a surprise. In discussions with Helmut Kohl and other European leaders, Major thought he had won their acquiescence for a partial easing of the ban. When that proved misguided, the prime minister reacted furiously to what he saw as a deliberate breach of trust. On Tuesday 21 May, he determined to retaliate. After hurried consultations with Rifkind and a lengthy meeting to 'square' a reluctant Clarke, Major announced in the House of Commons that Britain would adopt a policy of non-cooperation with its European partners. It would obstruct all legislation requiring unanimity in the Council of Ministers until other governments agreed a framework for the progressive dismantling of the export ban. In effect, European decision-making would be paralysed until the beef issue was addressed to Britain's satisfaction.

Major's announcement marked the gravest crisis in Britain's relations with its partners since it had joined in 1973. Several cabinet ministers were appalled at his precipitate action. The pro-European John Gummer learned of the move only when he was telephoned by Clarke a few hours before the announcement. It was a bad decision, taken in anger. According to Major's officials, it was also taken without any clear 'exit strategy'. It was designed to slake the thirst of the xenophobes on the Tory back benches rather than lead to a solution of the beef dispute. Everyone in Whitehall, these officials remarked, knew that there was no prospect that other European nations would buy British beef. The Foreign Office was appalled. It had fought off earlier proposals from 10 Downing Street that the government should adopt an 'empty chair' strategy, comparable to that of France's General De Gaulle in the mid-1960s. Now Rifkind's officials felt obliged to answer telephone calls from their European counterparts with the greeting 'How can I *not* help you.' Some blamed Norman Blackwell, who had replaced Sarah Hogg as the head of the No. 10 policy unit, for encouraging Major to fight a battle he could not win. Others said the prime minister had once again lost sight of strategy in his desire to win tactical points. Yet some Tory MPs appeared so distanced from reality as to believe, at least initially, that a 'beef war' could provide the platform for a snap general election

victory. Tony Blair was among those who failed to grasp the absurdity
of this proposition. Labour refused to condemn the confrontation.
Paddy Ashdown, the Liberal Democrat leader, alone among opposition leaders, was prepared to make the distinction between posturing
and pursuit of the national interest.

A month later, at the Florence summit on 21 June, the prime
minister was forced to stage the inevitable retreat. After a month of
deepening embarrassment in Brussels which saw British officials and
ministers block scores of decisions unrelated to the beef crisis – some
of them initiatives Britain had long favoured – Major was offered a
fig-leaf by his European partners. A programme would be put in place
for the progressive lifting of the ban, subject to European scrutiny of
the massive cattle slaughtering programme introduced by the government to eradicate BSE. Major claimed the deal would lead to the
complete removal of the restrictions by November. Other governments openly ridiculed that suggestion. They had given only the
loosest of undertakings. Germany and France had no intention of
buying British beef. The conflict had achieved nothing. It had also
inflicted severe damage on Britain's standing in other capitals. His
counterparts in Florence, Helmut Kohl and Jacques Chirac most
prominently, made no secret of the fact that they had given up on the
prime minister as a politician with whom they could do serious
business. They were waiting for the general election, their officials
remarked, and for Major's replacement by Blair. Meanwhile the
European leaders underlined once again their determination to press
ahead with EMU. The Dublin summit in December 1996 was set as
the deadline for completion of preparations by finance ministers,
including agreement on a fiscal 'stability pact' between those countries
in the vanguard of a single currency. As for the relationship between
those countries which joined and those which remained outside, the
summit leaders agreed the euro should be linked to the remaining
national currencies by a new exchange rate mechanism. The only
concession to Britain was an agreement that this revamped 'ERM'
would be 'voluntary'. Major would not be obliged to risk a repeat of
Black Wednesday. Yet there was no hiding from the reality of
Florence. Britain was now alone.

*

The bunker mentality in Downing Street was reflected in another extraordinary ministerial meeting at the end of May. Against all official advice, the cabinet's European sub-committee decided to defy the law if Britain was defeated in another entirely separate dispute with Brussels. The episode centred on an impending judgement of the European Court of Justice on an EU directive to establish a 48-hour working week. The Commission had pushed through the directive some years earlier under the provisions of the Union's health and safety regulations. This required only a majority vote in the Council of Ministers, rendering worthless the government's supposed veto on the application in Britain of such social legislation. The court's Advocate General had subsequently issued a preliminary ruling rejecting the government's case that the directive should not have been tabled under rubric of the health and safety legislation. Now ministers were told that the full court would soon endorse that judgement. Papers prepared by officials for the discussion reminded ministers that the World Health Organisation specifically included employment conditions in its analyses of public health.

The meeting considered a range of responses to the expected court judgement. They could accept it on the basis that the government had anyway succeeded in removing the most restrictive elements from the directive. While it stipulated that most workers could not be compelled by contract to work for more 48 hours, it did not ban voluntary overtime. Alternatively, ministers could seek to kick the issue into touch by deferring legislation beyond the general election, pleading the need for consultation with industry as justification for the delay. In the meantime it could insist in the Intergovernmental Conference that the treaty be amended to transfer working hours to the social chapter of the Maastricht treaty from which Britain had opted out.

But the mood was not for compromise. With the beef war already underway, the cabinet's sceptics were joined by several others in demanding open defiance of the court. There were some suggestions too that the non-cooperation policy should be extended from beef to cover a satisfactory resolution also of the dispute over working time. John Major shared the anger. He had negotiated the social chapter opt-out and considered that Europe was reneging on the deal. In his eyes, the governments which had pushed through the directive had reneged on the Maastricht accord.

Some at the meeting, however, were horrified at the outcome. One spoke later of 'swords glinting in the sun'. Another said his colleagues had been gripped by a 'fevered mania'. If the decision stood, the government would be in clear breach not only of European but of British law. That hardly sat comfortably with the Conservatives' claim to be the party of law and order. Robin Butler was dismayed. So too were the Attorney General Nicholas Lyell and the government's law officers. Lyell realized that, as the minister charged with upholding the law, he could not be associated with a cabinet decision to defy it.

Two weeks later the cabinet sub-committee was reconvened. Before they sat down each of the ministers had received a note from the law officers. It informed them that if they flouted a decision of the European Court, the government could be certain it would be sued for damages in the British courts. And it would lose. The legal challenge might extend still further. Each and every minister associated with the decision might be sued individually and be held liable for damages in respect of public sector workers. This clinched it. The ministers retreated, opting instead for the policy of delay when the judgement was made. They also resolved to take the issue to the intergovernmental conference. They had stepped back from the brink. But the episode provided a graphic illustration of the extent to which the atmosphere of government had now been poisoned by Europhobia.

There were moments when John Major himself drew back in apparent alarm at the direction his party was taking. In late April, he sought to calm suggestions that Conservatives were destined to abandon Europe. He told an audience of businessmen in London that there was no prospect of withdrawal: 'Some suggest that we could just negotiate a trading relationship with Europe. But frankly, the idea that if we were outside the EU we could somehow become a trading haven on the edge of Europe with all the benefits of that vital market of 370 million, while others fix the rules without any regard at all to our national self-interest, is cloud-cuckoo-land.'[7]

Clarke, bruised by the referendum row, continued to swim against the tide of Euroscepticism, singling out sections of the Tory press as well as back-bench MPs for criticism. 'The former Conservative press is now almost without exception edited by way-out Eurosceptics – as way out as our more difficult people in the House of Commons,' he told a radio interviewer in late April. As for the notion that participation in EMU would herald the end of the nation state, that was 'a diversion from the realities of late twentieth-century politics'.[8] In a speech a few weeks later, the chancellor took the opportunity to spell out at length why Britain could not detach itself from its European partners. 'The European Union is vital to our national interests, both commercial and political,' he insisted. 'It has been that way for centuries and will remain so for centuries. I simply do not believe that you can separate economics from politics. The economic and trading interests of a nation are at the heart of politics: political decisions affect a nation's economic and trading environment. When you consider Britain's future in Europe, you are considering Britain's economic and political well-being. The two are inextricably linked.'[9] Clarke's evidence during the same month to an inquiry by the all-party Treasury committee into EMU further enraged the sceptics. The chancellor declared that he had been 'sympathetic' to the goal of a single currency.[10]

Douglas Hurd meanwhile showed increasing irritation with the prime minister's willingness to dance to the sceptics' tune. In government, he had played the role of conciliator. The freedom of the back benches now encouraged him to stand up for the European cause. There was a note of apology in his speeches as the former foreign secretary insisted that the pro-Europeans would not allow the Conservative party to be hijacked. He lamented the decline of British influence abroad. The BSE row was accompanied by an outbreak of virulent Germanophobia among a vocal group on the Conservative back benches. Lady Thatcher's visceral distrust of Chancellor Kohl had infected many others in her party. EMU was seen by the sceptics as the instrument of European domination. Bill Cash, among others, spoke of Bonn's ambition to create a 'Germano-Russian condominium', of which the European Union would form the western pillar. Hurd despaired of such crudeness. The Germans, he said, had 'given up trying to understand or sympathize really'. They saw no point in paying heed to British ideas.[11] Sir Bryan Nicholson, the outgoing president of the Confederation of British Industry, made the point more graphically. 'In this pungent atmosphere of romantic nationalism and churlish xenophobia, I sometimes wonder if there are some among us who have failed to notice that the war with Germany has ended.'[12] Some detected a certain contrition as Hurd later assumed a high profile role in a new grouping of One Nation MPs, Conservative Mainstream, which pledged to fight the pro-European cause.

The sceptics were not dissuaded. As John Redwood, at the helm of his own think tank, the Conservative 2000 foundation, saw it: 'The aim of European integration is to create a country called Europe. For it to work, we would all have to swear allegiance to Europe. Of course that means weakening our sense of belonging to Britain. We would look to Frankfurt rather than to the City of London for our economic prospects. Our armies would go into battle under the European flag, marching to the European anthem. We would be represented abroad by the European rather than the British ambassador.'[13] In June, seventy-eight Tory MPs voted in favour of a bill tabled by the veteran Eurosceptic Bill Cash calling for a referendum not on the single currency but on Britain's place in Europe. The vote had no legislative significance, but it underlined once again the extent to which a significant section of the Conservative party now favoured disengagement. Norman Lamont and Kenneth Baker joined Redwood in backing the bill after Cash declared that Britain risked drowning 'under a tidal wave of federalism'. A month later a middle-ranking minister at the Treasury, David Heathcoat-Amory, added fuel to the fire of dissent by resigning from the government because of his opposition to a single currency. The first minister to leave the Major government over the issue, Heathcoat-Amory declared that equivocation over a single currency was damaging the party and confusing the public. 'When something is clearly against the national interest, it is our job as the party of the national interest to make our position clear and resist it now,' he said.[14] For all his growing personal antagonism to the project, Major insisted that it would be foolish to close off the option. Britain could not avoid the consequences of a single currency for the whole of Europe. It had to preserve its role in the shaping of EMU even if it decided eventually to stand aside. 'How could I defend to the City of London, British business, British industry, quite apart from the British individual, that I was going to say, on the most important economic issue for fifty years, I am going to withdraw from the debate and let the Europeans, on their own, with no British input, decided what is going to happen?'[15]

The sceptics, however, found further ammunition in an acknowledgement in Whitehall that Britain's decision on whether to participate in a single European currency could no longer be pushed into the dim and distant future. Major had decided to delay the election until the following spring. A confidential paper prepared in the Treasury by officials working for Nigel Wicks concluded that there would be precious little time after that for an incoming government to make up its mind. The Treasury paper identified two crucial pieces of important legislation which would have to be passed if Britain were to participate in EMU from January 1999. They included a parliamentary bill required by the Maastricht Act before the government could notify its European partners of its intention to join; and legislation to give independence to the Bank of England and to transfer ownership of the foreign exchange reserves to the Bank. In the case of the Conservatives at least, provision for a referendum would have to be made in one of the bills. There were also deadlines. The Maastricht treaty required Britain to notify its intention to join by January 1998 and to grant independence to the Bank by, at the latest, July of that year. The officials concluded that the new government would have to make its choice within months, if not weeks, of the election. The sceptics claimed that the timetable reinforced the case for the government to rule out in advance of the election any move to scrap sterling. It could hardly go into the election campaign saying it did not know, when the decision had to be made so soon after polling day. Within the cabinet, Michael Howard and Peter Lilley were among those arguing that the issue should be reopened. But Clarke argued strongly that the start-date for EMU might yet slip. And, in any event, if other European governments wanted Britain to join they would be flexible over deadlines.

There were divisions too within Labour. Tony Blair had decided at the outset of his leadership that the party must sustain the Europeanism of his predecessor John Smith. His policy towards a single currency was framed in terms of pragmatism rather than principle. A

Labour government would carefully weigh the economic arguments before deciding, but there was no fundamental constitutional objection to the replacement of sterling by the euro. Blair believed that, if successful, EMU would define the political core of Europe. Britain could not remain outside indefinitely without sacrificing vital political influence across the range of European policies. But he was conscious also that the electorate showed little enthusiasm for closer European integration. A promise to abolish the pound could leave the opposition dangerously exposed at the general election. A Labour government would also have other priorities for its first two years: devolution for Scotland and Wales, reform of the welfare state, significant shifts in education and health policy. So Blair was content to adopt Major's wait-and-see policy, and to exploit at every opportunity the disarray in the government. Labour would also seek the 'consent' of the voters if it decided to give up sterling, through a referendum or through a pledge in its general election manifesto. As shadow chancellor, Gordon Brown showed greater enthusiasm for the project. Participation in a single currency would buttress the tough monetary and fiscal policy he promised for the incoming Labour government. And there would be a clear penalty for remaining outside: higher interest rates, a vulnerable currency and, quite probably, a higher inflation rate. But others in the shadow cabinet struck a more sceptical note. Robin Cook, the foreign affairs spokesman, and John Prescott, the deputy leader, voiced fears that a leap into a single currency would impose a deflationary straitjacket on an incoming Labour administration. Blair, though instinctively convinced that Britain must remain in the European mainstream, echoed the doubts over whether it was ready to join the vanguard of EMU. In November 1996, Labour too promised a referendum on the issue.

The indecision and divisions within Labour were obscured by the open warfare within Conservative ranks. A mood of fatalism gripped Tory MPs. Many were by now concerned not about the outcome of an election they deemed to have already been lost but their positioning in the leadership contest which would follow such a defeat. Around the cabinet table more than half a dozen potential candidates began practising their lines, Michael Howard and Malcolm Rifkind among them. One senior minister joked that meetings of the cabinet's European sub-committee had become like a dress rehearsal for the looming leadership contest. The would-be candidates drew notes from their pockets before addressing colleagues in the manner of a public meeting. The tension between Europeanism and nationalism concealed also a steady improvement in prospects for the economy. After a slowdown late in 1995, the rate of growth picked up pace again in mid-1996. Kenneth Clarke, who had announced tax cuts worth £3bn in his November 1995 Budget, faced a deteriorating outlook for public borrowing. There were also disputes with Eddie George over interest rates. In June 1996, the chancellor defied both the Bank of England and most of his Treasury officials to cut borrowing costs from 6 to 5.75 per cent. But in the autumn Clarke prepared for the last Budget before the election against the background of healthy rises in output, falling unemployment and subdued inflation. On the foreign exchange markets, sterling rose steadily around DM2.50, its first sustained recovery since Black Wednesday. The return of the economic 'feel-good' factor brought an improvement in the Conservatives' standing in the opinion polls. A Labour lead which had previously stood at more than twenty points fell in some surveys to fifteen or fewer. Major's personal standing with the electorate also improved. Labour retained an unprecedented lead but some in the cabinet began to wonder whether the election might, after all, be saved.

Each burst of optimism, however, was clouded by further public flare-ups over Europe. In September 1996, Clarke's determination to preserve the single currency option through the general election brought fresh tensions with his Downing Street neighbour. Angered by some transparently sceptical comments delivered by Malcolm Rifkind, Clarke offered a public warning to his cabinet colleagues that he would not back down. He described as 'pathetic' the suggestion that the government should close off the option of joining EMU at the outset in favour of deferring a decision on participation until a single currency was seen to work.[16] In this particular interview, Clarke chose his words badly, but the target of his scorn was clear: the renewed suggestion by cabinet colleagues that Britain might yet rule itself out from the first wave of EMU. He was aware that Brian Mawhinney's aides in Conservative Central Office were briefing against him, and concerned lest John Major once again be tempted to give way to the sceptics. The reaction to Clarke's remarks – Norman Tebbit demanded his departure and Nicholas Bonsor, a middle-ranking Foreign Office minister drawn from the ranks of the sceptics, publicly attacked him – heralded a new bout of infighting. But the prime minister had struck a deal in April when the cabinet had endorsed a referendum. His chancellor was determined he would keep it. Clarke knew that the Conservatives could not go to the polls in 1997 as guarantors of a sovereign pound and then decide to surrender sterling a few years later. The option had to be kept open in 1997 to prevent his party from permanently discarding it. Isolation in Europe over EMU would also risk a much broader disengagement. Like Blair, he saw that if the single currency zone was successful, those within it would form a new political core. To remain indefinitely on the outside would be to opt for a policy of progressive detachment. This, the chancellor realized, was the ambition of the sceptics, Major understood that Clarke was in deadly earnest. If he bowed to the sceptics and fought the election on an anti-EMU platform, he would do so without his chancellor. Rifkind too saw the risks of a fatal cabinet battle. Tough words were exchanged between Clarke and Major, but by the time the party gathered in Bournemouth for the last party conference before the election, the chancellor had won. On the conference fringe, Redwood, Lamont and Tebbit once again raised the spectre of a European superstate dominated by Germany. But in the conference hall, Major and Rifkind backed Clarke in insisting that the party would make its decision on the future of sterling only after the general election. The chancellor meanwhile gave the political speech of his life. But nothing was resolved. After more than seventeen years in power the Conservatives were still haunted by sterling.

The British electorate is not much fussed about the value of sterling on international foreign exchange markets. The activities of the fund managers and speculators who trade hundreds of billions of dollars each day have a higher profile than when Harold Wilson railed against the gnomes of Zurich. The City dealing room has become one of the images of our time. But what counts to most people is the value of the pound in their pockets – the prices in the supermarket rather than the exchange rate at Thomas Cook.

It is the link between that rate and internal purchasing power of the currency, however, which confounds the politicians. Measured against

the Deutschmark, sterling's decline during the past thirty years mir-
rors almost exactly the much faster rate of inflation in Britain than in
Germany. Since 1964 the pound has lost over 80 per cent of its value
against the Deutschmark. Its purchasing power in Sainsbury's has
fallen by about 90 per cent. Cause and effect operate in tandem.
Sometimes sterling's depreciation has driven up prices in Britain
relative to those in Germany. On other occasions the fall in the
exchange rate has followed faster increases in Britain's relative costs.
The mistake made by the Conservatives since 1979 has been to assume
at different moments they could ignore the exchange rate or they
could fix it irrevocably.

During the early 1980s, the first Thatcher government suffered for
a brief period the rare embarrassment of an overvalued exchange rate.
North Sea oil and the tightest monetary squeeze in the postwar period
briefly re-established sterling as a strong currency. The damage that
the appreciation inflicted on Britain's industrial base was as inevitable
as the exchange rate's subsequent fall – neglect is never a benign
option. Subsequently, Nigel Lawson and then John Major sought to
fix the pound's level. Making the same error as Winston Churchill in
1925, they assumed the economy would adjust to the exchange rate
rather than vice versa. Major was right in his assessment that sterling's
devaluation over successive decades had brought no benefits – if a
weak currency was a panacea, Britain's economy would have emerged
the strongest in Europe. But likewise a fixed exchange rate has no
magical qualities. Major might have learned, if not from Harold
Wilson, then from Keynes, who wrote of Churchill's return to the
Gold Standard, 'The fundamental blunder of the Treasury and the
Bank of England has been due from the beginning to their belief that
if they looked after the deflation of prices, the deflation of costs would
look after itself.'[17] To the average voter DM2.95 meant nothing. But
John Major's administration insisted that any change in that exchange
rate would be a catastrophe, a national humiliation. A parity for
sterling plucked from random circumstance became a badge of
national pride. It was hardly surprising then that after sterling's ejection from the ERM, the electorate took the prime minister at his
word: devaluatioin became a terrible failure of government. Hardly
surprising then that Black Wednesday was the catalyst for the subsequent miseries of the Major government.

Sterling is a useful indicator and an instrument of economic management but the currency markets can be as destructive as they are powerful. For now there seems only the slightest prospect that Britain will join EMU in 1999. A re-elected Conservative government would not survive such a decision. Tony Blair would almost certainly have more pressing priorities. But if the rest of Europe does create a single currency, sterling's future will look bleak. Once again Britain is likely to follow Monnet's advice. It will watch from the sidelines to see if the venture works and, if it does, will join. Until then politics and the pound are destined to remain dangerously entangled.

APPENDIX

A Sinking Pound

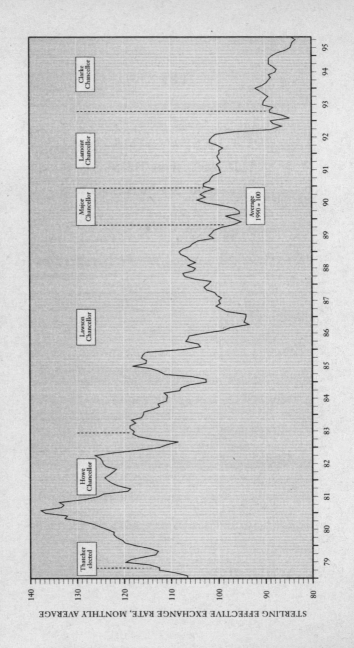

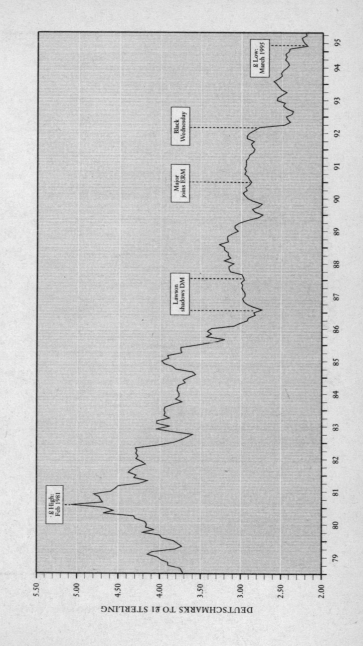

DEUTSCHMARK DOLDRUMS

£ High:
Feb 1981

Lawson
shadows DM

Major
joins ERM

Black
Wednesday

£ Low:
March 1995

DEUTSCHMARKS TO £1 STERLING

5.50
5.00
4.50
4.00
3.50
3.00
2.50
2.00

79 80 81 82 83 84 85 86 87 88 89 90 91 92 93 94 95

THE DOLLAR SWITCHBACK

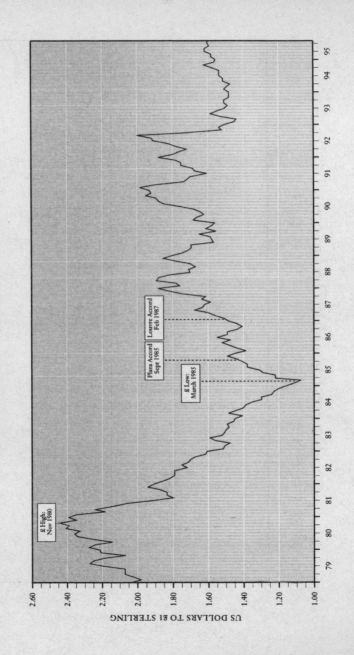

A RISING YEN

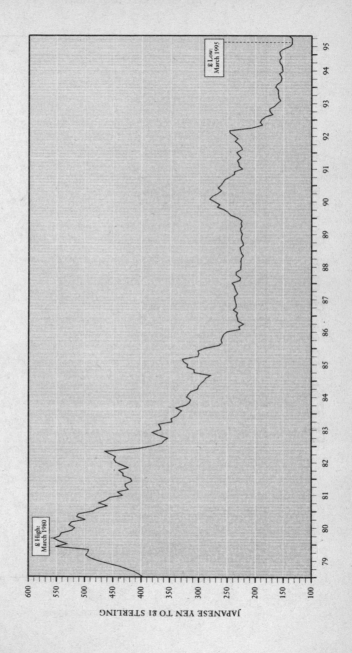

JAPANESE YEN TO £1 STERLING

£ High:
March 1980

£ Low:
March 1995

The Pound in Your Pocket

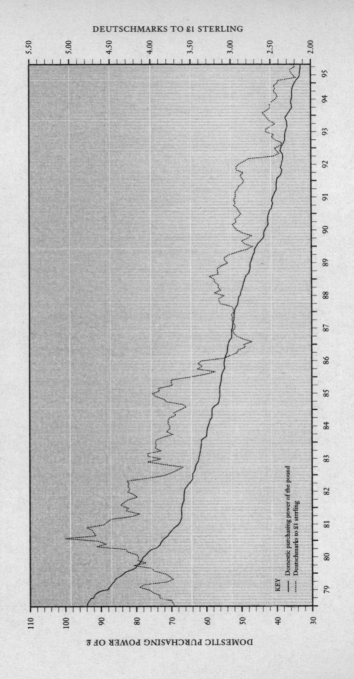

A Falling Pound and Rising Interest Rates

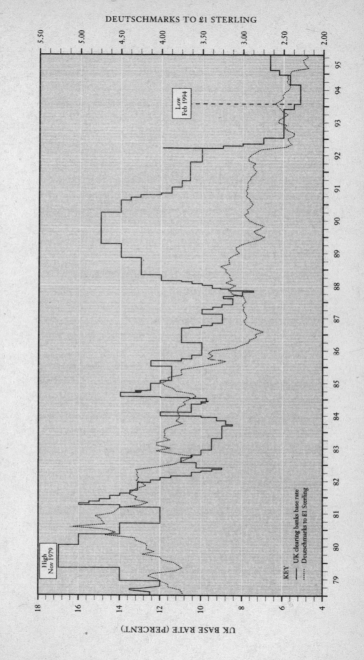

DEUTSCHMARKS TO £1 STERLING

UK BASE RATE (PERCENT)

High
Nov 1979

Low
Feb 1994

KEY
—— UK clearing banks base rate
.... Deutschmarks to £1 Sterling

REFERENCES

ONE CONVICTION

1. Bernard Donoughue, *Prime Minister* (Jonathan Cape, 1987)
2. James Callaghan, House of Commons, *Hansard*, cols. 1421–38, 6 December 1978
3. Denis Healey, *The Time of My Life* (Michael Joseph, 1989)
4. Margaret Thatcher, House of Commons, *Hansard*, cols. 1421–38, 6 December 1978
5. Geoffrey Howe, House of Commons, *Hansard*, cols. 473–87, 29 November 1978
6. *Conservative Manifesto for the European Election* (Conservative Central Office, May 1979)
7. Quoted by David Smith in *The Rise and Fall of Monetarism* (Penguin Books, 1987), which provides a good analysis of the academic debate.
8. Charles Goodhart, *Money, Information and Uncertainty* (Macmillan, 1975)
9. Healey, *The Time of My Life*
10. Geoffrey Howe, House of Commons, *Hansard*, cols. 1439–90, 26 March 1980
11. Nigel Lawson, The New Conservatism – Lecture to the Bow Group, August 1980
12. *The Right Approach to the Economy* (Conservative Central Office, 1977)
13. William Keegan, *Mr Lawson's Gamble* (Hodder & Stoughton, 1989)
14. Christopher Johnson, *The Economy under Mrs Thatcher 1979–1990* (Penguin Books, 1991)
15. Nigel Lawson, *The View from No. 11: Memoirs of a Tory Radical* (Bantam Press, 1992)
16. Nigel Lawson, Thatcherism in Practice, A Progress Report – Speech to the Zurich Society of Economics (HM Treasury, 14 January 1981)
17. Middleton, Peter, *The Relationships between Monetary and Fiscal Policy* (Institute for Fiscal Studies, 1978)
18. Lawson, *The View from No. 11*

19. James Prior, *A Balance of Power* (Hamish Hamilton, 1986)
20. Geoffrey Howe, *Conflict of Loyalty* (Macmillan, 1994)
21. Johnson, *The Economy under Mrs Thatcher*
22. Simon Wren-Lewis, *The Role of Money in Determining Prices* (HM Treasury Working Paper, 1981)
23. Ian Gilmour, *Dancing with Dogma: Britain under Thatcherism* (Simon & Schuster, 1992)
24. Margaret Thatcher, *The Downing Street Years* (HarperCollins, 1993)
25. Howe, *Conflict of Loyalty*
26. Ibid.

TWO NAVIGATING WITHOUT A COMPASS

1. James Callaghan, *Time and Chance* (Collins, 1987)
2. Keegan, *Mr Lawson's Gamble*
3. Ibid.
4. Robin Leigh-Pemberton, Some Aspects of UK Monetary Policy – Lecture to the University of Kent, 28 October 1984; reprinted in *Bank of England Quarterly Bulletin*, December 1984
5. Keegan, *Mr Lawson's Gamble*
6. *The Times*, 14 September 1978
7. Lawson, *The View from No. 11*
8. Nigel Lawson, Chancellor's Speech at the Lord Mayor's Banquet for Bankers and Merchants of the City of London (HM Treasury, 28 October 1983)
9. Nigel Lawson, Chancellor's Speech at the Lord Mayor's Banquet for Bankers and Merchants of the City of London (HM Treasury, 18 October 1984)
10. Lawson, *The View from No. 11*
11. Nigel Lawson, The British Experiment – the Fifth Mais Lecture (HM Treasury, 18 June 1984)
12. Nigel Lawson, Evidence to the Treasury and Civil Service Committee, Session 1984–85, The Exchange Rate, Minutes of Evidence, House of Commons, 28 January 1985
13. George Blunden, Evidence to the Treasury and Civil Service Committee, *The Role of the Bank of England* (HMSO, 2 vols., 8 December 1993), vol. 2

14. Terence Burns, 'The UK Government's Financial Strategy', in *Keynes and Economic Policy*, ed. Walter Eltis and Peter Sinclair (Macmillan, 1988)
15. *Financial Times*, 21 March 1985
16. Nigel Lawson, House of Commons, *Hansard*, cols. 783–800, 19 March 1985
17. Robin Leigh-Pemberton, Treasury and Civil Service Committee, *The 1985 Budget* (HMSO, 22 April 1985)
18. Margaret Thatcher, House of Commons, *Hansard*, col. 166, 16 July 1985
19. Gilmour, *Dancing with Dogma*
20. Nigel Lawson, Chancellor's Speech at the Lord Mayor's Banquet for Bankers and Merchants of the City of London (HM Treasury, 17 October 1985)
21. Lawson, *The View from No. 11*
22. Treasury and Civil Service Committee, *The European Monetary System* (HMSO, 19 November 1985)
23. Lawson, *The View from No. 11*
24. Thatcher, *The Downing Street Years*
25. Lawson, *The View from No. 11*
26. Alan Walters, *Britain's Economic Renaissance, Margaret Thatcher's Reforms 1979–1984* (Oxford University Press, 1986)

THREE A DEVALUED CURRENCY

1. Lawson, *The View from No. 11*
2. Healey, *The Time of My Life*
3. House of Lords, *Report of the Select Committee on Overseas Trade* (HMSO, July 1985)
4. Nigel Lawson, Speech in Cambridge – What Are We Going To Do When the Oil Runs Out? (HM Treasury, 9 April 1984)
5. Lawson, *The View from No. 11*
6. Nigel Lawson, House of Commons, *Hansard*, cols. 166–84, 18 March 1986
7. *Financial Times*, 20 March 1986
8. Ibid.
9. Nigel Lawson, Chancellor's Speech to the Lombard Association (HM Treasury, 16 April 1986)

10. Margaret Thatcher, House of Commons, *Hansard*, cols. 419–20, 24 April 1986
11. Margaret Thatcher, House of Commons, *Hansard*, col. 171, 10 June 1986
12. Lawson, *The View from No. 11*
13. Nigel Lawson, Chancellor's Speech at the Lord Mayor's Banquet for Bankers and Merchants of the City of London (HM Treasury, 16 October 1986)
14. Robin Leigh-Pemberton, Speech at the Lord Mayor's Banquet, 16 October 1986; reprinted in *Bank of England Quarterly Bulletin*, December 1986
15. Robin Leigh-Pemberton, Financial Change and Broad Money – Lecture to Loughborough University, 22 October 1986; reprinted in *Bank of England Quarterly Bulletin*, December 1986
16. Treasury and Civil Service Committee, *The 1986 Autumn Statement* (HMSO, 3 December 1986)
17. *Financial Times*, 19 November 1986
18. Nigel Lawson, Evidence to the Treasury and Civil Service Committee, *The 1986 Autumn Statement*
19. *Sun*, 31 October 1987
20. *Financial Times*, 23 February 1987
21. Lawson, *The View from No. 11*
22. *Financial Times*, 19 March 1987
23. Thatcher, *The Downing Street Years*

FOUR SHADOWS IN DOWNING STREET

1. Nigel Lawson, Chancellor's Speech to the International Monetary Fund (HM Treasury, 30 September 1987)
2. Nigel Lawson, Chancellor's Speech at the Lord Mayor's Banquet for Bankers and Merchants of the City of London (HM Treasury, 4 November 1987)
3. *Financial Times*, 23 November 1987
4. Treasury and Civil Service Committee, *The 1987 Autumn Statement* (HMSO, 14 December 1987)
5. Thatcher, *The Downing Street Years*
6. *Bank of England Quarterly Bulletin*, February 1988

7. Lawson, *The View from No. 11*
8. Nigel Lawson, House of Commons, *Hansard*, cols. 512–15, 10 March 1988
9. Margaret Thatcher, House of Commons, *Hansard*, col. 517, 10 March 1988
10. Nigel Lawson, House of Commons, *Hansard*, cols. 993–1013, 15 March 1988
11. *Financial Times*, 17 March 1988
12. Margaret Thatcher, House of Commons, *Hansard*, col. 1219, 17 March 1988
13. Lord Young, Remarks at Manchester Business Conference, 21 March 1988
14. Geoffrey Howe, Foreign Secretary's Speech to Swiss Institute for International Studies, Zurich (Foreign and Commonwealth Office, 24 March 1988)
15. Treasury and Civil Service Committee, *The 1988 Budget* (HMSO, 20 April 1988)
16. Ibid.
17. Margaret Thatcher, House of Commons, *Hansard*, col. 465, 21 May 1988
18. Howe, *Conflict of Loyalty*
19. Lawson, *The View from No. 11*
20. Thatcher, *The Downing Street Years*
21. Margaret Thatcher, House of Commons, *Hansard*, cols. 798–9, 17 May 1988
22. *Financial Times*, 19 May 1988
23. Nigel Lawson, Chancellor's Speech to the Annual Meeting of the International Monetary Fund, Berlin (HM Treasury, 28 September 1988)

FIVE HUBRIS

1. Lawson, *The View from No. 11*
2. Margaret Thatcher, House of Commons, *Hansard*, col. 988, 12 January 1989
3. *Financial Times* and *Daily Telegraph*, 25 January 1989
4. Jacques Delors, Speech to the European Parliament, 6 July 1988
5. Margaret Thatcher, *Jimmy Young Programme*, BBC Radio, 27 July 1988

6. Margaret Thatcher, Prime Minister's Speech to the College of Europe, Bruges (Press Office, 10 Downing Street, 20 September 1988)

7. Hugo Young, *One of Us* (Macmillan, rev. edn 1991)

8. Howe, *Conflict of Loyalty*

9. Lawson, *The View from No. 11*

10. Committee for the Study of Economic and Monetary Union, *Report on Economic and Monetary Union in the European Community* (European Commission, Brussels, April 1989)

11. Nigel Lawson, What Sort of European Financial Area? – Chancellor's Speech to the Royal Institute of International Affairs (HM Treasury, 25 January 1989)

12 Geoffrey Howe, Foreign Secretary's Speech to the CBI (Foreign and Commonwealth Office, 16 May 1989)

13. Lawson, *The View from No. 11*

14. Thatcher, *The Downing Street Years*

15. *Daily Telegraph*, 24 June 1989

16. Thatcher, *The Downing Street Years*

17. Howe, *Conflict of Loyalty*

18. Margaret Thatcher, House of Commons, *Hansard*, cols. 1107–1222, 29 June 1989

19. Margaret Thatcher, BBC World Service interview, 19 May 1989

20. Nigel Lawson, BBC Radio interview, 24 May 1989

21. Nigel Lawson, Evidence to the Treasury and Civil Service Committee, 12 June 1989, *The Delors Report* (HMSO, 19 June 1989)

22. Nigel Lawson, House of Commons, *Hansard*, cols. 257–66, 7 June 1989

23. Margaret Thatcher, House of Commons, *Hansard*, cols. 698–700, 13 June 1989

24. Michael Heseltine, *Where There's a Will* (Hutchinson, 1987)

25. Michael Heseltine, *The Challenge of Europe: Can Britain Win?* (Weidenfeld & Nicolson, 1989)

SIX FAREWELL

1. Geoffrey Howe, Speech to the Radical Society (Foreign and Commonwealth Office, 19 July 1989)

2. Kenneth Baker, *The Turbulent Years: My Life in Politics* (Faber and Faber, 1993)

3. Bernard Ingham, *Kill the Messenger* (HarperCollins, 1992)
4. *Sunday Times*, 8 October 1989
5. Baker, *The Turbulent Years*
6. *Financial Times*, 18 October 1989
7. Nigel Lawson, House of Commons, *Hansard*, cols. 208–10, 31 October 1989
8. Lawson, *The View from No. 11*
9. Baker, *The Turbulent Years*
10. Nigel Lawson, House of Commons, *Hansard*, cols. 208–10, 31 October 1989
11. Nigel Lawson, Evidence to the Treasury and Civil Service Committee, *The 1985 Autumn Statement* (HMSO, 2 December 1985)
12. Lawson, *The View from No. 11*

SEVEN TOO LATE

1. John Major, Public Service Management: The Revolution in Progress – the First Audit Commission Lecture (HM Treasury, 21 June 1989)
2. John Major, Extract from a Speech in Northampton by the Chancellor of the Exchequer (HM Treasury, 27 October 1989)
3. Margaret Thatcher, *Walden*, LWT, 29 October 1989
4. Geoffrey Howe, Speech at Anglo-Spanish Conference, Bath, 28 October 1989
5. Robin Leigh-Pemberton, Interview on Channel-4 News, 30 October 1989
6. John Major, House of Commons, *Hansard*, cols. 200–207, 31 October 1989
7. Treasury and Civil Service Committee, *The 1989 Autumn Statement* (HMSO, 13 December 1989)
8. John Major, House of Commons, *Hansard*, col. 594, 28 November 1989
9. *Financial Statement and Budget Report* (HM Treasury, March 1990)
10. Thatcher, *The Downing Street Years*
11. Michael Heseltine, Speech to the British Chamber of Commerce for Belgium and Luxembourg, Brussels, 22 February 1990
12. Robin Leigh-Pemberton, Evidence to the Treasury and Civil Service Committee, *The 1990 Budget* (HMSO, 23 April 1990)
13. *Financial Times*, 15 March 1990

14. John Major, *On the Record*, BBC Television, 25 March 1990
15. *Financial Times*, 26 March 1990
16. Thatcher, *The Downing Street Years*
17. Margaret Thatcher, Speech to the Scottish Conservative Conference, Aberdeen, 12 May 1990
18. *Financial Times*, 12 June 1990
19. John Major, reported in the *Financial Times*, 11 July 1990
20. Margaret Thatcher, House of Commons, *Hansard*, col. 132, 12 June 1990
21. Alan Walters, *Sterling in Danger: The Economic Consequences of Pegged Exchange Rates* (Fontana, 1990)
22. Treasury and Civil Service Committee, *The Delors Report* (HMSO, 19 June 1989)
23. John Major, House of Commons, *Hansard*, cols. 488–95, 2 November 1989
24. Thatcher, *The Downing Street Years*
25. Douglas Hurd, Speech to Scottish Conservative Conference, Aberdeen, 11 May 1990
26. Margaret Thatcher, House of Commons, *Hansard*, col. 1111, 21 June 1990
27. Anthony Meyer, *Stand Up and Be Counted* (William Heinemann, 1990)
28. Ian Gilmour, Speech to the Cambridge University Reform Group, 9 November 1989

EIGHT NEMESIS

1. Press notice, HM Treasury, 5 October 1990
2. Margaret Thatcher, Prime Minister's Speech to the Aspen Institute, (Press Office, 10 Downing Street, 5 August 1990)
3. *The United Kingdom*, OECD Economic Surveys (OECD, Paris, August 1990)
4. John Major, *Today*, BBC Radio, 7 September 1990
5. John Major, Chancellor's Speech to the International Monetary Fund (HM Treasury, 26 September 1990)
6. Baker, *The Turbulent Years*
7. Thatcher, *The Downing Street Years*
8. *Bank of England Quarterly Bulletin*, August 1990

9. John Major, Evidence to the House of Commons Treasury and Civil Service Committee, 25 July 1990

10. Robin Leigh-Pemberton, Speech to the Keidanren, Tokyo, 8 October 1990; reprinted in *Bank of England Quarterly Bulletin*, November 1990

11. John Smith, House of Commons, *Hansard*, cols. 929–31, 15 October 1990

12. William Keegan, *Observer*, 14 October 1990

13. Nigel Lawson, House of Commons, *Hansard*, cols. 214–19, 23 October 1990

14. Nicholas Ridley, *My Style of Government: The Thatcher Years* (Hutchinson, 1991)

15. Margaret Thatcher, Speech at the Conservative Party Conference, Bournemouth (Conservative Central Office, 12 October 1990)

16. Conclusions of the Presidency, European Council, 28 October 1990

17. Margaret Thatcher, Interview with BBC Radio, 28 October 1990

18. Geoffrey Howe, *Walden*, LWT, 28 October 1990

19. Margaret Thatcher, House of Commons, *Hansard*, cols. 869–92, 30 October 1990

20. *The Times*, 31 October 1990

21. Press Statement, 10 Downing Street, 1 November 1990

22. Margaret Thatcher, House of Commons, *Hansard*, col. 29, 7 November 1990

23. Geoffrey Howe, House of Commons, *Hansard*, cols. 461–5, 13 November 1990

24. Anthony Teasdale, Review of *Conflict of Loyalty*, Tory Reform Group, *Reformer*, Spring 1995

25. Norman Lamont, Speech to the Bruges Group, 15 November 1990

26. John Major, Prime Minister's Speech to the Konrad Adenauer Foundation, Bonn (Press Office, 10 Downing Street, 11 March 1991)

27. Norman Lamont, House of Commons, *Hansard*, col. 413, 16 May 1991

28. National Institute of Economic and Social Research, August 1991

29. Sarah Hogg and Jonathan Hill, *Too Close to Call* (Little, Brown, 1995)

NINE SLEEPLESS NIGHTS

1. Robin Leigh-Pemberton, Speech to the Annual Dinner of the Eastern Region of the Confederation of British Industry, 8 October 1992

2. *Bank of England Quarterly Bulletin*, February 1991
3. Terence Burns, Evidence to the Treasury and Civil Service Committee, *The 1990 Autumn Statement* (HMSO, 17 December 1990)
4. Maastricht Treaty, Protocol 11: On Certain Provisions relating to the United Kingdom of Great Britain and Northern Ireland (Council of the European Union, Brussels, 1991)
5. John Major, House of Commons, *Hansard*, cols. 264–73, 10 May 1992
6. Future Development of the EEC, House of Commons Order Paper, 3 June 1992, Motion 174
7. John Major, Prime Minister's Speech to the Ayrshire Chamber of Commerce (Press Office, 10 Downing Street, 1 June 1992)
8. John Major, House of Commons, *Hansard*, cols. 827–40, 3 June 1992
9. Margaret Thatcher, *Breakfast with Frost*, BBC Television, 28 June 1992
10. Healey, *The Time of My Life*
11. Norman Lamont, Evidence to the House of Commons Treasury and Civil Service Committee, *The 1992 Autumn Statement and the Conduct of Economic Policy* (HMSO, 13 January 1993)
12. Norman Lamont, Britain and the Exchange Rate Mechanism – Chancellor's Speech to the European Policy Forum (HM Treasury, 10 July 1992)
13. Callaghan, *Time and Chance*
14. *The Times*, 14 July 1992
15. Norman Lamont, Evidence to the House of Commons Treasury and Civil Service Committee, *The 1992 Autumn Statement and the Conduct of Economic Policy* (HMSO, 13 January 1993)
16. Robin Leigh-Pemberton, Evidence to the House of Commons Treasury and Civil Service Committee, *The 1992 Autumn Statement and the Conduct of Economic Policy* (HMSO, 13 January 1993)
17. *Bank of England Quarterly Bulletin*, August 1992
18. *Fortune*, 16 November 1992

TEN HUMILIATION

1. Norman Lamont, Chancellor's Statement (HM Treasury, 26 August 1992)
2. *Financial Times*, 27 August 1992

3. Statement by European Community Finance Ministers (HM Treasury, 28 August 1992)
4. Statement by European Community Finance Ministers (HM Treasury, 5 September 1992)
5. Helmut Schlesinger, *The World this Weekend*, BBC Radio, 6 September 1992
6. *Financial Times*, 11 December 1992
7. Norman Lamont, Evidence to the House of Commons Treasury and Civil Service Committee, *The 1992 Autumn Statement and the Conduct of Economic Policy* (HMSO, 13 January 1993)
8. John Major, Prime Minister's Speech to a Dinner of the Scottish CBI at the Forte Crest Hotel, Glasgow (Press Office, 10 Downing Street, 10 September 1992)
9. Penny Junor, *The Major Enigma* (Michael Joseph, 1993)
10. John Major, House of Commons, *Hansard*, cols. 2–11, 24 September 1992
11. *Financial Times*, 21 January 1993
12. *Handelsblatt*, 16 and 17 September 1992
13. Callaghan, *Time and Chance*
14. Junor, *The Major Enigma*
15. Interview with author
16. Norman Lamont, Chancellor's Statement (HM Treasury, 16 September 1992)
17. Lawson, *The View from No. 11*
18. *Bank of England Quarterly Bulletin* and *Financial Statistics*, HMSO
19. Norman Lamont, House of Commons, *Hansard*, cols. 281–5, 9 June 1983
20. Robin Leigh-Pemberton, Speech to the Annual Dinner of the Eastern Region of the Confederation of British Industry, 8 October 1992

ELEVEN BROKEN PROMISES

1. Norman Lamont, House of Commons, *Hansard*, cols. 281–5, 9 June 1993.
2. Malcolm Balen, *Kenneth Clarke* (Fourth Estate, 1994)
3. Eddie George, Governor's Speech at the Lord Mayor's Dinner for the Merchants and Bankers of the City of London, 14 June 1995

4. Norman Lamont, Chancellor's Speech at the Lord Mayor's Dinner for the Merchants and Bankers of the City of London (HM Treasury, 29 October 1992)

5. Norman Lamont, Chancellor's Letter to John Watts MP, Chairman of the Treasury and Civil Service Committee (HM Treasury, 8 October 1992)

6. *Evening Standard*, 21 September 1992

7. John Major, House of Commons, *Hansard*, cols. 2–11, 24 September 1992

8. Fixed Exchange Rates, House of Commons Order Paper, 24 September 1992, Motion 47

9. *Financial Times*, 1 October 1993

10. Statement from HM Treasury, 30 September 1993

11. *The Times*, 7 October and 21 October 1992

12. *Bank of England Quarterly Bulletin*, November 1992

13. Nigel Lawson, Evidence to the Treasury and Civil Service Committee, *The 1988 Budget* (HMSO, 20 April 1988)

14. *The Right Approach to the Economy* (Conservative Central Office, October 1977)

15. Lawson, *The View from No. 11*

16. John Major, House of Commons, *Hansard*, cols. 297–305, 9 June 1993

17. Callaghan, *Time and Chance*

18. Norman Lamont, Speech at the Conference of the Scottish Conservative Party, 12 May 1993

19. Norman Lamont, House of Commons, *Hansard*, cols. 281–5, 9 June 1983

20. Balen, *Kenneth Clarke*

21. Kenneth Clarke, Chancellor's Speech to the Parliamentary Press Gallery (HM Treasury, 9 June 1993)

22. *Financial Times*, 25 June 1993

23. *Official Responses to the ERM Crisis: Reports from the Committee of Central Bank Governors and the EC Monetary Committee* (European Council, Brussels, May 1993)

24. Quoted in Andy McSmith, *Kenneth Clarke: A Political Biography* (Verso, 1994)

25. *The Economist*, 24 September 1993

26. House of Commons Treasury and Civil Service Committee, *The Role of the Bank of England* (HMSO, 2 vols, 8 December 1993)

27. Eddie George, Governor's Speech to the American Chamber of Commerce in London, 22 September 1993; reprinted in *Bank of England Quarterly Bulletin*, November 1993

28. Eddie George, Governor's Speech to the Association Cambiste Internationale, 4 June 1994; reprinted in *Bank of England Quarterly Bulletin*, August 1994

29. Minutes of Monthly Monetary Meeting of 5 May 1995 (HM Treasury, 21 June 1995)

TWELVE A SOVEREIGN POUND

1. Margaret Thatcher, Speech to CNN World Economic Development Congress, Washington, DC, 20 September 1992

2. Margaret Thatcher, Interview in *The European*, 8 October 1992

3. Norman Tebbit, Speech to the Conservative Party Conference, 6 October 1992

4. Douglas Hurd, Speech to the Conservative Party Conference (Conservative Central Office, 6 October 1992)

5. John Major, House of Commons, *Hansard*, cols. 381–2, 25 June 1992

6. John Major, Speech to the Conservative Party Conference (Conservative Central Office, 9 October 1992)

7. John Major, House of Commons, *Hansard*, cols. 283–96, 4 November 1992

8. *Independent*, 24 September 1993

9. Harold Wilson, Labour Party Conference 1968

10. John Major, Speech to the Conference of Conservative Women (Conservative Central Office, 4 June 1993)

11. Leon Brittan, The Proudfoot Autumn Lecture, 17 November 1994

12. Margaret Thatcher, *The Path to Power* (HarperCollins, 1995)

13. Michael Portillo, GMTV, 1 May 1994

14. Eddie George, Churchill Memorial Lecture, 21 February 1995; reprinted in *Bank of England Quarterly Bulletin*, May 1995

15. Kenneth Clarke, Chancellor's Speech to European Movement Gala Dinner (HM Treasury, 9 February 1995)

16. John Major, House of Commons, *Hansard*, col. 1068, 1 March 1995

17. Tony Marlow, House of Commons, *Hansard*, col. 802, 29 March 1994

18. John Major, William and Mary Lecture, Leiden University, Netherlands (Press Office, 10 Downing Street, 7 September 1994)
19. Thatcher, *The Path to Power*
20. *Kingsdown Report* (Action Centre for Europe, 8 June 1995)
21. John Major, House of Commons, *Hansard*, col. 316, 8 June 1995
22. John Major, Prime Minister's Statement (Press Office, 10 Downing Street, 22 June 1995)
23. John Major, *Breakfast with Frost*, BBC Television, 2 July 1995
24. John Major, House of Commons, *Hansard*, cols. 893–909, 28 June 1995

THIRTEEN ALONE

1. Michael Portillo, speech to the Conservative Party Conference (Conservative Central Office, 10 October 1995)
2. Malcolm Rifkind, speech to Royal Institute for International Affairs (Foreign and Commonwealth Office, 21 September 1995)
3. John Major, House of Commons, *Hansard*, col 1225, 18 December 1995
4. Press release, Cabinet Office, 15 February 1996
5. John Major, House of Commons, *Hansard*, col 450, 7 March 1996
6. Cabinet Statement, Conservative Central Office, 3 April 1996
7. John Major, speech to the Institute of Directors (Press office, 10 Downing Street, 24 April 1996)
8. *Today* programme, BBC Radio, 25 April 1996
9. Kenneth Clarke, speech to German British Chamber of Commerce and Industry (HM Treasury, 14 May 1996)
10. Evidence to the House of Commons Treasury Committee, *The prognosis for Stage Three of Economic and Monetary Union* (HMSO, 23 July 1996)
11. *Financial Times*, 25 May 1996
12. Sir Bryan Nicholson, Confederation of British Industry, 21 May 1996
13. John Redwood, *Financial Times*, 16 May 1996
14. David Heathcoat-Amory, Resignation letter, 22 July 1996
15. John Major, *The Times*, 25 July 1996
16. Kenneth Clarke, *The World this Weekend*, BBC Radio, 22 September 1996
17. John Maynard Keynes, *The Economic Consequences of Mr Churchill* (Hogarth Press, 1925)

SELECT BIBLIOGRAPHY

Anderson, Bruce, *John Major: The Making of a Prime Minister* (Fourth Estate, 1991)

Baker, Kenneth, *The Turbulent Years: My Life in Politics* (Faber and Faber, 1993)

Balen, Malcolm, *Kenneth Clarke* (Fourth Estate, 1994)

Barnet, Joel, *Inside the Treasury* (André Deutsch, 1982)

Brittan, Samuel, *Capitalism with a Human Face* (Edward Elgar, 1995)

Brittan, Samuel, *A Restatement of Economic Liberalism* (Macmillan, 1988)

Brittan, Samuel, *Steering the Economy: The Role of the Treasury* (Penguin Books, rev. edn, 1971)

Burns, Terence, 'The UK Government's Financial Strategy', in *Keynes and Economic Policy*, ed. Walter Eltis and Peter Sinclair (Macmillan, 1988)

Callaghan, James, *Time and Chance* (Collins, 1987)

Connolly, Bernard, *The Rotten Heart of Europe* (Faber & Faber, 1995)

Galbraith, John Kenneth, *A History of Economics: The Past as Present* (Hamish Hamilton, 1987)

Gilmour, Ian, *Dancing with Dogma: Britain under Thatcherism* (Simon & Schuster, 1992)

Gorman, Teresa, *Dirty Tricks and the Challenge to Europe* (Pan Books, 1993)

Grant, Charles, *Inside the House that Jacques Built* (Nicholas Brealey, 1994)

Healey, Denis, *The Time of My Life* (Michael Joseph, 1989)

Heseltine, Michael, *The Challenge of Europe: Can Britain Win?* (Weidenfeld & Nicolson, 1989)

Heseltine, Michael, *Where There's a Will* (Hutchinson, 1987)

Hogg, Sarah, and Hill, Jonathan, *Too Close to Call* (Little, Brown, 1995)

Howe, Geoffrey, *Conflict of Loyalty* (Macmillan, 1994)

Ingham, Bernard, *Kill the Messenger* (HarperCollins, 1992)

Jay, Douglas, *Sterling: A Plea for Moderation* (Sidgwick & Jackson, 1985)

Johnson, Christopher, *The Economy under Mrs Thatcher 1979–1990* (Penguin Books, 1991)

Kavanagh, Dennis, *Thatcherism and British Politics* (Oxford University Press, 1990)

Kavanagh, Dennis, and Seldon, Anthony (eds.), *The Major Effect* (Macmillan, 1994)

Keegan, William, *Mr Lawson's Gamble* (Hodder & Stoughton, 1989)

Keegan, William, *Mrs Thatcher's Economic Experiment* (Allen Lane, 1984)

Lawson, Nigel, *The View from No. 11: Memoirs of a Tory Radical* (Bantam Press, 1992)

Lundberg, Kirsten, *Black Wednesday in Britain: The Politics of the ERM Crisis*, (John F. Kennedy School of Government, Harvard, USA, 1995)

McSmith, Andy, *Kenneth Clarke: A Political Biography* (Verso, 1994)

Major, John, *The Power to Choose, the Right to Own: Selected Speeches* (Conservative Political Centre, 1991)

Maynard, Geoffrey, *The Economy under Mrs Thatcher* (Basil Blackwell, 1989)

Meyer, Anthony, *Stand Up and Be Counted* (William Heinemann, 1990)

Pearce, Edward, *The Quiet Rise of John Major* (Weidenfeld & Nicolson, 1991)

Pliatzky, Leo, *The Treasury under Mrs Thatcher* (Basil Blackwell, 1989)

Prior, James, *A Balance of Power* (Hamish Hamilton, 1986)

Pym, Francis, *The Politics of Consent* (Hamish Hamilton, 1984)

Riddle, Peter, *The Thatcher Decade* (Basil Blackwell, 1989)

Riddle, Peter, *The Thatcher Government* (Basil Blackwell, rev. edn, 1985)

Ridley, Nicholas, *My Style of Government: The Thatcher Years* (Hutchinson, 1991)

Roll, Eric, *Where Did We Go Wrong? From the Gold Standard to Europe* (Faber and Faber, 1995)

Smith, David, *From Boom to Bust: Trial and Error in British Economic Policy* (Penguin Books, 1992)

Smith, David, *The Rise and Fall of Monetarism* (Penguin Books, 1987)

Spicer, Michael, *A Treaty Too Far* (Fourth Estate, 1992)

Thatcher, Margaret, *The Downing Street Years* (HarperCollins, 1993)

Thatcher, Margaret, *The Path to Power* (HarperCollins, 1995)

Walker, Peter, *Staying Power: Peter Walker, an Autobiography* (Bloomsbury, 1991)

Walters, Alan, *Britain's Economic Renaissance: Margaret Thatcher's Reforms 1979–1984* (Oxford University Press, 1986)

Walters, Alan, *Sterling in Danger: The Economic Consequences of Pegged Exchange Rates* (Fontana, 1990)

Watkins, Alan, *A Conservative Coup* (Duckworth, 1992)

Whitelaw, William, *The Whitelaw Memoirs* (Aurum Press, 1989)

Young, David, *The Enterprise Years* (Headline, 1990)

Young, Hugo, *One of Us* (Macmillan, rev. edn, 1991)

INDEX